YOU HAVE A LOT TO LOSE

YOU HAVE A LOT TO LOSE

A MEMOIR 1956–1986

C. K. STEAD

AUCKLAND UNIVERSITY PRESS

For Kay with love

The path is narrow
the tide is beginning to run
and the sun
makes light of it.

Also by C. K. Stead

Poetry

Whether the Will is Free
Crossing the Bar
Quesada
Walking Westward
Geographies
Poems of a Decade
Paris
Between
Voices
Straw into Gold
The Right Thing
Dog
The Red Tram
The Black River
Collected Poems 1951–2006
The Yellow Buoy: Poems 2007–2012
In the Mirror, and Dancing
That Derrida Whom I Derided Died

Fiction

Smith's Dream
Five for the Symbol (stories)
All Visitors Ashore
The Death of the Body
Sister Hollywood
The End of the Century at the End of the World
The Singing Whakapapa
Villa Vittoria
The Blind Blonde with Candles in her Hair (stories)
Talking about O'Dwyer
The Secret History of Modernism
Mansfield
My Name was Judas
Risk
The Name on the Door is Not Mine (stories)
The Necessary Angel

Memoir

South-West of Eden: A Memoir 1932–1956

Criticism

The New Poetic
In the Glass Case
Pound, Yeats, Eliot and the Modernist Movement
Answering to the Language
The Writer at Work
Kin of Place: Essays on 20 New Zealand Writers
Book Self: The Reader as Writer and the Writer as Critic
Shelf Life: Reviews, Replies and Reminiscences

Edited

Oxford New Zealand Short Stories (2nd series)
Measure for Measure, a Casebook
Letters and Journals of Katherine Mansfield
Collected Stories of Maurice Duggan
Faber Book of Contemporary South Pacific Stories
Werner Forman's New Zealand

First published 2020
Auckland University Press
University of Auckland
Private Bag 92019
Auckland 1142
New Zealand
www.press.auckland.ac.nz

ISBN 978 1 86940 912 8

Published with the assistance of Creative New Zealand

creative nz
ARTS COUNCIL OF NEW ZEALAND TOI AOTEAROA

A catalogue record for this book is available from the National Library of New Zealand

Design by Carolyn Lewis

Cover images: Front – Karl, Mansfield Menton Fellow, heading for the Villa Isola Bella, 1972; Back – Karl addressing an anti-Vietnam War rally in Myers Park, Auckland, 1968; both photographed by Marti Friedlander, courtesy of the Gerrard and Marti Friedlander Charitable Trust

Printed in China through Asia Pacific Offset

FSC www.fsc.org MIX Paper from responsible sources FSC® C136333

Contents

Note by Way of Introduction

This is an account of myself from the end of *South-West of Eden*, when I first left New Zealand at the age of twenty-three, to my leaving the University of Auckland to become a full-time writer at the age of fifty-three. During all of those thirty years I had been writing – and that work and the responses to it figure here. But there was always in my mind the hope I would reach a position sufficiently secure to allow me to be a writer only, with employment obligations to no one but myself. So these are my years as graduate student, teacher, professor, but equally as poet, critic, and fiction writer. In part it is the record of one struggling to get out – but out of no bad place, and managing pretty well right where he was. If there was conflict between the writer and the academic, and between a commitment to New Zealand and temptations to be somewhere else, these seem not to have been destructive. They were just my life – even an expression of my temperament – but also in some ways illustrative of New Zealand and its place in the world during those years.

This is a literary biography – a story of books and how they come about, of teaching and learning, of writers and how they interact with one another. It is a truthful account of my experience of those thirty years; nothing is deliberately misrepresented. But I have left things out, most often in the interests of economy, but sometimes for reasons of discretion, or privacy. There are significant people in my life who don't figure in these pages. I claim to be a truthful recorder, not a comprehensive one.

After the end of my university employment there is another thirty years of my writing life, a further story which may have to tell itself, and perhaps has largely done so in my books published since 1986.

Part One

Getting There

1.
Booloominbah and Beyond

'Overseas'

At the beginning of 1956, aged twenty-three, one year married and with a first-class honours MA from the University of Auckland, I was appointed to my first academic job, a temporary lectureship in English at the University of New England (UNE) in Armidale, New South Wales. The salary was £1,200 p.a., so at a stroke I had become what my father called 'a thousand-a-year man' – his measure of something distinctly better than merely a working wage, and which he had possibly never achieved himself. UNE had been established in 1938 as a college of the University of Sydney, but in 1954 it had been granted autonomy on condition that it undertook all the extramural teaching for the state of New South Wales, and a large part of my work would be dealing with students at a distance, setting and marking exercises, occasionally visiting outlying areas to hold weekend schools.

So Kay and I packed all our belongings, as you did then, said our goodbyes, and a sad farewell to our little £3-a-week glassed-in flat on Takapuna Beach, and set sail for a three-day journey from Auckland to Sydney on the P&O liner *Orsova*. It would be my first experience of 'Overseas'.

I thought of Australia, as everyone who didn't know it well did (and perhaps does), as unstratified, democratic, egalitarian. In fact it was rife with divisions, rankings and snobberies – Catholic and Protestant especially in those days, which meant roughly Irish stock and English stock, poorer and richer, lower and upper castes.

The university too seemed to be divided – especially between 'before 1954' and 'after 1954', the 'before' being appointments made when UNE was only a college of Sydney, lecturers now considered rather shop-soiled and out-of-date; the 'after', younger staff, better qualified academically. In the September before my appointment H. W. Piper, the university's 'Foundation Professor' of English, had opened his inaugural (public) lecture: 'I have today the duty and the honour of delivering the second inaugural lecture to be given in this University and the first from the Faculty of Arts.' Previously, as a college of Sydney, Armidale had no professorial chairs and consequently lacked the status that went with them.

Along with this distinction went an element of social, and even military, snobbery. The new Vice-Chancellor, R. B. (later Sir Robert) Madgwick, though the son of a Sydney tram driver, was an Oxford DPhil, and had been an army officer, a colonel. Professor Piper (Herbert, but known to his colleagues as 'Pip'), also an army officer, Rhodes scholar and Oxford graduate, had come from Adelaide with his intensely 'social' wife Marie – a pretty and ample blonde with perfect pink and white skin, by whom he appeared to be dominated, and with whom he was deeply in love. He once, in an untypical and unguarded moment, explained to me that watching Marie sleep had made him realise that in 'Composed upon Westminster Bridge' (which begins 'Earth has not anything to show more fair') Wordsworth had really been writing about watching the woman he loved sleeping. I thought (though of course didn't say) that this was touching but mistaken – an example of reading *into*, rather than reading what was there on the page.

Professor Piper exists in my mind as a semi-comic figure, partly confused with the absurd Professor Welch in Kingsley Amis's first novel *Lucky Jim*, just then becoming a best-seller, in which I found something of myself in the trouble-prone character of the young lecturer at a provincial university, Jim Dixon. Although the parallel with Dixon's professor was no doubt quite unfair to mine, it was enhanced when Piper requested (almost, I felt, commanded) that Kay and I should join his Scottish country dancing group – a near-enough parallel with the fictional professor Welch's enlisting his staff, including the reluctant and musically dyslexic Jim Dixon, in music-making. Apart from the Pipers and the Steads the dancing group included the wife of Armidale's mayor, two games mistresses from a local ladies' college, the very queenly Professor of Philosophy Denis Grey (whose inaugural lecture would be remembered for declaring a 'lifelong dedication to passionate celibacy'), and a botanist whose father owned a brewery in Tasmania and who possibly had the product on tap.

Country dancing was a kind of social engagement; and it's true that when Mrs Piper – Marie – saw me slightly inebriate and jolly at a faculty occasion, she crooned, 'I thought you were a solemn young man, Mr Stead. If I'd known you could loosen up like this, I would have invited you to our Left Bank party.' But since the party was already over and gone, and if there was another she had by that time forgotten my talent for 'loosening up', our relations remained distant and formal, seniors to juniors. The only other encounter I remember with the lovely Marie was when Kay and I were invited to the house for dinner and she mentioned that she knew New Zealand's then Governor-General, Sir Willoughby Norrie, '. . . rather well, actually', and asked, in a sort of artificial contralto, 'How *is* dear Willoughby?' – a question that might have elicited, inwardly, one of Jim Dixon's funny faces – the Edith Sitwell face, for example, or perhaps the Martian Invader.

Armidale itself represented, at least covertly, another Australian division, the one that drew a line between kinds of political conservative, the urban Liberals and the rural Country Party. These two were (as they are still) conjoined in the federal Parliament and in confrontation with their political enemies of the left, but were otherwise divided in style and in their degrees of conservatism: Liberals right, Country Party further right; and there were ambitions still alive among Country Party stalwarts in the Tablelands for a New State, distinct from New South Wales (which tended too often to elect a Labor government) and free of the dominance of Sydney. Getting the university at Armidale disconnected from its urban parent had been a symbolic step along the way; and the new university Chancellor, Sir Earle Christmas Grafton Page,* was a prominent New Stater. So was its Deputy Chancellor, Phillip Arundell Wright, father of the well-known and much-honoured poet Judith Wright who was born near Armidale and who had written lyrically of the region as 'my blood's country' –

> . . . that tableland, high delicate outline
> of bony slopes wincing under the winter,
> low trees blue-leaved and olive, outcropping granite –
> clean, lean, hungry country . . .

It was an open secret that Armidale Teachers' College, constructed in 1928 in Italian Renaissance style on a hill overlooking the town, had been designed, with a grand entrance and iconic columns, to be the building that might become in time the Parliament of the New State.

The New England Tablelands were grazier country and the graziers, whose scions played polocrosse and went to posh schools like TAS (The Armidale School), NEGS (New England Girls' School), and even PLC (Presbyterian Ladies' College), considered themselves a cut above the Sydney-siders who were seen as having still the smack of the old penal colony – a mix of larrikin lawlessness and forelock-tugging. So the newly independent university, despite

---

* It was said his full name derived from having been born at Grafton early on a Christmas morning.

the ankle chain of its extramural responsibilities, aimed at a kind of Oxbridge equivalence. Full-time students, all of them in residence, drifted about the ample grounds wearing undergraduate gowns against a backdrop of brown grass and grey-green eucalypts, while the presence of wallabies and kangaroos, lounging or loping, the mothers sometimes snatching up their joeys and jamming them anyhow, even upside down, into the pouch, seemed to compromise the intended superior effect of the university's 'deer park'. I and my younger colleague, Margaret Bell, daughter of a doctor from Lismore in the Northern Rivers and an honours graduate from Queensland, would be largely responsible for the English Department share of the ankle chain. We might tutor the students in residence; but lecturing to them was reserved for the more senior and permanent staff.

The university's central administration building was a fine red-brick mansion, Booloominbah, said to have been in its time Australia's largest country house, built in the 1880s for the White family, and donated by Frank White to be a college of Sydney University. That was in 1938, a decade after the Teachers' College was built, and probably likewise with the New State in long-term prospect. Frank was the uncle of the novelist Patrick White ('a grazier's heir' as he would describe himself in his late memoir, *Flaws in the Glass*), whose fourth novel, *The Tree of Man*, having run through a number of reprints in the United States, was just now (1956) receiving the kind of praise in England that would get him the serious attention he had so far lacked. This was the beginning of the acclaim that would lead to his winning, in 1973, Australia's first Nobel Prize for literature.

Finally there was the division – mile-wide, world-wide – between Australians and Australian Aborigines. The only time we saw these ill-clad, shabby, brown-black and bewildered fellows in significant numbers, looking like aliens from another planet rather than, as they were, aliens in the world that had once been their own, was on a Monday morning outside the police court, where those arrested over the weekend, most often for drunkenness and related offences, gathered to be arraigned. They lived somewhere out of town, close to the rubbish dump, where they built themselves shacks or 'humpies' of scrap iron, old water tanks, kerosene cans, and random pieces of timber. They had no running water, and the women often trudged long distances carrying it. The men looked for work on road gangs and cattle stations, but not on the railways which had a policy against employing them. In cold weather their clothes didn't seem to change and always looked inadequate. They were often to be seen walking into town in ones and twos, or occasionally, when one or another had scored some cash, riding in a taxi. But they were never on the bus – that seemed to be quietly understood and accepted. No law was needed to enforce it; any more than there had to be one saying that in the cinema they sat only in the two or three front rows.

Kay's first employment in Armidale was as shorthand typist to a public accountant and there she saw graziers' tax returns which always included an amount paid to 'Jackie'. 'Jackie' was the generic name for whatever 'Abo' was employed for 'general duties'. Thus the actual incumbent could change, or even be more than one person at the same time, without needing to be individually identified.

The university had a branch of a society that aimed at 'Aboriginal assimilation' – not an acceptable term now, but well-meant at the time; and perhaps some good things were done, some assistance given where it was needed, some small progress made towards healing the damage history had done to these people. When the novelist Kylie Tennant came that year to give the annual Commonwealth Literary Fund lectures on Australian literature, and was invited to a meeting of the Staff Wives Club, she asked what, if anything, they did for the Aboriginal people. She was told a visit to their encampment was planned. According to the story that went about later, Tennant said there was no time like the present and organised taxis and cars on the spot. I never heard how the visit went (Kay, a working woman, avoided the Staff Wives Club); but Tennant was said to have remarked that she was sorry she would not be there when the invitation she had issued for a return visit was taken up.

Awareness of 'the problem of the Aboriginal' in those days took mainly the form of embarrassment and avoidance – and I was guilty of both, telling myself it was their (Australians') problem, not mine; but it was not acute enough for the Sydney *Bulletin* (the '*Bully*', as D. H. Lawrence calls it admiringly in *Kangaroo*) yet to have abandoned its old banner, kept I suppose more out of loyalty to, and nostalgia for, its own frontier past than as a statement for the present or future, but nonetheless shocking. It read simply: 'AUSTRALIA FOR THE WHITE MAN'.

The 'New Australians'

Armidale was about equidistant between Sydney and Brisbane, getting on for 500 kilometres from each but, up on the inland plateau, almost 1000 metres above sea level; and I remember how our first long slow train journey up from Sydney began in the almost insufferable humid heat of the harbour city, and ended with us shivering, inadequately clothed for the chill of evening in the Tablelands.

There were a few hits and misses finding permanent accommodation. We spent a couple of weeks in a house whose owners, going on holiday, wanted it occupied for security. This was somewhere along the road to the university which was 5 kilometres out of town. Huge moths with luminous eyes, attracted by the lights, beat on the fly screens at night, and dogs howled in the distance. The postman came on a horse, wearing a broad-brimmed hat and riding boots. The days were beautifully clear until they turned to thunderstorms in the late afternoons, with vivid forked lightning.

Next came a small flat back in town. It had an outdoor (across the yard) bathroom with a wood-burning water heater, and housed a very large hairy spider of the kind popularly known as a tarantula, but in fact a huntsman, harmless to all but its natural prey. Finally we scored a 'modern' (i.e. recently built) flat at 93 Donnelly Street, with uninsulated wallboard partitions painted in pastel colours (green mainly), too thin to keep the cold out in winter or the heat out in summer.

By now it was well into April and the long avenue of elms leading in to the university was turning yellow in sudden vivid patches. The days were clear and hot by midday, but at night there were the first signs of the frosts which would challenge our kerosene-burning heater, all we had to keep the cold at bay.

Our next-door neighbours at Donnelly Street were 'New Australians', as post-war immigrants were called – a German Jewish couple, Israel Getzler, lecturer in history at the university, and his wife 'Ada' (Agathe). Ada had survived in Germany, her Jewishness hidden right through the war, and she seemed still fearful of venturing out into public places. In their kitchen she conjured exotic and delicious snacks; and Israel liked to make dumplings of chicken livers fried in deep oil. It was our joke that we had together a 'garlic pact' against Australia, which was still predominantly Anglo and conservative in matters of cuisine. Israel was a tremendous talker, and the flow of ideas and anecdote, the stories, didn't stop even when he was at the wheel of his Holden, the first Australian-manufactured car. Each day, after Kay got a post in the university library, he would drive us to work, still talking. But he had been brought up in Germanic proprieties, and didn't like to speak without meeting your eye, so there was constant anxiety as he clung to the wheel with both hands while casting his eyes away from the road towards the interlocutor beside him, or even over his shoulder to the one behind.

He had been a member of the Jewish Young Guard in pre-war Germany, an admirer of Stefan George and of the poems of Karl Wolfskehl who had come to New Zealand as a Jewish refugee, and had been Frank Sargeson's friend. Israel's stories were of life in Nazi Germany through the 1930s, growing always darker and more threatening; of his family's escape, walking east through Poland into Russia; of the war spent in Siberia; and then the post-war escape westward, again often on foot.

It was with the Getzlers and Margaret Bell that Kay and I went to hear the 'world-famous' historian Arnold J. Toynbee, on a tour promoting the recently completed tenth volume of his *Study of History*, a lecture circuit that was clearly taking him to the ends of the earth. His message was that civilisations died if they were confronted by radical challenges and did not make a 'creative response' – something that could only come from an enlightened minority, usually imbued with the regenerative force of a religion. None of us was much impressed by this, and Israel, a staunch socialist, was particularly outraged by the idea that the general franchise had been a 'dilution', undermining the creative influence of the 'educated middle class'. It was this same essentially fascist idea of 'creative response' by a favoured minority that, fifteen years later, I would give to the dictator Volkner in my political fantasy, *Smith's Dream*.

Other new appointments to the university enlivened our social life. In one letter home I reported, 'an Austrian physics lecturer has arrived – bearded, fierce, intolerant and brilliant'. This was Otto Bergmann, appointed to a research post as a theoretical physicist, and we seemed to attach ourselves to one another almost at once. His doctorate was from Vienna and he had taught for a time in Ireland and then Adelaide. His temperament was restless. He drove the classic VW of the time, and we would soon be on the move with him, making visits down to the Pacific coast (where we swam at night at Valla Beach, trying not to think about sharks), up to the Northern Rivers, as well as to and from Sydney. It was with Otto that we first saw Brisbane, with its suburban houses on stilts, and Queensland's Gold Coast, then only a glorious strip of untenanted sand with a few low-rise buildings, and no hint of the real-estate dream (and nightmare) it has since become. Of that northern region in general I still have strong but rather unspecific memories of flame trees, poinsettias, bananas, pineapples, sugar cane – and the heat – and still brown water that might have hidden crocodiles.

The country we were seeing by car seemed to run on and on, its bush lacking the density and greenness of New Zealand's rainforest, but loping and sprawling and grey-blue forever into distance, as if leisure, even in the patterns of local speech, came naturally because hurry was pointless: this was a continent not an island, and no one was going anywhere fast or getting anywhere soon. Furthermore (and further yet) somewhere in there, over there, away 'back of beyond' and out of sight, you knew was the red desert and the bones of its hapless mapmakers.

Really what we were exploring, though thousands of miles long and hundreds wide, was hardly more than the coastal strip. But even this, habitable Australia's capacity for extremes – flood and fire and drought – was something you were not quite allowed to forget. There was a documentary we all saw at the university Film Society that year, *Back of Beyond*, some of its commentary taken from Douglas Stewart's poem sequence, *The Birdsville Track*. The central image, or the one that stayed with me, was of sheep dead from drought under a tree containing, in its upper branches, the carcass of a cow deposited there during a flood.

Otto introduced us to the music of Richard Strauss, and had the complete LP set of *Der Rosenkavalier*. Sometimes he cooked for us, and this involved much careful shopping and preparation. The item which impressed and surprised me most was a grand Austrian torte which was not cooked, but somehow compounded of various kinds of imported biscuits, assembled into the right shape, and then left to absorb the brandy (and possibly also liqueurs) poured over them, to be topped finally with whipped cream.

In the last two years of the war, aged eighteen and nineteen, Otto had been conscripted into a tank battalion of the German Army. He had had some miraculous escapes from death after the D-Day landings; and in the final two weeks before Germany's surrender, was involved in ferocious infantry battles with the Russians advancing in the east. He and Israel Getzler had a language in common which, so far as I can recall, they never spoke when together; and though they were not impolite or uncivil with one another, there was a wariness between them. It was as if the

German language, if they had slipped into it, might in some way betray what they were concealing; the guilt on one side, and the pain on both. I think there was suspicion on Israel's part: was Otto telling us the full story of his war? – and this was something Otto was aware of and resented. I think too that Otto, who enjoyed verbal jokes and making light of things, considered Israel rather heavy going, too relentlessly serious. Maybe there was even a small residue – who knows? – of the anti-Semitism he must have grown up with. At some time during that first year Joyce Dunn, an Australian, joined the History Department and she and Otto were soon a couple.

On one occasion, during a visit to Sydney, Otto took me with him to visit Harry Messel, Professor of Physics there, and we were shown the computer Messel and his team had built, said to be the first in the Southern Hemisphere, a very large contraption filling one room and with ancillary components in two more. I had not at the time the faintest notion of how computers would figure in our lives, imagining this must be some sort of machine for doing mathematical calculations, and faintly puzzled that Harry and Otto should speak of it in such reverent tones, and look at it with such respect. It was on the same visit I saw, in a hotel foyer, a set broadcasting what was probably Australia's first TV programme – again without any idea of what effect this new device would have on social life in the second half of the century.

Otto and I drove on to Canberra where he had academic business to do at the Australian National University. There we ran into Bob Chapman, one of my former teachers in the History Department at Auckland. Bob was on leave working towards a PhD that would never be finished, and learning to be a psephologist, which would in time give him a television identity in New Zealand and earn him appointment as Auckland's first Professor of Politics. But at the time he still aspired to be a poet and literary critic, and had recently, together with Jonathan Bennett, edited the Oxford *Anthology of New Zealand Verse*. After a dinner in the college he invited us to his room, with an English doctoral student, Ruth Butterworth. Hungry to exchange New Zealand news, and drinking more than enough, Bob and I reminisced and gossiped the other two into silence. At last I was silent too, and it was just Bob, running fluently on towards a peroration about New Zealand as 'the new, the better, Florence – the fulfilment of the philosopher's dream'. Nationalism, and particularly literary nationalism, was strong among New Zealanders at the time. I was infected myself, though not so badly that I didn't feel embarrassed by this excess.

Canberra is a strange, manufactured federal capital, grandiose in design and celebrating warrior triumphs – like Washington, DC, on which it is partly modelled. If it is now an adolescent hoping to grow tall and fill its adult clothes, in those days it was still an infant in a sailor suit. The grand reflecting lakes had been dug but not yet filled with water. The boulevards lacked the buildings they had been designed for. Many of the suburbs were still only sketch maps bulldozered into a scruffy, rather arid landscape.

I don't know what it was persuaded me it would be a good idea while there to call on A. D. Hope, Professor of English at the ANU. He was widely considered to be the finest living Australian poet, though for a variety of reasons his promised first full collection had been long delayed and only published the previous year. This was *The Wandering Islands*, beautifully produced and everywhere acclaimed – except in New Zealand's major literary journal, *Landfall*, where I had treated it with undisguised cool. Even though I must have supposed (and probably wrongly) that Hope would not have seen this review, it was quite out of character for me to visit a notable person uninvited. I was too shy for such literary venturing. Perhaps ease of access explains it: I simply found his office, knocked, and was commanded to come in.

I said who I was, and tried to make conversation. Nothing I said elicited much more than one-word, or single-sentence, responses. The frost was palpable, and I retreated, glowing with embarrassment. I never met him again.

On the road back to Sydney, through the repetitious scenery of brown grass and blue gums, Otto told me about a dream he'd had: Joyce was in her car driving away from him and he was running to catch up, panting, feeling she hadn't seen him, that she was departing and wouldn't be back, when all at once he turned into a kangaroo and was bounding fast through the landscape and keeping up with her.

Among visitors to UNE in that first year was Wallace Robson, an Oxford don in Australia to give the British Academy lectures. He did this with few notes and remarkable fluency, while at intervals casting his eyes up and tugging at the front of the yellow knitted sweater he was wearing, which had perhaps shrunk from inexpert laundering – pulling it down over his lower stomach, from which, however, it at once sprang back towards his waist. It was the slow movement of the eyes *up* while the hand pulled *down* I found so distracting. A year or two later, visiting Dan Davin (whose 'fine intellect' Robson had praised in conversation), I was to learn that this undoubtedly brilliant though physically unattractive blob of a man had been 'secretly' engaged to Iris Murdoch, whose novels I would soon be reading regularly, one by dependable one, as they emerged. Some years later again I was to meet her with the stammering don, John Bailey, who had replaced Robson in Murdoch's affections and married her.

Nineteen fifty-six was the year of Hungary and Suez, and we lived through those crises, from a distance and yet feeling deeply concerned and thoroughly engaged.

Doing the job

Lucky Jim Dixon's closest colleague is Margaret Peel.[*] Mine was Margaret Bell. There was not much likeness. Bespectacled and

* Based, one has learned since, on Philip Larkin's friend Monica Jones, whom Amis didn't like or approve of.

dressing in arty clothes, Jim's Margaret tends to neurosis or hysteria and is constantly sending out ambiguous signals – a not wholly attractive character but one to whom Jim feels obscurely bound until, at the novel's end, her dishonesties and stratagems are exposed and he is free to win the altogether more desirable (i.e. better-looking and less 'difficult') Christine.

My Margaret was an unambiguous handsome well-formed young Australian woman, with whom I shared a task and an office. She became a friend, an ally, and often came home with Kay and me to share our meal, sometimes to take a turn cooking it, to gossip and exchange stories of our respective pasts, and share routine complaints about the boss. As the winter drew on and the nights became colder, she sometimes shared our only bed (and a toothbrush) rather than walk home in the icy night.

Margaret and I were largely responsible for first-year extramural work in English in the state of New South Wales. We set and marked exercises, sent out 'advisory letters' about set books, marked essays on them and, sometimes together, sometimes separately, conducted weekend schools, both in Armidale and in centres around the state.

In that first year there were weekend schools at Grafton, Sydney and Dubbo. In the pub that housed us in Grafton I was shown the mark, high up the wall behind the bar, where the last floods had gone through. To reach Dubbo I had to travel first to Sydney, then north-west to the town – a total of 1320 miles, as I recorded in letters home. There was heavy rain throughout the weekend, and the Macquarie River rose 23 feet in twenty-four hours. Its waters were just beginning to flow into the gutters of the main street as my train pulled out again.

I was continuing to publish poems and reviews at home, and poems in Australia (*Meanjin*, the Sydney *Bulletin*, the *Jindyworobak Anthology*). When Douglas Stewart took a poem for the *Bulletin*, it appeared with others under the heading 'Poems from the Six States', making me momentarily New South Wales' representative poet. Allen Curnow signalled he would be taking poems (including one written in Armidale) for the *Penguin Book of New Zealand Verse* he was working on. From Frank Sargeson came information about Janet Frame, still his (free) lodger but soon to be *dis*lodged and sent to London, to make her way in the world with what consequences Frank didn't dare think too closely about. Never far from his mind was Robin Hyde's suicide there – but his patience with Janet had pretty much run out, though he was still doing all he could to raise money to assist her on her travels.

'Have you read', I asked him,

> Angus Wilson's new novel, *Anglo-Saxon Attitudes*? It creates the scholarly world in a completely convincing way and is artistically flawless – rather like a stage play in the way it's worked out to suit the movement of the plot – a perfect example of the good novelist who is not a great one. It creates the surface of life without being superficial but also without bringing you up against anything truly universal. In fact it is so sane and wholesome and tidy and well-arranged and interesting that while reading it you tend to think of the Lawrences and the Melvilles as a rather mad tiresome bunch. Wilson is a better novelist than Patrick White, perhaps even a better one than Lawrence, but not as important as either.

I sent the Wilson to my parents. As the daughter of a Swedish sea captain, my mother tended to identify with anything or anyone Scandinavian; so I thought she would find a way of seeing herself in the character of the Danish woman Ingeborg; and that my father might see himself as Ingeborg's unhappy and defeated English husband, and feel sorry for himself. So both parents might be gratified, but in quite different ways that could never be acknowledged.

Margaret Bell's and my appointments had been 'temporary', and when a permanent appointee, Harry Heseltine, was found to begin in 1957, hers was not renewed. She was not altogether happy about this, but cheered herself up by booking a passage to London for what would be her first trip abroad. She would go, not to do further academic work, but on a working holiday. She promised she would be there to greet us in a year's time. Together with Otto, Kay and I saw her off from Pyrmont Wharf on 25 January of the new year. The Suez Canal was still closed, so her ship would have to take the long route, around the Cape of Good Hope. We would miss her. Armidale would be quieter without her.

Kangaroo

Sydney was our escape and playground. We came and went in university vacations, often by car with friends, sometimes by rail, once by air – my first experience of flight, which took us at no great altitude and in the heat of summer over some areas of bush fires, with consequent turbulence. Kay's older sister, Aileen, had married an Australian, Clem Schuller, so there was always accommodation for us in Sydney. They had one little daughter and a second was born during the summer of 1956–57.

In 1956 when the state of New South Wales announced that the Danish architect Jørn Utzon had won an international competition for the design of an opera house to be built on the Sydney waterfront, and the design was revealed in the *Sydney Morning Herald*, there was an immediate clamour – of celebration from the intellectual community, surprised and delighted that something so brilliantly avant-garde and beautiful should have been chosen; of derision and alarm from the anything-but-silent majority who, though they seldom went to operas, knew what an opera house should look like and it wasn't like this. To begin with brother-in-law Clem was with the opposers. Later he recognised that something wonderful had happened *for Australia*, and was able to change sides without acknowledging that he had ever said a word against the design or its enormous cost.

Though not a 'returned soldier', Clem had some of the qualities of the Diggers as represented in D. H. Lawrence's *Kangaroo* which I had never read before crossing the Tasman. It was surprising how much of the Australian character, and the feel of the landscape too, Lawrence had managed to capture during a visit of scarcely more than three months, and how he had made the two, man and land, interactive. He caught the flavours of Australian politics, with its extreme tendencies, left and right, and its obsession with mateship and male bonding in war and at work.

Of course Somers was Lawrence and Harriet was Frieda; and Lawrence's messianic self-importance can become, in any of his novels, almost intolerable. But *Kangaroo* is such a frank book, and so self-revealing. The scolding Frieda is constantly there in the character of Harriet, mocking Somers' intellectual pretensions, dissecting them, curbing them. She is the hectoring counter-statement to the Lawrentian grandeur. Looking outward, Lawrence caught the weird mix of rebel and conformist that I saw at least something of in Clem Schuller; looking in, he saw both his own vision of human greatness, and the ridiculousness of himself as its little ginger-bearded purveyor. And strangely, he found a corrective to his own extremism in the Sydney *Bulletin*:

> Bits, bits, bits. Yet [Somers] read on. It was not mere anecdotage. It was the sheer momentaneous life of the continent. There was no consecutive thread. Only the laconic courage of experience.
>
> All the better. He could have kicked himself for wanting to help mankind, join in revolutions or reforms or any of that stuff. And he kicked himself still harder thinking of his frantic struggles with the 'soul' and the 'dark god' and the 'listener' and the 'answerer'. Blarney – blarney – blarney! He was a preacher and a blatherer, and he hated himself for it. Damn the 'soul', damn the 'dark god', and above all, damn his own interfering nosy self.

Re-read now, far from that first Australian encounter, *Kangaroo* can seem in parts grotesque, illogical, not quite sane; but it has still the unmistakable streak of genius that was Lawrence. Alan Ross calls it 'the most intuitive and imaginatively resolved of all Lawrence's novels'.* In his memoir *Flaws in the Glass*, Patrick White writes, 'the little that is subtle in the Australian character comes from the masculine principle in its women, the feminine in its men'. If that is true, it's something Lawrence saw and represented in *Kangaroo*. The novel's last sentence reads: 'It was only four days to New Zealand, over a cold, dark, inhospitable sea.' I wasn't sure whether to be glad or sorry that when he crossed those waters he hadn't stayed long enough to write a sequel called *Kiwi*.

Digging in

Letters kept arriving, including copiously from Margaret Bell who kept her 'Dearest Steads' up to date, and in intimate detail, with her experiences as the young Australian coping with the shock of London, where she was school teaching, 'sometimes homesick for 93 Donnelly Street', but already attached to the British seaman she would later marry.

Looking through a great collection of these letters from family and friends (they were always kept) I notice a recurring manner, jocular, tending often to obscenity and self-deprecation, sometimes daft to the point of surreal, meant to entertain, but informative too, full of facts. I'm surprised to recognise how much time we all spent writing them – how conscientious we were, and how subject to guilt about delay or failure in reply. Most wrote news – what they'd been doing, what was going on around them. Among contemporaries only my slightly younger poet friend Rob Dyer, currently in Oxford on a scholarship from Auckland, wrote what I suppose could be called 'intellectual' letters. One was an account of his own

* *The London Magazine*, July 1980, p. 17.

> . . . diligent study of Plato's *Republic*, which I have found rewarding and a thing of great pathos – to see a man so in love with beauty led on so inevitably by his own, at first tiny, mistakes to a strange world where only he and his creations can live. [. . .] My construction of sentences goes to pieces completely under his influence. I am living out in the country at the moment with nothing but Plato, Thucydides, the clothes I stand up in, and the assembly of nerves from which I profess to distil my particular lust for knowledge – not to project myself on to the world as I conceive it, but to stamp whatever are its springs and patterns of being on myself, and achieve communion in its highest form.

This was a serious young man who still seemed to be heading somewhere. But I was not altogether surprised, a little later, when the Oxford scholarship, and his work there, all seemed to fall apart and come to nothing. And in fact there had always been, at intervals, statements I thought of as 'Rob's Grand Manner', which must have made his teachers anxious if they ever encountered it. These, coincidentally, signalled that he still thought of us (I suppose I did too) as competitors:

> I am glad when I hear that the world gives you her favours, for you were ever her lover, more intimate and more honoured but perhaps less powerful than I, her priest.

This might have warranted one of Jim Dixon's faces – the Sex Life in Ancient Rome face, or perhaps the Chinese Mandarin.

It was Rob who had sent me Philip Larkin's first major breakthrough collection, *The Less Deceived*, which I continued to read with close attention, even telling Sargeson, 'of course the century has produced greater poets, but none better'. To Rob I wrote:

> Basically there is only one experience behind the half dozen best poems – a tension, not so much between desire and

> fulfilment, as between all the possibilities of a situation which resolve themselves into two opposites, both of which are 'fulfilments'. And it's the ability to hang between them, to have a foot in both camps, that makes the poet. He must never choose one side or the other. That would negate the self – it would be a death-wish.

Now that Larkin's life is known, as it was not then, one can see from that intuited summary how much of it was already visible in the poems, and how true to it they were.

Armidale fostered friendships of a strange kind, sometimes so intense they could seem, however briefly, like falling in love. One was with a young poet, Iain Lonie, my exact contemporary, a New Zealander and Cambridge graduate, lecturer in classics, who translated Euripides' *Alcestis* and persuaded me to put the choruses into semi-formal verse, which he didn't feel he could do himself. He had a wife, Jean, and a number of children, but Kay and I saw little of them – only Iain himself; and I remember the three of us spending a long evening together which we enjoyed so much we were reluctant to end it. So in the small hours we walked him home from our flat to his, and then, still not ready to go our separate ways, he walked back with us, came in for another drink and more talk, after which we walked him home a second time as the first signs of daylight were just creeping into the cold sky. Our version of *Alcestis* was performed by the University Players in the Armidale Town Hall, and later a version of it was broadcast by the ABC.*

Iain was always uncertain about his poems, and slow in writing them, but they mattered to him more than anything; and he wrote to me, after getting an appointment at Sydney University,

---

* Two of these choruses survive in my *Collected Poems, 1951–2006*, Auckland University Press, 2008, pp. 24 and 511.

> You seem to have started something off again in me, the night I saw you last. Since then I've been churning out poems and receiving rejection slips from all over the place.

In the same letter he sent ten of the forty guineas the ABC had paid for our play, money which he needed more than I did, and which was more than my fair share of the work. He still had little success with poems offered to literary journals, though he was to have more later on after his return to New Zealand.

In March 1957 I wrote to Frank Sargeson about new friends, Lee and Jack Bartley – he a veterinary scientist on a Fulbright scholarship to study toxaemia in pregnant ewes; Lee an arts faculty graduate – both from Berkeley, California.

> They are both beautiful – small, healthy-looking, clean-cut, with the sort of hair and teeth that win animals prizes in shows [. . .] The weather is exciting now too – cool nights and fresh clear sunny days. We go on picnics with them in their little Morris. The landscape, which can sometimes seem so drab in the daytime, looks wonderful under the moon, especially if you have a fire and the smell of eucalypt burning.
>
> Joyce and Otto got married in Melbourne at Christmas and Margaret Bell reports from London.

It was about the middle of the year that James McAuley came to give the year's Commonwealth Literary Fund lectures. McAuley and A. D. Hope were currently the dominant poets on the scene, working together,* deeply committed to a neo-Augustan anti-Modernist poetic, not just for themselves but for everyone, and it seemed for the good of the nation. This had its parallel in Britain's Movement poets, but the Australian version, in no sense an offshoot, was more dogmatic, grimmer, more extreme. McCauley's

* Hope's collection, *The Wandering Islands*, was dedicated to McCauley.

poems were undoubtedly accomplished, but seemed to me sterile, machine-made; and he read them, not just well, but with alarming passion, wringing blood out of stones as if his life (and lives beyond his own) depended on it.

McCauley had recently become a Catholic and was now a stalwart right-wing Cold Warrior, editor of the new (in 1956) magazine *Quadrant* which would later be revealed as secretly funded by the CIA. The favourable attention Patrick White's *The Tree of Man* was getting in London was one of the matters currently upsetting him. The book had caught on overseas, he argued, with people who knew nothing of Australia and were not qualified to judge. Hope agreed and, not mincing his words, had dismissed the novel in the *Sydney Morning Herald* as 'pretentious and illiterate verbal sludge'.

But what McCauley was most famous for, and by now perhaps wished it was not so, was as the author, together with Harold Stewart, of the Ern Malley hoax. This was a group of sixteen Modernist poems, *The Darkening Ecliptic*, written in 1943 and offered to the avant-garde periodical *Angry Penguins* as the complete poems of Ern Malley who had died of Graves' disease aged twenty-five leaving them for his sister Ethel to have published if she could find an editor to take them. *Angry Penguins* editor Max Harris published them, hailing a major talent tragically lost to Australia. The real authors then declared themselves, claiming the poems were worthless, and that they had exposed the sham that passed for poetry under the Modernist banner.

Anyone who reads the Malley poems now will probably recognise at once elements of false, fake and funny. Once you know, they're hard to miss. But it has to be remembered how much those poems were *of their time* – a time in which T. S. Eliot could publish lines like

> Midnight shakes the memory
> As a madman shakes a dead geranium

which would look entirely at home in *The Darkening Ecliptic*. Fashion is something which to a certain extent sets its own standards and imposes a degree of blindness. Also relevant is the fact that these poems came to Harris from a person claiming to be the young poet's grieving sister. Harris was hoaxed as much by the fiction surrounding the poems as by the poems themselves. Publishing them was, among many things, an act of kindness.

It was a case that became famous internationally, with pundits on both sides (but most, including Herbert Read, on Harris's) lining up to express an opinion. Ocker Australia, its anti-intellectualism given aid and comfort, enjoyed the laugh. The state of Victoria prosecuted Harris on the grounds that the poems were obscene. He acquitted himself admirably under cross-examination in court and was nonetheless convicted, which only increased, in the eyes of his supporters, the honour due to him and the hoaxers' shame. Sidney Nolan painted Ern's portrait.

This was an event in our visitor's fairly recent past which had had the effect of driving him further into the neo-classical cage he now defended as the sole and proper frame for poetry. In his lectures he insisted that poetic Modernism was a dead horse, a delusion, the literary reflection of a larger moral and spiritual decay, and offered A. D. Hope, who had himself attacked the 'shuffle' and 'vomit' of Modernism, as his example of poetic virtue and promise for the future.

I thought the hoax had rebounded on the hoaxers – more particularly on McCauley, who had written most of the Malley lines, and in writing them had released moments of casual or accidental lyricism nowhere else apparent in his work. I remember his reading clearly, but cannot bring a single line of his to mind. On the other hand there are lines of Ern Malley's I can't forget – not least

I am still
the black swan of trespass on alien waters.

The 'here' and the 'there'

Around the middle of 1957 I received word I had been elected to a Commonwealth exhibition to Cambridge, and even assigned a college, Trinity, and a tutor, M. G. M. Pryor. Claire Tomalin writes of receiving a telegram offering her a place at another Cambridge college, Newnham, 'No one forgets that moment'. It did seem an exciting possibility; but soon after came news I had won the Hiatt Baker scholarship to the University of Bristol. The Bristol scholarship was £450 p.a. for an initial two years, all university fees covered, and with a possible extension. I don't have an exact figure for the Cambridge one but it was not sufficiently different to decide the matter. The British Council had awarded me a free passage to and from the UK. We had lived mostly on Kay's earnings and saved most of mine so were not going to be poor – in fact planned to buy our first car and learn to drive as soon as we got to England. I liked the thought of Cambridge and the mana that went with the name and the degree. But Oxford's and Cambridge's refusal to recognise any degrees apart from their own meant that I would be technically an undergraduate, and would need to enrol first for their BA, in effect repeating what I had done already in Auckland, rather than getting straight on to the critical and scholarly work that enrolment as a PhD candidate at Bristol would permit.

Bristol's Winterstoke* Professor of English, L. C. Knights, was known in academic circles for his *Drama and Society in the Age of Jonson*; but he was better (more widely) known for an article with the ironic title 'How many children had Lady Macbeth?', which became something like a banner for the New Criticism and for the journal *Scrutiny* of which for many years he was editor. This article was an attack on the nineteenth-century habit of treating Shakespeare plays – and more widely, works of fiction – as

---

* It was from this title I derived the name for my character, Bertie Winterstoke, in my novel *Talking about O'Dwyer*, Harvill Press, 1999.

repositories of 'characters' who had a life beyond the text. So the question in the title would have been, to a nineteenth-century critic like A. C. Bradley, a reasonable one; and if the text of *Macbeth* did not give you a direct answer, one might be inferred by an imaginative exploration of the lady's behaviour and the 'character' it revealed. (She did, after all, talk about 'giving suck' and plucking the baby from her breast.) The reform Knights called for was an end to this kind of abstraction of 'character', 'plot' etc. from text, and a more complete focus upon the words on the page. Without the words, there was nothing; and *in* the words lay the key to the 'rich and controlled experience' which was the play.

But Knights, though formidable and important, was not the dominating presence in what by now was famous as the *Scrutiny* group. That presence was F. R. Leavis. Writing home I said Knights was one of the more brilliant of F. R. Leavis's *Scrutiny* group, 'but I think without too much of their narrowness' – so it seems I had made preliminary enquiries. Leavis was famous as an acute and demanding critic, guardian of the highest literary standards, but known equally for dogmatism and a messianic temperament that seemed to require conformity from his disciples. His declared principle was that literary criticism should be a dialogue. A. would present a proposition, to which B. would respond, 'Yes, but . . .' and offer a qualifier or an alternative. Nothing could be more reasonable. But in reality Leavis's tone and behaviour seemed to require that in response to any proposition of his, only 'Yes I see that', and 'Yes I agree', would be appropriate and acceptable.

At a time when, and in a place where, tie-less was next-to-naked, the cover shots to Leavis's books usually showed him striding about Cambridge with shirt collar wide open over lapels. I took literary criticism very seriously. Indeed, the somewhat ruthlessly analytical reviews I had been sending home to Charles Brasch for *Landfall* were taking it, or myself, perhaps too seriously. It was not that my breakdown, for example, of the elements in Alistair Campbell's poems was wrong, or even unfair; but it was unkind – and it would have been better if I could have somehow also built into it an acknowledgement that, before cool analysis set in, I had been charmed and moved by the poems I was now taking apart*. I had grown up under the influence of T. S. Eliot and others, including Leavis himself, whose analysis of literary works was subtle, usually persuasive, often compelling. That was my apprenticeship; and I neither regret it, nor wish to unlearn its lessons. Leavis was a major intellectual force; but he was also, temperamentally, a puritan and a bully, and I was neither.

For Leavis, D. H. Lawrence was one of the greatest English writers. He described *Kangaroo* as a 'fictional experiment' in political action, and added that it represented 'with an insight and an integrity which can be poignantly affecting, the drama of his relationship with Frieda'. Milton, on the other hand, did not measure up to Leavis's high standards and was, if not banished from the canon, at least given a much lower place than hitherto. Dickens was only seen at full stretch in *Hard Times*; the rest of his work did not deserve the attention of a serious mind – until, that is, Leavis changed his (requiring his acolytes to change with him), and Dickens too became one of the giants. Virginia Woolf wrote novels of 'extraordinary vacancy and pointlessness'. T. S. Eliot was accepted as one of the great poets of the English language, but W. B. Yeats was not, or not *quite*. Nor (certainly *not*) was W. H. Auden. And Leavis seemed to reserve a special phial of bile for Stephen Spender whom he saw as the prototype of the worthless leftish London book world that posed as the life of literature.

I could of course have chosen Cambridge, though not Downing, Leavis's college, since Trinity had already been chosen, or had chosen me; but I could have put myself somewhere in range of his teaching and his influence. Bristol, however, was already my preference because it would enrol me at once for postgraduate work and leave me so much freer to pursue my own course.

---

* *Landfall* 40, December 1956, pp. 355–56.

My mind now was never far (or not for long) from the thought of our departure. Once again Kay and I would have to pack everything we owned, some marked NOT WANTED ON VOYAGE to go in the hold; some, to be available at intervals, marked BAGGAGE ROOM; the rest CABIN BAGGAGE. My free passage required me to have a medical check including chest X-rays. Inoculations against diseases prevalent in some of the countries we would pass through, including smallpox, were required, and we both reacted badly to these. The effect was like a very bad flu, with temperature, muscular aches, depression – just *illness.*

Kay's fare was £158.15.0. That 15 shillings was significant enough to be tagged on to the £158 is as much an indicator of the inflation since as is the actual fare, which covered one's accommodation and meals for the nearly five weeks at sea. Only the very rich could afford to go by air; and even that was slow and complicated. It was as if every journey made you a migrant – and that was how it felt when the distances were so great and took so long. We would travel from Sydney with shore stops at Melbourne, Fremantle (the port of Perth), Colombo and Aden; then through Suez (the canal just recently reopened), into the Mediterranean, going ashore at Naples and Marseilles, calling at Gibraltar, and onward to Tilbury Docks. We would then be as far from home as you could go without being on some kind of return journey.

And yet we would not be far from home at all: we would be in England. Not that we, twentieth-century New Zealand nationalists and anti-monarchists, would have dreamed of using the word 'Home' in the old colonial sense to mean England, as it did in the conversation of some of our grand- or great-grandparents' generation. But there was a sense in which it *was* – a home to the literary mind, the source of a very large part of our education, reading, history – our law and our lore. This was not, as it was often (and is still) said to be, a kind of colonial subservience. To have two homes, like two languages, can be better than just one, and I am too old now to pretend otherwise. Undoubtedly the primacy of the one where I spent my formative years was absolute; but the second, also formative, was hardly to be dismissed as unimportant or a burden. However subtle the rights and wrongs of the matter might be, and however delicate the national pride, I approached the thought of setting foot in England with immense excitement.

I had good academic contacts in Australia now, and was confident I could come back to an academic job if that was what I wanted. There appeared to be no obstacles, either, to my becoming an Australian writer – as New Zealanders like Douglas Stewart and Ruth Park* had done. But I was almost equally sure that if it came to choosing between *here* and *there*, the *here* would be New Zealand and the *there* England. Australia had been good to me; but I was still burdened with that naïve idealism I have described in *South-West of Eden*, about 'creating a New Zealand literature' – the idea that had been planted, not by injunction but by example, in particular that of Curnow and Sargeson. Charles Brasch, as founder and funder of our one good literary quarterly, *Landfall*, was also an important part of that literary-nationalist project.

Yet none of what these men wrote to me seemed to urge me to come home soon. Brasch had written,

> Don't throw up Armidale lightly [. . .] For almost all writers writing must be a vocation not a profession; this is a hard truth one has to face. I can't give you any good advice; but don't act hastily; and do please tell me what you think of doing.

And from Curnow:

> From all accounts your move has turned out well. It's a bleak way of putting it but I can't think of anything worse for you

* Park's 1948 novel, *The Harp in the South*, had established her as a significant figure on the literary scene. When she died in 2010 aged ninety-three the *Australian* described her as author of 'classic Australian novels'.

> than staying here would have been. There's too much fake erudition about this Department; some day there will have to be a big house-clean, we'll stop posing as savants in three centuries of Eng. Lit. & teach what we know or have time to read.

I can't have taken a lot of notice of this warning because on the eve of leaving Armidale I was writing to Sargeson that I intended to spend just two years in England and then come back to Auckland, 'even if there's no job for me'. It was early to announce this with such certainty. The '*here*' was known; the '*there*' had yet to be experienced.

Brasch, who was making a brief trip to England and had hoped to meet me there, wrote,

> So you are going to England! Alas we shan't meet for I sail again about 2 August [. . .] It's a great disappointment to be missing you; I'd so hoped to see you there. Please don't forget *Landfall*; New Zealand will always need you. This sounds like goodbye again, so I wish you the best of fortune with all my heart.

I wrote a 'Last poem in Australia', which was fond enough but certainly not suffused with regret – I was too focused on what lay ahead. A group of eight or ten people came to see us off at the Armidale station. It was a night train and we had booked a sleeper. Among those there to say goodbye were Ada (pregnant) and Israel Getzler, and Otto Bergmann (without Joyce, who had taken a temporary lectureship in Auckland). There was a lot of noise, promises of letters and meetings-again, hilarity and some tears. Otto hugged us both, the whistle was blown, we climbed aboard, were waved away and settled for the night. Next morning early, when we emerged on the station platform at Sydney central, there was Otto again, welcoming us. It was a joke and a generous gesture. He had driven through the night to surprise us and say goodbye one more time.

Two or three days later we were at sea on the *Oronsay* (from memory 28,000 tons), P&O sister-ship of the *Orsova* that had brought us from Auckland.

Postscripts:
We never saw either Otto and Joyce Bergmann nor Israel and Ada Getzler again. Otto reported by letter that the Getzler baby was a boy, born soon after we left, and would be named David. Joyce kept up Christmas messages. She and Otto moved in 1958 to Baltimore, the following year to the University of Alabama, and finally in 1962 to George Washington University in Washington, DC, where Otto was promoted to a full professorship in 1968, by which time they had two children, 'Toni' (Anton) and 'Lizzie' (Elizabeth). Joyce reported (card undated but a year when Lyndon Johnson was lighting the National Christmas Tree and the students were rioting) she had had a radical mastectomy. She died in 1977. Otto's distinguished career, with papers on particle physics, special and general relativity, plasma physics, and material science, continued until he retired in 1988 as professor emeritus. He died in 2013 aged eighty-eight.

We lost contact with the Getzlers and what I know of him comes from an obituary in the *Guardian*. He went from Armidale to Adelaide, then to London. He became an international expert on modern Russian history, arguing in several important books that the Russian Revolution need not have gone the way it did, that totalitarianism was not inevitable. In 1971 he was appointed Professor of History at the Hebrew University of Jerusalem. This, the obit writer says, had been his 'lifelong dream', but he raged constantly against his country's treatment of the Palestinians, and against the settlement policies of both the Likud and the Labor parties. His marriage to Ada ended in divorce and his second wife, to whom he had a daughter, was a political journalist and peace activist. He was a member of the Peace Now movement, and continued protesting into old age. He died in 2012, aged ninety-one.

Iain Lonie returned to New Zealand where his first marriage foundered, and his second ended tragically with the sudden death of the new wife. He lived on for some years after that, writing poems about grief and loss, and then in 1988 killed himself. His best book, *Winter Walk at Morning*, was published posthumously in 1991.

2. Woodbines with Lionel Knights

Further 'overseas'

Kay and I calculated once that we had spent almost six months of our lives at sea simply coming and going between New Zealand and the United Kingdom. People pay large sums to travel that way now, not to go anywhere in particular, just to 'travel'. It has its moments, especially when you come into a new port in the early morning after many days at sea; but mostly I was bored and uncomfortable. Though I never threw up I felt often close to it when the seas were rough. Days passed during which I felt sickish, sleepily unfocused, rather like the condition many women report during pregnancy.

We travelled twice to England by P&O through Suez, returning by the New Zealand Line through Panama. Our third voyage to England took us north by the Chandris Line, past Pitcairn Island and through the Panama Canal; then up America's east coast to New York, and across the Atlantic. That was 1972, with three small children, and that time we returned by air.

The sea voyages usually divided into three parts – rough in the Southern Ocean, mainly (but not always) calm and hot through the middle latitudes, then rough again out of the Mediterranean into the Bay of Biscay, or across the Atlantic from New York. There was a certain oppressive and intrusive jolliness on board, with a professional entertainment officer to keep you occupied, exercised, and 'happy' – bingo and quizzes in the evenings, dances and parties, ceremonies of 'Crossing the Line' when Neptune dunked the younger ones in the pool and issued certificates. There was a great deal of food, many meals and sub-meals, and boredom, which meant everyone ate (and drank too – booze was duty-free) more than was good for them.

As the cabins grew hotter and more uncomfortable many – the young especially – took to sleeping on deck. This was sanctioned and stretchers or deck mattresses were provided. I do have fond recollections of watching the tropic stars through such rigging as there was, hearing the engines drumming, the sea swishing by, and feeling not just soothed, but excited too, to be on the move, to be going so far 'overseas' – not just to Australia, which was only a visit to your cousins 'across the ditch'. Men had joined up for war just so they could do this – get away from home, out of the cage, experience the adventure of foreign climes and languages, as well as the thrills of battle.

And it was travel at a human pace. Those ships, which were hardly in the 'slow boat to China' class and got along, indeed, at a fair clip, travelled only as far in twenty-four hours as a modern jet covers in one; so instead of the great leaps in time zones the body clock has had to learn to accommodate with east–west air travel, the ship's clocks were adjusted usually at a rate of about one hour each day or second day. I remember on my first return to New Zealand my dreams during the first part of the journey seemed mostly to happen in England; then New Zealand began to appear – dreams of childhood, mostly. By the end of the journey England, still very much in my daily thoughts, seemed to have been expelled from dreamland. Some part of the mind, quite independent of the will, was making its own adjustments.

On that first journey the days beyond Melbourne, getting through the Great Australian Bight, were given over to finding one's 'sea legs', and learning how a 28,000-ton ship can, not just roll, but pitch from end to end, so one moment a lower deck appears like a shaft going steeply down into turbulent sea, and the next is pointing up, equally steeply, into turbulent sky; and how the screws can shudder and complain when lifted clear of the water and given nothing to drive against.

On the long many-days' haul across the Indian Ocean between Perth and Ceylon (as it then was) we passed into calm navy-blue ocean, with flying fish sprinting out from the white bow wave like a small silver artillery.

The Suez Canal was once again open but tension remained in that region as a result of Anthony Eden's failed attempt to wrest it back from Egypt and into Franco-British hands. In Aden, a British colonial port, a place of military uniforms and swagger sticks on the one hand, skinny brown legs and loincloths on the other, a group of us who had gone into the town for sightseeing adventures, were suddenly surrounded by a hostile crowd and had to escape back to the ship in taxis, with men hammering on the roofs and windows with their fists and shouting 'Limey bastards'.

Suez was some hundreds of kilometres on, up the Red Sea. The canal, when you reached it and entered, was entirely desert on one side, and on the other lush green fruit- and flower-filled gardens; and because the canal was not a straight line but, for its first few kilometres at the Red Sea end took a dog's-leg route, there were moments when you looked across desert from your deck or cabin and saw another ship appearing to be on the move through, or over, the sands. There was still some wreckage from the recent fighting, but very little. The scene was peaceful and orderly and the canal was working in a way Eden had argued simply could not happen if the Egyptians ever got control of it. But there was to be no going ashore at Port Said – it would not have been safe.

In the Mediterranean there were shore visits at Naples and Marseilles, and in both places, though World War II was now some years over, some of the damage, and evidence still of distress and poverty, remained. It would be another fifteen years before we would begin to be truly at home in this region of citrus and cypress, olive and grape, and I could not have imagined how strongly and continuously it would figure in my life thereafter. And now it was out into the rough-house of the Atlantic, up the Portuguese coast, across the Bay of Biscay into the Channel, and so to Tilbury Docks.

I no longer have any memory of the arrangements we must have made for the delivery and/or storage of the large amounts of stuff everyone travelled with then – a cabin trunk full of bedding and linen, crockery, cutlery and God knows what. But they must have been settled there on the dock after the passage through Customs, and we were soon on a train to London. We took that journey with a middle-aged New Zealand man, Jack or Fred or Bill, we'd got to know and to like on the voyage. He was single, quiet, thoughtful, kindly, a relatively uneducated, unsophisticated working man, who had no wife, family or attachments – a character out of a Frank Sargeson story, who had decided in middle life he would 'go to England'. Maybe he'd missed the war; or it had not taken him far from home. He was 'travelling on a shoestring', he said, had taken the cheapest fare, sharing a six-berth cabin with strangers.

We would not see him again after that day, but I remember him so clearly, I think, because I felt we were in the same state of mind – a sort of astonishment that here was London, becoming real. There were no beautiful or remarkable sights – mainly brick, the brown backs of houses you see from English trains, and sometimes longer views, whole streets of terrace houses, glimpses of very green parks, trees still in lush full leaf, and playing fields, gasworks, murky canals. But what it was, recognisably and beyond doubt, was *England*, a realm of magic. This was our secret and (one might have felt but would under no circumstances have acknowledged) our treasure, not vouchsafed to those merely born there.

Bristol

There was a week in London with old friends from Takapuna, John and Patsy Dutch, living in Sidcup (south London). Each day for most of a week we took the train in with them to Charing Cross, they to go to their workplaces, Kay and I to go wherever our feet took us, to see the things tourists see, palaces, art galleries, the river and its bridges, the parks of the West End, the churches and cathedrals, Parliament; but more, just to see what we came upon, to be taken by surprise. There were still scars, craters, areas of wasteland from the World War II bombing, especially around St Paul's – these areas covered in weeds and self-sown buddleia, and patrolled by feral cats. It was the beginning of an ongoing connection that has made London my second city, where my 'other' self has lived its flickering shadowy and occasionally vivid 'other life' for more than half a century. I suppose during these days too I made arrangements for getting our luggage to Bristol.

We were soon in a flat there, in the suburb, or outlying village, of Westbury-on-Trym – 'very old', I reported home the day after my twenty-fifth birthday, 'with a trickle of water we take to be the Trym running under innumerable stone bridges'. There were woods, a castle, an ancient church, and I had my hair cut in a building that had been a priory in 715. A five-penny bus ride took you to the university, sixpence to the town centre.

The flat was the upper floor of a semi-detached house, owned by a very posh English horsewoman and her very large hunting dog and seemingly also somewhat posh German husband. She ran a 'School of Equitation', and there were hunting prints on the walls downstairs, and the stuffed head of a fox she had killed on Durdham Down in 1939. The husband appeared to do little apart from watching programmes on television about tribal customs, a fact which clearly displeased her, though there must surely have been times when he did 'mucking out' at the stables. Our flat had its own bathroom and a second bedroom. The weekly rent was £4, and the first handing-over was cause for embarrassment: she shivered visibly receiving the banknotes, and made it clear that if, from now on, it was to come in the form of cash, this was to be placed in a plain envelope on a small table in the hallway.

Like London, Bristol still had many scars visible from the Blitz, but the city was charming, full of ups and downs, the 'downs' in fact being ups – or 'rolling uplands' as the *Shorter Oxford* defines the word – broad generous grassland parks. It had names and institutions redolent of its past – the Red Maids' School, Whiteladies hill, Temple Meads station, the Merchant Taylors' School where the boys wore a long black cassock tied around the waist by a rope. The university sat grandly at the top of George Street, which runs steeply down to the centre. There was also Isambard Kingdom Brunel's famous Clifton suspension bridge, matching his Hammersmith Bridge in London, but more dramatic, built as it is over the deep gorge of the Avon. And there were the docks from which famous sailors, real and fictional, had put to sea, and which to me had a familiar feel about them if only because it was here the *Hispaniola*'s crew had been recruited, with the help of Long John Silver the one-legged sea cook, before they sailed for Treasure Island. Down there too was the old eighteenth-century Theatre Royal which had been, since the end of the war, home to the Bristol Old Vic. Later during our stay Kay would work in that area as a shorthand typist for the Bristol Steam Navigation Company, in sight of the church where Coleridge was married, St Mary Redcliffe with its dramatic and elegant spire.

The Bristol accent was charming, with a lot of 'oi' sounds and a burred 'r'. A phrase I overheard stuck in my head as a kind of touchstone for mimicry – 'Going up here Saturday', which I heard as 'Goonoop'ere suturr-dee'. There was also a tendency to put an 'l' on the end of some words – gypsies, for example, were gypsols – which was how the name Brightstowe had evolved into Bristol.

We bought our car, registration number 576AHY, a grey Ford Popular, the cheapest on the market at £450 new, which included £150 tax. Neither of us had ever driven, and I remember the night we bought it, looking out at it under the street lamp in the swirling mist and wishing it would just go away, leave us, disappear. I paid for a few lessons, put my name down for the driving test, got myself an L plate, and drove. There were some bad moments, but the licence was earned eventually and I still have it, the only one for which I was ever tested. You had to drive with your window down in all weathers so the compulsory hand signals could be made, including a strange circular motion of the whole right arm, indicating a turn left was about to be made.

We were soon loving our tall skinny brutally sprung car and the places we could go in it. There was a regular tour we made with friends who visited from London – Patsy and John, other New Zealand friends, but also Margaret Bell, and, on their way home via Europe, Lee and Jack Bartley. This was a circuit taking in Bath with its elegant Georgian crescents and terraces and its Roman remains; then Wells Cathedral with its imposing façade and its Bishop's Palace where swans on the moat tugged at a bell rope to be fed; and Wookey Hole, a system of limestone caves with a rich history. Sometimes the Cheddar Gorge was also included. Later we went further afield – north-east to Gloucester and Berkeley Castle; across into Wales by the Aust Ferry (no bridge across the Severn Estuary in those days) and up the Wye Valley to find Tintern Abbey. I had most of Wordsworth's poem about the abbey by heart from school days, but I complained in a letter to Charles Brasch after the visit that Wordsworth had not had to pay sixpence to a man in a peaked cap.

On 7 November 1957, the fortieth anniversary of the Russian Revolution, the USSR, locked in a space race with the USA, put a dog they called Laika (Barker) into orbit on board Sputnik 2. I stood on the Downs at night staring up at the stars and trying to imagine the poor pooch circling the globe every ninety minutes – something we have since got used to but which at the time seemed both sad (how would they ever get it back? – they didn't of course) and technologically brilliant.

There was a new poet just beginning to be noticed and praised, Ted Hughes, and for Kay's twenty-fourth birthday I gave her a copy of his first book, *The Hawk in the Rain*. Hughes had dedicated it 'to Sylvia', a name which as yet had no resonance for us. I was thinking of offering a collection of my own for publication and dithering about what to include and what was an appropriate length. I notice I have written '41 poems, 974 lines' in pencil at the end of the Hughes book, and '29 poems, 630 lines' (which seemed better, more 'achievable') at the end of Larkin's *The Less Deceived*. To Charles Brasch (it was Christmas, and there were, I told him, carol singers under the street light outside 'looking like polar explorers') I wrote about current poets and poetry in Britain:

> Somewhere one has to find an intermediate point between the hammer and the Chinese vase. Ted Hughes is the latest Book Society choice and some of his poems are strong and good. Thom Gunn less so. The Movement poets are too dry and mechanical – but I still have a high opinion of Larkin. Amis and Wain are clever but I don't know that either will produce poems that matter – they haven't so far.

But writing in New Zealand was never far from my thoughts. I told Sargeson that working on Yeats had given me 'the conviction that a great literature could grow up in N.Z. if only our literary world would grow more self-conscious, more critical, and more confident'. These were the ruminations of a serious literary nationalist!

There were always places to go, things to do and to see in the West Country; but London pulled, and it was just a few days before Christmas Eve when we drove through Marlborough and Slough, through Hammersmith, Kensington and Piccadilly (two-way in those days), two or three times around the Piccadilly Circus (still possible then), down the Haymarket – and then . . . where? Unsure, I stopped beside an island among the traffic circling Trafalgar Square (that too has changed), and got out under the lights to read our map. A gentle snow was drifting down, the big Christmas tree was up in the square, and there was a sound, above the traffic, of angelic voices singing carols. I should not have stopped there of course, but it was one of those moments of desperation when you're new to driving, and in a strange place, lost. A policeman, unable to get to me through the traffic, was signalling fiercely as I drove off again – on along the Strand and over Waterloo Bridge. Somehow we got to Sidcup where John and Patsy Dutch were expecting us.

John, whose short story 'Death of a Bullock' I had published two years before in Auckland University's student annual, *Kiwi*, was trying journalism, working for a trade magazine called *White Fish* while writing a deeply Faulkneresque novel. I had already been through three of his short stories with him to get them into presentable shape, and they had gone off to Brasch for *Landfall* with a strong recommendation from me. Brasch had seemed interested but returned them.

Patsy worked for a small jewellery firm, H. H. Plante – 'by appointment to her Majesty', so the horses' silverware was sometimes brought from the Palace in a taxi for cleaning. One day a gent in a bowler brought in a silver épergne which he wanted gilded, and Patsy noticed the name on the order: Evelyn Waugh – a case of absurd 'poshing up' which struck Sargeson as so perfect, and typical of Waugh when he heard about it, he put it into the third of his memoirs.*

There was an untypically large amount of Christmas snow that year, and after making a snowman in the morning at Sidcup we had the dinner – turkey with chestnut stuffing, pudding with burning brandy, and champagne – in a big flat in Castelnau Mansions on the south side of the Hammersmith Bridge, with seven New Zealanders and one Ethiopian Greek-Cypriot, Evrodiki Michaelidou. We were,

* *Never Enough: Places and People Mainly*, Martin Brian & O'Keefe, 1977, p. 107, though he had forgotten the details and made the item a set of cuff links.

it seemed, in *England*, truly, unbelievably, having the kind of Christmas our greeting cards and decorations at home had told us, since childhood, was 'proper' and made Christmas 'real'.

But it was on the Downs in Bristol Kay and I discovered that we both invariably made the wrong assumption about directions, picking east as west and west as east. It was, I decided, because in the Southern Hemisphere when you face the sun's path you face north, so the sun moves from right to left; in the Northern Hemisphere looking to the sun's path you face south and it moves from left to right. This was somehow built-in and permanent 'knowledge', so your immediate (usually unconscious) assumptions, if there was no correcting indicator, were wrong.

We were, then, and forever it seemed, indelibly of the Southern Hemisphere, where the sun when you face it travels right to left, and where the proper place to be at Christmas is outdoors in the sun, at the beach and in the sea.

The graduate student

But all this time I was hard at work – 'hard', and yet it seemed effortless. Everything was a joy. Bliss was it in that dawn to be alive – and so on . . . Bristol's university, or rather its principal building, was like a larger version of Auckland's – a neo-Gothic monster of similarly recent vintage, endowed by the cigarette manufacturers W. D. & H. O. Wills, who had begun in Bristol. Auckland University's Arts and Library building was known as the Wedding Cake; Bristol's (in those days without embarrassment about the cigarette connection) as Wills Castle. Both featured a tower. I smoked Woodbines, certainly not out of loyalty to W. D. & H. O. (I doubt I knew they were the makers) but just because they were the cheapest you could buy; and at our first social meeting my professor, L. C. Knights, joked about middle-class boys who affected working-class habits by smoking that brand. How English! It had to be an affectation, and to do with class – not an economy.

But my relations with him, then and thereafter, were good. He got me to write something about my research intentions, and then declared he was 'giving himself the luxury' of appointing himself my supervisor. He was gentle in manner, formidably articulate in public, and it was possible to get on a personal, or less impersonal anyway, footing quite early. It was not, however, until later in my stay in Bristol that a further step towards relaxation of the codes was signalled, and in a very English way – a letter about the work I was doing which began 'My dear Stead' and then '(may we drop the formalities?)'. This meant he wouldn't any longer address me as 'Mr Stead', and I would not have to address him as 'Professor Knights'. Now we would be 'Stead' and 'Knights' – or in letters always 'My dear Stead' and 'My dear Knights'. The unlikely further advance into the frightful intimacy of first names, 'Karl' and 'Lionel', could only come, if it were ever to happen, after some years of recognising one another as colleagues.

Knights and I met at intervals, sometimes at Bristol's Kardomah coffee house, sometimes at his house, or his university office, to discuss my work. If it was at his house he would often begin by reading to me the most wonderful discovery he had just made in Wordsworth. I was usually called to these meetings by postcard – and these little notes, which always arrived promptly, sometimes even on the day posted, remind me how comparatively little phones were used when they had to be attached to something, and when many flats didn't have one. Knights appreciated that I had ideas of my own, particularly about T. S. Eliot, and would hope to pursue them critically; but he stressed there would have to be 'a research component', and I think it was his idea, or his extension of a suggestion of mine, that I should explore what was going on in literary periodicals in the early years of the century when what came to be known as Modernism was first appearing. This became an important element in the finished thesis, my first published critical work, *The New Poetic*.

Once, when the subject of F. R. Leavis came up in conversation, Knights told me, with clear evidence of pain, how Leavis had attacked him in print, in their own periodical, *Scrutiny*, for a piece he had written about *Measure for Measure*. It was an attack I was aware of, typical of Leavis in its not letting up, and in its total absence of that 'Yes, but . . .' tone he was supposed to favour. Knights was bruised: it must have felt like being one of the Twelve and hearing yourself chastised in a sermon by the Master. But for the moment, and despite that wound, Bristol's was still an indelibly Leavisite English Department, which meant, among other things, that Yeats, whose work I wanted to figure prominently in my thesis, was not favoured. This was something I decided to meet head-on.

Knights had an essay on Yeats in his 1946 collection, *Explorations*, thorough in its reading and respectful of the later Yeats, who had replaced the language of Romantic yearning with a poetry capable of expressing the life of 'the personality as a whole'. But Knights concluded, nonetheless, that there were only two Yeats poems, 'Sailing to Byzantium' and 'Among School Children', 'which, without any qualification, deserve the title of "great poetry" '.*

There were all kinds of mock one might make of this: for example, if you were speaking of 'greatness', were two *enough*? And how close did one or two (or ten or twenty) others come? Did they miss by a whisker – or by a mile? Were they like the classic Oxbridge 2:1? Was he sure he'd got the *right* two? And so on. There was something absurdly Leavisite about the precision of it, and the *narrowness*. But of course I had no intention of making mock. I wanted, rather, to make Knights take seriously the degree of seriousness I was going to pay to Yeats who, quite apart from the Leavis influence, was also, I noticed, sometimes slighted simply as 'Irish'. This was in an England where recent flat-hunting had familiarised us with the sign, NO IRISH, NO COLOUREDS.

Knights's broad argument was that even in his later poems, where he did escape from the languor of the Celtic Twilight into the

* L. C. Knights, *Explorations: Essays in Criticism Mainly on the Literature of the Seventeenth Century*, Penguin, 1964 (first published 1946), p. 185.

hard light of the Modern, Yeats still resorted to 'Romantic glamour as an escape from difficult or painful problems'. And in citing a number of examples, he mentioned in passing the refrain of 'Easter 1916', Yeats's eloquent tribute to the sixteen men executed by the British for their part in the 1916 rebellion:

> All changed, changed utterly:
> A terrible beauty is born.

This refrain, Knights argued, 'represents an escape from full realization'.

Knights conducted graduate seminars at regular intervals, attended also by most of the lecturing staff. 'Easter 1916' was a poem I particularly admired in those days. In my research I was paying the closest attention not only to Yeats's poetry but to his essays and autobiographical writings, and I saw a chance here, when my turn came to present a paper, to make a case for the poem – not just for its rhetorical power, but precisely for the intellectual backbone my professor had suggested it lacked. This was the exposition which later went into *The New Poetic*, and into so many subsequent anthologies of Yeats criticism it can now, I think, be called the poem's definitive reading.*

I had not, of course, set out to represent Knights as guilty of a critical sin, or lapse of taste – I was employing, I thought, the proper Leavisite 'Yes, but . . .' approach to a critical question. In fact I was keenly intent (not just because he was my professor, but because I liked him very much) on treading carefully and politely. But I felt

---

* C. K. Stead, *The New Poetic*, Hutchinson University Library, 1964, pp. 35–38. The reading is reproduced in (for example) *W. B. Yeats* (Penguin critical anthologies), ed. William H. Pritchard, Penguin, 1972; *William Butler Yeats: A Collection of Criticism*, ed. Patrick J. Keane, McGraw-Hill, 1973; *Yeats: Poems, 1919–1935, A Selection of Critical Essays*, ed. Elizabeth Cullingford, Palgrave, 1984; *The Poems of W. B. Yeats, A Literary Sourcebook*, ed. Michael O'Neill, Routledge, 2004; *The Poetry of W. B. Yeats, A Reader's Guide to Essential Criticism*, ed. Michael Faherty, Palgrave, 2005.

that somehow this challenge had to be made, and in the department, because Yeats was such an important part of the work I wanted to do – and there was a tone of casual dismissal of him that prevailed there. 'Consoom me horrt away' I'd heard Henry Gifford, the senior lecturer, intone, mocking a famous Yeats line for comic effect.

Knights was more than good about my paper. He not only acknowledged generously that my case had been made; I think he saw me now as someone who could be turned loose with minimal supervision, and with confidence there would be an outcome. But there must have been some slight wince, because I notice that a later one of those postcards (this one sent to me in London) by which I was summoned to a supervision meeting, begins:

> I have read your new chapter with enjoyment (and with rather less than usual of the masochistic pleasure of having my corns trodden on), and have only a small number of minor comments. Would it be convenient for you to come to Bristol for a meeting on the afternoon of the 24th, or the morning of the 25th, or morning of the 2nd – but, within limits, I can adjust to suit you. Let me know.

This can only have referred to the 'Easter 1916' paper because I don't think there was another occasion where I made a clear point of disagreeing with him. I should add that when that reading of the poem was published I removed all mention of the Knights essay as its occasion.

The university had distinguished visitors from time to time. One of these, who came in the winter of 1958 as Churchill Professor, was Edwin Muir, often described (with Hugh MacDiarmid) as one of the two major Scottish poets of the first half of the twentieth century; and because he'd admired something of mine Knights had shown him, and (more important) because we had a car, Kay and I were put in partial charge of him for the month he was there, picking him up from his hotel and driving him about. The piece of mine he'd been shown was about T. S. Eliot, and Muir entertained us with stories Eliot had told him about his time in Paris with James Joyce. He joked that at the age of sixty-eight Eliot had prepared for his recent marriage to his young secretary Valerie by taking dancing lessons. The marriage had happened in secret early on a winter morning, without guests or any celebration apart from the couple's own. Eliot, Muir said, was a very strange and secretive fellow – mysterious, like his poems . . .

Another visitor to the department was the Canadian-born, American-by-adoption, critic Hugh Kenner, already a notable Eliot scholar. I don't now remember much of his lecture but I recall his natty bow tie and mop of curly hair, and how his at first disconcerting speech (a consequence of deafness in childhood) contrasted with Lionel Knights's smoothness and fluency introducing him; and yet how the keen intelligence and originality shone through. This was the man who made me aware I needed to know more about Ezra Pound, and who gave the idea of 'Modernism' an intellectual edge – made a puzzle and a challenge of it.

One purpose of Kenner's Bristol visit was to cement his association with Charles Tomlinson, a junior lecturer in the department, and the only British poet whose work Kenner felt was in tune with important things that were going on in American poetry. I can't now quite disengage my present overview of Kenner from the much less I would have known about him then.* He is author of one of the great books of twentieth-century literary criticism, *The Pound Era* (1972) – great not only for its intelligence and scholarship but for liveliness, originality and readability. Yet Kenner can also seem at times a critic with quite extreme quirks and crankiness, prone to clever but absurd overstatement, like a brilliant drunk in full flight. In that year he was giving Charles Tomlinson

* See my review of Kenner's *Historical Fictions: Essays* for the *Times Literary Supplement*, 25 January 1991, reprinted in my *Shelf Life: Reviews, Replies and Reminiscences*, Auckland University Press, 2016, p. 121.

a start he might never otherwise have had, putting him in direct touch with American poets he admired, William Carlos Williams and Marianne Moore, and persuading his own American publisher, McDowell, Obolensky, to take Tomlinson's collection of poems, *Seeing is Believing*, which no publisher in England (Charles said he'd tried them all) would touch.

This was the time when the British poets of the Movement, in reaction against the flamboyance of Dylan Thomas, George Barker and the 'new Romantics' of the 1940s, were being defined and displayed in anthologies, from which Tomlinson had been excluded. Hell hath no fury like a poet shut out of a currently fashionable anthology, and Tomlinson was busy scourging the Movement in journals on either side of the Atlantic – in *Poetry* (Chicago), and in *Essays in Criticism* (Oxford) where he devoted no fewer than nine pages to the punishment of what he called 'the Middlebrow Muse'.*

To me Tomlinson appeared as an interesting specimen of one kind of Englishness, a man whose father sometimes believed, and liked to claim, he was of royal blood on the wrong side of the blanket, and that he had married beneath him in that his wife, the poet's mother, had been a Leicestershire mill girl. Tomlinson senior had lost his job as foreman in a factory that made jam pots, but was expert at fishing in the canals – which must have made the Eliot lines especially redolent to the son when he first encountered them in 'The Waste Land':

> While I was fishing in the dull canal
> On a winter evening round behind the gashouse
> Musing upon the king my brother's wreck.

As a student at Cambridge where he had won an exhibition, Tomlinson had not been happy until, in his second year, Donald

* *Poetry* (Chicago), January 1957; and *Essays in Criticism*, April 1957.

Davie became his tutor. Davie, who can't have been many years older than his charge, was also a poet, alert to what was happening in the American poetry scene, a critic as readable as Kenner but less eccentric, and interested especially in the syntax of poetry which he characterised as 'articulate energy'. He and Tomlinson formed a bond that lasted a lifetime.

After graduating, and teaching unhappily in a school in Camden Town, Tomlinson scored a post as private secretary to the British writer Percy Lubbock, then living in Italy, in Lerici; but he was dismissed after three weeks, probably, he thought, because his genteel employer found his flat Midlands 'a' vowel unacceptable. Lubbock, he said, believed even 'ants' should be pronounced 'aunts' – but he allowed Charles and his wife Brenda to stay on there in a *villino* adjoining the gardener's cottage, thus giving the Tomlinson sensibility an Italian airing from which it never looked back. It was a region the couple were to return to often.

Tomlinson was seven years my senior and, though only a junior lecturer, was my senior also in status. We were amiably aware of one another without being close, and met regularly in graduate seminars. In 1958 he and Brenda had just moved to a rural location with the wonderfully English address of Brook Cottage, Ozleworth Bottom, Wotton-under-Edge. Many years later, at a conference in Tübingen on poetry and regionalism, he and I would reminisce warmly about the L. C. Knights days in Bristol. Tomlinson had stayed on in the Bristol department his whole working life, in the end I think occupying the Winterstoke chair, the one Knights had held.

But in 1957 I was (perhaps without good reason, certainly without careful consideration) put off his poetry partly just by his manner in person, a look of depleted energy, in fact of such profound, unrelenting weariness, I felt if it was not an illness it had to be an affectation; and by something in the lines themselves – a kind of *dis*engagement, as if the words had been picked out with immense care, but with a faint feeling of distaste.

Janet

I'd had messages from Janet Frame. One of these, excessively metaphorical as she admitted herself, about gratitude and pot plants, thanked us for our contribution to her travel costs. A second, an aerogramme also sent to Armidale, had had to limp back after us surface mail, all the way to Bristol. It told us she was now in the Maudsley psychiatric hospital in London and was being psychologically treated. She added something to this about having all the trappings, and I thought she might have intended it as a latent pun.

Now came another little message from the Maudsley, postmarked 15 December, rather scrappy and desolate-looking on a torn piece of yellow paper, saying she had been sick in hospital but thought often of us both and would so much like to see us. A PS said she had changed her name to Janet Clutha. I replied, signing myself Karl Waikato, and promising to visit.

I knew from Sargeson that she had been a year or more in Spain (Ibiza mainly). Having sent her packing,* Frank was now in a constant flap – about her luggage when it was briefly lost, about her shortage of money, her precarious situation and state of mind – trying, now that she was out of reach, to be still 'hands on' and in control. I was urged to visit her, to extract information about her welfare, and especially, if possible, to get hold of any literary manuscripts she could be persuaded to release, for which posterity, Frank assured me, would thank me eternally.

Kay and I had been Janet's close friends in 1955. I felt slightly reluctant, or resistant to this pressure from Frank; but the appeal from Janet herself was touching. Late in January we called at the hospital to see her. To Frank I wrote:

> Janet had got into bed and put on sun-glasses and had the bed-covers up to her chin, but these were soon removed, and she

* In recommending *Owls Do Cry*, which he had sent to us, he had written, 'But it's fortunate for myself that I have managed to ship the author abroad.'

> quickly got used to talking to us. I couldn't see that her mental state was any worse than when we knew her at your place.
>
> She says she had a love affair on Ibiza – with a friend of an artist who lived upstairs – and then another one in (I think this is right) Andorra. She finished a novel (all very *Daily Mail* and no good at all) about Ibiza, and then began another which she couldn't get straight. There has been what she describes as a traffic jam and this is the cause of her present trouble. The Ibiza novel is locked away (where? Maybe the bank?) and the more pressure she feels from N.Z. to produce it the less inclined she is to do anything with it. [. . .] She says she regrets publishing *Owls [Do Cry]* but I think there wasn't much conviction in the regret.

She was not thinking of coming home yet, she said, but seemed to like the idea of Ōamaru, with the mayor and the town council and everyone knowing everyone. This last was a characteristic Janet remark. Her voice trembled very slightly on the brink of what might have (but didn't) become a laugh. Conversation with her was full of such moments – just as her writing is when it's at its best. Things she said, and truly meant, also seemed to be faintly mocked – as if there were two Janets, a sentimentalist and a satirist, speaking with one voice. She was a person who seemed always eager to live inside the social reality, obeying its norms and codes, but carrying at the same time the tragic-comic knowledge that came of having lived for a time quite outside it.

Soon after hearing of this visit from me, spider Sargeson at the centre of his web was receiving Janet's report. She told him that Kay, with a red-and-white spotted handkerchief on her head, looked like a little gypsy, and Karl's forehead was transparent. We had said we were homesick for our evenings at Esmonde Road, and Janet exclaimed at the tragedy of little gypsies and poets.

I think (in fact I'm certain) the fondness we both felt for her was returned – the feeling that led her to write many years later that our friendship, during that year in Takapuna, had filled her life, giving her at last a place in her own years; but it seems clear also that, towards the little gypsy and the scholar with the transparent forehead, there must have been mixed feelings. Perhaps in some meaner compartment of her richly ambiguous (and world-wounded) mind she half hoped that, as in her story 'The Triumph of Poetry', Kay might prove to be suburban and barren, and that poetry would fail me as I became just one more dusty academic.*

It was to be almost a year before we saw her again.†

Colonial / post-colonial

We'd been six or seven months in Westbury-on-Trym when the landlady's hunting dog was run over in the street and killed. She was distraught – in fact set up the most extraordinary howling and sobbing that was strange because, though wordless and even canine, it still sounded unmistakably posh. The right accent, it seemed, if you had it, was not lost even *in extremis* – something to do with the purity of certain vowels and the diphthongisation of others, in the right combination. She didn't appear to recover her composure in the following days, and I had the impression she blamed the German for the death. She decided the house must be sold – she couldn't stay on there being reminded every moment of her poor dead pooch and his hideous end – and to facilitate the sale process we were asked to leave.

Our new flat was in Cotham – Elmgrove Road, which had no elms, no grove, and much grey stone, but was easy walking distance from the university. It had no second bedroom, but there was a double day-bed for visitors in an ample sitting room, with a broad outlook from the top of the house under high sloping ceilings. The

* This story will be discussed in Chapter 4 under 'A baby, New York, Maurice, Barry, and Janet again', p. 112.

† Michael King, *Wrestling with the Angel*, Viking, 2000, pp. 188–89 and note 26, dates a further report of mine about Frame as 4/3/58. The letter comes in fact a year later and is clearly postmarked 4/3/59, which is where it will occur in this account.

rent was £3 a week, a saving of a pound. There was a church next door which rang its deafening bells on Sundays and sometimes during the week. The bathroom was on the middle floor and we shared it with a couple there, and with a bachelor on the ground floor. He was a fish delivery man whose name, Harry Pulsford, soon became in our conversation How Repulsford because of the odour that went with his work, and grew stronger as the week went on. (Fish in England never smells truly fresh to a New Zealand nose.) How Repulsford took a long strong bath once a week on Sunday morning, so heavily perfumed it pervaded the house and one longed for the tart smell of dead fish. He appeared to be the boyfriend of the landlady who lived away from the premises.

By this time we had a number of friends among the graduate students, including Robin Marleyn who had introduced himself on the Wills Castle stairs on my first day there. He was a small, nuggety handsome fellow with a strong beard. His German grandfather had been a minor opera singer who claimed to have shared the stage with Chaliapin and Galli-Curci, and Robin had inherited a fine baritone voice, though so far as I know he never used it solo, only as a member of Bristol's University Choral Society. His father had recently decamped in mysterious circumstances from a university in Wales to take up a lectureship in German in Auckland. Robin had been a student at King's College London, whose senior staff, he soon decided, were unbearably stuffy and conservative. But it was there he came under the influence of two young Cambridge men, both strong Leavisites. Robin became in effect a convert, and wanted to escape King's College. Since there was no chance (despite what he described as his 'ardent allegiance') of getting into Cambridge and putting himself directly under Leavis's tutelage, he tried for the next best thing – to come in under the Bristol English Department's umbrella, where surely he would be kept warm and dry. He applied for admission to 'a little-known non-graduate MA course' there, and, supported by 'formidable' (Knights's description) references from the young London tutors, was admitted by our professor who consigned him to the care of the senior lecturer, Henry Gifford. Robin, it was decided, would write a thesis on 'Principles and Practice in the Novels of Henry James and D. H. Lawrence'.

Robin's thesis was never submitted – in fact I wonder how much was written. There was at least one substantial chapter completed, because Kay typed it for him in spare moments (of which there were quite enough, she said) at the Bristol Steam Navigation Company. Robin was the perfect Leavisite, very high and mighty about the sins of popular culture, the press, the BBC, the British Council, the publishing industry. He knew which few books were to be respected, and which few authors revered, and that the rest could be ignored or deplored. Once, hearing me whistle a Bach Brandenburg Concerto, he remarked that mine had been 'the *Reader's Digest* version'. He was probably right – I had no doubt skipped a few bars where memory failed or the notes were too difficult for my whistle.

I was certainly not above my own outbursts of assertive or competitive arrogance and literary snobbism. But listening to Robin's dismissive pronouncements about this or that book or writer I was sure he hadn't read, I felt that Leavis, like every messiah or guru, could become an easy route to virtue without ever putting yourself to the test. The Master's confidence replaced your own, and catered to some failure of the will – an ultimate timidity.

But Robin was clever, with a lively sense of humour, and an Ezra Poundian tendency, in conversation and on the page, to torment the language into comic form by remorseless puns, spoonerisms, mispronunciations. Kay and I enjoyed his company. He and Elisabeth Woods, another member of the graduate seminar known as Liz, were a couple, and we were soon taking them on the Bath-Wells-Wooky Hole circuit, Robin keeping up a sort of humming baritone semi- or sub-verbal comic accompaniment, Liz reading a book, not bothering to look at the scenery as we bowled along the almost empty roads through those lovely green West Country landscapes. Liz was clever and eccentric, warm, attractive and likeable. She said of Robin that he had 'a whim of iron'; and I remember her murmuring, parodying Blake as we had coffee and after-dinner mints, 'The *dinnermints* of gratified desire'.* When feeling affectionate they called one another Nig and Nog.

Among our graduate friends there were three from Sheffield who had brought their unvarnished northern accents with them. Brian Mapplethorpe and his wife Marguerita seemed both down-at-heel (struggling, no doubt, on Brian's scholarship) and consciously, or perhaps conscientiously, working class. Brian affirmed Leavisite principles, but he also liked to mock them, as if speaking for the workers against the intellectuals. One of Leavis's touchstones of great literature was what he called 'felt life', and I remember Brian saying '*Felt life?* 'Ave you ever seen Knights at a football match?' It was the flat northern vowels – '. . . laafe . . . Knaaghts . . .' – that made it at once comic and dismissive.

Brian's fellow-northerner was Peter Middleton, another grammar school boy now studying statistics after graduating from Sheffield University with first-class honours in economics. He used to sing, in the accent of his region, a song that went:

> 'Where's tha bin lud?'
> ' 'awkeen papers.'
> ' 'oo for?'
> 'Me ooncle Benjamin.'
> 'Wha's 'e gin thee?'
> 'Skinny old 'ate'ny.'
> 'Silly awl blawk
> 'e ought ta dee.'†

---

* William Blake's line is 'The lineaments of gratified desire'.

† i.e. 'Where've you been, lad?' 'Hawking [news]papers.' 'Who for?' 'My uncle Benjamin.' 'What did he give [pay] you.' 'Skinny old ha'penny.' 'Silly old bloke – he ought to die.'

Peter sang this with unmatchable tunelessness, but it was so consistently the same non-tune, I learned it and can 'sing' it still, exactly as he did – a sort of Modernist piece eschewing melody. He was tall, clever and good-humoured, and seemed purposeful.

Liz Woods' accent was 'RP' – the one least frowned upon, the one earning general social approval without being 'posh'. Robin's, as I remember it, was the same, but with a lilt from a childhood spent in South Wales. Liz liked to call me 'Stid', and get me to say, 'egg sandwich' in my broadest Kiwi, which she heard as 'igg senwudge'.

With spring K & K and the Ford Popular were on the move again, further afield, camping first with John and Patsy Dutch. John was feeling time was short for them in England. He could have elected to stay permanently, as you could in those pre-EU days when our passports described us as 'New Zealand citizen and British subject'. He was tempted, didn't want to go home; but he would have to do National Service,* and the thought of two years in the British Army, taking up the 'white man's burden' of a diminishing Empire, facing angry crowds demanding independence in Cyprus, or Mau Mau freedom fighters in Kenya, or backing up the police in Nyasaland – it was, or might prove to be, a high price to pay for the privilege of being 'British'.

We crossed into Wales, went up into the Snowdon area, then back south to Dylan Thomas's village, Laugharne. It was with John and Patsy two years before we had marched along Takapuna Beach in the night chanting Thomas poems. To Charles Brasch I reported:

> Under Milk Wood is still fantasy but not so fanciful as one imagined. I'm sure we met Mrs Dai Bread I and II in the local bakery – Mrs I insisted on giving us more rolls than we had paid for, and Mrs II on taking them back. I looked through

* I don't recall that I was threatened with this requirement and suppose this must have been because I had already done compulsory military training in New Zealand.

> a crack into Thomas's old writing shed which looks out over beautiful land- and seascapes. It has been locked up and left – a photograph of D. H. L. on the wall, that old Chinese picture of an angler sleeping in his boat among reeds, a stove heater, a chair and a table with bundles of paper. The shed is built out over a small bluff, and windows look out on to the waters of a wide tidal inlet. Thomas's grave is on a hill slope at the other end of the village, and has just a grass mound and a thin white wooden cross. In the local pub there's a photograph of him sitting pugnacious behind a pint, Caitlin beside him very sexy. I'm glad to have seen it all before it becomes National Trussed.

John and I sang old favourites at the grave – 'Sweet Beulah Land' and 'Softly and Tenderly Jesus is Calling' – in my case learned in childhood from my atheist grandmother, in John's from his Māori street-preacher father and their church. I took the melody and he slipped into the descant. Our mood in these renditions was always ironic and mocking; and yet the music was given full force, and something like real feeling came with it.

Contact had been renewed with Don Smith, my fellow student from the 1955 MA class in Auckland, now at Merton College, Oxford, where his first reaction to the social climate (this was while Kay and I were in Armidale) had been one of horror, withdrawal and near breakdown, causing him to return to athletics with renewed ferocity. Before long he was winning races and being praised in the press as a 'tall handsome New Zealander', compared to Lovelock and credited therefore with a Rhodes scholarship, which Don did not have. He was elected in his second year a member of Vincent's Club (described in Oxford-ese of the 1950s as 'frightfully OK' – i.e. socially desirable), and was pursued and written to by pretty undergraduate young women whom he claimed to rebuff. So Kay and I were there with two or three of the young New Zealand women from Castelnau Mansions cheering as he won a big international event at White City on 24 May, beating the European champion, Szengali of Hungary. In the Great Britain v. the Empire match that followed the 1958 Commonwealth Games, he came fourth in the 880 yards behind Herb Elliott (Australian world record holder), Hewson (Great Britain) and Kerr (Jamaica) in a time of 1:49.4, equalling Doug Harris's New Zealand record.*

Don came to stay with us for a few days in Bristol; and we were in Oxford visiting him early in June. I was reading Henry James, and those novels, the English summer and Oxford were having a combined effect that would set in train my first substantial fiction, a story called 'A Race Apart' about (unsurprisingly) a young New Zealand athlete whom I called Andrew Nicholson – fortunately before the presently well-known New Zealand Olympic horseman of that name was born.

I rang Dan Davin, an established port of call for literary and academic Kiwis. Davin at once invited us around to his home in Southmoor Road, saying yes, we must bring our New Zealand friend too. So an early connection was made which would lead, ultimately, to Oxford University Press publishing Don's edition of Andrew Marvell's satire, *The Rehearsal Transprosed* – and also to my own editing of the second *New Zealand Short Stories* in the World's Classics series, of which Davin himself had edited the first. Winnie Davin welcomed us, enacting effortlessly the miracle of the loaves and fishes when the house was further invaded by a homecoming of young Davins, three daughters with the boyfriend of one, Luke, whom I described in a letter home as 'a Balliol freshman, ex-Eton, scruffy, with a lot of hair'. They had been to an anti H-bomb march. It was a time when the anti-nuclear movement was very strong in Britain and constantly in action.

Finally we continued a well-established Davin ritual by retiring to their local, where Dan occupied the chair always reserved for

---

* For an image of D. I. B. Smith in action at White City over the half mile, and winning, not in the May '58 race but I think in the British Olympic trials of 1959 or '60, see http://www.britishpathe.com/video/test-for-olympics/query/hewson

him. It was positioned (as Don noticed) in a corner, so his back was to the wall and he commanded a view of everyone entering and leaving – perfect for the man whose whole life his biographer would later describe metaphorically as 'A Fighting Withdrawal'. Davin had the kudos of the returned soldier and of having won a Rhodes, the scholarship our university had nominated Don for.* His name was associated with John Mulgan's, with whom he had worked at Oxford University Press. Mulgan had distinguished himself during the war and then, mysteriously, had taken his own life. So he was celebrated for his one novel, *Man Alone*, which had a certain dour force, and had greatly excited me when I'd come upon it in the Mt Albert Grammar School library, because it was a 'modern novel', meaning one by someone who had evidently read and learned from Hemingway and Scott Fitzgerald, but set in my own New Zealand landscapes. Davin too wrote fiction, and I had just read his novel *The Sullen Bell* which I described in a letter to Sargeson as 'essential reading for N.Zers here in England', but 'curiously stodgy . . . its prose is lifeless'.

The embarrassment of riches

All this time we were going regularly to theatre and concerts in Bristol, and also Bath (a festival there in May–June '58) and in London. We saw every change at the Bristol Old Vic during our period there. A young and brilliant Peter O'Toole, as yet relatively unknown, had been Vladimir in *Godot* in December '57, and its Hamlet the following April. By 1959 when we were living in London we would see him at the Royal Court in the play that seemed to make him famous almost overnight, Willis Hall's *The Long and the Short and the Tall*. But there was during those few

* Along with my other good friend John Edwards, Auckland's science nominee, neither of them successful. I would have wanted a shot at it myself but was ineligible because married. The Rhodes in those days did not admit women or married men.

years another young star who outshone even O'Toole. At the Lyric Hammersmith in 1959 we saw Patrick McGoohan, first in *Danton's Death* by Büchner, then in Ibsen's *Brand* – two extraordinary performances. Both these actors went on to movies, O'Toole soon famous as Lawrence of Arabia, McGoohan (the more powerful actor I thought – if that means anything when both were so good) never as famous, and possibly best remembered now for a cult TV series, *The Prisoner*.

I thought always in terms of what might be done in New Zealand. My ideas were influenced too by all the Yeats I'd been reading, because his later plays, and the theories he evolved to explain them, seemed more sophisticated than most of what passed for 'thinking' in the modern theatre. Plays like *The Herne's Egg*, *Purgatory*, and *The Death of Cuchulain*, written in the last couple of years of his life, seemed both richly weird and tightly disciplined – written with a great poet's steely economy. In a letter I told Sargeson I was 'sick of prose realism' (should I have said that? but I think he was sick of it too), and that Bristol Old Vic's *Waiting for Godot*

> ... excited me because it shows a possible way out of the 'Tennessee Williams-or-Noel Coward' alternative. Eliot disguises poetry as West End and [Christopher] Fry disguises West End as poetry. The Godot sort of thing could make a break. I've heard about a new surrealist dramatist, Ionesco, who might have something [. . .] It doesn't have to be verse so long as it's stylised, formal, symbolic and intelligent.

Shortly after writing that letter I saw Ionesco's two plays, *The Chairs* and *The Lesson*, and Mayakovsky's *The Bedbug*, described as 'a pantomime comedy in nine scenes', done by London University Drama Society. Even a version of Aristophanes' *Lysistrata* at the Duke of York's, with a richly husky Joan Greenwood in the title role, pushed in that direction – all of which is to leave out Shakespeare (*Lear*, *Macbeth*, *Julius Caesar* at the London Old Vic, Gielgud in

The Tempest at the Theatre Royal Drury Lane) . . . the constant and ongoing force in the theatre, suggesting always both freedom and economy, linguistic inventiveness and linguistic discipline.

Associated with these excitements there were certain locations that increased them – in particular the Dove, a pub on the river at Hammersmith where we went to drink after watching plays at the Lyric. I remember watching Mai Zetterling there, the glamorous Swedish movie star we'd just seen in *Creditors* by Strindberg, another playwright whose work suggested liberation.

There were also movies, and we were all addicted to Westerns which in the '50s and '60s reached a high point, almost Japanese in its ritualised unreality. Don Smith and I loved their absurdities, and practised shoot-outs in the Castelnau Mansions flat, tolerated by the landlady as one or other, or both, crashed to the floor shot through the heart. And then, as if in quite a different world, there was Fellini. I still remember coming out into a car park in Bristol at night having seen my first – *Nights of Cabiria* with Giulietta Masina in the title role – and the sense of astonishment and elation it had produced.

We had been to one of the rich offerings at the Bath Festival at the end of May that year and were back at Elmgrove Road about to sit down to a meal with Robin and Elisabeth, Peter Middleton (he of the 'Where's tha bin lud?' song), and Barbara McKay (Kay's old school friend and my fellow history student from Auckland), when the doorbell rang and it was Louise and Hubert Henderson – Louise the French-born painter (later Dame Louise), and Hubert, former Director of Education in Auckland, the parents of Diane, friend of my student days.* Hubert had been working as a UNESCO education advisor in Jordan, Lebanon, Iraq and Iran; and Louise's work had profited from new scenes and exotic subjects. Now they were taking the long way home via London and Paris. An outcome of this visit was that they offered us the use of their bedsit in London while they went to Paris for a month. This was really the beginning

---

* See *South-West of Eden*, Auckland University Press, 2010, mainly Chapter 16.

of a transition from Bristol to London, necessary because of the direction my PhD research was taking, but sought also because, though Bristol was pleasant London was . . . *London.*

We spent all of June there, and it was in the middle of that month our old friend, Kay's from school days, mine from university, Jill Evans arrived for an OE that might have led to opportunities in the musical world if she had pushed her luck. She had a beautiful lyric soprano voice and had been singing in operas in New Zealand; and when I told Charles Brasch she was now in London he wrote that he had seen her in Gian Carlo Menotti's *The Medium*. 'She was lovely to look at and to listen to,' he said, and so she was. We met her at Southampton and drove her to the Castelnau Mansions flat where she would become a regular among that itinerant mainly Kiwi population. Next day we took her to White City to see Don Smith run (and win) the half mile in the Oxford-Cambridge v. Pennsylvania-Cornell university match.

It was with Jill some time during the summer of 1958 we made our first trip to the Lake District, including Grasmere and the Wordsworths' Dove Cottage, where you could see the very small 'port' in which he carried his few travelling needs – clean linen, spare shirt, one book and, I imagined, notepaper – though possibly not much was needed since he had the habit of composing in his head while walking, a feat of memory in itself, and one which partly explains the beautiful on-running syntax of his *Lyrical Ballads*. We camped in a field just out of Grasmere on the edge of the lake. In the Red Lion pub in the evenings we played darts and drank cider, a taste acquired in Bristol where it was called scrumpy. I found that whereas, sober in daylight, it took me a stop, a reverse, a wheel-turn and second go to get through the narrow stone gates at the entrance to the field, at night after a few scrumpies I could take the Ford through without a stop.

At some time during the summer vacation I told Professor Knights I'd seen an advertisement for a lectureship in the Auckland English Department, and that I'd decided to apply. He said of course he would write in support, but did I need to do this so soon? I told him I wasn't sure how often lectureships would come up. He asked did I need to do it at all. When I didn't have an answer he made it clear that he meant I could have an academic career in Britain. If things went on as well as they were going now there could be a place for me in the Bristol department, which would please him; or in some other one of Britain's better universities. I thanked him and told him I would certainly think about these possibilities, but meanwhile thought the application should go forward.

That response from Knights brought out something I had feared – the sense of it as a temptation. It was as if some part of me was hell-bent on rushing back to New Zealand out of fear of another part that wanted, and might want more and more, to stay. It was during this same conversation Knights agreed that, after Christmas, I would be permitted to move to London so my work at the British Museum could be accelerated. I would spend one more term in Bristol and then be released from the residency requirement, and simply commute down to Bristol by train for graduate seminars and for talks about progress on the thesis.

With Jill Evans we made a trip through Devon and Cornwall, including the region so precisely described by Coleridge in his note on the writing of 'Kubla Khan' that had been interrupted by 'the man from Porlock', and then on to Zennor in Cornwall where Mansfield and Murry had lived side by side with Lawrence and Frieda in dual cottages. Jill sang as we drove – the Irish folk song 'The Lark in the Clear Air', the Mozart aria from *The Marriage of Figaro* ('Gone for ever those hours of gladness'), Adele's song from *Die Fledermaus* protesting that she is not a lady's maid disguised but a real lady, 'Four black swans' from Menotti's *The Medium* . . . We camped along the way, got lost, slept a night in the car in what turned out at morning to be a quarry, and got all the way to St Ives, more for the Frances Hodgkins connection (Kay and I had read Eric McCormick's *The Expatriate*) than for the Barbara Hepworth cottage

Early in December we made the agreed move to London. I gave a new thesis chapter to Knights and that evening there was a *'Farewell (but not Forever) dinner'* with 'the usual suspects'. Kay and I had cleaned and scoured the Elmgrove Road flat. On the morning of 3 December we said our farewells to the How Repulsford and the forgotten-named couple on the middle floor, paid the landlady and, with all our worldly goods packed into 576AHY, we left Bristol for London where, as I wrote to Charles Brasch, the streets were paved with New Zealanders.

3.
London and Dr Johnson's Stone

The BM and Lit. Hist.

The Hendersons' bedsit had been in Phillimore Gardens, a street of many embassies and a few somewhat up-beat rooming houses just off Kensington High Street. We had already secured a bedsit in the same street, in a house owned by the quite genteel Misses Curwen, who might have preferred not to be landladies but were compelled by 'circumstances' – eccentric siblings whom Kay, remembering Mansfield, referred to as 'the daughters of the late colonel'. It cost 5 guineas a week, our highest rent yet, and we paid for gas for cooking and heating one shilling at a time in a gas meter with a slot from which one of the sisters extracted the coins at irregular intervals. If we found ourselves without shilling coins I picked the padlock with one of Kay's hairpins and recycled a coin. This could only be done infrequently or coins and consumption would have been noticeably out of sync. Our tube station was High St Ken on the District and Circle Line, and we were only a short drive from Hammersmith, Castelnau Mansions, the Lyric, the Dove. In the street outside (a measure of how long ago this was) there was always parking, and no fees. In Kensington High Street conveniently close there was, as we might have said then, 'one of those new *supermarkets!*'.

Each day I went on the Circle Line, changing to the Piccadilly at Gloucester Road, and getting out at Russell Square, then walking around past number 24, hoping to catch a glimpse of the newly married grand old man of Faber and Faber, perhaps in his bowler hat. I was working on the emergence of the new poetry out of the aestheticism of the 1890s (socially discredited by the fall of Oscar Wilde), through the cheerfully manly, frequently pompous verse of the Edwardians ('his Captain's hand on his shoulder smote'), on through the Georgians ('The cool kindliness of sheets'), and into Modernism ('The river's tent is broken: the last fingers of leaf / Clutch and sink into the wet bank.'). The Georgians, I soon discovered, were of two sorts – the backward-looking conservatives who clustered around J. C. Squire at the London Mercury, and those favoured by Edward Marsh, editor of the Georgian *Anthology*, who thought of themselves as forward-looking, 'modern', and of liberal tendency. This recognition of a division between kinds of Georgian poetry rescued the term itself from the aura that surrounded it at the time I began my work, of a use-by date already past. One might soon be able to write of Georgian poetry without necessarily suggesting disparagement.

Rupert Brooke, of the forward-looking liberal strand, was not just rather gorgeous – he was also free-thinking and somewhat risqué, with his Pacific Island sexual adventuring (including a visit to New Zealand) and his unromantic poem about chucking up on a Channel crossing. He would be briefly a public hero for greeting the outbreak of the 1914 war with 'Now, God be thanked Who has matched us with His hour'; and even more, in death, for his 'corner of a foreign field / That is for ever England'. Churchill spoke eloquently of him in the House of Commons and wrote his obituary in *The Times*; and Henry James, who had met him in Cambridge, where the beauty of that 'splendid setting' had been matched by the 'reconciling vision' of the man himself, had clearly fallen in love with the image.*

But it was a septic mosquito bite, not a bullet, that killed Brooke; and he would be upstaged, if not in the popular mind, certainly in the literary one, by the 'real' war poets, especially Wilfred Owen, with his dicta 'the true poets must be truthful' and 'the poetry is in the pity'; and by Siegfried Sassoon, author of *Memoirs of a Fox-Hunting Man* who, on leave wounded from the trenches, had tried to get up a soldiers' rebellion against the war. If he had not been an officer and a toff, he would have been shot for this; as it was he was hospitalised and treated as briefly deranged.

This was literary history I was engaged on, but it was also British history, and it was complicated by the powerful presence – intrusion even, invasion – of the Americans. British poetry in the twentieth century was never going to be entirely Modernist, but it was powerfully influenced by those who were – and at the same time somewhat resistant. There were confusions. How, for example, did F. R. Leavis's 'Great Tradition' (the title of one of his books, and the theme he harped on), which was essentially a British, even an *English* tradition, take on board, as it seemed to do, Henry James, T. S. Eliot, and even Joseph Conrad? A perfectly clear descriptive picture was impossible; but one thing was unarguable, that in the period I was studying, and beyond, T. S. Eliot had mysteriously and comprehensively come to rule the literary roost. Everyone deferred to him; everyone was intimidated by his manner and his intellect. As he wrote himself:

> How unpleasant to meet Mr Eliot
> With his features of clerical cut
> And his brow so grim
> And his mouth so prim . . .

---

* See James's preface to *Letters from America by Rupert Brooke*, Charles Scribner's Sons, 1916

How unpleasant, but how exciting. I was enjoying going back into, and over, the years I chose to focus on closely, 1909 to 1916, reliving the debates, watching the developments, the excitement and confusion, measuring and recording something like progress as the new century defined itself and the new poetry emerged.

My place of work was the famous Reading Room of the British Museum, known because of its shape as 'the gasometer', where Karl Marx had worked and written – G. B. Shaw, too; and where Eric Partridge, the New Zealand-born lexicographer, could be seen every day, compiling his works on the English language, its slang, its uses and abuses. Partridge was one of several regulars who, like Davin in his Oxford pub, were always conceded the same seat. Though no rule said no one else could sit there, no one did. One of these recognised regulars was a woman who always wore a khaki shirt and baggy khaki shorts, brown woollen socks and tramping boots. I never discovered who she was, but everyone deferred to her. Knights had arranged a card giving me permission to work there.

The Reading Room was arranged concentrically around the catalogues, large leather-bound books with the entries pasted in by hand, one by one, the catalogue racks themselves forming a circle around a central desk where you took your requests after finding what you needed in the catalogues. The working desks radiated out from that centre to the perimeter. Like miners, the porters spent the whole day going God-knows-where underground and coming up with yet another trolley-load. You claimed a desk for the day and your requests were delivered there.

In one of his notes to me from Bristol (beginning 'Another good chapter, and as usual a pleasure to read') Knights wrote, 'And of course there's nothing like the B.M. Reading Room on a foggy winter's day – when the fog penetrates a bit – but the light seems especially welcome and the guardians of literary decorum, round the base of the dome, hold the fog and the world at bay.' To this warm reminiscence he added, however, 'But don't spend all your time there.' One can go there now as a tourist and see it as a relic of past times. The British Library at King's Cross has completely replaced it. It is vastly superior, the facilities admirable, efficient, necessary. But there used to be a special pleasure in finding things by patient hunting through those unwieldy catalogue books, and the feeling of achievement is not really matched by having technology do the hunting for you.

It was the kind of concentrated work from which one has to take breaks. For the first time in my life I learned to read fast – to skim-read looking for some particular item, a skill I'm glad to say I have since lost. Mid-morning I walked up and down between the Doric columns outside, smoking a Woodbine. Or I walked through the galleries of the museum itself – so often that over time many things became familiar, from the Elgin Marbles (which in their tragic and semi-smashed incompleteness and beauty could have been Modernist works), to the tiny gods lining certain display cases in phallic salute. Very close to the museum were Little Russell and Museum Streets, and Bury Place, with their shops selling rare books and prints.

I was happy in my work, extended, and somehow 'brewing up'. The PhD went ahead. But I began to write something else, a poem – not one poem but a sequence – and in a state of mind that was like holding the breath, watching it happen. I was the observer, and I was also the someone to whom it was happening – the other Karl, the better, slightly inebriate one who could drive through the stone gates at Grasmere without stopping. I would call it 'Pictures in a Gallery Undersea'. I sent it to Brasch some time in December 1958.

Charles had given me G. S. Fraser's address and urged me to call on him – he was one of the New Apocalypse poets and had good literary connections in London. Kay and I drove there and climbed the stairs to his door, then asked one another did we want to do this, and crept away without knocking. Charles told me the Canadian poet Earle Birney was in London, and 'I think you should look him up'. He gave each of us the other's address, and Birney wrote suggesting a meeting. I liked the idea, but never got around to replying. Charles asked me to call on his old friend in Oxford Jack (J. A. W.) Bennett, now a don at Magdalen College. 'He will have read you in *Landfall*,' Charles wrote. 'I've told him you might call.' I wrote back:

> 'Yes, I will visit Bennett. Thank you. He wrote our school hymn which begins
>
> Dusk on the walls and the twilight lingering,
> Darken yet lighten our half-dimmèd gaze,
> While on the panels still bright with his fingering
> God writes this legend in golden rays.
>
> 'Don't worry though, I won't remind him.'

Charles was opening doors for me – or at least showing me doors that might be opened. But I didn't do that either.*

One responsibility, however, did weigh on me – Janet Frame – and Sargeson continued asking had I seen her and how was she. On 18 August I had written to him saying I felt guilty that I hadn't been in touch with her but there had been 'a hell of a lot to do and a consequent state of semi-permanent exhaustion in which some things keep getting put aside'. More than four months later (2/1/59), after the permanent move to London, I added a PS to a letter in which I said only, 'Have seen Janet. She is not well – is locked in for the moment.' That was all. A few days later, 11 January, my diary has 'SNOW' in caps and then 'Shadbolts for dinner' – no mention of Janet; but I had visited her again, and her biographer Michael King records that on that same day she wrote to her friend John Money, '[Karl] talked in such a rich New Zealand accent of mountains and creeks and snow, snow, snow. I think I myself have

* Bennett was a Mt Albert Grammar old boy, and on 20 June 2008, long after his death, he and I were together inducted into the school's Hall of Distinction.

tied in my heart a remembrance knot of snow-grass.'* This is so recognisably Janet's own 'rich New Zealand accent' – Janet at her lyrical best.

On 4 March I wrote to Frank saying I had put off replying to his last because I wanted to see Janet first. I had now visited her and found her

> ... now in a locked part of the hospital. She said the last time we visited that she had been 'high' and is locked up for the time being – the time being how long I hate to guess. She pointed vaguely to some marks on her wrist which I took to be the marks of a straight-jacket but Maurice [Shadbolt] pointed out they are designed to leave no marks and that she must have slashed her wrists.† I hope this doesn't disturb you too much. She hasn't changed at all and is just as sane as ever. I will get around to going again before too long.

Janet had told me the doctor she liked and trusted, R. H. Cawley, thought it would be good for him to meet and talk to someone who had known her in New Zealand – someone she trusted – and that she had mentioned my name. She wrote his name and address for me on a card (one from Knights, dated 17 April).

Cawley and I met on 15 May and the first question he asked was did I think Janet was insane. I said I thought she was entirely sane, but that it was as if she lacked one layer of protective skin – like an extremely sensitive and timid teenager. He told me she was regarded as their most interesting patient, and that opinion was divided 50/50 among the hospital specialists. There were those who thought she was classifiable as schizophrenic, and those like himself who

---

* *Wrestling with the Angel*, p. 197.

† In fact one learns now from her biography that Janet had threatened to throw herself into the Thames and had been arrested, so the marks on her wrists might have been from handcuffs. She never seemed insane, but was (then, and throughout her life) adroit at creating anxiety and commanding everyone's attention.

disagreed – didn't think she was 'classifiable' at all: that she was just a sensitive artist who would always respond to kindness and the opportunity to use her talent.* He told me he considered the number of ECGs she'd had in New Zealand was 'barbaric'.

Stay or leave – and Shadbolt

A lot of my exchanges with Frank were about books, as if we were still meeting and talking at 14 Esmonde Road, as we had done when Frame was there in 1955. A typical letter from him contained:

> [Davin] doesn't seem to understand that if you belong to the wholesome school and write about the eternal commonplaces, you require a major talent not a marginal one. Tolstoy brought it off but if he hadn't been Tolstoy he would have been a thundering bore. [. . .]
> I got quite in a rage over Anthony Quinton's insulting Kerouac and his positively golden novel [. . .] *On the Road.*
> Every now and then I peck at the new clever novelists – the latest Iris Murdoch (Oxford don-ess) [. . .]
> By the way I'm getting the hang of some of the newest poets – among others I must discuss with you are Thomas Blackburn and Hilary Corke. [. . .]
> Have you seen Sinclair's headlong Pelican *History of N.Z*? It's readable and radical but slipshod. [. . .]
> I thought the portrait of the boy in *The God Boy* [Ian Cross] pretty good even though it seemed to have been composed with Salinger's *The Catcher in the Rye* propped up for model. [. . .]
> If you ever see the *Collected Stories of Isaac Babel* don't overlook them.

* I told this to Michael King when he was doing her biography but he couldn't use it. The writing was being overseen by Janet, and if she was to cooperate it had to conform to the story as she told it herself, that all her troubles sprang from an early misdiagnosis of schizophrenia.

Was Sinclair's important work ever so crisply characterised? We exchanged thoughts about Wordsworth; and Milton too – on 18 January he reported, 'I've gone through *Paradise Lost* since Christmas.'

He was worrying about how he was going to respond to a new novel by James Courage, sent to him by the author, which deserved, he thought, 'heavily scented brickbats'. About my reviews in *Landfall* Frank clearly had mixed feelings:

> You terrify me with the way you use the scalpel which you have learned to handle. I can't imagine a worse fate than to be reviewed by you. I hope Charles congratulates himself that a couple of years back he survived so handsomely. Nevertheless this is critical mastery and my somewhat more than awed congratulations.

But then in response to one written around this time in which I said 'Your letter restored our faith in the possibility of living sanely and intelligently in a spiritual dependency of Europe', Frank replied,

> I'm sorry but one doesn't live sanely or intelligently in this community. If you could conceive how isolated I've been lately! I have a novel to finish of course. But apart from that, sane and intelligent items such as your letter are very very rare.

In another he wrote, 'Think carefully about coming back to this country sooner than you're pushed into it.'

Shouldn't these have been warnings? But the thought of him writing and reading in his little fibro bach, with all its books and papers, the whole section one big vegetable garden hidden from the road by trees, tomatoes, peppers and sunflower seeds ripening or drying in the sun on the window sills and Takapuna Beach only a walk away – and Frank himself with his keen bright eyes and wicked humour – it all seemed heroic and wonderful. There was news too of a new book of poems by Curnow. Sargeson and Curnow: they were the two, heroically or tragically, or maybe just *necessarily*, hanging on out there in the South Pacific, and I wanted to be part of what they represented, to be part of what Keith Sinclair called 'the intense gladness of being at the beginning'.* And yet I had written to Frank on New Year's Day 1959, 'I don't really want to come back now that it's staring me in the face. I suppose I will settle to it.'

Maurice Shadbolt had written to me the previous September, a friendly letter giving his phone number and suggesting we meet. This had come shortly after I read his report in the June *Landfall* of his travels in China, Russia and Bulgaria, a view from the other side of the Iron Curtain that was unusual and informative – in fact, seen in retrospect, sometimes astonishing. For example he reported that a novel called *Doctor Zhivago* by Boris Pasternak, publication of which had been 'halted abruptly' in the Soviet Union, had been obtained by the Italian publisher Feltrinelli, and consequently might soon be available in the West. Especially arresting, like an authentic voice from the dark cellar, were anecdotes repeated from listening to the writer Alexei Surkov: on duty in the Hall of Columns when Stalin's body was lying in state, Surkov recalled how dangerous the floors had been to walk on because wet and slippery with human tears; and then describing Khrushchev's denunciation of Stalin at the Twentieth Party Congress as 'the day the mountain fell on us'.

These were gems of a kind seldom available in the West, gathered by a young man who had been bold enough to go into the heart of the Eastern bloc, using his strong left-wing connections to gain access to writers there. It was a good moment to be there, so soon after the Khrushchev 'thaw', and before a new freeze began. It meant Shadbolt could report dissent, but from within the ranks, and still seem, and feel himself to be, loyal to the left. It was

* 'The Muses', *A Time to Embrace*, Paul's Book Arcade, 1963, p. 53.

possible now, post Twentieth Congress, to deplore the extremes of 'Stalinism' without sounding like a 'capitalist lackey'.

In a second letter Shadbolt revealed he was in the state of uncertainty about staying or going home that was the endless topic of discussion among New Zealanders in England:

> To convince myself, in this autumn mood, that I don't really want to go back to that place, I've taken to reading 'Truth'; it helps a great deal. On the other hand, to convince myself that there are compensations for living in this place [. . .] I went to the theatre last night and saw O'Neill's *A long day's journey into night*. I enjoyed it immensely; so much so that I've been thinking all day of writing a play. But I expect that mood, like so many others, will pass too. Anyway I have successfully neutralised myself: I swing, in a state of apathy between this place and that place. And not really caring

I evidently wasted no time getting in touch because our first visit to the Shadbolts' basement flat in Chelsea was 4 December, the day after we arrived back in London. After that, meetings were frequent – dinners at one another's flats, meetings in pubs, plays, parties. In a letter to Sargeson I said he would laugh to hear this but I liked Maurice and was enjoying his company This was true. Maurice was easily (and often) flustered, and tended at such times to shouting and waving his arms about. He was also prone to depression, and needed constant propping up – something his wife Gillian did loyally. But we talked constantly about politics, all four of us, seriously committed to the left, disagreeing a lot, often vehemently; but our interests coincided, Maurice was a good talker, a companion, and for the time being he and I simply 'got on well' – with one another and one another's wives.

There was a great deal about literature that Maurice didn't know and would never know; but he was up with what was going on in the world of contemporary fiction in a way I was not. He was soon telling me about Nadine Gordimer and Doris Lessing, whose work he admired not only for the strength of the writing but, in each case, for radical politics, particularly in the context of southern Africa. Gordimer was holding on in South Africa, battling it out bravely with Afrikaner nationalism which was now in government. Lessing had left Southern Rhodesia for London and was making it clear she would not return.* These two represented the burdensome choice, the alternatives still open to those of us from the 'White' Commonwealth: was it to be home, or England (which, as Lessing said, meant London)? Shadbolt was for returning to New Zealand. So was I, but unlike him I felt under pressure to act now, because I was keen to have a university lectureship, and uncertain how often such posts were offered.

Maurice's wife, Gill, working as publicity officer for the National Union of Students, was for the moment the household's dependable money-earner. She could laugh at Maurice's extravagances, yet never in a way that undermined him. She was practical, friendly, easy-going, and he was looked after, sometimes like an invalid. Even his lunch was usually prepared and left ready before Gill departed for work. His hypochondria sometimes seemed extreme: when we told him that our friend Ted Sturmer had contracted tuberculosis, Maurice looked panic-stricken, and for days afterwards, Gill told us, he was reporting mysterious and sinister pains in the chest. Kay thought Gill probably saw her, in her Jaeger suit and good shoes, as 'bourgeois'– while she saw Gill as a good-natured wry-toned hippie before hippies had been invented. They too got on well.

Because Maurice and I both thought about writing plays we went to hear John Osborne talk at London University, but were distracted by Osborne's wife at the time, Mary Ure, a glamorous stage actress (as she would then have been called), who seemed to position herself towards the front and to one side, half-facing the

---

* Each of these women would ultimately receive the Nobel Prize for literature.

audience, and posing as if to be noticed, 'deep in thought'. It must have been a good performance because afterwards we admitted we remembered her rather better than anything the playwright had said. We went to social realist plays by Brendan Behan and Shelagh Delaney – more to his taste than mine. Though entertaining they seemed to me rough-house and artless; but they were the kind of play Maurice thought he might try to write.

We visited David Ballantyne on one occasion, and Kasmin (as he has since become known) on another. I had published one of his poems in the student annual *Kiwi* in 1955 when he was still John Kaye, and taken him with me to visit Louis Johnson in Wellington. Johnson had viewed him darkly and referred to him in a follow-up letter as 'the wee narcissus'. In London Kasmin had a large round washing basket which he climbed into, and then, requiring his guests to make music like Hindu pipes, would rise sinuously up, being the cobra. He has long since grown rich and famous as an art dealer, painted by Hockney whose work he was one of the first to promote and profit from.

Maurice had his first collection of stories ready to offer a publisher. It was called *The New Zealanders*, a title which seemed typically audacious, even preposterous, as if he could claim, and speak for, us all; but it was a choice that turned out to be astute. He gave me the typescript and I spent three days going through, making ten pages of notes, stylistic mainly, but trying to be encouraging. My doubts, which were considerable, were omitted, except in the form of suggestions for improvement. I told him I thought the book would be accepted, which was not true. I would not have accepted it.

Maurice spent the next few days making, he said, virtually all of the suggested changes* and sent it off to Gollancz. Three and a half weeks after that, 7 March, he had a letter of acceptance. There

---

* Though Philip Temple in his Shadbolt biography (*Life as a Novel: A Biography of Maurice Shadbolt*, David Ling Publishing, 2018, vol. I, p. 130) says he made very few.

was a party that night to celebrate. To Sargeson I sent a somewhat scornful message with news about Gollancz acceptance, to which Kay added the Yeats line, 'We that look on but laugh in tragic joy'. Frank must have reproached me for this because my next letter said:

> You are right about Maurice. Also no doubt there was a fair whack of jealousy in my bitchiness. After all he has had the courage to sit in Chelsea writing his own work while I have been preparing for my future. [. . .] Maurice's book will be better than I thought – Gollancz have asked him to take out four of 15 stories which will improve the general level enormously.

In the same letter I wrote that Charles was still hovering 'like a great hairy B above the nectar of my verses'. This was a jaunty pretence of indifference about the poem 'Pictures in a Gallery Undersea' which had arrived so mysteriously, nearly complete, its genesis and therefore its 'meaning', if it had one, not entirely clear to its author. It was the debt to Eliot that was causing Brasch to hesitate;* and it was that debt which had taught me so much about Eliot's composition of 'The Waste Land' – how sections of a long poem can emerge whole, in some sense from one's reading, and yet re-processed into 'something rich and strange'; and that even arriving in this way 'from the depths', the sections had still to be edited and assembled into some kind of order by the conscious mind. In the case of 'The Waste Land' the conscious mind had been, finally, Ezra Pound's – a fact which Eliot had acknowledged by dedicating the poem to him as 'Il miglior fabbro', the better craftsman.

We now had bookings to return to New Zealand and I wrote,

* The hesitation was resolved, the poem published and received the *Landfall* Reader's Award for *Landfall*'s most admired poem in its first fifteen years of publication.

> We leave on June 5 and arrive Wgtn July 7. We have indeed many regrets – both of us – and I have been kicking myself periodically for racing into the shafts as soon as I saw a set empty. But on the other hand there is the danger that if one leaves it too long one will never come back, and finish up a Davin [. . .] Anyway I suppose we're all happy to feel crucified on the crossed staves of European and Pacific consciousness.

Meanwhile I had been working on the novella, the idea for which had come to me in Oxford the previous summer about a young New Zealand runner (bearing some resemblance to Don Smith) and an English upper-middle-class country-woman, Emily Summerscroft. It was to be called *A Race Apart*.

In March I read it to Kay and the Shadbolts and my diary records that it was 'Well received'.

Looking forward, looking back

I could say of myself, as Doris Lessing says, 'No one brought up as I was can ever really shed politics.' Politics was always serious, a preoccupation, even an obsession, and Kay and I followed the domestic scene under Harold Macmillan ('Supermac', the papers called him) in detail, with passion and loyal-to-Labour convictions. But 'domestic' in the case of British politics at that time was international in its concerns and effects. As Macmillan would say in a famous speech the following year, 'the winds of change' were blowing through Africa and elsewhere, and British policy-makers were constantly having to decide what should be hung on to and when to let go. Cyprus was a 'British' problem of these years – a crown colony wanting 'Enosis' (union with Greece) which the UK government was reluctant to allow because the island was an important military base – and in any case complicated by the fact that union with Greece was not wanted by the island's Turkish population. Violent confrontations between British soldiers and demonstrators, and 'terrorist' actions by Colonel George Grivas and his EOKA movement, were in the news.

The Kenya problem continued, with Jomo Kenyatta locked up, continuing fear of the Mau Mau (freedom fighters), and the commitment of British troops in effect to repress the movement for independence and protect the rights of settlers to go on holding land and privileges at the expense of the local population. I remember that when I told Knights, and then his deputy, Henry Gifford, that I was planning to go back to New Zealand, Gifford said at once, 'What about the Maoris?' I could see that he was thinking of current troubles in Africa, and probably India too where he had spent some time, even keeping a caged mynah in his kitchen as a memento. At the time I thought his anxiety on my behalf well-meant but amusing. New Zealand was not Africa. And yet, though he was wrong and there was no exact parallel, he was at least more nearly right than I recognised. There was a Māori problem. We were settlers; and like the white settlers in Africa, we thought we belonged there and nowhere else, and had, consequently, the 'rights' of being native born. It was a deep emotional attachment. Our problem was not as bad as white-settler Africans because we outnumbered the tangata whenua, and because, unlike black Africans, Māori had democratic rights. Also relevant was the fact that the Treaty of Waitangi had established a kind of legitimacy to the European settlement – nothing of the kind had happened in Africa. And finally was the fact that there was so much intermarriage in New Zealand the question of who could claim any special rights accorded to 'Māori' would become increasingly difficult and, over time, ultimately impossible.

Our (mine and Kay's) support for those fighting for independence from the British in Africa was genuinely felt, and right, but it was not quite clearly thought out in relation to our own homeland. Looking at it now I sometimes ask myself should we not have had more feeling for the native-born settlers whose position in African countries, and attachment to their lands, was similar to our own.

But that gap in our consciousness was, I think, because the degree of discontent, and the sense of wrongs suffered, had not in the 1950s yet been clearly expressed among Māori; or at least had not been heard and given public recognition among Pākehā. So Henry Gifford's question, 'What about the Maoris?' was not stupid; and my reaction to it, I would learn as the years rolled on, had been unduly complacent.

Britain during these years seemed constantly shaken by the demands of the old Empire clamouring to be free, and yet seldom wanting complete severance. British universities taught graduate students of all colours from all around the Commonwealth; and at the other end of the social spectrum, many came looking for work – particularly, at that time, London bus drivers recruited from the West Indies. Doris Lessing wrote that for her England was 'a grail'. 'The horizon conquerors' set sail or took wing for London, 'determined to conquer it, but on their own terms'.

That was the spirit of the 1950s, and it would come to an end a decade later when Britain opted for the EU, hoping to keep the Commonwealth attachment, but at the same time closing the door on us, 'kith and kin' as those who cared deeply were inclined to bleat, while opening it to Europeans.

Our interest in all these matters became keener and more narrowly focused when Kay began to work for Canon John Collins of St Paul's. Collins had set up Christian Action after the war, with the idea of achieving some kind of reconciliation with Germany. The movement had changed with the issues of the time and had transmogrified into the Southern Africa Defence and Aid Fund, which became important in supporting Nelson Mandela and the ANC at the time of their trial. But the hot issue in 1959 was Nyasaland.

Kay was general office assistant to Collins, collecting and recording the money that poured in from all over Britain and beyond, and banking it, typing letters for him, sometimes even collecting the youngest Collins boy (there were four) from school and giving him his tea – because the office was in the basement of the Collins house at Amen Court, Ave Maria Lane in the shadow of St Paul's. The area around the great cathedral was still very largely in ruins – there were bomb sites everywhere,* a constant reminder of what modern warfare meant. Collins was a stalwart (possibly founder) of the British anti-nuclear movement, and Kay remembers him, his sore feet in slippers the day after the big Aldermaston march of that year. He was tall, strongly built, with horn-rimmed glasses and a large pipe, the accent of a public school and Cambridge man, good-humoured, even hearty, with the air of a clergyman who had found, since the war, and by means of war experience, a radical way of life that he could continue to believe in and believe was truly useful in the world beyond prayers and sermons, baptisms, marriages and funerals.

Increasing tension in what was called the Central African Federation (Northern and Southern Rhodesia and Nyasaland)† had led to the arrest of the Nyasaland leader, Dr Hastings Banda and his political associates, the banning of their political party the Nyasaland ANC, and the declaration of a state of emergency. There was outrage from Labour in Britain when one of their MPs, John Stonehouse, on a fact-finding mission in the course of which he told the ANC that they had Labour's support, was arrested and deported. I reported to Sargeson that we had been to Parliament to hear the consequent debate:

> An interesting study in Tory psychology: on the front benches the tall, Riviera-bronzed South Kensington Jaguar-type smart-Alecks who really know what is happening but pretend to have secret information about a conspiracy by the African National Congress to murder whites, coloureds and loyal

* The ruins have all been cleared away and replaced over the years by modern buildings. Only one remains – the ruin of Christchurch Greyfriars, its wrecked walls and open roof now enclosing a beautiful garden kept, I suppose, as a reminder of what was lost in the 1939–45 years.

† Now Zambia, Zimbabwe and Malawi.

> blacks ('the vast majority'); and on the back benches the red-faced white-moustached blimps who reminisce about the territory when they knew it twenty years ago, insisting that 'the Nyasa boy was a good boy, a very trustworthy boy' if he wasn't allowed to be swayed by 'rabble-rousing intellectuals'. At the end, when they had all scrambled off to vote, a large round-faced hairless bewildered baby toddled with great difficulty into the chamber, looked blindly around, flopped backwards into his seat, and dozed off: Winston Churchill.

A few weeks later Kay was included (and I with her, as spouse) as members of the official party on the stage of the Albert Hall when a vast rally in support of the Nyasaland ANC was called. Among the party was the veteran woman Labour MP Bessie Braddock. John Stonehouse was one of the speakers. They were stirring times.

I HAD OFFERED MY COLLECTION of poems to Chatto and Windus, and received it back with a faintly (but I don't think intentionally) patronising, and not altogether discouraging, letter from Elizabeth Jennings, herself a poet at that time associated with the Movement, that loose grouping of neo-formalists whose best rep (though denying he was one of them) was Philip Larkin. So, still before 'Pictures in a Gallery Undersea' had arrived to strengthen the mix, I had sent the collection to the Hogarth Press, and got a letter back, also from Elizabeth Jennings, who, it now appeared, was the 'we' at both publishers. Charles Tomlinson, who had tried them all, told me the London literary scene was 'tight-knit and almost impenetrable – unless you go to the right parties'; but if Jennings went to parties you couldn't tell from her poems – and I thought probably not.

Meanwhile life was going on for me, at the British Museum daily, and in the evenings with friends. When I skim the diary that reveals plays, operas, orchestra concerts, two or three, even four times in a week, often at the Old Vic, Covent Garden, the Royal Festival Hall, and imagine what all this would cost now, I wonder, not so much how a couple living on a graduate student's scholarship and irregular secretarial temping could pay for it – because I know we could and did – but rather why the gap between those who can afford such luxuries and those who can't has so widened over the years that to live like that now you would need to be quite significantly affluent. One of the standard jokes against communism was well represented by Peter Sellers as the trade union idealist looking dreamy at a mention of the Soviet Union and murmuring, 'All that corn, and bally in the evening'; and of course it is a joke – the price for such cultural riches as were permitted in Russia was unthinkable. Yet it does seem that the welfare state, established in Britain by Clem Attlee's Labour government at the end of the war, had achieved a much more nearly equal society, one which, alas, permitted Macmillan to campaign in 1960 on the slogan 'You've never had it so good', as if the new prosperity was the Tories' doing, and so to win another five years in office, setting in motion the beginnings of a drive back towards a social model which would, over decades, reverse the process of equalisation and bring back the old extremes of poverty and wealth, as if they were the 'natural' order of things.

IN MARCH KAY'S OLD SCHOOL FRIEND Yvonne married an Englishman, Michael Riley. Yvonne had driven us to Takapuna Beach after our marriage, and now we drove her and Michael to the registry office, and then to the evening reception. I had hired a dinner suit – the first time I had ever worn one. Michael tried to help me with the bow tie, but I found I could only tie it lying flat on my back. At the proper hour we drove in to the front entrance of the Savoy, in those days a very grand institution, and I handed the keys to the parking person, who behaved in a manner that might have been scornful or charming – it seemed so extreme, and outside the range of my experience, I couldn't be sure how I was to understand it. He might have been just a comedian, matching the Ford Popular-at-the-Savoy joke with appropriate antics.

It was at this time that Kay and I brought Jill Evans and Don Smith together. We took Jill with us up to Oxford on Good Friday, stayed a night there, and then drove on, taking Don too, to see Tintern Abbey again. So our two friends, the singer who could be quite sporty, and the decidedly tuneful sportsman, were jammed for hours at a time into the back seat of our car, a form of intimacy that could only lead to discomfort or accommodation. Accommodation triumphed, and Don became a regular visitor to the benign coven at Castelnau Mansions, and a fourth fellow-traveller in the Ford. They were married (not without the usual beforehand alarms and retreats) in London the following year, after we had returned to New Zealand.

At intervals over this period I went back to Bristol by train, met with Knights for lunch and a talk about my work, or attended the graduate seminar, and spent a night there with Robin and Liz and 'the usual suspects'. On one of my visits Knights told me he had arranged for me to be interviewed by the Professor of English at Nottingham, Vivian de Sola Pinto, who had himself written on modern poetry and was to be my external examiner.

The five completed chapters of my thesis, and an outline of the direction the two yet to be written would take, were duly sent to Pinto, and a day and time agreed when he would examine me. On 21 May Kay and I set off with Don and Jill, through Oxford to Loughborough, where we stayed a night, and then on to Nottingham. At the university my three friends lay on the grass in the sun while I went in to be examined.

By now I knew a little more about my examiner. Vivian de Sola Pinto had been the once-gassed and twice-wounded second-in-command to the World War I poet Siegfried Sassoon, and figured in Sassoon's memoirs as 'Velmore', the subaltern who had introduced his captain to the poems of James Elroy Flecker. I could expect something military, then, but not militaristic – cool, like Sassoon himself, towards jingoism: not, in other words, unsympathetic to the line my thesis was taking, which I supposed was why Knights had selected him. I tried to imagine him in advance – a no-nonsense Robert Graves, for example. Perhaps it would, after all, be the kind of peppery engagement I'd hoped for.

So I knocked at his office door with some excitement. He called me in and came around his desk to greet me and shake my hand – a tall man with glasses and a military moustache, whom I described in a letter home as 'an old [he was in fact only in his early-to-middle sixties] Professor-type in a comfortable book-lined office'. He sat me opposite him and was soon telling me that he had read my chapters with considerable interest and how very much he admired them. That was most of what he had to say, though it was reiterated in various ways. There was, however, a rather sleepy reservation: he was very sorry I had not found space, or reason, to include the poems of Thomas Hardy.

I suggested Hardy was rather *prior* to my subject interest, Modernism, though of course ahead of his time, and admirable.

'Yes, quite,' the Prof agreed; but he did so admire Hardy, whom he had once met. It seemed a pity – 'particularly the later poems . . . The later poems . . . The later poems . . .' This phrase was repeated diminuendo, ending in a silence which might have been a brief nap.

So the conversation continued, I think for about an hour. We talked about Edwardians (bad) and Georgians (good on the whole – though with reservations . . . With reservations . . . Reservations . . .) Nothing he said seemed memorable – nothing except those repetitions which were memorably absurd. Nothing challenged me to think hard, or defend my thesis. If we'd been of an age we might have drifted off together.

He referred to his own book, *Crisis in English Poetry*, and I saluted it. He thought the ideas I was proposing for my final two as yet unwritten chapters were bold, 'unusual – original'. They would constitute a challenge in the writing – and, indeed, in the matter of finding the evidence necessary to support them – but one which, in the light of this work (patting the chapters still unopened on his desk) he felt sure 'will be quite within your powers . . . Within your powers . . . Within your powers . . .' And another brief doze.

Was this shell shock? Those war wounds? Gas? Friday afternoon-ism? It was certainly not F. R. Leavis, who had joked to his students (at once acknowledging the great poet's status but asserting his limitations) that he'd found Milton was the only major English poet whose lines he could carry in his head through a prolonged artillery bombardment. How much I would have preferred to be saying, or hearing, a Leavisite 'Yes, but . . .'

It was disappointing – and yet also a relief. What was being done for me, allowing this to pass for the viva examination before the thesis was written, probably pushed at the boundaries of regulations governing the degree. Of course the thesis would still have to be completed, and would have to be good. But this nominal 'examination' would save me the expense and difficulty of sailing half way around the world just to go through what Knights was convinced would be a mere formality.

So it would be up to me now to complete the doctoral thesis at home 'in my own time', insofar as the new job offered any. I was already reading *Measure for Measure*, and *Richard II*, the two Shakespeare plays I would have to lecture on first. But even that was put aside, and I spent a final week, perhaps ten days, desperately writing a novel about a young London real estate agent whose slogan was BUY WEST OF THE BEST WHERE THE DREAM IS ATTAINABLE. Nothing would come of it. I record the fact only to signal the peculiar, slightly frantic and divided, state of mind I must have been in.

Back in London there was a letter waiting for us at New Zealand House from Patsy Dutch in Auckland:

> Have you forgotten the one long main street, the funny little shops and low little wooden buildings? Or the beautiful

> harbour and the sunshine (and rain) and the ferries? Bring back ten gallons of Patna rice, yards of white elastic, cartons of ships' cigarettes, blankets, coconut, cocoa, books, prints and anything else you might want, as many things are hard to get here, the shops becoming empty – patterns of frocks if you see any, they are very difficult . . . And go to every play you can, and concert. Only a warning which you won't heed . . . Physically we are in better health and mentally in some ways more content, but there is not much to stimulate one to anger . . .

On 28 May we took the car to the Albert Docks. 576AHY was already a container for most of our 'effects' and was to come home with us. Next day I went down to Bristol and met Knights at 3.30 to make a final report and say goodbye – to him, and that evening other Bristol goodbyes.

So I would not be there to finish what I had begun – nor to see the others finish or fail to finish. I would not be in England for the wedding of the runner and the singer; nor for the publication of Maurice Shadbolt's first book, which I still could not altogether admire but had helped on its way. I would not be there for the summer that was coming in and promising to be a good one.

Two nights before our ship sailed we went to *Der Rosenkavalier*, the opera Otto Bergmann had introduced us to. This was the second time we'd seen it, but now, as a farewell present to ourselves, we were in the stalls at Covent Garden. I thought once again that the street singer's aria at the Marschallin's morning levée was Strauss's answer to the girl who asked 'Where are the tunes?' – and to any who thought he, Strauss, couldn't do 'that kind of thing'. It was lovely – a romantic melody the mind can slip in to, hold on to, exult in – and then the nameless singer was rudely bundled out, never to return. The presentation of the silver rose was a step beyond 'that kind of thing', as if into another dimension of music. (I had yet to discover Wagner.) And it was Strauss's music that put an end, for me, to the philosophical debate about whether there was something that could definitively be called 'beauty', or whether it was only 'in the eye (or ear) of the beholder'. It was like Dr Johnson kicking a stone on the road to answer the Bishop Berkeley question whether the world was real. How do I know the world is real? Because I kick that stone and it hurts my toe? How do I know there is such a thing as 'beauty'? Because I listen to Richard Strauss's music and feel an elevation of the spirit accompanied by a shudder in the spine and a prickling of the scalp.

There you are then – the short-cut of pragmatism – and now it was time to go home. There was a party at Castelnau Mansions the night before we left. And then . . . '*Ruahine* sails', my diary records, and there ends. There are no further entries.

Postscripts:

Dr Hastings Banda was released from detention and became Prime Minister of Nyasaland in 1963, and led the country to independence a year later when it became Malawi, soon to be a republic and a one-party state with himself as president. In 1971 he was declared president for life. He supported the West in the Cold War and was consequently supported in return – praised for his defence of women's rights and a well-maintained system of education. But he retained full diplomatic relations with apartheid South Africa, and his repression of any opposition, by means of imprisonment, torture and (it was said) murder, was ruthless. He was not removed from office until 1994, and died in South Africa in 1997.

John Stonehouse, the MP whose expulsion from Nyasaland had led to the Albert Hall rally Kay and I attended in 1959, faked his own 'death by drowning' in Miami in 1974 – at first successfully – and attempted to start a new life in Australia with his mistress, transferring large sums of money to himself under false names through the Bank of New South Wales and the Bank of New Zealand. He was arrested in Australia under suspicion that he might be Lord Lucan, the runaway British peer who had murdered his children's nurse. Stonehouse's real identity was thus uncovered and he was returned to Britain, tried and found guilty of fraud, theft and conspiracy, and sentenced to seven years' jail. After his release he married the mistress and fathered a son with her. It was not until some time after his death in 1989 that it was revealed Stonehouse had acted as a spy for the Czechoslovakian secret service.

Professor Vivian de Sola Pinto, external examiner of my Bristol PhD, dozed off finally ten years after our 1959 meeting, by which time the thesis had been five years in print as *The New Poetic* in the Hutchinson University Library series and had been reissued as a Pelican in England and a Harper Torchbook in the United States.

Robin and Elisabeth Marleyn stayed on in Bristol, bought a house there in Hope Square, Liz working as a journalist and Robin as a school teacher. They visited us once in New Zealand, and Kay and I stayed with them in Bristol and took them with us visiting Zennor and Higher Tregerthen in Cornwall when I was working on my novel *Mansfield*.

Peter Middleton, my fellow graduate student of the 'Where's tha bin lud?' song, went into the British Civil Service where he had a distinguished career, rising to be Permanent Secretary to the Treasury. After retirement from that, and duly knighted, Sir Peter became head of Lloyds Bank. Returning to home base (at least when not at home in London) he became Chancellor of Sheffield University.

The young librarian, Kay, 1955

The young graduate, Karl, 1955

Above: Kay in the West Country, 1957
Below: Karl and Kay camping at Lake Grasmere, 1958

Kay in a punt, Oxford, 1958

Left: Karl at Maunsell Road, Auckland, 1960

Below: Karl and Jill Evans 'making music', London, 1959

Jill Evans and Kay and Karl cleaning the Ford Popular, Elmgrove Road, Bristol, 1958

Right: Frank Sargeson, gardener, 1950s

Below: Frank Sargeson, Karl, Hone Tuwhare and Jim Baxter, reading at Auckland City Art Gallery (the fourth reader, out of sight, was Maurice Duggan), 1964, photographed by Marti Friedlander, courtesy of the Gerrard and Marti Friedlander Charitable Trust

Left: Maurice Duggan in a launch at Lilian & David Chrystall's place at Taupō, 1965, photographed by Marti Friedlander, courtesy of the Gerrard and Marti Friedlander Charitable Trust

Below: Charles Brasch, Janet Frame and Karl ('looking like a Viennese doctor') at Charles' crib at Broad Bay, photo by Ruth Dallas, 1966

Kay and Karl, Maunsell Road, reading Maurice Shadbolt's stories, 1960, photographed by Marti Friedlander, courtesy of the Gerrard and Marti Friedlander Charitable Trust

4.
In and Out of Auckland

Home again, home again . . .

Katherine Mansfield tells herself somewhere '*Risk! Risk all!*' I was not a risk-taker. I was scuttling home to safety – I thought; but also to something I'd thought I wanted most for myself, a lectureship in the institution that had seemed to open new worlds for me; and perhaps in due course a significant place in the making of a New Zealand literature. Some risks are not taken boldly, in full consciousness, as advocated by the young Mansfield; they are taken blindly – the man running from the metaphorical frying pan falls into the metaphorical fire. What action, or act of conscious will, does not involve risk? Even 'running for cover' may prove to have been a mistake.

Our ship, the New Zealand Line *Ruahine*, beat its way south and west down the Atlantic into the Caribbean, stopping, after many days, at the oil port of Willemstad on the island of Curaçao, where I wrote some lines that were only rediscovered when I was putting together my *Collected Poems*.

Curaçao

Willemstad's Dutch facades teach colours to meet and debate.
A black waiter brings ice-cream on a yellow plate.

The Caribbean breaks low on the old fort wall.
In there Ethel and the Doctor are swimming in a glass pool.

The road-bridge swings aside, lets pass another ship.
The waiter returns across the marble, helps me decide on a tip.

He and the mop-girl are at home. I am nowhere at all.
The blue sea breaks and breaks, white on the orange wall.

I lack a language. Colours all speak of the weather.
Goggled at, Ethel and the Doctor swim coolly together.

A lizard translates itself from a shadowy groove
To a sunlit patch of marble, and is not seen to move.

Somewhere deep under the reef I think an angel fish
Pauses in bright shafts, hangs weightless, without a wish.

I have dim recollections of Ethel; none of 'the Doctor'. Soon we were at sea again.

The Panama Canal takes you through from the east to the west of the Americas; from Atlantic to Pacific. More interesting than Suez (and no less politically problematic at the time) it takes you through jungle rather than desert, but has to lift you, by means of a series of locks, up to an artificial lake, and then down by another series, to sea level again, and on into the Pacific.

Then it was another long beat home, with only one stop, standing off Pitcairn while the islanders came out in small boats and sold souvenirs hauled up on ropes to the deck, wood-carvings of flying fish and seabirds. On the last few days towards New Zealand waters we were trailed by seabirds, I think albatrosses, certainly very large, which seemed to ride the warm draughts up from the ship, then veer off left or right and away, seeming to vanish in the far distance until all at once, there they were again, riding in our wake. To come home like that, and to come in sight of land at last, is to be reminded of remoteness, its beauty and the faint fear that goes with it; and to be reminded how Curnow had seemed to catch the fact of it.

> Always to islanders danger
> Is what comes over the sea;
> Over the yellow sands and the clear
> Shallows, the dull filament
> Flickers, the blood of strangers [. . .]

We arrived at Wellington in winter, and from the deck could see the painted iron roofs of suburban houses climbing the hills – hills with bush on them, or pine plantations – and feel the keen cold wind that might have been coming all the way from the polar region.

Everything we owned was packed into the little grey Ford, and we drove it up the island, rediscovering the blue and white and brown beauty, and the stillness and silence, of the landscape; the sense of skies widening into distance and something like emptiness.

Auckland, though not as extreme as Wellington, had likewise not entirely lost the feel of a frontier town, a Pacific port built so largely of wood and corrugated iron. We rented a flat, first in Crescent Road, Parnell, looking out over the harbour towards Devonport and Rangitoto; and then, driven out by noisy neighbours, found one in Masons Avenue, Herne Bay.

Kay found work again in the university, the Botany Department first, as secretary to Professor V. J. ('Val') Chapman, who was writing a book on salt marshes of the world which she typed up for him when there were periods free of other work in the department. Chapman was one of several English-born professors in Auckland at the time – a braying fraternity, many of them what we thought of as 'social Anglicans', who seemed to camp here as if it was not a place to be taken entirely seriously; so although it gave them the title Professor (and for life) which they valued greatly, their eyes, or their ambitions, seemed often to be elsewhere. Among these I would have to include my own professor, Sydney Musgrove, who rented a small flat in Devonport as if at any moment he expected to be off again.

I settled at once into the lectures on W. B. Yeats, and on Shakespeare's *Richard II* and *Measure for Measure*. There were reunions with family and friends, and with my former teachers in the English Department now to be my colleagues. Among letters to Charles Brasch in late 1959 is a flattering report of us from Sargeson. He complained that the new harbour bridge made him 'too readily accessible to people who drop in', but Stead and his wife were 'wonderful exceptions'.*

In November of that year there was an election. Labour had been in government since late 1956, with Walter Nash as PM and Arnold Nordmeyer as Minister of Finance. Facing a balance of payments crisis, and wanting to preserve and protect the welfare state, Nordmeyer had introduced a famously unpopular 'Black Budget'. Kay and I went with my parents to hear Nash make his opening campaign speech in Auckland's Civic Theatre. My father, who was a senior official in the party, introduced me to Nash, saying I'd been doing postgraduate work in Bristol. Nash at once told me that as a young man he had been a traveller for W. D. & H. O. Wills. He explained how much each carton of cigarettes was worth, and how his profits were calculated. He used his right hand, close to his portly belly with its watch chain and MP's 'free-travel-on-the-railways'

---

* Sargeson's letters to Brasch were copied for me by the Hocken Library when I was preparing my Michael King Memorial Lecture for 2006.

medallion, taking a certain amount of money from one pigeon-hole and, with a circular movement of the hand, pushing it into another. A few minutes later we were watching him explaining the country's budget from the stage, with exactly the same hand movement taking units from one account to put into another, but this time the amounts were millions, which he pronounced *millie-ons*.

Labour should not have lost that election, but it did. 'For an achingly brief moment', historian Chris Trotter writes, Labour Ministers in the 1958–60 government 'found themselves in a position to force open the door to a future in which the working people of this country would have enjoyed a standard of living comparable to those of Germany and the Scandinavian states.'* But the media's total, blanket, remorseless focus on Nordmeyer and his 'Black Budget' meant that the larger picture and that vision for the future were lost, and so was the election. This brought in the pompous and deeply conservative Keith Holyoake as Prime Minister – twelve years of essentially a farmers' government – and what Trotter calls 'the Keynesian moment of the early 1960s' passed New Zealand by. The welfare state which Labour had established in the 1930s would not be dismantled; but it would not be extended either – so for example eyes, teeth, and hearing, which in the UK were covered by the National Health Service, in New Zealand would remain the responsibility of the individual – as they still are.

Curnow, Sargeson, Brasch 'and so on'. . .

Allen Curnow was an unstoppable monologist. Once in full flight he was like Lucio in *Measure for Measure* who refuses to be shaken off and says 'I am a kind of burr. I shall stick.' Quite apart from the difficulties of his private life, balancing wife Betty at home and secret second-wife-in-waiting, Jeny Tole, away, Allen at this time was in a seriously disturbed state that seemed sometimes to take him right to the borders of sanity. He was obsessed with the fact

* Chris Trotter, *No Left Turn*, Random House, 2007, p. 239.

that his play, *Moon Section*, produced by Ronnie Barker for the 1959 Auckland Arts Festival, had been panned in both daily papers, the *Herald* and the *Star*, and had failed dismally. This was something he seemed unable to cope with, and he could only relieve the pain by talking about it to one he could trust to listen sympathetically.

His other obsession was the attempt that the fearsome Wellington troika of James K. Baxter, Louis Johnson and Alistair Campbell had made to sabotage his Penguin *A Book of New Zealand Verse*. In his official capacity as an editor of School Publications, Campbell had asked for and received advance notice of its contents, and the three had written to Penguin complaining that the work of recent New Zealand poets was grossly under-represented. This then became another theme of Curnow's monologues.

I was myself frantic with the amount of work that seemed to have fallen on me, all new lectures to prepare, and a feeling that the unfinished thesis might be slipping away from me. So although I was quite as admiring of Allen as I had been before, and pleased and flattered to be wanted and of use to him, I found myself avoiding him for fear of being (as I used to say to Kay) 'ancient marinered again'. I'm not sure that it wasn't at this time I began to resort to exchanges of notes in the hope of avoiding the monologues. Certainly later, when we lived in the same street, we fell into the epistolary habit, and became the rare case of two poets with a growing archive of letters to and fro, delivered not by post across distances (though they did continue when either was on leave), but by hand, letterbox to letterbox across the street. We talked too, of course – and I still miss that, as I do the letters. The appearance of that stylish hand on an envelope, often containing a new poem for comment, was always exciting and welcome. But it's also true that for me the written exchanges were a form of avoidance. I felt sorry for him at this time. His anxiety was real and his anger with the Wellington three was justified; but part of me looked forward to the fact that for most of 1961 he would be away on sabbatical leave.

My first year back was also the one in which I was to give one of the university series of Winter Lectures on the theme of New Zealand's 'remoteness'. My contribution was to be on our literature. It was my first ever public lecture and it put Curnow right at the centre of New Zealand's literary situation, and how it could be seen to be affected by our 'remoteness'. It began by quoting his lines

> Wholehearted he can't move
> From where he is, nor love
>
> Wholehearted that place . . .

It took issue with the Baxter, Johnson, Campbell group (and also my fellow-lecturers Sinclair and Chapman) who were challenging Curnow's authority as anthologist and what they were calling his 'South Island myth'; it argued that his was 'an achievement quite unequalled by any other New Zealand poet'; and it ended with a quotation from Curnow's poem 'When the Hulk of the World', which made the point about 'remoteness' and gave my lecture its title. Terry Sturm in his Curnow biography subjects that poem to two or three pages of close reading. I didn't analyse it. I simply kept it until last, and then hit the audience with its full force – a way of winding up the lecture to demonstrate how much 'remoteness' did affect us at that time, how deeply it was felt, and how Curnow at his rhetorical best could rise to it, make it felt, make you feel it:

> Seas will be seas, the same;
> Thick as our blood may flood, our opposite isles
> Chase each other round till the quiet poles
> Crack, and the six days top
> Totter, but catch us neither sight nor hold;
> Place will be place, limbs may not fold
> Their natural death in dreams.
> I pray, pray for me on some spring-wet pavement

Where halts the heartprint of our salt bereavement,
Pray over many times,
Forgive him the seas forgive him the spring leaf
All bloom ungathered perishable as grief
For the hulk of the world's between [. . .]

At some time during that same year the Curnows, Allen and Betty, and the Steads were at a party together on the town side, I think at the Lowrys', and Kay and I drove them home across the new harbour bridge. Allen invited us in for a nightcap, as you did in those days; and then, in the midst of our conversation, he remembered the bantams that roosted in their macrocarpa, and said he and I should go out and swing on the branches and 'shake them up' – or down. Many years later I put this moment into a very literary sonnet about Auckland's North Shore as an enclave of writers, a poem which began with an echo of *Macbeth* and ended with an echo of the lines from *Henry IV (I)* which are on Katherine Mansfield's grave (the ones quoted by Neville Chamberlain before his Munich meeting with Hitler):

To Maurice and to Maurice and to Maurice
Duggan, Shadbolt, Gee, how they load us down with fictions

And all our yesterdays maybe have lighted fools
The way to Dostoyevski. How many years ago was it

That Curnow's bantams roosted in his macrocarpa,
And he and I one midnight crept under the moon

And swung on the branches bringing those feathered half-wits
Down around our heads with a flapping and a squawking

That echoed over Big Shoal Bay. Do good poets
Make bad professors? Do many Maurices

Make light work, as one Sargeson made a Summer?
How many K.S's could the North Shore harbour

Before the Fall? I tell you my Lord Fool
Out of these nettle prophets we still pluck our safety pins.*

For me this bantam-shaking was a significant moment, revealing an aspect of the man that was always there somewhere just below the surface. It was what I've called 'the larrikin-radical' in him, Denis Glover's best mate though, unlike Glover, never too irretrievably far from sobriety. It was Curnow *ludens*, the comic spirit that would be let loose much later in poems like 'Organo ad Libitum' and the Raynor poem, 'A Fellow Being'. That Curnow would never be entirely absent from the poems; but it was to be gradually edited out of the public face. As time went on his behaviour became impeccable: no more shaking of sleeping bantams out of trees.

The following March Allen left on his first sabbatical after ten years in the job, and Kay and I were there on the wharf with Betty to wave him away. It was that extraordinary ritual of farewell at the wharfside that counted for so much, when travelling 'overseas' was still rare and dramatically significant; with the ritual streamers stretching from ship to shore; and then the final shuddering blast of the horn that signalled the ship was moving – and the streamers stretched and finally broke, and the two sets of human faces were slowly lost to one another.

What was odd on this occasion was that once we'd seen Allen on board and arranged ourselves with our streamers in the crowd on the wharf, with Allen up there at the rail waving, it became apparent that he was waving to us and then vanishing. Somewhere in the

---

* At the time I wrote this poem Maurice Duggan had sent me a letter signed Maurice with a triple bracket and Gee with an X, Shadbolt with an X, and Duggan with a tick. My reply was signed K. S. and a triple bracket, Keith Sinclair with an X, Kendrick Smithyman with an X, and Karl Stead with a tick. That exchange gave rise to the sonnet.

crowd at another point along the wharf there had to be another he was farewelling. Kay and I had known about the 'other', Jeny Tole; and as long ago as 1955, when I was an MA student, Betty had told me that she knew Allen 'had a mistress'; so I supposed she was guessing, as we were, that 'the mistress' was the other person being farewelled. But she said nothing about it; and neither did we. She just said she was worried that Allen might not have a change of underclothes. The Sturm biography reveals that Betty was hoping this leave would bring about a severance with 'the mistress'. What she didn't know, and neither did we, was that Allen was saying goodbye to her forever. He was planning to do what T. S. Eliot had done in 1933–34 when he used a lecture tour in the United States to effect a separation from his wife Vivien, and then while away wrote to tell her he would not be back.

When we next saw Allen he was living in what he characteristically called 'a mothel' in Grafton Road, preserving the necessary distances preliminary to divorce proceedings.

THE POEM SEQUENCE 'Pictures in a Gallery Undersea' appeared in *Landfall* in June 1959, and the long story written in London, 'A Race Apart', a year later. 'Flags are flying for you all over the country', Brasch wrote. 'I can't remember any story in *Lf* winning such praise before.' In the August Kay and I looked after him during his visit to Auckland and he wrote thanking us: 'And now I'm full of hopes and plans.' One of these plans was for his retirement from the editorship of *Landfall*, which he would soon have edited ten years, and for his replacement when the time came.

By the end of 1959 Frank had been describing himself as 'stale and fagged', and the following March he wrote, 'I have typed 50 000 words in triplicate and feel light-headed.' This was *Memoirs of a Peon*, the novel, now close to completion, he'd begun to write after despairing of finding a producer and a theatre for his plays. The business of simply preparing a work of fiction for submission to a publisher, when there was no photocopying, and second and third sheets had to go into the typewriter with carbons for your final draft, made the writer's task demanding in ways I don't think anyone who hasn't experienced it can imagine.* Frank was weary, struggling to keep up his daily routine, and this, I suspect, was reflected in what he wrote to me about 'A Race Apart'. His prognostications for me, and for the kind of success that lay ahead, were at once flattering and dire:

> As the author of 'A Race Apart' I think of you with awe – and fear and trembling – the latter because I see a long disorderly work-ridden life ahead of you [. . .] all finally killing you – by inches perhaps with strain irritation quarrels frustration and the unceasing solitary grind.

This, I thought, was Frank talking indirectly about himself. I thought my story had some passages of prose, and some scenic/atmospheric writing, as good as I was ever likely to do, but that there was something implausible, or naïve (or both) about 'what happened'. Nonetheless in 1961 I put it in for the first BNZ Katherine Mansfield short story award, which had just been announced, and it won.

In the same year the Winter Lecture series was published with the title *Distance Looks Our Way*, and alas, my contribution was not only about Curnow. It was about the larger picture of recent New Zealand literature, and I had used a Shadbolt story from *The New Zealanders* to illustrate, and deplore, a particularly prevalent kind of provincial romanticism. This (which I would have defended as critical 'honesty' – a kind of Leavisite scrupulousness, not favouring one's friends) must have seemed unwarranted, even treacherous, to the writer who had become a friend in London, 'Maurie', and he was to deliver the deserved revenge a couple of years later in his first novel, *Among the Cinders*.

---

* Only those who recognise the word 'twink' and what it means will fully appreciate this sentence.

But at first Maurice's reaction, or as much as he let me see, seemed eminently reasonable. He disagreed with me, and argued at length in a letter; but he concluded 'I'm hoping to see you next month', and the sense of a friendship seemed to have survived. There was a footnote to the letter saying that baby Sean 'gave me hell after you left trying to get me to sing the rhymes you sang to him'. Later he was writing to tell me about the marriage of Barry Crump and Fleur Adcock, and 'a rather violent sequel. They took a flat just up the road from us. Fleur finished up with a dislocated arm, now in plaster, and she's living here with us. Crump has gone off to live in a shearer's quarters.' In the same letter he says he is just back from Samoa and is sending me a lava-lava – 'excellent bedwear'.

I tried to shrug my criticism off as 'just a lecture – I give them all the time', and in the same letter invited him and Gill to stay with us if they needed a bed over Christmas. Philip Temple in the first volume of his Shadbolt biography comments, 'If Maurice was careless or unaware of the effect on others of his boasting and self-publicity, Stead seemed equally unaware or careless of his public dissections of others' work.'*

Looking back it seems everything during these early years of my lectureship in Auckland was turbulent, racing and not quite under control. There was a sense of excitement, of success – and there would never be another moment when anyone would have occasion to write, with neither irony nor exaggeration, 'flags are flying for you all over the country'. There was often regret about what had been left behind in England. New Zealand still didn't have weekend shopping; the pubs still closed at 6 p.m.; wine could not be served with meals in restaurants; theatre was struggling to become dependably professional; and music of the kind Kay and I liked was dependent on visits from the National Orchestra based in Wellington. It was a time when to criticise the Governor-General,

* *Life as a Novel*, vol. I, p. 165.

Lord Cobham (which I did publicly on one occasion)* was an act that bordered on treason and caused outrage.

But there were excitements, and new friends to enjoy and admire. One was Murray Groves, an Australian lecturer in anthropology. He had a flat at Belmont looking out across the blue expanse of the Hauraki Gulf to Rangitoto and beyond; and I remember a party there on a Sunday afternoon when someone put on the newly released LP of the Curnow/Lilburn 'Landfall in Unknown Seas' – and the extraordinary beauty of the scene, the music, the poem and the people gave me such a feeling of exhilaration I was sure I was in the right place at the right time.

It was Murray Groves who introduced us to his friend from Melbourne days, Barry Humphries. Barry had a New Zealand-born wife (Rosalind née Tong, his second) and they were visiting her parents in Takapuna. Murray arranged for Barry to put on a show in the Auckland University Hall, and this was one of the very earliest appearances of Edna Everage, who would grow over the years into Dame Edna, superstar and squillionairess. Kay and I went (I suppose you could call it) 'night-clubbing' in Auckland with Barry and Rosalind, and Barry's long hair and bizarre behaviour and appearance were later to go into my story 'A Fitting Tribute' in which the hero, Julian Harp, makes wings out of stolen umbrellas and flies away into history. Beneath the comedian and the clown Barry was an exceptional literary intelligence and sensibility, a serious reader, a natural critic, a collector of rare books, a connoisseur of fine art expert on the *fin de siècle* period. He was an intellectual, politically conservative, brilliant in conversation, and in those days heading for alcoholism. We became friends then, and for life.

In 1961 we moved from the flat in Masons Avenue to a little two-storeyed house, two rooms up and two down, that had been the manse of a wooden church (both long since demolished) on

---

* 'Speeches by Lord Cobham', *Auckland Star*, 1 June 1961.

the corner of Maunsell and Parnell Roads, just a few hundred metres from the Auckland War Memorial Museum. Allen Curnow meanwhile, after returning from leave, had been living in the 'mothel' in Grafton Road. In 1963 the divorce proceedings must have moved forward far enough for Allen and Jeny to move in together; so when we finally moved into the modest little house we had bought in Tohunga Crescent which, modified many times over, would be home from then on, Allen and Jeny took over the one in Maunsell Road.

Parties, poems, and letters by hand

Among friends of that time were Tom and La Rue Storm, Dick and Elsie Scott, Dent and Hilary Gardner, Walter and Danuta Pollard, Peter and Bobbie Swinburn. Tom and La Rue were Americans, Tom a lecturer in the university's Psychology Department. Walter Pollard was Irish but had grown up in Switzerland and lectured in French. Danuta, a medical psychologist, had been, with her twin sister, a child member of the Resistance in Poland at the end of World War II. Peter Swinburn was a doctor, and Bobbie had been 'Miss New Zealand, 1949'. Dick Scott had been an editor on the communist paper the *People's Voice*, and was still a hard-line leftist. We thought of these people as the Titirangi/west coast party set, and seemed to be forever, at night or in the weekends, jumping into the resolute Ford and heading west. La Rue was having an affair with Dick, and Tom with one of his students, Christine Orbell, whom he would later marry. A lot of the events and atmosphere of that time were to find fictional form much later in my novel *The End of the Century at the End of the World*, in which Maurice Scobie, a Dick Scott sort of character (but more benign than the original), figures as the man who has, despite everything that is weighing against it, preserved an affirmative vision of the great socialist adventure that, for his generation, had reached one of its peaks in the Spanish Civil War and the International Brigades.

It was a time of dinner parties as well as parties, and we did those – gave them and went to them – with Barbara and Maurice Duggan, Keith and Mary Sinclair, Bob and Noeline Chapman. These were our seniors by ten years, the born-1922 generation, which included also Bill Pearson and Kendrick Smithyman. Keith and Bob were the Young Turks and rivals in the History Department, and it was Bob's temperament that he needed to find acolytes. He would have liked to recruit me, because, like Keith, he aspired to write poetry and to figure in the New Zealand literary landscape. Together with Jonathan Bennett he had edited the 1956 Oxford *Anthology of New Zealand Verse*, and had published in *Landfall* a notable essay, 'Fiction and the Social Pattern'. In the *New Zealand Poetry Yearbook* he published poems that had their moments, but tended for the most part to be clunky and awful. That was nothing in itself – we could all in those days, and did, publish bad poems in Louis Johnson's generously welcoming and famously erratic annual; but, though I recognised, as I think most people who had to deal with Bob did, the raw force of his intellect, I could never understand him perfectly enough to simply agree with his weighty utterances. They always seemed to be muffled and spoiled in the undergrowth of exposition, cluttered in ever-branching metaphor; and though our conversations would go on late into the night, and into the morning hours, I knew I always disappointed him. If there was a theme and a point to these arguments, it circled around Bob's nationalistic determination to treat any mark of respect for 'Britain' (and 'England' especially) as colonial cringe, and to deplore my tendency to (as he saw it) defer to the British part of our intellectual and literary inheritance. I had been to a British university as he had not, and it was as if he wanted to purge me of its bad effects.

Sinclair, though his 'ear' for language was always less than perfect, was the better poet; and certainly the more successful historian. I was fond of Keith, and always impressed by his quickness. I was sometimes conversationally laborious, anxiously explanatory, and he usually raced to my point ahead of the exposition. He had an annoying ability to keep a conversation running while listening in on another going on somewhere close by, even contributing to it at intervals. He said he'd learned his conversational habits in a family of ten, the father a waterside worker. I think Bob's father was a medical man; and Bob prided himself (not without evident leftist shame) on being 'Remuera', while Keith was equally, and with no shame at all, 'Point Chev'. It was obvious that these two, though each considered the other uncommonly brilliant, could not get on together in the same department – a problem solved in the end by appointing Bob (whose PhD in psephology from Canberra was not, and never would be, finished) Professor of the new Department of Political Studies.

In his introduction to his *Penguin Book of New Zealand Verse*, Curnow had said of Sinclair as poet that his words seemed 'placed with a kind of careful absent-mindedness, lest he should compromise his meaning. He lets his limitations be seen, disarmingly; and they are considerable.' Keith asked me if I knew what this meant and, though I thought I did, I told him I didn't.

My exchanges with Maurice Duggan were not just in conversation but by letter, and we exchanged poems – something I was also doing at this time with Alan Roddick. Duggan was disabled, one leg having been amputated, I think just above the knee. He told me once, in a corner-of-the-mouth tone that did not invite further enquiry, that it was the consequence of a motorcycle accident, and I believed that until after he died when I was editing his *Collected Stories* and discovered it was caused, less picturesquely, by osteomyelitis, an infection of the bone. At this time Maurice was writing full-time, while his wife, Barbara, a physiotherapist, was the breadwinner; but he felt uneasy about this and was soon to go back into advertising which he was said to be very good at, but hated. With Duggan the old *here* or *there* argument, that had occupied so much thought and talk among Kiwis in London, was likely to come to the surface; and after one such, he wrote:

> My mind kept returning to the subject over the weekend and there were moments when, endeavouring to argue with your voice, I said for you, 'I don't find there's anything useful for me in rejection, any more than acceptance. The decision doesn't matter. I'll get away, and write, and publish. Put in terms of stay or go the whole question enters an area so personal as not to be available for logical analysis'.

It interests me that he spoke for me, rather than for himself – a fiction writer's device.

Around this time I read Kendrick Smithyman's collection, *Inheritance*, for Blackwood Paul and recommended it for publication, but suggested it should be bigger; so Ken and I sat together, outside the garden shed in Shakespeare Road where he did his writing, with the local stream running by while we enlarged the selection. Ken was a fine and original poet, already experimenting with syllabic form (often combined with complex rhyming) – as prolific as Baxter, more constantly productive than Curnow, but well known for 'difficulty', which for a time he had seemed to encourage in himself, as if he was afraid of being understood. He had a bluff up-front manner hiding, I thought, sensitivity and uncertainty. He'd been unsuccessful in completing a university degree, so earned his living (until the English Department found a niche for him as a stage one tutor) as a primary school teacher, I think of 'special needs' children. None of us knew as much as he did about what was going on in the world of contemporary English-language poetry. In those days when you borrowed a book from the library you signed a card; and it seemed I never borrowed a book of modern poetry in which the card had not previously been signed by Ken.

A colleague in the English Department was Bill Pearson, and only in recent years I've learned from his biographer, Paul Millar, that Bill, ten years my senior, resented my rapid promotion above him. It was not for himself, Bill claimed, that he was concerned, but for the injustice to Allen Curnow, a decade older again. None of these grumbles reached me at the time. As a student, before meeting Bill, I'd read and admired his essay 'Fretful Sleepers'; and I would soon (1963) be reading, with something more than dutiful respect, what was to be his only novel, *Coal Flat*. I knew nothing at this time, and not for several decades yet, of his agonies about his own homosexuality, and the fact that he reproached himself for having disguised it in the writing of the novel. There was always something intellectually solid about Bill, and a capacity for little rushes of recognition and affection – a sort of quick, boyish charm. But being a member of a university department with him, one encountered constantly his suspicion bordering on paranoia, his distrust, his anxiety, his fears. Bill had such a memory for wrongs done to him, real or imagined, that I suspected there must be a fretful* diary in which all such were meticulously set down 'for the record'. But he and I worked, together with Allen Curnow and without conflict, to get New Zealand writing recognised and gradually established in Auckland's Eng. Lit. courses.

On one of our visits to the Duggans' I told Maurice about my idea that all the human attempts to make wings had failed because the inventors imagined flying face-down, in effect on their stomachs, which meant the movement of the arms making the wingbeat wasn't right and would drive you backwards. I'd illustrated this to Kay on a walk in the Auckland Domain, lying first face-down, then on my back, on a park bench that was a single plank. If you wanted your arms to beat like a gull's, I argued, you had to lie on your back. Maurice looked at me quizzically and said, 'You're talking about a story you're writing, aren't you?' A story on this theme had not crossed my mind but now he had planted the idea.

* Millar's biography records that as a child Bill cried a lot. When I read that I imagined he was probably often chided for being 'fretful'; so when he called his countrymen 'fretful sleepers' he was, so to speak, turning the reproach back on those who had made it of him. We were crying in our sleep and not knowing why, and he was the wakeful one, warning us.

It would lie there for a while, the other element in the making of 'A Fitting Tribute', and would not be written until after my 1963 visit to New York, when I did feel I had briefly taken wing.

Late in 1960 I heard of Hutchinson's plan to publish a collection of short stories by new writers, under their New Authors imprint, which had already published Marilyn Duckworth's first novel. I offered them 'A Race Apart' which they liked and accepted; and they already had two or three stories by Diana Athill, herself working in the London publishing world, and much later to become famous for her series of editor's reminiscences. But at that point the plan stalled. Their call for stories by unpublished authors had brought nothing else they thought up to the mark. This seemed to me absurd and I wrote suggesting they send someone to the library at New Zealand House in the Strand and hunt out stories by Maurice Duggan, Maurice Gee and O. E. Middleton. In due course the two Maurices were accepted, but not Middleton; so *New Authors Short Story One* was published in September with three Kiwis and an Englishwoman. This gave all three of us our first book publication in the UK. Gee published his next two novels with Hutchinson, my own first critical book was to come from Hutchinson University Library, while Duggan moved on to Gollancz.

It was in the 1960–61 summer vacation I had returned to my thesis and completed the two final chapters. All the evidence I needed was ready in notebooks, and pretty well marshalled in my head, but the writing was hard work, leaving me exhausted at the beginning of the new year and the new term, pale and thin and looking, my mother thought, overworked and underfed. In the May vacation the writing, typing, checking quotations (there were many small mistakes because I relied so much on memory) were completed and the work sent off to Bristol. By October, a month after the publication of *Short Story One*, and the month in which I won the Mansfield prize, Knights was writing that he and de Sola Pinto found it a first-class piece of work, a pleasure to read, a contribution to Lit. Hist. and critical thinking – and so on.

The PhD was conferred in absentia the following January. Better than any of that, however, to the young man whose desire to prove himself as a writer mattered more, was a review of *Short Story One* by Edna O'Brien describing 'A Race Apart' as 'delicious [. . .] subtle, funny and dextrously written'.

A baby, New York, Maurice, Barry, and Janet again

'Each day brings on its common miracle':* the sun comes up, the rooster crows, we all get up and go to work, the leaves go on greening or browning according to the season. But then there are the things that are common only if you think of the world at large. People are born and they die in millie-ons; but each is singular, discrete, unique.

Throughout most of 1963 Kay was pregnant – the sleepy mother-to-be, her beautiful face and thick black hair on the white pillow; the early intimations, the scans, the ghostly Other in there, the beating heart, the kick-boxing under the growing bulge. There was less talking, for her more sleeping, and for me more reading – old favourites, not Henry James whose characters seemed not born of bodies but conceived in a mind – the mind of a master, but my appetite was for more primitive things: *The Last of the Mohicans, The Mill on the Floss, Moby Dick*.

'Call me Ishmael.'

In the meantime I had been invited to give a paper at the 9th Congress of FILLM – the International Federation for Modern Languages and Literature – to take place at New York University, fares and accommodation provided. People have said 'A Fitting Tribute' is my best story. It's many things, composed of many elements – fantasy, comedy, satire. But it's also about flying away, leaving loved ones behind, disappearing forever. What if I didn't come back!

---

* R. A. K. Mason, 'Miracle of Life'.

Oliver William was born in August 1963. Ken Smithyman's congrats were for 'keeping up a local tradition': he, Sinclair and Chapman had three sons each, and Duggan one – no daughters among them. Only a fortnight after Oliver's arrival I took off, feeling badly shaken by the excitements and anxieties of the birth, and by the very strong sense that I should not be going anywhere – that I should be at home and 'on guard'. But Kay was keen I should go; and her mother had moved in to be with her and help with the baby in my absence. My parents drove me to the airport, Mum and Dad in the front seats while I wept silently in the dark behind them.

There were no runways in New Zealand long enough for the Boeing 707, so you flew first by turbo-prop Auckland to Fiji, and then on by 707 to Honolulu, to San Francisco, and to New York, the last a night flight which gave me a very small poem I still like for its irony:

> Small towns unwoken pitted meagre lights
> In the huge dark. Perhaps their cocks foretold
> The unseen fire. If so, they did not lie.
> It pressed at the world's rim. It tinged my wing.
> So great a commonplace deserves a word.
> There's none commends itself. I sat so high!
> I saw the light come to America.

It was the first time that particular international conference had been held in the US, and everything was turned on to make it a grand affair. It was presided over by the great Henry James biographer and editor Leon Edel, and we received a message of welcome from President Kennedy. I was impressed to be in the presence of some of the grandees of American Eng. Lit. academia – M. H. Abrams, R. S. Crane, Ronald Bush. To Kay I wrote:

> . . . at a cocktail party this evening in the splendid Eisner and Lubin Auditorium the young sleek smooth handsome president of N.Y.U. and his likewise wife were hosts – lights dimmed,

just a few spots at angles from the ceiling – the welcoming party ranged at the top of the hall. Down two sides were long tables with white cloths, finger-food, punch, champagne, attended by [African-Americans] in bright scarlet livery, and at the far end the university quartet playing chamber music. All splendour and opulence.

One noted of course the imbalance of race – the waiting staff were all African-American (a term not then in use, and I have substituted it here). Their colour was like their livery – a uniform, a uniformity.

Having difficulty sleeping I wandered out one night and came on a free open-air concert in Washington Square. I found myself sitting with a group of five women school teachers, about my age or younger, New Yorkers. They took me to their favourite tea house afterwards, and joked that they were all looking for a husband. They were politically liberal and put their faith in John F. Kennedy. I too had felt the excitement of his election three years earlier; but then, during the Cuban Missile Crisis of the previous October (the only time I ever thought we were seriously, dangerously at the nuclear brink) I had felt he was as guilty as his two predecessors of the post-World War II American arrogance and inflexibility.* In just two months, however, he would be assassinated in Texas; and not far in the future for these young women (and for me at a distance) lay the 'liberation' of the '60s, flower power, and the long horror and protest of the Vietnam War.

Kay's letters were full of baby Oliver, doing well, eating and growing and sometimes bawling, and visits by family and friends. Bob Chapman had been appointed to the new chair of Political Studies and Kay wrote:

---

* My thinking had been that since the Soviets had to put up with American nuclear missiles on their borders, Khrushchev had only been levelling the odds when he put his into Cuba. But the whole story of the crisis, when it emerged, was complex, and Kennedy came out of it rather well in that he had held his military in check. It is partly told in Roger Donaldson's movie *Thirteen Days* (2000).

> I got brave yesterday and rang him to congratulate. We had an odd conversation. He talked in a funny way, very quiet and nonchalant so I couldn't always catch what he said. But humble – he can be very honest sometimes, as you know. He said for instance that his main feeling was relief. That I call honest. Also he's going to spend 1964 studying the teaching of Pol. Studs. in the U.K. and U.S.; and he had the grace to laugh about going to England and said you would be able to tease him about it. Good things put people in a good frame of mind.

Anticipating what would appear the following year in *The New Poetic*, the paper I had come all this way to deliver set out to demonstrate in effect that although T. S. Eliot had persuaded the literary world he was a 'classicist', immune to, and quite independent of, any notion of Romantic 'inspiration', there was in fact, buried among his writings over a long period, clear evidence of dependence on the 'inner voice', on the 'oracular expertness' he liked to mock, on states of 'ill-health, debility or anaemia', and even on 'a demon against which he felt powerless'. The question then was how could we reconcile his talk about the 'frightful toil' of literary composition with these very personal accounts of spontaneity, unpredictability, 'inspiration' and lack of control? It was really a question of two quite distinct phases of composition: the poet finding places for fragments that had come, often almost unbidden and out of nowhere, organising them into something ('The Waste Land' for example) that could be offered as a single work. This latter part was the hard labour.

It was a paper that created a strong impression, first because it contradicted Eliot and what it proposed was something most academics had not previously thought possible, and then because the exposition and the evidence were convincing. It attracted a lot of interest, elicited many questions and compliments. L. C. Knights, who must have had spies abroad, was soon writing to congratulate me on 'stellar reports'. I flew back from New York certain I'd made a mark.

I had been home a couple of months and was looking out from the kitchen at new bright green leaf on our plum tree, and on the grapevine around the old garden shed, when I heard on the radio the news that President Kennedy had been shot. I went into the bedroom where Kay was breast-feeding Oliver and told her the news. She went on feeding the baby but weeping, the tears falling on his small head. Later, when American power, its ubiquitousness and arbitrary violence, had begun to invade my poems with images of Rome and the imperial eagle, I wrote about that death:

Dallas, 1963

Caesar, you were everybody's baby
But not mine.
I thought the broken warhorse that doddered before
Alone made you shine.
But when your head leaked blood on the lap of the world
Like those your mistakes murdered,
I thought it was the golden apple
And the holy wine.

The 'broken warhorse' was Republican President Dwight D. Eisenhower, formerly Supreme Commander of Allied Forces in World War II, who preceded Democrat Kennedy. But what did the final two lines mean? Some years later again, when editors Michael Hulse and Simon Rae included the poem in their anthology *The 20th Century in Poetry*, they asked me that question. The 'But' in line five suggests a change of tone. I had not shared the enthusiasm for this young Caesar – but now? In Greek myth the golden apple (which had the words 'for the fairest' written on it) was the symbol of discord; the holy wine suggests the Christian sacrament and Kennedy's Catholicism – so there is an ambiguity, and the lines (perhaps) work better for being less than crystal clear. We shed tears at this death – but would what followed have been better if he had lived? It was, after all, Kennedy's own team – Dean Rusk, Robert McNamara, McGeorge Bundy, and his otherwise liberal Vice President Lyndon Johnson – who would initiate and prosecute the brutal and unnecessary war in Vietnam. Perhaps he would have seen sense and curbed them – but probably not.

New York and the world of international academia were left behind. At home I published a review article on R. A. K. Mason, and a longer one in *Landfall* on Curnow. But I had been bitten by the fiction bug. The success of 'A Race Apart' had set me writing more. There was a story, fifty-five quarto pages, called 'Finch Among the Shadows', and a longer version, novella length, called *Harry Riding*, about a young pianist. Nothing was to come of these; but when I got back to New Zealand, with the experience of flight, of 'flying away', in some way both troubling and teasing my imagination, I remembered Duggan's response when I'd told him my theory about human flight. So I wrote 'A Fitting Tribute', about Julian Harp* whose eccentric behaviour I based largely on those memories of Barry Humphries in Auckland. Julian constructs, out of stolen umbrellas, the first successful man-made set of wings, takes off from the Auckland Domain, flies out over the Hauraki Gulf, and is never seen again. It's a comedy about fame and provincial myth-making. Robie Macauley, editor of the American literary journal the *Kenyon Review*, liked it and it appeared there in 1965.

Around this time Barry Humphries came on his second visit to Auckland and Kay and I took him with Rosalind to visit Maurice Duggan. Both of the two men we were bringing together were at this time well down the road to alcoholism.† Duggan's limp was noticeable, even picturesque, but the loss of a leg which had caused it was something he was sensitive about. He was a great Irish talker who used to peak with a brilliantly funny story that would have

* The name was meant to suggest the 'Aeolian harp', symbol of poetic inspiration.

† Barry's alcoholism continued and got worse until a crisis in 1973 after which he joined AA and has never touched alcohol since.

everyone sick with laughter, and then lapse into alcoholic gloom and even sometimes violence.

Barry listened while Maurice explained about toheroa – the season, the limit on the bag, how it was minced to make an incomparable soup; listened too, and looked, while Duggan, quietly proud, pointed out the books on his immaculate shelves and how many of the modern fiction titles were hardcover first editions.

Maurice must have been up on his plateau ready to go into his usual entertaining anecdote-and-plunge when Barry pre-empted the moment, launching into a monologue about his own collection of hardcover toe-he-rowers, and about how short the season was on books and how tight the limit on the bag, but the great soups that could be made by critics who put them through the mincer. I remember it now only in crude outline; but in detail – in performance so to speak – it was bewildering and clever. It was the only time I saw Maurice driven backwards into sobriety. Afterwards, if Humphries was referred to, Maurice would dismiss him as 'a clever magpie'.

Sometimes in Barry's company I felt like Dame Edna's Kiwi suburban bridesmaid, Madge Allsop, and yet we always got on well. It was on this visit that after being taken out or entertained somewhere he turned up on our front lawn, due soon at the airport to depart New Zealand, with a 'thank you' present, a fine Italian silk tie (Testoni) he had chosen for me – not garish, but much more dashing than anything I would have chosen for myself. We all wore ties in those days, and mine must have seemed too dull and conventional. I still have it after half a century, still my best, and I have often worn it, always in his honour.

Meanwhile there were no new poems. Prose – critical and fictional – had taken over. Poetry had always been first base – what mattered most – but now the cupboard was bare, until early the following year when a visit to Auckland by a Fijian brass band gave me something which became for some days a total obsession – as if I had to wring it out of myself, painfully. Maybe it was just desperation – the Muse had abandoned me and I wanted her back. But the poem kept becoming, not just verbally more dextrous, but louder, less 'sensitive', more outlandish and brass-bandish. It was in my head night and day, being constantly worked on, constantly revised. 'The Fijian Police Band Performs in Albert Park, Auckland', was to be the last poem in my first collection when it was finally published in 1964. The following year when I was on leave in London organising a reading of New Zealand poems in the Royal Court Theatre, Maurice Duggan wrote to me:

> Poetry at the Royal Court Theatre – rather puts our little Auckland Art Gallery fest out of the picture. I still remember the Fijian band, though. Poom!

Poom! indeed. It was a performance piece, and rewarded extravagant presentation.

LATE IN 1964 I WAS COMMISSIONED by Oxford University Press to make the selection for a second *Oxford New Zealand Short Stories*. Janet Frame was alerted that I would be on the hunt for something of hers, and would look at what she'd published outside New Zealand. Alarmed, she confessed to Frank that there was a story in her double collection, *The Reservoir / Snowman Snowman*, that would give great offence to the Steads.* It was called (with heavy irony) 'The Triumph of Poetry', and was about a young poet, Alan Wakefield, and his wife Sylvia, who live in a renovated washhouse by the sea. So much of their early life, their friends and pursuits (his especially) were drawn from ours, there could be no doubt about the source. Alan is a first-class honours student, swimmer, tennis and chess player. Sylvia is a librarian. There is an unwanted pregnancy and a termination. Gradually (the story

* See my previous memoir, *South-West of Eden*, pp. 342–43.

is twenty-six dreary pages long) Alan's poetry is subverted by academia and the marriage. He loses his hair and becomes an arid academic critic, while Sylvia resorts to growing dahlias. There are no children. Their life is barren, and all that is left between them in the final paragraph is a nameless fear.

When Frank brought Janet to dinner, bearing the double stories collection in its George Braziller boxed set, with her own handwritten name and address crossed out in both volumes and re-inscribed 'to Karl, Kay and Oliver with my good wishes and apologies', we still didn't know what the story contained. Head down like a naughty schoolgirl, Janet was silent, while Frank's nervous chatter seldom stopped. It was a bizarre evening among four old friends who had been so happy and relaxed together in the past! As soon as they'd gone I read the story. It came as a profound shock. From one we'd thought of as a dear friend, and whom we'd helped, it felt like a malediction.

A few days later Janet wrote explaining that she hadn't wanted me, in doing my job as an anthologist, to come upon the story without being forewarned, and without knowing that she 'asked forgiveness'. The rest of the letter was full of the wonders of having known us in Takapuna where she'd spent some of the happiest evenings of her life, and how the latter years of her fictional poet Alan Wakefield were really based on her imaginings about an old lecturer in Dunedin.

As Janet said herself, 'The Triumph of Poetry' was not a good story. It combined naïve High Romanticism about 'Poetry' with satiric malice – a risky mix, like oil and vinegar, difficult to bring off without curdling. Frank's explanation was 'her insanity'. But Janet, though in certain situations socially dysfunctional, was never insane. Kay was convinced it was jealousy and thwarted love, and the story was a kind of revenge. I thought it was that burning, child-like envy which is sometimes the motivating force of her writing. Janet was a victim of her times, damaged by mistreatment, misdiagnosis and medical malpractice. We all knew what she had suffered because she was putting it vividly on record in her fiction. (*Faces in the Water* had appeared in 1961.) But pity was not a critical principle, and did not make her story better or worse. In any case I was still suffering from shock and hurt. I did not keep a copy of the letter I wrote in response to hers, but when Michael King was writing her biography he found it among her papers and sent me a copy. It was cool, but considering my feelings at that moment, restrained:

> Dear Janet,
>
> It's difficult to know what to say about the story – I hoped I wouldn't have to say anything. It had its effect, and still has, despite your letter. I hope it won't be published in New Zealand.
>
> I don't think there would be any point in my sending you the story about the man with wings. You would feel obliged to praise it, whatever you thought of it.
>
> I hope everything is going well for you.
>
> Karl

She had asked for forgiveness and hadn't received it. Now she didn't forgive me. She replied at once with a single-sentence letter telling me I could no doubt find consolation with 'novelettish Kay'.

The hurt passed, though the wound left a scar. Janet and I would meet as friends again in two years' time, with Charles Brasch in Dunedin. When King was at work on his biography, he sent me a copy of something I had written to Frank a few years later, after meeting Iris Murdoch:

> Iris reminded me of Janet, though on the surface much more formidable and commanding. But I detected the same disbelief in the world around her, the same dislike of being the subject of attention and dislike of not being it, the same apparent diffidence covering an enormous self-consuming ego.

'Very acute this,' Michael commented, 'but of course I can't use it.'

London again, and poetry, and Vietnam

I now had two books published. *The New Poetic* appeared early in 1964, and the long-delayed first collection of poems, *Whether the Will is Free*, later the same year. Typically they were published at opposite ends of the earth, and as if for entirely different sets of readers, one large, one small. I was to have two separate literary identities which for a very long time would seldom meet, in fact showed no outward sign that they even knew one another.

Enthusiastic letters about *The New Poetic* began coming almost at once, from both sides of the Atlantic, and there were good reviews. In the *Guardian* Bernard Bergonzi called it 'brilliant' and said it 'neatly demolished the bogus concept of the "neo-classical" Eliot'. Graham Hough in the (UK) *Listener* took the same view. In *The London Magazine* Roy Fuller was 'absorbed and instructed by it', and concluded (confirming my feeling that it had some of the narrative momentum of a novel) 'to append any brief account of his discoveries about Eliot's verse would be as unfair as giving away the plot of a detective story'.

By August there was news it would appear as a Penguin alongside the continuing Hutchinson hardcover, and there was interest from Harper in the US who would soon sign up to do it as a Torchbook. On 19 October, two days after my thirty-second birthday, I was promoted to Associate Professor, and Frank wrote, 'I can't get rid of my concern about your health and the way you are now placed at the university. I can't see Curnow ever really forgiving you.'*

I had sabbatical leave ahead for the whole of 1965 and had been awarded a Nuffield travelling scholarship, which provided first-class sea travel and a flat in London in Prince Albert Road on the northern

---

* That Frank's supposition about Curnow was somewhat closer to correct than I imagined has since been made clear in Terry Sturm's Curnow biography (*Simply by Sailing in a New Direction*, ed. Linda Cassells, Auckland University Press, 2018). I discussed this in a paper given at a symposium to accompany the publication of the biography and the *Collected Poems* and published in *PN Review* 241, May 2018.

side of Regent's Park. I was going to return to the work on Auden and the 1930s poets (originally intended as part of *The New Poetic*), while also making my choices for the new *Oxford New Zealand Short Stories*. But more serious than any of these declared plans was my intention to find my way back to writing poems.

Frank must have been suffering one of his bouts of nerves which made him feel he would soon die, because he wrote in November, 'As you will be away so long and it could be quite on the cards I wouldn't be here when you returned – yes, I would like to visit the pair of you before you leave if I could be conveniently fitted in. But only if convenient. Choose your own time.' Of course he could be 'fitted in' – he had always (as he knew well) a priority place in our life. He came (with a toy for Oliver in the rucksack along with the usual vegetables), and the talk was as warm and ribald as ever; but we also talked about the Oxford stories I was to edit, and he said he'd been asked by Dan Davin to advise on an editor and had recommended against me. He wanted me doing 'my own work' not other people's. Possibly he also thought I would do a rush job. Others were anxious about it too – Bill Pearson, for example, who didn't expect I would include him (he was wrong); and Maurice Shadbolt for the same reason (also wrong). There was so much anxiety about anthologies in those days, when they seemed to matter so much.

My book of poems appeared from Blackwood Paul in May and received the usual range of reviews, positive and negative; but I quote one in particular because in retrospect it seems unusually lively, and because I took it, with its casual dismissal ('who cares?') of Curnow's literary nationalism, to be by James K. Baxter.*

> C. K. Stead is one of the few poets who have managed to establish a name for themselves before the appearance of their first book. *Whether the will is free* serves to reinforce Stead's reputation in certain unexpected ways; firstly for the simple

* *PPTA Journal*, August 1964, unsigned.

lyricism of a few poems such as 'Winter Song', vaguely reminiscent of the earlier Alistair Campbell; and secondly for landscapes where old Curnow sits in a fold of the hills fondling his bone flute, while young girls, satyrs and Greek fish-shop owners sprawl on sands that belong to the Hauraki, perhaps, or to the Aegean, who cares? Overall the effect is overwhelming. Stead is never afraid to stage his raid on the inarticulate – in broad daylight in a London street, drunk in a toilet or on an Auckland divan, under a landscape window. Wherever it may be Stead brings it off, neatly poised between the sublime and the ridiculous.

BY JANUARY 1965 WE WERE AT SEA. Once again there was that sense of the immensity of distance between our *here* and our *there*. The series of Winter Lectures I had contributed to had taken as its title the Brasch line, 'Distance looks our way' – but Distance did nothing of the sort. It was an enormous barrier, and a severance to communication. Air letters took ten days, so twenty for a message and reply; phone calls had to be booked in advance and were so expensive they were hardly ever used except in the event of a crisis or a death. There was no email, no internet, not even fax.

Two famous men died while we were at sea – T. S. Eliot on the 4th of January, and Winston Churchill on the 24th. The fuss about the Churchill exit was inevitably immense (I remember parades we didn't attend, and thunderous fly-pasts we couldn't avoid); but London's literary attention, and mine, was focused on Eliot. He had been the dominant poet-critic of the age, and the centre of my literary and academic consciousness – author of the great Modernist poem 'The Waste Land', hero and villain, brilliant and flawed, High Anglican Royalist whose not-long-past (if it was past) anti-Semitism was still perceptible in poems and lectures.

There was a memorial service in Westminster Abbey on 4 February, and later in the year an extraordinary theatrical homage at the Globe Theatre in Shaftesbury Avenue, involving Stravinsky, W. H. Auden, Groucho Marx (reading from the *Old Possum's Book of Practical Cats*), Andrey Voznesensky, Henry Moore (in the form of an immense marble sculpture creaking around on a revolving stage), Cleo Laine and Johnny Dankworth (doing *Sweeney Agonistes*), Peter O'Toole, Paul Scofield, Laurence Olivier . . . On both occasions all London's biggest literary guns were present and on view, and I have a distinct memory of that crowd in the Globe foyer towered over by the one who had written 'I think continually of those who were truly great'.

Among all the copious pieces about Eliot's death there was one in the *New Statesman* by Frank Kermode which I found irritating, partly because it had his characteristic bland, authoritative tone, and yet (also characteristic at that time) lack of clarity. I was also irritated by a conviction that he was using *The New Poetic* without saying so or naming it. I discussed this with my friend Ted Sturmer, a young New Zealand lawyer now permanently based in London, and Ted wrote to the *New Statesman* asking how much Kermode's piece owed to my book and why it wasn't acknowledged. Kermode at first denied any knowledge of *The New Poetic*, and then, when pressed, told the editor (Karl Miller whom I would later know very well) that he had attended a seminar in which the book had been discussed and that he '*may have taken notes*'. When he reprinted the essay in a 1966 collection of essays on Eliot edited by Allen Tate he acknowledged the debt.

This was not to be my last engagement with Kermode; and I was reminded of it many years later when he wrote in his autobiography:*

> . . . for a while I continued to alter the facts to suit myself; fibs and distortions, all begetting further fibs and distortions, were for some time a recurrent feature of my moral life, continuing,

* Frank Kermode, *Not Entitled: A Memoir*, HarperCollins, 1995, p. 62.

> I suppose, until I had no further need of them and I could settle for the greater comfort, the relative intellectual ease, of veracity . . .

Evidently in 1965 veracity had not yet set in. But he was to go on soothing the literary world with that tone of authority, while flattering its sense that in reading him they were engaging with a significant intellectual. He was such a *British* phenomenon, the super-critic with *manners*, in due time *Sir* Frank of course, whose autobiography, which acknowledged 'fibs' in his past, was disarmingly entitled *Not Entitled*.

I was soon working regularly in the Reading Room of the British Museum; but there was also a study I could use behind and beneath our flat where I began to work on new poems. I'd been engaged to organise the New Zealand part of readings at the Royal Court Theatre as part of a Commonwealth Poetry Festival. Eighteen poets had been commissioned to write a poem, to be published in the programme, so that was one of the first things I went to work on. I sat in that study looking out on a car-park and the brown backs of London houses, and thought of Hobson Bay at the bottom of Tohunga Crescent when the tide was full and the weather good, remembering in particular a day when I'd walked along the old sewer pipe (since demolished) and seen three or four very big kingfish cruising in its shadow and making raids out into the sunlight where flatfish were doing whatever an unsuspecting flatfish does on a sunny day. My poem began:

> Hard. Bright. Clean. Particular.
> That kind of a day.
> Gable points picked out on the cliff-top, the tide
> Pumping through the causeway to the bay.*

---

* 'You Have a Lot to Lose', *Collected Poems, 1951–2006*, Auckland University Press, 2008, p. 35.

The fact that LBJ (President Lyndon Johnson) figured in this poem is an indication that what was to be my political (it is hardly too much to say) obsession for the next seven years was already creeping into my poems. There didn't seem, even then (and it has since become even clearer) any doubt that the US Navy, probably with White House approval, had invented or incited the Gulf of Tonkin incident, an exchange of fire with North Vietnamese naval forces, which had given President Johnson an excuse, and the approval he needed from Senate and Congress, to go to war in Vietnam. Previously there had been only US military advisors to the South Vietnamese; now there was to be an American army – and it was during 1965 that Johnson was advised to increase the force to half a million men, and began to move rapidly towards that figure. It was also the year when New Zealand committed troops to the war. This had already become the international issue of the moment, with right-wing politicians (including our own in New Zealand) propounding a theory which saw Vietnam as the first of a series of dominoes. If it fell, the rest could follow. The slogan in New Zealand was 'Better to fight them there than here'.

Already during 1965 protests were happening on American campuses, and in New Zealand there were 'teach-ins' opposing our participation. Keith Sinclair was prominent among opponents. The Americans were now bombing Hanoi and spreading Agent Orange over the jungles to destroy forest cover – something which would have horrifying long-term effects for the population. Helicopter gunships ranged over the southern provinces, raking paddies from the air, and landing troops to engage the Viet Cong. After each engagement a body count was announced, usually (in fact with such regularity one suspected it was the required success rate for US home consumption) ten Vietnamese dead for each dead American. Since it tended to be whole villages that were blasted and there was no way of distinguishing 'Viet Cong' from 'civilians', men, women and children were all counted and the required ratio was easily achieved. But the numbers climbed, and even counted in ones rather than tens, America's losses became alarming.

In Britain Vietnam was not yet a huge issue, because Labour Prime Minister Harold Wilson was determined to keep Britain out of an unnecessary war. His Foreign Secretary, Michael Stewart, kept up regular statements of support for America, probably insincere since, despite pressure from Washington, no troops were ever offered.*

Those seven years of my obsession with the issue of Vietnam were also the years of what came to be called 'the sexual revolution'. Philip Larkin was its comic historian:

> So life was never better than
> In nineteen sixty-three
> [. . .]
> Between the end of the *Chatterley* ban
> And the Beatles' first LP.

In the years before 1963 it had been a reasonable assumption that one's students who were not married were either virgins, or not engaged in regular sexual activity. After 1963 the opposite was the case, and the change was manifest in their behaviour, and even in their language. It was a time of both mini-skirts and long flimsy flowery dresses; of beads and beards and sandals; of the Beatles and long hair and flower power. It was the age of the Pill, and the freedom that went before the Fall that was the AIDS scare of the '80s. 'Bliss was it in that dawn to be alive'; and though I was no longer quite young there were indeed to be moments that would seem 'very heaven'.

Poetry and politics and a festival

The London skies were clearing, the Clean Air Act of the late '50s at last beginning to have real effect; and I remember lying in bed

---

* It was an example Tony Blair should have followed some decades later when America invaded Iraq; but Blair's vanity made him determined to be part of the big league.

with flu, looking up through the big sash windows astonished to be seeing a clear blue London sky. L. C. Knights had just left his Winterstoke chair at Bristol to take up appointment as King Edward VII Professor of English at Cambridge. He invited me there and we walked in his college gardens (Queens') which he entered using an ancient-looking key, like a small tennis racquet; and had lunch in the college. He was charming as ever, pleased with his former student's progress, but not altogether happy with his own. There was surely no more distinguished chair of English literature in Britain, but he gave the impression (though discreetly, and without names) that Cambridge was full of conflict, envy and malice. Certainly F. R. Leavis was such a contentious figure that to have edited the Leavisite critical journal *Scrutiny* for most of its life, as Knights had, must have created problems for him; and he did give the impression of a man who had been mysteriously elbowed and tripped in a crowd by no one in particular. There was also the difficult fact that Leavis would have liked that chair himself, and it was said he referred to Knights as 'Professor Judas' for having accepted it.

Correspondence with home continued. Sargeson's letters were like the man himself – busy, quick, full of 'quips and cranks and wanton wiles'. Brasch's were wearily dutiful and not always pleased. Maurice Duggan's were sometimes opaque, comically Catholic, much-mannered exercises in style. He could run on, free-wheeling for many pages, at times funny-frank about his own (recent) past:

> Oh well, you didn't in the end offend me. Anyway the fleures-cent tube is in Italy at the moment, under adverse weather conditions learning to speak to the natives like an Italian. O to this flower of common stock, ad cock. Yet after all these years and miles and countries I remain quite fond of the old sport.*

* The reference here is to Fleur Adcock with whom Duggan had a somewhat public affair in Dunedin while there on the Burns Fellowship in 1960.

The process of making choices for the *Oxford New Zealand Short Stories* was sometimes difficult. I felt Shadbolt had to be included but in every story there was something that for me created a block. I chose 'The People Before', and Professor Alex Calder has since called it 'a small masterpiece'.* Writing to Bill Pearson about these difficulties, including that of finding one of his own stories, I said:

> I'm surprised to find I'm a charitable anthologiser in the sense that I read everything hoping it will be good. This seems to me the reverse of Allen who I suspect reads everything (with a few exceptions) hoping it will be bad. This means I am more often disappointed than he is.

Untypically, Bill seemed to trust me more because I told him what I thought was wrong with two of his stories. He was even grateful. 'I was glad to have your comments on those stories [. . .] it enabled me to see them in a new light.' Subsequent to this I found his 'At the Leicesters', an E. M. Forsterish end-of-Empire decadence story set in Cairo, which seemed to me to work well, and still does.

Some choices were going to be easy. There were writers like Duggan, David Ballantyne, O. E. Middleton and Phillip Wilson represented in the earlier (1953) Oxford selection made by Dan Davin by a single example, who had gone on to better things and would be represented each by two stories in mine. Janet Frame was a problem because of what has been called her 'Mansfield complex' and a consequent reluctance to have a story about childhood in an anthology where most would be about adults. But I persisted with the one I wanted, 'The Reservoir', and finally she agreed, with signs in letters back and forth that the old affection was returning.

---

* *The Settler's Plot*, Auckland University Press, 2011, p. 126. I can't agree of course, but my choice is endorsed!

In London Kay and I got to know David and Vivienne Ballantyne. Dave, who had come from Auckland, was working for the *Evening Standard* and writing fiction, hoping to repeat the success he'd had with his first novel *The Cunninghams*, but struggling. He kept up the rough bluff front of the 'journo', concealing sensitivity with a breezy manner, booze and fags. In the years not too far ahead the booze would damage and the fags kill him. He is one of the male writers of his time for whom I feel profound sympathy. It was always their responsibility to be 'strong', never to complain, to do the heavy lifting and bring home the bacon, and to write only as 'spare time' permitted.

Vivienne was a painter, a gentle, slightly batty soul who was also (and unyieldingly as time and history went against her) a hard-line Marxist. Dave and Viv lived with their one son in a post-war jerry-built terrace house bought with a mortgage. Viv had papered the walls of the kitchen with *New Yorker* covers, in what spirit, jolly-and-decorative or Stalinist-satirical, I didn't like to ask. The house seemed of amazing flimsiness. When the front door slammed the whole structure shuddered.

I asked Dave's permission to use two of his stories, and he asked me would I read and comment on a typescript of his new novel, *A Friend of the Family*. I was busy and reluctant, but agreed and was impressed. At once and thereafter I was a supporter and admirer. He was still a few years away from writing his best novel, *Sydney Bridge Upside Down*, which I think has only received its due since his death.

Around this time I had a note from Jack Tressider, my fellow student-poet of the early '50s,* who had seen my name connected with the forthcoming poetry festival. We invited him to dinner, and the Ballantynes as well, knowing the two men had worked together at the *Auckland Star*. The evening passed off amiably until Dave reached a certain alcohol level beyond which anything might

* See *South-West of Eden*, p. 224, where I quote one of his poems.

happen, and there he chose to remember a review Jack had written of his collection *And the Glory*. Perhaps the fact that I was choosing two of these stories for the anthology increased his confidence in them, and his sense that the review had done them less than justice. Jack was puzzled because he thought he'd rather admired the book and had said so. Kay and I sat helpless while Dave raved, and the evening broke up. Next morning an embarrassed Vivienne called around with (needless) apologies and a toy for Oliver.

My work at the British Museum Reading Room was on the thirties poets – the MacSpaunday group as the South African poet Roy Campbell had called them: W. H. Auden, Stephen Spender, Louis MacNeice and Cecil Day-Lewis – especially the poetry they had written in the 1930s when they'd been, all but MacNeice, in full leftist flush, full flight and politically committed, yet already at odds with the Communist Party, which didn't like bourgeois obscurity and thought the drumbeat of the working class should be sounding without refinements or ambiguities. First Spender, and then Auden, had gone to join, or at least to see and report on, the International Brigades in Spain; and Auden's poem 'Spain 1937' had become a rallying cry for the cause.

Auden was the supreme technician of the group. But that, his great strength, also revealed (did it? – this for me was the question) a kind of shallowness. He could change his ground, alter his political opinions, adjust his stand and, with a few deft tricks, take the poem with him – or if it refused to go he would eliminate it. But if the changes were so seemingly effortless, was that to be admired, or did it cast a doubt on the earlier version, and on the whole process? 'Spain 1937', for example, had been first emasculated by radical cutting, and finally rejected altogether as 'trash' and eliminated from his collected poems.

Also there was the broader question of how far political commitment could be legitimately part of poetry at all, and how much the two, the poetic mode and the political, were different not just in purpose and emphasis but in kind. I was coming more and more to the view that they were different modes of thinking, of consciousness, of being. Insofar as politics involved feelings, those could be part of the tone and colour of poetry; but reasoned exposition, argument, debating points, taking sides, beating a drum – never! That was why 'Spain 1937' had worked so well as a poem – because it had given itself the vast space of 'history' on which to suggest the *feelings* people of the left had about the Spanish Civil War: 'Yesterday all the past . . . Tomorrow perhaps . . . *But today the Struggle!*' It didn't have to be 'right' or 'wrong', a good cause or a bad one. That was how people felt about it, and the poem caught their feeling. So Auden's adjusting, and finally eliminating, the poem were political acts. They were not the actions of the poet who had written it. They were acts against poetry and in favour of politics.

Auden, still a factory in regular production, was inevitably the central focus of my study. Step by step, and they were big ones, he had been leaving behind his commitment to the 'low dishonest decade', as he called the 1930s, and to the poetry of the left – not like Spender, to become an honest (fairly honest) Labour-voting liberal, but in favour of High Church Anglicanism and old fashioned Toryism – two isms that did not have to go hand in hand, but were certainly comfortable in one another's company.

But there was a sense in which that famous four were old literary hat. Ted Hughes had been photographed a year or two before with three of them and T. S. Eliot, like a pictorial admission to the Faber big league; and his wife Sylvia Plath had written to her mother to say how proud that photograph had made her. But the literary sensation of that 1965 sabbatical year was not a MacSpaunday, nor even Ted. It was the publication of Sylvia's *Ariel*. It came out around the time of the Eliot obsequies, and when I bought a copy in March it was already into its second impression. The high level of interest was partly because the writing was so good, so challenging – but it would have been purely a literary matter if Plath had not been already dead, and by suicide. More sensationally, she had been the wife, and mother of his two small children, of the poet Ted Hughes who had left her for another (or others); so in the eyes of journalists looking for a story, Hughes had to be in part responsible for her death – and this seemed to be confirmed by the poems with their dark malevolent images of the male, sometimes father, sometimes husband, often both-in-one. Hughes seemed present there as 'the vampire' who 'drank my blood' for seven years, and her own suicide was foreseen:

> Dying
> Is an art, like everything else.
> I do it exceptionally well.

It was the perfect merging of poetry and gossip, and has continued thus ever since. I have no clippings from the time, but a memory that the critic Al Alvarez was in the picture early, claiming friendship with Plath at her time of distress; and I have a sedate *Poetry Book Society Bulletin* (no. 44, February 1965) which begins with an 'In Memoriam' for T. S. Eliot by (inevitably) Stephen Spender, but followed by an article in which Hughes writes about *Ariel*, and Plath's habits of composition, and goes on:

> Behind [the *Ariel* poems] there is a fierce and uncompromising nature. There is also a child desperately infatuated with the world. And there is a strange muse, bald, white and wild in her 'hood of bone', floating over a landscape like that of the Primitive Painters, a burning luminous vision of Paradise. A Paradise which is at the same time eerily frightening, an unalterably spot-lit vision of death.

This did not seem to me a propitious start to the Hughes–Plath partnership in death. It was to be a long road for Hughes in which his own fame would increase together with, tethered to, for a time sullied by, his identity as the one who had wronged his more brilliant wife, and might even be held accountable for her death. By the time the poetry festival came towards the end of the year the gossip was rife, not diminished by the fact that the Canadian David Wevill, husband of Assia Wevill, one of two women Hughes was said to be having affairs with when Sylvia killed herself, was one of the eighteen poets commissioned to write poems for it. His book of poems, *Birth of a Shark*, published only the year before, was dedicated to Assia, who had now had a child to Ted; and it was even said that David took his turn looking after the Hughes child, and that he wanted to preserve his marriage to Assia. Wevill's commissioned poem began:

> Every man
> Carries a scandal
> At his heart.
>
> The woodpile hides
> A baby or
> A dead wife's bones.

And ended

> I,
> Down the same darkness
> Retrieve my lost diamond.

The alliance of Ted and Assia (David's 'lost diamond') we now know went through many ups and downs in the next few years until 1969 when she too killed herself. Sylvia in her suicide had taken special care that the gas did not reach the children asleep upstairs. Assia on the other hand took her and Ted's little daughter Shura with her – curled up with her on the kitchen floor so they died together.

There were, for us, other connections with all this. We were not far from Fitzroy Road, where Sylvia had killed herself, and knew the house for its blue plaque recording that Yeats had lived there.

We knew the phone box on the corner of Primrose Hill from which she had tried to call Ted on the fatal night. We were in earshot of the zoo's howling wolves and caged beasts that figured as part of Ted's poetic furniture. Our GP was Dr John Horder who described Sylvia as 'a model patient', and had phoned Ted and told him (brutally, and surely meant to be) 'Your wife is dead'. All this was 'just gossip', of no literary consequence; but one could not disentangle the pure stuff from the dross, or pretend one was 'above all that'. More than thirty years later I would write a sequence of nine-line poems, one of which was called 'Sylvia':

> Ten days after he was, you were born.
> Heading out past sixty he's still hanging on
> but you bailed out at thirty telling the world
> 'Dying is an art. I do it exceptionally well.'
> Now you're a young poet of deserved fame,
> he an aging one, forgetting reputation.
> From where he sits cool Daddy looks at you.
> He sees the pain, and the brat, and the brat in pain.
> Living is an art. He does it as well as he can.

A reviewer took the 'he' to be Hughes, which is probably what I intended in using 'he' rather than 'I'; but the clue is in the dates of birth, Sylvia's and my own.

Two novels published in London that year were of special interest to me, and to Kay too: Sargeson's *Memoirs of a Peon* emerged at *last* from MacGibbon and Kee, and Maurice Shadbolt's *Among the Cinders* from Eyre and Spottiswoode. In Shadbolt's the teenage anti-hero, Nick, has a balding academic and always ridiculous older brother, D. K. Flinders, writer of unintelligible literary criticism, an unmistakable caricature. Philip Temple's biography of Maurice tracks down an exchange on this subject:*

---

* *Life as a Novel*, vol. I, pp. 212–13.

> Everyone in the literary world knew that 'Derek' [D. K. Flinders] was a caricature of C. K. Stead. Stead was amicable enough in a letter from London. First there was the domestic connection between them, and Stead responded to Maurice's news of twins with 'We are lagging in the rear' with just one two year-old. But Stead moved quickly on to *Among the Cinders*. He had 'devoured' it in a day and a half, 'reading impatiently through the bits in which D. K. F. did not appear, and then reading rather irritably through the parts where he did' and wondered if the best parts were where he was absent. As one caricatured he was not the best person to judge but also wondered if the 'slight element of spleen (quite justified in personal terms no doubt) that crept in, didn't throw the whole thing a little out of balance . . . The important – and difficult – thing is to keep going isn't it? – whatever the bastards (me, in your case; you in mine!) say.'
>
> Maurice replied, 'D. F. K.'s solemnity about literature seemed to be mine, too; that is I often felt I was satirising myself. There is something in him of most New Zealand writers.'

Remarkably civil! Nonetheless, I was pleased when a reviewer in the *Spectator* wished that Nick Flinders 'would trip over one of his coke bottles and break his cute little neck'.

I WAS WRITING NEW POEMS. Were they good? One could never be sure. 'Only Time would tell' – and I would not be the one Time told. What I did know was that when I wrote a poem that seemed to be on my own terms successful, a kind of peace came with it, from the doing of it – a satisfaction which no public success or award or promotion could match. I recognised that there was probably something neurotic about this. One wanted to control the world and make it more orderly and beautiful than reality ever could be, so one created a world of one's own, and controlled that. But the job should not be easy – in fact the harder the better, because harder meant nearer to intractable reality.

News came that improvements to our Tohunga Crescent house were finished – two small rooms had been turned into one larger, and a new kitchen added – and that Allen and Jeny Curnow had bought and moved into the house directly across the street. Maurice Duggan wrote:

> Are you due back for beginning of term? And is your house all finished and waiting? It would be cheating of me to ride over and peep. And have you read Frank's *Peon*; and what in the world do you think? My feeling is that one knows Frank too well to give the book its proper reading. Though I've read it. [. . .] With meantime a barbershop trio of greetings from the lot of us.
> Remember: *You have a lot to lose.**

Writing to Brasch in December about poems of mine he was going to publish I finished:

> Whatever happens, anyway, I feel I've finally established in my own mind this year where I want to go. The direction isn't academic, and I don't think I'll be easily put off.

We stayed on as long as possible into the English winter, and with the usual mixed feelings were back at sea in January, once again with a new car in the hold, this time the 'professorial Morris'. Walking the decks in rough weather I composed (in my head, Wordsworth style) a poem about art and life, which was to be the title poem for my next collection:

---

* This was the title of my festival-commissioned poem which had also been published in the *Listener*.

Crossing the Bar

Poetry: second best.
It represents. It speaks
Truest from a broken house.
Only the whole man
Jumps his own height.

Brumel, crossing the bar,
Represents nothing.
A singular wit
Shrugs gravity a moment off
And falls on foam.

Poets at the last are deft.
I contract to that end
My second-best art.
It will serve to praise the first.
The first served only itself.

I don't think I knew clearly what the poem was saying while I was composing it. It went past thinking, past 'working it out', straight to meaning, and by a route that was indirect. That indirection was 'the fascination of what's difficult'.

Now, all these years later, I read it as a commitment to poetry, parallel to what I'd said to Brasch in that letter – like a renewal of vows.

Part Two
The Professor

5.
Poetry & Politics, Children & Vietnam

Domesticity, 'and so on'

The direction ahead, I had told Brasch, was not to be academic; and there was that shipboard poem, 'a commitment to poetry'. But I was about to embark on a full seven unbroken years of university teaching. I was now Associate Professor, and by June 1968, aged thirty-five I was appointed Professor. I soon had a spacious office on the third-floor corner of the new library building, looking north-east over the harbour and west over Albert Park.* So poetry and fiction were going to have to compete with the academy. I could have been described as a man divided against himself, or in competition with his own ambition.

Charlotte was born at the end of 1966 and Margaret in 1970, and Kay had embarked on what was to be a decade away from the library as a full-time mother. 'The pram in the hall' was one of Cyril

* Something the current managers who have taken over the running of the place now would not permit – yet it was efficient. With stacking chairs I held all my tutorials in there with groups of up to ten students.

Connolly's 'enemies of promise'. But I have a very clear recollection of walking home from the university, reaching the top of the rise that led down to our house, and there, beautifully calm and unruffled, was Hobson Bay with the tide full and the moon rising, and the sounds of children's voices coming up from down there – and feeling for a moment (a primitive, animal sense, as birds must feel when the nest is secure) that everything was 'right' with my world; that everything was as it should be. This was not a constant, or even a common, state of mind: an epiphany, perhaps; or just an irrational rush of internal chemistry.

Academic work used energy that would otherwise have gone into poems and fiction – I have no doubt about that; and it's true I never found cruise mode or a way of doing the job in the 'at ease' position. The lectures, tutorials, essay-marking and preparation, the examinations, setting and marking – it was all hard work. Bill Pearson told me he'd heard a workman, possibly a window-cleaner, who had looked in at him in his office, say to a mate, 'These guys get paid high salaries to sit and read books!' It was true – we did, and would not have preferred to be cleaning windows. But it was hard work.

I also went through a committee phase. I was on Dennis McEldowney's University Press Committee for a number of years; also the Academic Committee, and a member of the Promotions Advisory Committee where, among other things, I was able to steer Allen Curnow's application for promotion to Associate Professor through to success against obstacles – not least of these the reference he'd relied on each year from a Wellington friend, James Bertram, whose recommendations did him no favours.

There were mornings when I walked around Albert Park first thing and the beautifully laid-out gardens, the city and the harbour humming below, gave me another of those epiphanies about place, time and circumstance. I was, after all, exactly where I'd wanted to be; and yet I was also bored and restless – still a youngish male, wanting drama, action, what Blake calls 'war and hunting'.

Domesticity itself was not just 'the pram in the hall', the changing of nappies, the walking the wakeful baby up and down the room for an hour or hours until she slept, the pushing of strollers and the unspeakable *longueurs* of 'quality time' in the toddlers' playground; nor was it just the delights and pleasures, the hugs and romps, the high jinks and silly name-games that were the other side of the chore-factor. Kay and I read and talked and listened to music, went to plays and concerts and were good companions. We usually managed a Friday-night dinner alone together, often at the Colosseo restaurant in K Road, where Antonio Ola treated us as special guests, and would cook for a family group when there was an occasion.

Married life was also, among the academics and writers who were our friends (most of them a few years older than us), an arena of adventure, conflict, theatricality and experiment; a place in which pleasure and pain were almost inseparable, always with a potential (depending on who was looking and commenting) for comedy – but equally for disaster. Our friends' lives were like a Woody Allen movie, or one of those Iris Murdoch novels where, to remind yourself of how the cast of characters are interrelating, you draw a diagram at the back of the book with arrows going diagonally this way and that, crossing and recrossing between beds. Right through this period we bought and read her novels, until I reached a score of about ten, and decided no more.*

Out west Tom and La Rue Storm were gone but the parties raged on. Dick and Elsie Scott had split. Maurice Shadbolt was for a time abandoned with four children by the much-wronged Gill, and was soon to embark on a sequence of affairs and marriages that turned his book dedications, panting to keep up with his life, into (unintentionally) comic poems. This one was for *An Ear of the Dragon*:

* Recently Kay re-read them all and, though she thought them often implausible, admired Murdoch's talent for narrative.

To Sheena for living
Beverley for loving
and Barbara for caring.

And this for *Season of the Jew*:

With great gratitude to Bridget
all the wild way.

Three of the four women named there – all the Bs – were wives or live-in partners subsequent to Gill who came first, and prior to Elspeth the penultimate. Bridget was to come back a second time as the last before Alzheimer's took him away.

On the North Shore Keith Sinclair was visibly restless and flammable, and would soon move on to fresh fields and pastures new. Maurice Duggan was turbulent, drunk and unfaithful, leaving home and returning at intervals. He'd had his much-talked-about affair with Fleur Adcock in Dunedin – and then with her sister Marilyn Duckworth, who also favoured the other Maurice, Shadbolt, very nearly becoming one of the wives, and who has put all this commendably and rather beautifully on record.* Bob and Noeline Chapman seemed securely together. Allen Curnow and Jeny told us they hoped to have a child but years passed, none came, and Jeny had to content herself with being stepmother to Allen's previous three as far as they would permit this. The Smithymans appeared to be in always anxious and sometimes angry lockdown.

Bill Pearson's private life was darkly angst-ridden and secret, and the little we heard of it came more often from Frank Sargeson, to whom Bill did not confide, than from the Curnows to whom he did. Bill would take us to dinner sometimes at the Pearl Garden restaurant in Newmarket, and would tell us about his troubles with the formidable Dr Elizabeth Shepherd, who would sometimes invite

* See *Camping on the Faultline: A Memoir*, Vintage, 2000.

us to a dinner of confidences at the same restaurant. Loyalties in the department changed like the Auckland weather, but the enmity between these two, Bill and 'Betty', was close to constant.

The department, notable at the time for its writers, was sometimes described by those further south as 'a nest of singing birds', but the songs were not always harmonious: feathers were often ruffled and sometimes flying. Bill reviewed Mike Joseph's first novel cruelly, and consequently appeared as an absurd drunk at a party in his second. Allen's poem 'Dichtung und Wahrheit', a denunciation of Mike's novel *The Soldier's Tale*, was so brilliant and vicious it must have left poor old Mike reeling. And meanwhile Ken Smithyman, our senior tutor, became the self-appointed departmental laureate and court jester, writing poems to celebrate arrivals, departures, anniversaries, anything at all.

There were also 'interesting times' further down the hierarchy. One addition to the department I found especially rewarding was Kay Davenport, an American engaged to teach in the Old and Middle English courses, with a strong interest (and talent) in visual representations and the art of the Middle Ages. She was one of those people whose high intelligence seems kept just out of sight, a concealed weapon, but always there, possibly threatening, but witty and capable of great fun. Kay was a friend, and was to become another of our baby-sitters. The kids loved her and so did we.

A Dutch interlude

John and Patsy Dutch who had been our neighbours across the yard in Takapuna (the models for Jim and June in my novel *All Visitors Ashore*), our first welcomers in London (to Sidcup, where they designated themselves the Dutches of Kent), our first out-of-town visitors in Bristol and our fellow-travellers to the grave of Dylan Thomas in Wales, had returned to New Zealand ahead of us.

John's father, Tom Dutch, was a Māori street preacher, whose Pākehā wife, Nancy, supported him on a portable organ, singing with him and handing out leaflets. On his way to the tennis club at Glen Eden, where Kay had known him as a teenager, John would pass this pair, the father preaching to the empty air, or the two singing hymns together. John would pretend he didn't know them, and hope whoever he was with would not know of the connection, or would pretend they didn't. He had run away from home without completing School Certificate, and worked for a time on an Australian cattle station.

John's family came from Northland. He was descended from Captain John Martin of the Hokianga and Kiriora (known as Māori Kate), and John looked surprisingly like Winston Peters to whom he may well have been related. He had the same good looks and inability to suppress a broad grin at moments he meant to be entirely serious. He had been given no second or middle name, but began to sign himself John M. Dutch. When I asked him what the M. stood for he said, 'Martin, of course'. When I first knew him he was socially unpredictable and often used to offend people. I found him entirely charming and great company.

Lacking educational qualifications for jobs, and back from his big OE in the UK, John enrolled at Auckland University as an *ad eundem statum* student for a BA, doing English and psychology, and I had to get used to him in my classes. He behaved as if he was not there, and never mentioned the lectures afterwards, so I had no idea what he thought of them; but I remembered a wicked parody he'd written in 1955 called 'Paws', when a poem of mine called 'Pause' appeared in the *Listener*, so I tried to avoid his eye. It was as if I had a student in my class who looked exactly like someone I had once known well. I might have been his father, preaching as he passed me by on the other side.

Once during this period John left Patsy, and Kay and I were involved in bringing them back together. He and I still liked to sing the old Sankey hymns, heavy with irony and yet rich in feeling, John slipping always effortlessly into harmony. I was immensely fond of him; and at any time a communication might come from him, posing as a letter, a random 'piece', an eructation, always undated, peculiarly clever and funny. He passed his papers (I'm jumping ahead now), did an MA in psychology (he was a Skinnerian behaviourist working with rats), then a PhD, and as Dr Dutch became a lecturer, first in Professor Laurie Brown's Psychology Department at Massey in the Manawatū, and then, still with Brown, at Victoria in Wellington. He and Patsy bought a house in Khandallah and had one child – a son, Nicholas. In 1971 I dedicated my first novel, *Smith's Dream*, to them.

Dunedin and the genes, Vietnam and another baby

Early in 1966 Kevin Cunningham writing for the Otago University Students' Association invited me to Dunedin. I was to be there for a weekend. On the Friday night there would be a lecture by James K. Baxter and a poetry reading in which he and I would take part, with two others, Brasch, and my friend from Armidale days, Iain Lonie; on the Saturday evening I would give the lecture and this would be followed by more poetry reading. Baxter's paper was one he subsequently published* – an account of the writing of his poem 'Henley Pub', step by step, almost matching in its detail, and its claims of deliberateness and calculation, Edgar Allan Poe's famous account of the writing of 'The Raven'; a match too, I thought, in being less than entirely believable.

Baxter was impressive as always – that shaggy presence, the oversized head and hunched shoulders, the peculiarly resonant voice, the seriousness and weight of utterance, the sense of ancient, and even divine, authority invoked: it was all to my eye and ear more than faintly absurd – while at the same time I yielded to it as to a natural force, a phenomenon, the Poet with a capital P talking about Poetry and how he had put one of his Poems together.

* 'The Virgin and the Tempter', *The Man on the Horse*, University of Otago Press, 1967, pp. 65–89.

I loved every minute of it, but considered it, intellectually, tosh – the Catholic new boy (he was a recent convert) demonstrating a sophisticated grasp of sin and redemption, with a twisty Graham Greene-ish unorthodoxy, and a 'liberal' ability to shock the old dears of the Church, male and female, lay and clergy alike – and yet all of this in a fervently Marian, golden wrapping; a poem that could move from 'Hail holy Queen!' and the 'glory and the doom / Of Israel' to

> I thought, shoving my muscle through black hair,
> 'What is a man, this glittering dung-fed fly
> Who burrows in foul earth?'
>   And that is all;
> All; Jehovah's sky
> And earth like millstones grind us small.

I don't any longer have a copy of my own paper of the following night, but its central argument was reproduced, with the title 'Poetry and the Criticism of Poetry', in the *Critical Quarterly*.* It was not, I think, an anti-Leavis argument, certainly not opposed to critical rigour, but a plea for critical flexibility and tolerance:

> Am I saying the critic should never condemn? I hope not. But […] a weed-killer is not a fertiliser, and at the moment it is weed-killers our universities seem bent on promoting.

From there it went on to a rather fancy 'close reading' of a passage from *Four Quartets*.

Janet Frame was in the audience for all this and reported to Frank (the guilty conscience speaking) that I was 'magnificently lucid, illuminating'.† That night and the one before Charles had

* Vol. 8, no. 4, Winter 1966.
† King, *Wrestling with the Angel*, p. 306.

cooked dinner which he and I ate alone together. All I remember is that it ended with chocolate fish for dessert, and coffee; and that both nights after the university event we sat over his gas fire and toasted crumpets, having not so much a man-to-man as a heart-to-heart. *Crumpets!* Charles was very serious and very kind. I need to acknowledge that, because I'm sure I was in his debt, and felt that I was; but I have to say also that he was very precious. One felt he was almost certainly gay, but probably not happy about it, and not active. There was none of the easy openness that could prevail with Frank on the subject of sex. I was not at ease with Charles, and I remember nothing of our talk – only its slight discomfort, and that I tried very hard to make it go well, and not to displease or disappoint him.

On the Sunday morning we drove to his crib at Broad Bay with Janet Frame and Ruth Dallas. Janet was skittish in this company. I'd had a warm letter from her in London the previous November, and it seemed we were to be friends again. Ruth took a photo of three of us, which I described later: 'Janet sitting smiling at the camera from behind the safety screen of dark glasses; Charles clinging to a verandah post and smiling down at her; me leaning back against another post, pencil-thin and formal, with a goatee beard, looking like a Viennese doctor'.*

But it was Baxter who made the strongest impression on that visit. I wrote a poem about him but didn't publish it until long afterwards:

Dunedin

(Remembering James K. Baxter, 1966)

Evening where Taieri moved
between dark McCahon hills

---

* Ibid.

fog threatened. You were back
in your aquarium town

wearing your flesh and blood
as if it belonged to you.

Would I get out? Would
it close on Momona?

In the womb we were all
fish. Once was enough.

Any bad-coloured sky
I'd have risked climbing,

scaled any barnacled chain –
yet there you went, at home,

submariner for God
telling the squid and the skate

'Open your gills, my brothers.
'Enjoy the life of the Deep.'

The sense of Baxter as a literary force, like a force of nature, is there; and yet at the same time I considered his solemn convert-Catholicism only a little short of idiotic, not least when he wrote lengthy, convoluted, self-contradictory defences of the Church's rulings on birth control. 'Your correspondent', he wrote in one such, 'has astonished me by the claim that artificial birth control "rests with every woman's individual choice"'; and he went on to invoke 'Christ's injunction to His followers to remember their bodies were the temples of the Holy Spirit'. Baxter's own temple of the Holy Spirit was known to be widely available, and quite frequently sought by young women with an appetite for Poetry-in-the-flesh. At about this time the Catholic paper, the *Tablet*, had caused concern to the Church by questioning the Pope's teaching on these matters, and the laity were warned to avoid it. I wrote to the *Listener*:

> Catholics in Auckland are not only required to renounce the Pill. They are not allowed to take the *Tablet* either. Would James K. Baxter please write another of his very long letters justifying this?*

I wrote to Charles thanking him for having me, and more important, for twenty years of *Landfall* – and it was true that over those years New Zealand writers had needed a periodical they could respect, admire and aspire to, in the same way that actors needed a theatre. I sent good wishes to Janet and Ruth, Jim and Iain, and suggested Charles might think about Robin Dudding as *Landfall*'s new editor. He replied that he'd been worried about me (I'd been coughing): 'Even in Ruth's photos you look a little less than yourself.' The house was being painted – 'bathroom and passage are now a gorgeous red with white ceilings and woodwork'. And yes, he had 'thought about Robin Dudding, and he won't be forgotten'.

Before leaving London I had sent him a group of poems which he'd accepted for *Landfall*, including 'A Small Registry of Births and Deaths', which begins with the birth of Oliver, but expands outward and becomes a poem about Vietnam; but now Charles had to hold the group over for publication until June. As soon as they appeared I offered the 'Small Registry' poem to Karl Miller for the *New Statesman* and he accepted it. 'Can I take it *Landfall* won't mind?' he asked. I thought *Landfall* would be delighted. *Landfall* was not. Charles was, he said, 'dismayed' and wrote me a reproachful letter about it.

---

* This, and also the Baxter letter quoted, were in the *New Zealand Listener*, 18 October 1968.

Alan Roddick, a recent father, was moved by the 'Small Registry' poem, and wrote about it at length, including:

> I must confess [. . .] it has nudged me quite off balance in my opinion about Vietnam – which you'll remember was rather opposed to yours. Balance had been increasingly harder to maintain; your poem may have toppled me entirely.

But it had not and this conversion did not last. Alan and I were soon at serious loggerheads again on that (as it was) central political issue of the 1960s.

My father had always subscribed to the *New Statesman*. He got his running knowledge of the wider political world from it; and for me as a schoolboy the back pages of the same paper had given me an early sense of what was happening in modern literature. It was there I had first encountered new poems by Louis MacNeice, Dylan Thomas, Geoffrey Grigson, Stephen Spender. So for Dad to find me there, in a poem and later in prose, must have been a confirmation of the worth of the (to him) mysterious and unfamiliar path I had taken. Around this time he came with my mother to hear me address an anti-Vietnam War gathering in the Auckland Town Hall. I described Air Vice-Marshall Ky, the current head of the South Vietnamese government, as 'the worst kind of traitor – the kind that calls in foreign troops against his own people' – and challenged the local papers to report what I'd said. Only the *People's Voice* did. Dad said afterwards only that he was surprised I 'had seemed so in charge'.

All this, and my being now not just a 'thousand-a-year man' but a good deal more, pleased him, I'm sure – and yet I think made him envious too; or perhaps I should say regretful, for himself. I was the product of the Labour welfare state he had worked for – free education, free health care, a fair tax system to keep the differences between rich and poor from widening too far, and the promise of a pension on retirement. These were the advantages his generation had lacked, causing him to leave school and become a worker at the age of twelve or thirteen.

I think his ambition to represent Labour in Parliament had died. He sat in his armchair and read endlessly, and smoked, sometimes cheerful and funny, but often morose, now and then angry. I felt sorry for him, which is not the first, or the best, thing to feel for one's parent. Other father figures had partly replaced him; and yet he was still the father I dreamed about anxiously, with his garden and his chooks, his meetings and minute books, his gun-damaged right arm and paralysed right hand, and the consequent steeply sloped left-hand writing. What a weird thing parenthood is. I had his physique, but we were temperamentally so unalike.

My mother and I were much less alien to one another; we understood one another. But the sense of a distance between us increased with the years, and I felt she blamed me for this, thought I considered myself to have outgrown, 'got above', my family, and in her pride she did not forgive me for it.

Kay was pregnant again through most of 1966, sleepy and slightly unwell as pregnant women mostly are, the body, like Occupied France, going about its regular business as best it could while the invader was really in charge. Oliver would be three in August and was not only talking but singing perfectly in tune, the one who had inherited what I would call 'the singing whakapapa'.

The war, immoral, unlawful and obscene, raged on, and I was involved deeper and deeper in writing and protesting about it. In October President Lyndon Johnson arrived with his wife, Lady Bird, and though protesters turned out in large numbers in Wellington, the welcomers exceeded them by far. New Zealand had at first only sent a civilian medical team to the war; but under pressure for a more significant contribution (it was the symbolism the US cared about, and a medics-only team might suggest neutrality on the moral/political issue) we had sent military engineers, and finally an artillery unit, now blasting and bombardiering away in the jungles of southern Vietnam. We had not followed Australia in conscripting an army – ours were all Regular Force volunteers – but President Johnson was here to thank us and ask for more. He was clearly delighted by the warm reception and keen to shake the hot hands everywhere held out to him.

During these years we sometimes stayed with Keith and Mary Sinclair and their boys in their bach at Wyuna Bay, Coromandel; and sometimes in the bach next door owned by Jack Northey, Auckland University's Dean of Law. We went out with Keith in his little launch, fishing and collecting shellfish, and helped him make fish-head soup or seafood chowder; and those experiences, together with ranging about and over the hills to the other coast, formed the basis for a lot of my political fantasy *Smith's Dream*, in which the librarian Smith (surname only – the novel does not give him a first name) escapes to live his Kiwi dream, and wakes from it to find the country taken over by a fascist dictator backed by the American military. We bought a section at Wyuna Bay intending to build our own bach, but later sold it in favour of land on Lone Kauri Road, in the bush a mile up from the beach at Karekare, where Allen and Jeny had their bach.

I visited Frank regularly, and sometimes he came to us. He and I kept up reading one another's new work and sending encouraging notes and letters back and forth across the harbour – his sometimes frolicsome and camp: 'Anyway, although I should probably strike you a cruel blow across the cheek with my fan for flattery your letter pleases me.' Frank was particularly struck by a poem of mine, 'Letter to the Enemy', in the *London Magazine* of February 1967. He prided himself on hearing echoes, half-rhymes and assonances, and reading subtle subtexts in my poems. These were effects which were really there, but which had often gone down in the writing, not quite consciously and deliberately as he supposed, but by a kind of musical instinct, the aural imagination working at top speed. Seven Baxter poems, versions of Catullus, appeared in the same issue. To Frank they seemed careless, rough-shod. 'Mr B' Frank wrote 'too lightly assumes that if his ear is satisfied the reader's is bound to be as well.' But to me those poems were a revelation, and another nudge towards what was to become an important part of my poetry – the Catullus persona. That issue of the *London Magazine* was also possibly the reason for a fraternal letter from Baxter, the prelude to a number of later mendicant visits when he was in Auckland.

Sometimes Allen and Jeny came to our house for a meal, or we went to theirs. In the department he and I worked closely, together with Bill Pearson, to advance the cause of NZ Lit. He continued (with much groaning on Wednesdays, delivery day) his always cleverly pointed and often brilliant weekly satirical *Whim Whams* for the *Herald* and the *Press*. There were no new poems from him, and would be none until the early 1970s; but there was a verse play, *The Duke's Miracle*, a fiction that developed out of his reading of Browning's poem 'My Last Duchess'. Allen's note on the subject of this play when it was performed on radio in 1967 I found strange and even slightly disturbing:

> It offends [my Duke's] pride to grow old; soon he can't bear the sight of his wife's beauty; his intellect despises the infatuation of his senses. [. . .] If my Duke is a little mad, he is no madder than we. Like him, we can pull the curtain over our murders while we relish an occasional peep behind.

Which murders were they? Possibly he had Vietnam in mind, since we were all obsessed with it. And it was Vietnam, not poetry, that put a barrier between me and the other Alan, Roddick. My principal fault in our correspondence was impatience and consequent rudeness; his, I would of course have said, was obtuseness. If he could be so clever with poems, why so dumb when it came to politics and world affairs? When, after an angry exchange, he sent a conciliatory PS, I replied 'I don't think there can be "negotiations" between us until you remember, or I forget, that Ho and the Viet Cong are Vietnamese fighting in their own country and that LBJ and his armies are not.'

That must have seemed like an end to our correspondence, but before very long it had started up again with a note from Alan that began:

> Reading your well-made little poem in the *Listener* some weeks ago reminded me that we once corresponded about such things; and it is I must apologise for not continuing to do so.

He was sending me new poems with this note, hoping for responses; and so we began again, but always now about poetry and our growing families, no longer about Vietnam, a subject we avoided.

For relief during the later months of 1966 I read Tolstoy including, for the first time, *War and Peace*. Charlotte was born on the 14th of December, ten days before Kay's thirty-third birthday, three months after my thirty-fourth. As usual Marti Friedlander (by now, and for a very long time yet to come, almost a member of the family) took photographs of beautiful Kay with the beautiful new baby who would one day be the novelist Charlotte Grimshaw. A few months later Frank wrote Kay one of the skittish letters he liked to write to the women among his friends:

> Would some Wednesday evening be convenient for a visit? I should love to come – I hate to think of your Charlotte instead of a lamb may become a female hogget before I ever set eyes on her. [. . .]
> I got some new glasses the other day and now have about 8 pairs, using this one for typing (not very effectively you see), this for eating fish, and that for opening the door to visitors. I asked the optician could he suggest a pair for making love, and we agreed it would be of course contact lenses. Then he thought no, perhaps bi-focals. But I thought he wasn't quite right – by-by focals.

Deaths and entrances – and Vietnam

There were not many new poems, but the literary flame burned on, and the positive response to my story 'A Quality of Life' in *Landfall* gave me confidence and hope. It was about my youthful love for Diane Henderson,* and I had tried to conceal its autobiographical base by setting it on a mythical South Pacific Island, Nova; but I learned from Eric McCormick that it had upset his friend the painter Louise Henderson, Diane's mother, and so probably also Diane. Eric delivered what seemed like a tentative rebuke about it as Kay and I were leaving a party, and then wrote apologising for his 'muddled remarks', saying he admired my courage as a writer. 'Instead of retreating into "scholarship" as I do, you make something of your experience. [. . .] I can't say what a pleasure our few brief meetings have given me.' And in fact many years later when I came to write the part of my memoir, *South-West of Eden*, that would cover that part of my life, Diane asked me not to be completely frank about an episode recorded and interpreted in the story which might, she thought, 'upset our families'. It was hard to see how our families might be upset, unless she meant her husband who I think would not have read it, and who has since died; but I let the fiction stand for the facts – which in a way it still does. I am the narrator (disguised as a famous old Novan writer, and a grandfather looking back – neither of which I was at the time of writing); Diane is Veena; Mike Mileage is Neil McKegg the man she married; and Tusker, who intervenes to turn dramatic climax into anti-climax and defeat, is Rob Dyer. So I give the earnest researcher, if there should ever be one, my warrant to find that story† and make free with these connections.

I was thoroughly 'inside' the academic institution now, and Frank, whose dislike of the university was unwavering (though he would later accept an honorary doctorate when we contrived to get him one) liked to remind me of what he called 'your supermarket

---

* See *South-West of Eden*, Chapters 15 and 16.

† 'A Quality of Life', *Five for the Symbol*, Longman Paul, 1981, pp. 113–38.

apron around your legs' – his image of the grocer in the big store, selling stuff. It was an image better fitted to the university as it is now than as it was then, when we did not think of students as 'customers', or 'clients', sources of revenue, and were not reluctant to fail them if they didn't come up to the standards we set.

Frank could be bitchy at times, thinking long and hard about something that annoyed him and setting conversational traps. There would be a lot of preliminary palaver while he made tea and whisked away any floating leaves from the cups. The eyes would be keen as always, but with a little more steel than usual, as you were led, step by prepared step, along the path he'd contrived to where the trap was waiting – and you duly fell into it. I was much more tolerant and patient with Frank than I would have been with anyone else. He had been a mentor and was now a friend, and even his bitchiness was a show worth watching. I was like one of those victims of Dame Edna Everage, so enchanted by the cleverness and the concentration of focus on *myself*, I was able mostly to take it in good part. But we did once or twice quarrel with more than an edge of malice, and after one such, when he wrote me a letter that was supposed to be conciliatory but was still full of half-veiled insult, and I replied thanking him for the olive branch 'even if you do rather hit me with it', he wrote back,

> O.K., O.K., I'm a sharp-tongued lout. But I wouldn't mind being hit with an olive branch if it stimulated me into inventing that expression (I hope you didn't in fact borrow it from anyone, as *I* have now done that.)

But unlike writers who were more or less permanently alienated (Keith Sinclair most notably, and I think also Maurice Duggan) I would let a little time go by and then return to visiting as if nothing had changed.

In 1969 Keith stood for Labour in the Eden electorate, and Kay and I did door-knocking for the cause, and were with him on

Takapuna Beach for a photo session with Marti Friedlander for publicity pictures. Keith brought the Labour leader Norman Kirk to the university senior common room – a sociable visit for a sandwich lunch and a chat with senior academics. To me Kirk was like familiar Labour figures of my childhood – A. S. Richards for example, MP for Roskill, for whom my father had been campaign manager – burly men in heavy suits and with secret springs of soapbox eloquence. There was something strange about Kirk's breathing which seemed to affect his speech, as if (though this can hardly have been the case) the sounds were being made by breathing in rather than out. His education had stopped at the end of primary school, and he was wary in a university setting, not at ease or at home with us. I only ever saw him in person on one other occasion, and that was in Wellington airport four or five years later, when Kay and I were waiting to board a plane, and there was Kirk, by now Prime Minister,* patiently waiting his turn in a queue with a tray.

On 27 July 1968 we put on a farewell party for Keith and Mary Sinclair who were heading overseas. Keith had won a Smuts fellowship to Cambridge, and the party invitation, designed by Kay Davenport, showed them riding a Kiwi with a sign 'To EDEN via CAMBRIDGE'. Keith's plan was to take up the Cambridge post for nine months, and return still in time to fight the election in Eden.

National won in 1969, its fourth successive term, though the numbers were close, and Keith won the Eden seat on the night from the Cabinet Minister John Rae. He attended his first Labour caucus meeting in Wellington while still waiting for the final count, which included special and overseas votes, and alas, reversed the result. Keith had mixed feelings. He was too impatient to have been happy sitting out three years in Opposition, so the Eden outcome was both a disappointment and a relief. He'd had his shot at

* It was something that could only happen in New Zealand. When Keith Holyoake was PM his home phone number was listed in the telephone directory, and he was seen walking to work every day.

politics, and now went back to being New Zealand's most notable historian.* His marriage to Mary ended in 1972, and his partnership with fellow-historian Raewyn Dalziel became public.

Towards the end of 1969, while waiting for our third child, we had the Parnell house enlarged again. Parnell was one of the inner-city suburbs that had been frowned upon in the 1920s when fear of the 'Spanish flu' that killed so many after World War I sent people scurrying for what were then the outer suburbs. Now Parnell was in transition, becoming slowly gentrified. The house we had paid £3,250 for was absurdly rocketing in value. For us the position seemed perfect. We could walk to the university in half an hour; and the children loved Hobson Bay and were able to range about the gully that was Tohunga Crescent, a blind street ending in the bay and with no through traffic. Parnell Primary School in those days was roughly 50/50 divided between Māori/ Pasifika and Pākehā.

The house enlargement on our small section was achieved this time by using space at the front twice over, having an entrance and lower bedroom half a floor below, and an upstairs sitting room or study half a floor above, the level of the main floor. Frank, who had once expressed interest (not encouraged) in the fibro shed in our back yard 'for my old age', came to visit. It was still a modest dwelling, though with four bedrooms and two sitting rooms, and I could see at once he didn't approve. It did not at all suit his preference which was that writers and artists should live in a sort of picturesque poverty, like his own. McCahon-style indigence or Dudding-style squalor would have been preferable. This was 'too boo-geois' (as he mispronounced that word), the most absolute of put-downs in his vocabulary. Yet he was by now (as he had written to me in 1967) 'a man in a dilemma'. He had begun to inherit money from dying relatives, and this was an embarrassment.

---

* He was knighted in 1985 for services to New Zealand history.

> Cheques begin to arrive from the Estate, nearly a thousand and a half [dollars]; & over 3000 soon to follow. Never in my life have I known such a thing. I faint under the thought of all my promises of help – and does it all mean the end of my sitting 2 to 3 hours daily at the grind which produces the only thing that in any way will distinguish me, given some sort of civilised community.

Of course it meant nothing of the kind, and although with this bequest from an uncle, and then a bigger one from an aunt, he was never to be really short again, he contrived in his remaining years to give away, indeed often, I thought, to squander on recipients of doubtful merit, most of the money as it came in. It was an ongoing problem, and he found it difficult sometimes to keep up appearances necessary to the image of poverty he had created over many years.

In February 1970 when Margaret Hermione was born my parents came to see the new baby and the enlarged house. My father, who I remembered had tried to conceal his uncertainty about the property when we first bought it, approved of course. He sat in the new upstairs room holding the baby and told us he hadn't expected to live to see this grandchild, his seventh. He was only sixty-six, but physical damage in youth (the gunshot wounds) had combined with years of heavy smoking to cause heart failure.

His death came suddenly only a few months later. At home with my mother, he got up suddenly from watching television and hastened towards the door, I suppose for medication, and fell. My mother phoned me and I was there within twenty minutes. Dad was still on the floor, too heavy for my mother to move, staring up sightlessly. I knelt beside him and stroked his brow, certain that he was past comfort. When the doctor came I asked was my father dead.

'Oh he's dead all right,' the doctor said with hearty emphasis, looking down at the colourless immobile features and lifeless eyes. He made it sound like an achievement and didn't seem to think it necessary to check for a pulse, or do any of the professional things one thought a death called for.

My sister Norma was soon there (our younger sister, Frances, was somewhere overseas) and we three, wife and two children of 'the deceased', sat in a stunned unspeaking row on a couch in the dining room, waiting for the undertaker. It was hard to believe that all that turbulence, affectionate good humour, morose ill humour, ambition and bad luck lying now unattended in the next room, could have been so abruptly switched off. I wrote in a notebook:

> [...] The previous Sunday I had been gardening for him. It started to rain and we crouched under a bush for shelter. He was wearing rubber boots and a windbreaker, and I thought although he looked unwell he looked stylish – it suited him to lose weight and he looked rangy. I thought it might be the last time I would see him alive and I was glad that Charlotte (I had only her with me) gave him a big hug and a kiss. And when I got home Oliver phoned to thank him for the map he had sent of Cook's voyage around New Zealand.
>
> I have a vivid image of him coming down the ramp and grinning ironically. I feel as if I might have become a weight on his mind – that he might have found me heavy weather. We weren't easy with one another. It's a pity he didn't have another son – easy going, more of a companion.
>
> At the graveside it was clear Autumn weather, the sky very blue, the priest's surplus very white, the prayers intermittently audible over the noise of trucks going by along the road ...

THESE WERE EXCITING YEARS for universities, at home and around the world. Stephen Spender called 1968 'the year of the young rebels', managing typically to be at Columbia in New York, at the Sorbonne in Paris, and in Prague and Berlin, moving from one to another all in the same year at the height of the troubles, and writing a book about it. At the centre was always Vietnam and (I don't think it's too much to say) the hatred of America for its war there. In New Zealand student activism, frowned upon by the National government, made Labour nervous, and was deplored by probably a majority of a population which considered it got on very well, thank you, without tertiary education, and that those who earned this privilege should apply themselves to their studies and not waste public money or disrupt civic order. The students were volatile, suspicious of authority, keen to right wrongs and (now and then if necessary) to break things. These were the years when I discovered that I was radical politically and conservative academically, a division which felt quite comfortable and reasonable, but which at times made me the object of wrath from one side or the other, and often from both.

One fuss that blew up in Auckland was caused by the discovery that there was an undisclosed member of the Security Intelligent Service enrolled in the Political Studies Department, and that he had tried to engage a student, Honey Martin, to report to him on the opinions, behaviour, and plans for action of student radicals. He had chosen badly – Honey, one of a trio of redoubtable sisters, would not help him; and soon the student body had been told that he was there and began to call for his removal. How could free discussion of political matters go on in the department in the presence of someone who was taking note and reporting to the SIS? The protests grew strident and produced counter-protest in Parliament, where senior Ministers were outraged at the university, students and staff for hounding an 'honest civil servant' (i.e. the spy) and railed against 'communist or near communist activity', especially in the Department of Political Studies. The department did, in fact, teach many of the members of the Princes Street Labour Party, several of whom would go on over time to be MPs, government Ministers, and two of them (Lange and Clark) Prime Ministers; but Bob Chapman could not be fairly blamed for what his students did in their spare time, or for the fact that knowledge very often leads to the recognition of wrongs, and hence to indignation and protest. Bob tried hard to sustain academic impartiality, and deserved sympathy because he was quite unfairly maligned. He was in fact (or I thought so) rather timid – determined not to put a foot wrong.

Early in the year of my father's death the US Vice President, Spiro Agnew, visited Auckland and was housed in the Hotel Intercontinental just across Waterloo Quadrant from Old Government House, now a part of the university. Of all the hotels available in Auckland, this was a strange one to choose. The anger about the war in Vietnam was by now red hot among people of liberal persuasion in America and throughout the world. Nixon himself was pretty much confined in the White House, as Lyndon Johnson had been in the last year of his presidency; and to send his deputy out to face people in public places anywhere was to trigger protest and violence. Nixon was still hanging on to the war, resorting to new strategies seemingly thought up for him by his National Security Advisor, the sinister Henry Kissinger – most notably invading and bombing Cambodia, which led directly to the rise of the Khmer Rouge there and the subsequent horrors of the killing fields, without in the least improving America's military situation.

The lovely gardens and grounds of Old Government House were going to be difficult to keep free of invading protesters, and the police, unable to distinguish between university personnel, who had a right to be there, and the public who could be legitimately excluded, decided everyone would be denied access. In his *A History of the University of Auckland* Keith Sinclair records that staff members joined the demonstrators, and that 150 to 200 police, having warned us to leave and receiving no response, attacked with boots and batons.

This, then, had become the undertone to our lives – one of indignation but also of ongoing excitement, a sense of involvement, of caring and of action, which Kay and I shared constantly. It found its way obliquely into my poems, in the images of Imperial Rome, and of the suburban back garden as a sort of Sabine farm, preserving aesthetic values and the rhythms of the natural world, yet under threat. It was there in my worrying at that old problem of poetry and politics, and how they could be made to mix – a problem equally present when I wrote about Andrew Marvell and Oliver Cromwell, and when I wrote about W. H. Auden and 'Spain 1937'.* It was the preoccupation behind, and the reason for, my novel *Smith's Dream*, which, thanks to the persistence of Phoebe Meikle at Longman Paul, would soon be published despite the refusal of a grant from the New Zealand Literary Fund, a refusal which Phoebe and I were led to believe had been caused by Advisory Committee member Helen Garrett's objecting to the Fund subsidising a work she said was 'blatantly political'. 'Thank God', Robin Dudding wrote to me, 'Longman Paul are going to make good the Lit Fund's idiocies.'

Smith's Dream was not a prediction of what would happen in New Zealand's future (though often read as if that had been my intention) but a political fantasy which created a Vietnam situation here and was meant to set readers asking themselves: If this should happen in New Zealand, where would I stand, which side would I take? Behind this lay the Auden argument of the 1930s, that these were times when every good citizen must make a commitment, must take sides. 'Yesterday all the past . . . Tomorrow perhaps . . . But *today the Struggle*.'

But the problem was that imagination led me to the opposite conclusion: towards the end of the first version Smith decides, like the old headmaster who makes an end-of-year speech on this theme, that taking sides is furthering the destruction, not ending it, and he walks away, puts commitment and action behind him, and after days of walking comes to a beach and what seems a perfect moment in a perfect place. A girl is sitting facing the sea:

---

* 'The Actor and the Man of Action: Marvell's "An Horatian Ode Upon Cromwell's Return from Ireland" ', *Critical Survey*, vol. 3, no. 3, Winter 1967, reprinted in *Book Self*, Auckland University Press, 2008, p. 392; and 'Auden's Spain', *London Magazine*, March 1968, reprinted in *Answering to the Language: Essays on Modern Writers*, Auckland University Press, 1989, p. 84.

> She was pale-skinned, lightly tanned. She sat perfectly still. From where Smith watched the highest waves appeared to lift above her. He saw her framed in green. Then as the wave broke and shot forward up the sand he saw her against the white froth and the blue of the sky. Sometimes in the relative quiet between breakers he heard faintly the sound of music and guessed that somewhere among her things scattered about on the beach towel on which she sat was a battery radio.
>
> She faced the sea. She seemed to offer herself to it. It thundered and approached but did not touch her. She did not move, and the sun shone on her back and on her hair.

'The end' (so to speak) – and very Hemingway; but very Stead too I suppose. A review referred to it as 'sentimental', and I was stung by the feeling that it might well be. Wasn't I one who argued for, preached, commitment? So when I was offered a paperback reprint, I rewrote the end. This beautiful moment is only Smith's dream; and he must wake from it to the continuing responsibility. He cannot disconnect from the action, but remains committed, and dies; and that is the ending that has remained through many paperback reprints – and is how *Sleeping Dogs*, the Roger Donaldson/ Sam Neill/ Ian Mune movie made from the novel, ends.

Later again, writing an essay about John Mulgan's novel *Man Alone*, I recognised a contradiction between Mulgan's theme of the 'man alone', and his theme of 'men marching together' – the existential individual against the socially and politically committed one; and that there was the same contradiction in my novel, which could not be resolved by either ending.* It was simply there in the fiction as it is in life. If I had a choice now I would prefer the earlier ending.

---

* See *Kin of Place: Essays on 20 New Zealand Writers*, Auckland University Press, 2002, pp. 180–82. At the time of writing (2018) a new movie version of *Smith's Dream* has been proposed and an option taken.

But there was something else about the writing of *Smith's Dream*. I was concerned at this time to avoid what I thought of as 'conventional fiction'; and one example of this I always went to in my head was Maurice Shadbolt. I thought of it as a kind of cruising, a default mode which it was easy for competent writers to put themselves into, and in response to which readers had a parallel mode, so you cruised mindlessly, uncritically together, the reader often in bed heading for sleep. I had some notion that this could be avoided, partly by avoiding dialogue which could sometimes tend to be mindlessly self-generating, and partly by 'telling a story' as if it were a fairy tale – from the outside rather than from within as conventional fiction seemed to require. These were ideas that were encouraged by my reading of Alberto Moravia, not Iris Murdoch. Both, M and M, could be described as intellectuals; but Murdoch's was high-calibre conventional middle-class fiction. Moravia was not more readable, but more sophisticated, always anxious about the provenance of a story, the question of what was its source and who was telling it, since (as he argued) in the modern world with no God, the 'voice of God' novel was not possible, or at least could not be taken seriously.

That, then, indicates the spirit in which I approached the writing of *Smith's Dream*; and my memory is that I wrote a couple of chapters very fast during a long vacation, and then had to set it aside as my lecturing work fell on me again. When I came back to it months later I felt I could never quite recover the sense of freshness and purpose I'd had. I thought of it as being like the difference between the look of the snapper when you first pull if from the sea, the brightness and shine of its colours, and the dullness when it has been dead an hour or two. It was still a good fresh fish and excellent eating; but the life had gone. It was one of the reasons why I didn't quite believe I would ever satisfy myself as a novelist until I managed to extract myself from the university.

But Vietnam could intervene in other ways. As was the convention at the time, I had been absent from the labour room at the birth of my first two children. It was usual for the father to be bundled out at the crucial moment in case he became emotionally involved and caused problems. Now the view was changing with the times. Father should be present, of course he should – involved, engaged, *committed!* So I was to be right there for the birth of our third. But the doctor attending Kay at National Women's Hospital, Herbert Green, knew of my involvement in the protests against the Vietnam War and wanted to talk to me. He had served with that first New Zealand contribution, the medical team sent in 1965, and was keen to tell me about it. He said the birth was still some way off, Kay was in good hands and he and I should walk together in the corridor and he would tell me about his experience. I was not keen and not attentive, and have no recollection at all of what he told me. I remember only my anxiety about the birth, and asking him repeatedly whether we shouldn't get back to the delivery room; and then that a young Asian doctor came to tell him the baby had arrived –so I did not see any of my children's entry into te ao mārama.

Green was later to be involved/exposed (depending on who was describing it) in what came to be called 'the unfortunate experiment', in which women with early signs of lesions (carcinoma in situ) on the cervix were not treated. This was based on Green's belief that surgery in such cases had been done unnecessarily, and that if the lesions were left alone cancer would not develop. In some cases this proved to be correct, and the woman was saved invasive surgery; in others it was wrong, and more extensive surgery, or death, resulted. What was worst about it was that decisions were being made by the medical team without consultation and consent.

Kay of course knew nothing of this – it would only emerge some years later in a *Metro* article by Sandra Coney and Phillida Bunkle. Kay liked Green and thought he was kind and helpful; but she did not like his involvement with Professor William Liley in SPUC (the anti-abortion league). In fact the birth of Margaret was a trauma for her, because there was a woman somewhere nearby, in the last stages of lung cancer, who had just given birth and who died in the night. Dr Green saw it as heroic and beautiful that the woman had not had an abortion early in the pregnancy and had lived long enough to give the foetus the life she was losing. Kay thought he was more emotionally attached to the foetus than to its carrier, and that this was sentimental and unpleasant.

'The door was open'

This was a period when one of the fashionable intellectual preoccupations was 'the two cultures' as propounded by the British novelist C. P. Snow. Snow was a literary man who knew his science; and his idea was that we literary folk should all be like him. I suspected he did not really want this so much as to be able to propound his own advantage over those who had only one culture. His 'two cultures' lecture was a great public success, lauded in the British press and around the world. There was a worthiness and shallowness about it which was bound to be welcomed by the worthy and shallow makers of public opinion.

Snow was stalwartly opposed in a public lecture by my old mentor's mentor, F. R. Leavis, who called Snow's lecture 'a document for the study of cliché' and analysed its language with rigour. A typically vigorous attack, it caused shock and was widely deplored; but I thought the fact it was less than polite and more than necessarily trenchant was not so important as that it was right.

Snow said among other things that anyone who did not know the second law of thermodynamics was uneducated; so I set to and learned it, remembered it for a time, and then forgot it except the general sense that it had something to do with loss of energy and the universe 'winding down'; and l later I wrote an ironic poem about it, and about having once been 'educated'.*

* 'A matter of time', published in *PN Review*, and subsequently in my collection *That Derrida Whom I Derided Died: Poems 2013–2017*, Auckland University Press, 2018.

I felt it was this atmosphere of togetherness between the arts and the sciences that had brought about the intense interest surgeon Sir Douglas Robb, currently the university's Chancellor, showed in poetry. He had been Fairburn's friend, and Fairburn had dedicated 'To a Friend in the Wilderness' to him. He came to one or two of my readings and wrote to me wanting a copy of my poem 'Myrtle', after which we exchanged letters and recommended books and articles to one another. I lent him a copy of *The Double Helix* and we discussed articles by Peter Medawar and the Snow/Leavis controversy. I recommended a Tolstoy story, 'The Death of Ivan Ilych' and he wrote in reply, 'although I have been present at many deaths – no doubt even contributed to them – I have never been personally curious or interested in the subject'. In one of his letters he wrote that *Landfall* had been 'conceived in our weekend house at Stanmore Bay after W. War II by Jim Bertram and Charles Brasch who planned it there. Rex Fairburn was also a visitor – almost a habitué.' On the Snow/Leavis dispute he wrote 'I think it a good thing for each of us [i.e. scientists and arts people] to want to know what the other is doing. My regret personally is that I have not had more opportunity all these years.'

Sir Douglas was an important man, and when the new vice chancellorship was still to be decided he wrote:

> I would like to chat if you could stand it – would 4.30–6 over a beer at the SCR or the U. Club ever suit? There are other things to talk about than the ones mentioned above – new V.C. for example. Give me a ring before 8.30 a.m.

Kenneth Maidment's retirement as Vice Chancellor had been announced and I knew my own stakes were high at this time and my chances would, I thought, have been fair. Two years later, over dinner in Menton, Maidment would ask me why I hadn't gone for it. 'The door was open,' he said. I think he thought I might have been afraid of failing – but that was not the case at all. I had never been one of those for whom the expectation of success was imprinted. Success always came as a surprise, failure as a disappointment but not really an embarrassment. I tried to explain that although it would have been nice to be King of the Castle, and though the signs had seemed fair to favourable, my writing came before everything else. I was employed because I needed to be; but my ambitions were elsewhere. Probably he didn't believe me. Those who have power always believe that others want it.

The following year the safe, bland Colin Maiden, an Auckland engineering graduate and Rhodes scholar to Oxford who had worked in America on heat shields in space rocket re-entry, was appointed to the post. I suppose one can say that over the next three or more decades he presided over the gradual transformation of the university from a place in which learning and research were self-directing and self-justifying, to one in which education became a commodity, an item for sale and for profit, and in which the managers slowly but surely became more important than the educators. I don't think Maiden (Sir Colin as he became) can be blamed for that; it has been a general trend worldwide over that past half century. What one can say is that he was never seen to oppose or take a stand against it. Heat shields had been his field, and metaphorically they continued to be.

Postscript 1:

John Dutch's ambition to be a fiction writer never wavered. In the end (as predicted in *All Visitors Ashore*) 'Jim and June' split. John married again, took early retirement from his lectureship at Victoria University, and went on writing. He completed novels but publishers declined them. Patsy continued teaching at the Correspondence School in Wellington and bringing up their son Nicholas. John wanted worldly success for his fiction but seemed willing to wait for it. When he died of cancer in his sixties his second wife published one of his novels privately, *April and Anderson*. It was dedicated

To Kay and Karl Stead
With fond memories – and always looking forward.

'Always looking forward' characterised him. A brief phone conversation I had with him just before his death, and the death notice itself, suggested he had returned at the last to the primitive Protestantism of his street-preacher parents, and had 'died in hope', still looking forward. I was astonished by that – but he was always unpredictable, and inscrutable. Was this return to the Protestant fold serious, half-serious, or a joke? He knew, I'm sure, that only he would know – and even he might not be quite sure.

That was my friend.

Postscript 2:
Kay Davenport left the department in 1972 and I never heard from her again for more than forty years until 2018 when she emailed me from her home in Ireland about my novel *The Necessary Angel*. Here is part of the exchange:

> Dear Karl,
> Congratulations, *mille fois*, on all your successes. I just read your latest [*The Necessary Angel*], prompted by the enthusiasm of *The Sunday Times* literary section which believes it should receive the Booker, and I would not disagree. [. . .] Hats off to you for handling life and teaching in Paris at university level so effortlessly, and for creating such fascinating likeable characters, any one of whom, I feel sure, I could have hated. And their depth. Adlestrop (an exclamation mark is called for here). You are quite brilliant.
>
> Good heavens Kay!!! From so long ago – and how well and fondly remembered. I once thought I caught sight of you riding a bike in London I think it might have been 1972 but she was

gone before I could arrest her – and never seen since. [. . .] I hope you're happy and remember your time here without too many shadows. For some reason I associate you with a maxim: 'The spirit of comedy must prevail'. I wonder why/what that was all about.

Dear Karl
Thrilled to hear from you. I think of you so often, useful advice you gave and funny things you said; my most vivid memories are of anarchic laughter. The difficulties you had taking Henry James out of the library without being grilled by Dr. Shepherd, and Allen Curnow's competitive and secretive approach to writing poetry. And do you remember saying, 'Just wait until I meet a PhD from Cambridge!' In the coffee room?

6.
Allez Mansfield! *Allez* Menton!

One life / three lives / more . . .

I had been granted sabbatical leave for the whole of 1972, and the previous year I explored possibilities of how and where it might be spent. But I was hoping I might manage to get the (as it was then) Winn-Manson Menton Fellowship, set up to honour Katherine Mansfield, which offered a New Zealand writer the opportunity to spend six to eight months in that Côte d'Azur town where Mansfield had written some notable stories.

On one of my visits to Sargeson that year he told me about the novelist he'd discovered, Ronald Hugh Morrieson. Frank would lend me Morrieson's two published novels and suggested we both write pieces about him for *Landfall*. I thought they were, though rough-hewn, something new and fresh, a sort of boozy Dickens-effect.* The articles appeared in June 1971, and one effect was that

* It seems Brasch had declined to have *The Scarecrow* or *Came a Hot Friday* reviewed, another example of his prissiness. Maurice Shadbolt had also tried to draw attention to Morrieson's work.

Kay and I began to get late-night calls from the seriously alcoholic author, thanking me profusely for my part in something that had given him new heart after many disappointments. It seemed he didn't have the courage to phone until he was well down the booze path, by which time he was almost unintelligible. Kay would take the call and say to me, 'Oh God, it's Ron again'; or she would deflect him. We worried about the costs – toll calls were not cheap – and I would try to think of ways, without offending him, to urge him to get out what he had to say and finish.

'Thanks Ron. All good. All understood. No need for more – off to bed now.'

'Oh yes Karl but one more thing . . .'

In August of that year at a writers' conference at Massey University (Palmerston North) I met him, a sad shabby figure whose clothes hung on him as if they had been bought long ago for a once much larger man. Ron's one contribution to one of the discussions on that first day was hardly more intelligible than his late-night phone calls. That night, having been out drinking with a friend, he fell down in the mud at the hostel door and had to be picked up and helped into bed by students. Next morning he left early before the second day's proceedings were under way. I didn't see him again and he died the following year; but his work had something of a revival – or one might say New Zealand discovered it – in the decade after his death.

Friends and literary associates at the conference included Robin Dudding, Marilyn Duckworth, Ian Cross, O. E. (Ted) Middleton, Phyllis Gant, Maurice Gee and John Reece Cole. Ian Milner was there from Prague. Maurice Shadbolt was expected but was detained by the birth of a new child to his current partner Barbara Magner. Marilyn Duckworth had been involved in a protracted attempt throughout the previous year to bring together their two families (hers and Shadbolt's – eight children in all) so they could become a couple; but this had been frustrated by a custody dispute between Marilyn and her second husband which, it was thought, could have been compromised if her association with Maurice had been publicly exposed; and so Barbara had moved in to fill the breach. I knew only a little of all this and did not fully understand what deep wounds and sensitivities remained. Marilyn records, 'Karl broke the news that Barbara had just given birth to Maurice's daughter. I cried at him. The pain was still there.'*

Somehow my life then which seems, when I reflect on it from the quiet distance of half a century, more like three lives, continued. The children saw me at breakfast, and I was there again in the evenings, often in time for us to watch a TV programme together before our meal. Weekends took us often to the west coast surf beaches, Karekare especially, and holidays to Tauranga. There is a notebook full of literary/critical ideas that might one day be enlarged upon; and a list of books read (apart from reading done for preparing lectures) that would be quite beyond me now. In 1970–71 my extracurricular reading seems to have focused especially on Alberto Moravia who had nothing to do with anything apart from my own wish to write fiction. Often books were read in turn by us both, Kay and Karl, and talked about at great length. We listened to a lot of music together; and daughter Margaret remembers giving this classical stuff a generic title – 'VIVALDI' – 'Oh God there they go: it's Vivaldi again.' It was not a quiet house. We were all somewhat inclined, though in varying ways and degrees, to turbulence; and some (Oliver and I especially) to song. In fact Oliver had inherited the voice and the 'ear' I thought of as my grandmother Karlson's gift, and I wanted to encourage him, as I thought I should have been encouraged, to be trained to use it – classically. But in the coming years I would never be able to divert him from his wish to be a rock musician.

Vietnam was ongoing and relentless, a commitment, an obsession, teaching us the practice, the tactics, and the willingness to take, when the cause was good, a step beyond what the law allowed

---

* *Camping on the Faultline: A Memoir*, Vintage, 2000, p. 201.

which we would use again during the 1981 Springbok tour. When I look around our house now I see so much evidence of that period, not only the books our friends were writing but their paintings – McCahon, Hanly, Hotere, Binney, Henderson, Woollaston, Pamela Woolf, Peter Siddell, Gretchen Albrecht, Richard Killeen, Michael Smither, Dennis Knight Turner – and Tony Stones' green watercolour portrait of Frank – paintings worth so much more now than we paid for them, bought not with the least idea of 'investment' but in a spirit of solidarity, a common enterprise, new directions. Marti Friedlander figures too, our 'family photographer' who was also becoming photographer to the New Zealand family, showing us the sides not usually recorded in pictures – including the down-side, the suburban banality, the dairies and pubs and shearing sheds, the old Māori women with their moko – and the protest.

Since my engagement with Baxter in Dunedin Jim had moved into his full hippie phase. He had established his commune (he preferred to call it a community) at Jerusalem on the Whanganui River and now, using that as his base, went about New Zealand with bare feet, long hair, an untrimmed beard and clothes from St Vincent de Paul – though his deserted wife Jacqui, who wrote as J. C. Sturm, and in whose name he was making his way into Māoridom, made it known he had good shoes and one or two nice suits in the wardrobe at home in Wellington. He called the young drop-outs and drug-addled acolytes he gathered around him 'nga mokai' –explaining that this meant 'the fatherless ones'; but I think a more accurate translation would have been his 'tribe of followers' (the disciples of Jesus could equally have been called 'nga mokai'); and sometime he referred to them romantically as 'the tribe of the wind'. In Auckland there was a sort of crash pad in Boyle Crescent and he was there from time to time. It was there he wrote his 'Ode to Auckland', which begins 'Auckland, you great arsehole', and also the 'The Ballad of the Junkies and the Fuzz' with its Ginsberg/Howl echoes and its grim view of suburban folk going 'home to their well-lit prisons'. Now and then he would knock at my office door in the English Department and I would be wrapped in a hug and asked for 'bread, man'. 'Bread' was money of course, and it was understood he had to be received as a sort of semi-official self-appointed Catholic mendicant. Jim made his own rules, and he was famous enough for the Church to be glad to claim him. This was the time of the *Jerusalem Sonnets* which I hugely admired, and I still value my copy inscribed with his 'Arohanui, Hemi', and its characteristic hand-drawn insignia/design. I loved the poet in him and found the high-toned hypocritical moralist absurd, and at times almost intolerable.

And then there was Jenny . . .

> Jenny, I'd like to show you
> A path dropping through native trees that shelter
> A pool so clear the small fish seem to hang
> In sun-shafts over its shingle floor.
> You weren't born when I said goodbye to that place.
> I'd loved it, as I have loved you
> With a wild sweet self-consuming passion.
> Last night I dreamed you were standing
> Beside a dark unruly river.

These lines were written in 1971. When they reappeared two years later in the sequence called 'Quesada', 'Jenny' had become 'Dulcinea', the first person had become third person (Quesada himself – a Quixote figure), and the trees would be 'ancient' rather than 'native'. The feeling would be unchanged, and the lines the centre point of a sequence which I felt took my poetry into new territory.

The 'Jenny' was a student, Jenny North. She was twenty, I was thirty-eight. Looking back in the light and shadow of the 'Me Too' movement of 2018 it's perhaps important to say there was nothing that could even remotely be called coercion or harassment; and it would be as wrong to say that I exploited age and status as that she exploited youth and beauty. We were two adults equally smitten, for a long time hesitating silent and embarrassed on the brink of saying so. She had been our baby-sitter since 1970 and at some time early in 1971 the words were spoken and the sexual rapport which had been simmering took us the next small step for a man and the giant step for mankind of a moon-landing. Jenny came from Hamilton and lived with one or two other students in a house on Grafton Road, long since vanished under the Grafton Gully motorways. It is described in my story, 'True Love',* in which a man murders the woman he loves and then, in prison, endlessly paints pictures of the house interior and the woman. Jenny had the front room that looked out on to the street. It had a high stud, a wide bunk bed that you climbed to by a ladder, and there was no second bunk below. There was a table where she worked at essays and letters and her own pieces of writing. Dresses and scarves hung from hooks in the ceiling, their colours and patterns swirling and swaying when a breeze went through. There was an old battered chest of drawers, and her guitar propped in a corner. I think the floors were bare scrubbed wood with a rug or two. Everything was clean and only disorderly in a clever orderly way.

I walked past that house on my way home which took me up a path into the Domain. Jenny would often run out and walk with me, holding my hand or skipping along beside me like a child, unburdened, full of enthusiasm and popular songs (Joni Mitchell, and especially 'Both Sides Now') which she liked to sing and play on her guitar. She was a flower child, a child of the '60s, sexually liberated by the Pill. It was the age of the mini-skirt and equally of those ankle-length flowing floral dresses; of Woodstock, of Vietnam protest and Richard Nixon and Kent State. These were the years of the young rebels, before AIDS and the dark cloud of the

* *The Name on the Door is Not Mine: Stories New and Selected*, Allen & Unwin, 2016, pp. 113–28.

late '80s sailed over and everything changed. In one of the fictions that sprang from this time I wrote (quoting and then misquoting Wordsworth) 'It was in the days of euphoria and Dionysus before the new cool. [. . .] Bliss was it in that dawn to be alive, but to be young was absolutely necessary.'* I was not young and I was not free; I was a husband and family man, not, it now seemed, a faithful husband, but certainly a loyal and committed one. Jenny would walk with me as far as the Scented Garden for the Blind on the eastern side of the museum, where she would turn back and I walked on home. There was a large and beautiful wooden house (now gone) on the corner of Domain Drive and Titoki Street and it was one of her fantasies that she and I would one day live in a flat there. I must have sighed over her a lot because Sigh became her nickname for me – 'My secret Sigh'. She gave me a copy of *The Catcher in the Rye* and inscribed it 'For Karl, my Catcher'. She was full of the fashionable cant of the time – Gurdjieff (and consequently Mansfield), Zen Buddhism (which had long interested me too), the I Ching, transcendental meditation, horoscopes and Hermann Hesse, Kahlil Gibran – and clogs. She was not a vegan thank goodness, but there was an inclination to rare seeds and nuts and green veggies. There was also numerology, which I engaged in with her, not believing as she seemed to, or pretended to, in its arcane efficacy, but because it was entertaining. We were both Librans which was 'important', her birthday the 8th of October, mine the 17th. It was therefore significant that my 1 + 7 equalled her 8. And there were more complicated and equally significant number facts: for example that if the numbers of our ages were reduced to a single digit, they were always the same: my 38 reduced to 3 + 8 = 11, which became 1 + 1 = 2 – the same as her 20, 2 + 0 = 2. This had begun at her first birthday when she was 1 and I was 19

* *The End of the Century at the End of the World*, Harvill, 1992. This was one of three of my novels and one novella in which one or another emanation of Jenny North can be found.

(1 + 9 = 10; 1 + 0 = 1); and could only continue. My 39 would come to 3 + 9 = 12 and 1 + 2 = 3, while her 21 would be 2 + 1 = 3; at my 40 (4 + 0 = 4) she would be 22 (2 + 2 = 4) – and this would go on as long as we both were alive. It was destiny – we were numerologically bound with no escape. I don't think she thought about either of us dying – certainly not that she would be first. Once she said, perhaps in a moment of uncertainty about the imminence of that flat on the corner of Titoki Street, 'I'm certain at least that we'll spend our old age together.'

With her friend Camilla During she sometimes attended the sessions of a guru on the North Shore, whose schtick was mainly Gurdjieff, but with extras. It was all, as a cynic of the time would say, 'a bunch of arse' – a kind of egotism, which puts the self at the centre of the universe, able to turn it in one's favour by the right 'in-the-know' mantras and rituals. What saved Jenny was high intelligence and a sense of humour; and her conviction, as she told me more than once, that one must keep always a little stone of irony in the left hand. The little stone of irony was always there for her, in everything – so she could play love to the hilt and stay sane.

Once when she was with me on my walk home she told me Kay would be waiting for us at the Scented Garden for the Blind to tell us our affair must stop. She would be accompanied by the three children – in sailor suits. *Sailor suits!* She could be tragic about herself; but she could turn her dilemma into comedy.

Two years later, when I had returned from my year in France and our affair briefly resumed, I had visited her late afternoon in her flat which was by then in Princes Street, and as I was leaving, lit up by the visit, she put on my raincoat, several sizes too big for her, and marched ahead of me down the path to the street, then turned suddenly back, holding the coat by its flaps and advancing on me in the guise of a flasher.

these white flowers grow only in the moonlight
their yellow stamens are the spokes of prayer-wheels

truth-tellers of the unbidden sun
they bloom in a garden in a dream

down the path comes the girl wearing my old raincoat
pretending to be a flasher
she is like electricity
like fresh spring water

out in the street the first leaves of autumn sidle down
from the tallest trees in the world
the clock in the tower has taken another minute from her youth
and added it to the sum of my age

the waxen cups on their shadowy stems
seem to float unsupported in the moonlight
fragile they look
but I know they will outlast us

She said once that her mother had told her, 'Never forget you are beautiful.' What sprang to mind at once, though I didn't say it, was, 'Not beautiful. Magic. You are *magic!*'

Jenny was only partly (but an important part) the model for Louise, the second wife of Professor of Philosophy Harry Butler in my novel *The Death of the Body*. Louise has taken over the room in their house where Harry was to write his great book on 'the Mind-Body Problem' and has decorated it as a shrine in which she performs her meditations, chanting 'I am not this body, I am not this body . . .' Harry has had a previous wife, and is already involved with another student, and it is from the dangerous consequences of this new attachment that the ever-resourceful Louise saves him. It was as if, after the affair with Jenny was over, I had written a serio-comic account of 'what might have followed'.

I was 'in love' – we both were – but I had much more than a little stone of irony in my left hand; I had a wife I loved very much and a family I was determined to keep together. Once, I told her she was a tourist. This was unfair and unkind. If there was one in this relationship, I was the tourist. She had ditched her boyfriend and was ready for anything. She told me her mother had said that *if* she was having an affair with a married man, and *if* there had to be a divorce so she could be married to him, that would be understood and accepted. So that was all right then! Her mother had psychic powers and I would have her on side with me. I never met her, or wanted to, having no such marital ambition. But I was in pain; we both were – and so, soon, was Kay.

Once when Jenny and I quarrelled she shoved essentials into a small petulant backpack, marched and scrambled her way down over the roadworks in the gully to the motorway heading south, and hitched a lift. From that front-room window on Grafton Road I watched her go, supposing she was heading for Hamilton and that reassuring mother; but no, she went further, south to Whanganui and west to Baxter's commune at Jerusalem. Jim (or Hemi as he had become) asked, 'What brings you here?'

She said, 'Karl Stead.'

He said, 'Tell me about it.'

So she did. It would have been a long story, well told, because when she was herself the subject she always took the scenic route, never the short cut. At the end of this narrative his advice was, 'Tell him to fuck you or fuck off.'

I don't know what there could have been in her narrative to prompt exactly this gnomic pronouncement, and I don't think she did either; but that night Hemi offered to join her in her sleeping bag. She declined, or said she did, I hope because she found the idea unpalatable and not because she'd forgotten to pack her pills. I have only her account for any of this, but it sounds plausible. Certainly she didn't stay more than a day among the 'nga mokai', whom she found grubby, dopey and disorderly. She was soon back in Auckland to tell me about it, which explains the poem addressed to her, and why in the dream she is standing beside a wild unruly river.

When Kay detected clear signs and asked questions there were no denials. Foolishly perhaps, I felt the whole thing was so important we had to share it, as we shared everything – as we had shared the fact of my brief but significant infidelity with a colleague in Armidale. But this was more serious, and the result was tears and anguish, and resolutions accepted also by Jenny, that our affair must stop. In my novel *The Singing Whakapapa* there is precisely this situation. The affair is discovered, acknowledged, and resolutions made. But the married couple, Hugh and Harriet, are about to go overseas, as Kay and I were close to departing for France and the Menton fellowship; and here the novel, though possibly with some fictional extravagance, describes what happened in reality. The resolutions were secretly broken, the sex did not stop, and, as Hugh does in the novel, I gave Jenny *poste restante* addresses in Menton and London where letters could reach me. The novel, when I came to write it, even used, with only minimal editorial improvements, her actual letters which I'd kept.

Jenny had her twenty-first birthday in Hamilton on 8th October. I didn't send flowers. I sent the biggest collection of Mansfield letters currently in print, the ones written to John Middleton Murry, inscribed 'To one Libran from another, the letters of a third, with fondest love.'

SMITH'S DREAM WAS LAUNCHED in a hardcover on 28th October, eleven days after my thirty-ninth birthday. Answering the launch toast I mentioned that its length was just 55,000 words, the same as my previous prose work *The New Poetic*, which, though a work of criticism and scholarship, I liked to describe as my first novel, because I thought its success had depended as much on a sort of narrative momentum as on its critical analysis; and now my new book was truly a novel, and I thought the narrative momentum was there again, but this book too could be seen as an exercise in analysis – political and social. At least I hoped so.

It received some slightly puzzled but mainly warm reviews; and it was to be the first work of fiction to win one of the New Zealand Book Awards.* It was something unexpected in our writing, and I had a feeling it puzzled people who knew me. Sargeson was silent, and I guessed it puzzled him. Clearly it was political in intention; but such an unabashed *story*, as if E. M. Forster's precious and more than faintly disdainful, 'Oh dear yes, I'm afraid the novel tells a story', was being flouted. What was I aiming for? John Buchan? Graham Greene? *Entertainment?* This kind of thing from a poet who had so far made his mark as a literary critic, an academic – something of an *intellectual*, was confusing. It was the beginning of the separation of the identities of 'C. K. Stead', which continued for many years, the gap that may not even now quite have closed. The local left were (at least for a time) to embrace me as their own, while international academia which admired *The New Poetic* knew nothing of the local left, nor of *Smith's Dream*, and might not have thought either worthy of notice.

On a Saturday a few weeks later the phone rang and an unmistakable patrician voice told me it was Hemi. He had spent yesterday and this morning reading my novel. It was an important book, he said, and we needed to talk about it. So he was soon at our door and, after greetings and hugs all round and a quick survey of the house, he had established himself comfortably on the floor of the small upstairs sitting room that caught the morning sun. Kay, who felt a certain affection for him but would sometimes interrupt his monologues with 'Oh come off it, Jim', welcomed him. Lunch was soon ready and he preferred to take his up there where he'd made himself at home. Charlotte has recorded a memory of the outrage the almost five-year-old felt finding her favourite space in the house occupied by this 'lordly bossy hippie' with his beard and bare feet.

* At that time they were the Wattie Book Awards, sponsored not inappropriately by the canners of fruit and baked beans. It came third in 1972. In the previous three years the awards had been running all the prize-winners had been works of non-fiction.

The talk was mostly about the war in Vietnam – what else at that time, with Nixon and Kissinger still recklessly in charge of the mayhem it had become? – and the *Smith's Dream* idea had been inspired or incited by it. No mention was made of Jenny North. Kay and I got on with our day, stopping off to chat with the guru and then continuing our preparations for departure. We were to leave in December and would have Christmas at sea somewhere between Auckland and Panama, so the preparations were beginning to seem urgent. In addition was the fact that Kay's nephew John Laurie had had a serious motorbike accident. His mangled leg had been saved, but only just, the repair was going to take time, his parents were living in the Waikato and we – Kay in particular – were his regular visitors. A visit was scheduled for today and we had only one car. What was to be done with Hemi, who was already known for moving in with friends and taking up residence for indefinite periods?

I decided our situation had to be explained with the clear implication he should move on. This was received in silence but with unmistakeable and dark displeasure. It was a breach of the protocol he had invented for himself, which he conceived to be Māori. He phoned Stephen Chan* to come and collect him, and drove off beside Stephen, staring ahead, refusing all warm waves and signals of fond farewell. Just on a year later I was to feel the sadness of that departure: it was the last I ever saw of him.

Côte d'Azur

It was mid-1971 when I learned I had been awarded the Menton fellowship for the following year. The award was an amount of $1,750 for living expense, with a free passage to Europe on the

* Stephen Chan, already a remarkable student literary entrepreneur and publisher, and rebel, is now Professor of World Politics at the School of Oriental and African Studies, University of London.

Chandris Line that had to be taken during December, the off-season; and a return by UTA French airline. Celia and Cecil Manson, with support and money from Sheila Winn (founder of the Hannah Playhouse in Wellington) had initiated the idea. They had negotiated it with the Menton authorities, and a Wellington committee had been set up to administer it at this end. I was soon in touch with Margaret Scott, the current holder, and from her I learned that the award was fraught with problems. The terms said the fellow would work in the Villa Isola Bella where Mansfield lived for a time in 1920 and wrote a number of significant stories. But the fellow's room, set aside as a memorial and marked as such with two brass plaques, was unsatisfactory and unready. It was dark and cold in winter, and the free passage meant you had to arrive in December or January. It had neither power nor running water, the plaster was flaking, and the town authorities were inert on the subject.

I was called to Wellington for the announcement of the award. Problems with the room were acknowledged. I wrote to Margaret describing the event, and concluded:

> ... one could make a fuss. Why should the Committee here and the authorities there, join forces in such a deception, and require the fellow to play along with it? On the other hand the arrangement is somewhat fragile. It does for me what I chiefly want – lifts me out of an academic environment and gives me an identity as a writer.

That was my resolve and I would stick to it. I was not going to rock this particular boat. I was going to make the most of it. It had already a certain public recognition, so it was an excuse for me to be less the academic, more the writer.

We had previously travelled, both times, by P&O *to*, and the New Zealand Line *from*, the UK. Chandris was a Greek line, the ship the *Ellinis*, on which (it was later revealed) the Great Train Robber Ronnie Biggs had, around this very time, made his second escape

– from Melbourne via Auckland to Panama and then a flight to Buenos Aires where he remained safe from capture for many years. Ronnie had even been appointed the ship's entertainment officer, supervising deck games and the rituals of 'Crossing the Line'. I would like to think he was the one who christened our kids for their first (or in Oliver's case third) crossing.

All the children on board had their evening meal together first, so the adults could have a formal dinner. Charlotte was somewhat adopted by a Greek steward, Costas, who from time to time would drop a packet of chocolate biscuits into the hood of her duffle coat when we were out on deck. We had a porthole cabin, and after Panama, going up the east coast of America, I kept a transistor radio at the gap, its aerial out so we picked up the local stations beaming across the water, and got used to, even addicted to, Don McLean's 'Bye bye Miss American Pie', a hit of that year. The lyrics grew more surreal and ridiculous the longer they went on, but the chorus was compulsive, and we all sang along with it in the cabin.

We sailed into New York, greeted by its remarkable skyline on a clear winter morning and spent a day or so there, where going up to the top of the Empire State Building seemed to establish in Oliver and Charlotte a taste for heights, or at least for being able to say like Hillary we had 'knocked the bastard off', which later in the year would take us up the Eiffel Tower and the Leaning Tower of Pisa. We visited the two great galleries, MoMA and the Guggenheim, which I'd seen in 1963 but were new to Kay. Picasso's *Guernica* was still in MoMA and would not be returned to Spain for another ten years. There was even a visit to Macy's – and the kids trailed around with us, uncomplaining, seeming alert to everything after their weeks at sea.

The Atlantic crossing was typically rugged, the ship rolling and heaving, smashing into the waves, sending squalls of spray over the decks while the overhead wires whined in the gale. In London Marti and Gerrard Friedlander met us and took us to their flat in Redcliffe Square. Gerrard, taking a sabbatical from his dental practice in Auckland, helped me with the transfer of our luggage to the night train on which we'd booked a *wagon lit* to Paris. Marti promised herself a stay with us in Menton – 'a week, or ten days if we still like one another' – when the summer arrived.

The train went to Dover, boarded the ferry, crossed with it and continued on the other side of the Channel; so we slept undisturbed overnight between London and Paris where we were met by Alan Goodyear from the New Zealand Embassy and his wife Peggy. We spent a day with them at Saint-Germain-en-Laye on the outskirts of Paris – and then we were whizzed to the train in Alan's Volvo and once again we were on the move, clickety-clacking south. The day in Paris was cold, there was ice on the puddles and clouds in the sky, and one of my great travel moments, the kind that stays with you for ever, was waking in our compartment (a *couchette* this time, fold-down beds, rather than the flash *wagon lit* of the previous night) to the sight of the blue of the Mediterranean, the yellow walls and orange roofs of its houses, the scarlet and purple bougainvillea and yellow mimosa, the hill-slopes of vines and olives and citrus – those classical landscapes which seemed, and can still seem (and perhaps not only to the Eurocentric mind) the real centre of the civilised world. It was Dr Johnson's stone again. Beauty existed; it was not just an idea, or a subjective and personal preference, but a human fact, an aspect of 'reality'. What I was seeing at that moment was beautiful. Whatever lay ahead in my life (and a significant part of it would have connections here) this shock of excitement marked a moment. The line in Keats's 'Ode to a Nightingale', the poem which had meant so much to me as a grammar school boy, took on new life: 'O for a beaker full of the warm South!'

It was January, mid-winter, and the warm South was not warm; but on this day the sun was shining, sky and sea were brilliant blue, and as we got down from the train at Menton and gathered ourselves at an outdoor café for breakfast and to wait for our land-agent contact who would, we hoped, have a flat to offer us, I held still to the exhilaration of that waking moment, vivid, never to be extinguished. Who is it says *chacun a deux pays, le sien et puis la France*?[*] I had felt something like that before ever setting foot there; now I felt it more, and it was a feeling which, despite vexations and frustrations, would take hold over time.

The estate agent, whose name had been given me by Margaret Scott, was Dutch-born Monsieur Wegnets, and he that day installed us in a quite lovely villa in central Menton not far from the station in a street called the *allée des Acacias*. It was owned by two ladies, Madame Allaria (renamed by Oliver Madame Malaria) and her daughter. They kept one room at the back where the daughter stayed from time to time to check on their tenants. Soon she was complaining that she heard our unruly children shouting at one another and jumping on the beds, creating mayhem and wreckage. She told us to go and, when we argued, threatened to cut off power and water and call in her lawyer and even the *gendarmes* – but she kept changing her mind, because the 1,300 francs a month we were paying was very attractive. While the drama continued over several days I was already surveying other possibilities, learning the language of *appartements et villas meublées à louer*.[†] It was seeing all these furnished interiors with their ornate furniture and lamps, stuffed birds and fancy cushions, knick-knacks and gew-gaws, that persuaded me Flaubert's fussiness over the details of his prose, his obsession with *le mot juste*, was really itself an expression of the bourgeois temperament he affected to hate.

So we moved to what was to be our permanent place, a spacious apartment at Garavan, only a short walk from the Mansfield memorial room, and on the edge of an ancient olive grove, *le Pian*, now preserved as a public park. The rent was the same, which used up the whole fellowship; but I had my sabbatical salary as well so we would be solvent, and would even buy a modest car. The apartment was slightly ramshackle, not so well furnished or finished as

* Everyone has two countries, his own, and then France.
† Furnished flats and villas for rent.

Madame Malaria's, but it was in almost every way more suitable. It had a 14-foot stud and a wide tiled hallway like a cricket pitch, and the cost of its central heating was included in the rent. Our space ran front to back on the western side of a building known as *la Garavan Palace*, a hotel in Victorian times now divided into private apartments. At the front we had a sitting room with a balcony that looked south and seaward over the Garavan port, east to Italy and the great orange rock-faces that leaned over the frontier, and west to Menton's old town and *vieux port*. There were three bedrooms and a kitchen along the western side, all looking out on the olive grove. The concierge brought us armloads of mimosa, just now in full yellow bloom, and the garden at the front had exotic plants, cacti, date and phoenix palms, a cypress, and a walking track down to the primary school Oliver and Charlotte were able to reach without stepping on to a roadway. Charlotte had her first five-year-old experience of school in this charming pink Spanish-style building with a courtyard, where she reacted as children of that age often do, as if school was a place where a different language was spoken – so she learned it. For Oliver aged eight it was more of a challenge, but he rose to it bravely and did not complain.

Our street was the *avenue Blasco Ibanez*, named after the Spanish novelist who had built himself a grand baroque house there, *Fontana Rosa*, as a memorial to the great novelists, in particular Cervantes, Dickens, Balzac – and himself! Over the gate there were portraits of these giants, a *bas-relief* of Blasco himself, and many enamels of scenes from what he considered to be the all-time masterwork, *Don Quixote*. Through the trees you could see fountains, and another bizarre representation of Blasco, his head on a plinth. Much of the garden was covered in creepers and falling slowly into ruin, and the villa was riddled with bullet holes where World War II gun battles had been fought. The great man had died there in 1928, and typically the town of Menton liked to claim him, and had named the street after him, but probably looked to Spain to pay for the upkeep; and since Blasco had been a great supporter of Spanish Republicanism, help from the Franco dictatorship, still in power there since the Spanish Civil War, was unlikely.

We had soon established a routine. Each morning I walked to the memorial room to work, Oliver and Charlotte went to school at 8.30, and Kay wheeled Margaret in a pushchair along the seafront promenade to the main market with its stunning displays of every kind of fresh food – vegetables and fruit, meat and poultry, cheeses and wines. Most of what was on offer came direct from the small farmers round about, often no distance at all, in gullies and corners of land that have in the years since been sold to, and built upon by, developers and wealthy holidaymakers. At midday we all gathered for the two-hour school break, had lunch and a rest or a sleep, and returned, I to work, the kids to school, Kay to minding the two-year-old and cooking dinner. There was school Saturday morning but none on Thursday. As the summer came on we began to go to the swimming beaches in the late afternoon and on the free days. We seemed to have been quick to adjust to the new life. It was challenging with three aged eight, five and two, but there was so much about it that was instantly attractive.

I was photographed as *l'invité d'honneur de la ville de Menton* being welcomed by the Senator-Mayor, M. Palmero, in front of a Cocteau mural on the wall of his office. Palmero was a man of sinister, subtly perfumed power, a sort of Mafia type I thought, who had a personal bodyguard and was later to be (without relinquishing his hold on the smaller town) also the mayor of Nice. Together with this photograph there appeared an interview in the *Nice Martin*. Asked about my work,

> *Je ne sais pas encore ce que je vais faire. En attendant de choisir, dit il, je vais perfectioner mon français.*[*]

[*] I don't know yet what I'm going to do. In the meantime, he said, I'm going to perfect my French.

What a diplomat! For this I was rewarded with, '*Mais le professeur parle fort bien notre langue.*'*

All this was fantasy. I had never met the journalist who 'interviewed' me, and I did not speak French well. One of the frustrations was knowing the language so well on the page and not being able to convert that knowledge into fluent speech. Some days later, when French journalists were on strike, Bernard Tardy, the town's well-named director of tourism, introduced me to my interviewer.

'Are you on strike?' Bernard asked him.

He shrugged and opened his hands in a way that signalled yes he was.

'You interviewed me,' I said. 'But we hadn't met. Where did you get that stuff?'

He nodded towards Tardy. 'Did I get something wrong?'

I said no it was okay. But it wasn't true I was fluent in French.

He shrugged. 'It will come.'

That exchange seemed to me another flavour of France – the off-the-cuff casual informal France, so different from the flannelled rhetoric and propriety that prevailed in public places.

In February came the *Fête du Citron*, the annual orange and lemon festival, where the town turned out into the streets and paraded up and down among bands and floats, streamers and balloons and *tricolor* bunting, shouting, singing and throwing confetti at one another. The children wore masks and we walked with them (Margaret in her pushchair) to the *Jardins des Biovès*. There the parade was started by Geoffrey Rippon, Minister in charge of negotiations for British entry into the EEC, who pressed a button to set a windmill in motion, its blades studded with oranges and lemons, and a Swiss band struck up (in honour of Rippon) 'God Save the Queen'. I felt we'd had an initiation into one of the traditional splendours/absurdities of French life – the street action. Other parades were soon to follow – *Mardi Gras*, then *Paques* (Easter).

---

* But the professor speaks our language very well.

Kay with Oliver in London, 1965

Karl addressing an anti-Vietnam War rally in Myers Park, Auckland, 1968, photographed by Marti Friedlander, courtesy of the Gerrard and Marti Friedlander Charitable Trust

Photographs by Marti Friedlander, courtesy of
the Gerrard and Marti Friedlander Charitable Trust:
Kay with baby Charlotte, 1967

Left: Oliver aged four or five, 1968 *Right:* Charlotte aged two, 1968

Margaret, aged two, in Menton, 1972

Karl with Margaret and Charlotte
Menton, 1972

Kay with Margaret, Oliver and Charlotte going through the Suez Canal, 1971

Karl meets the Mayor of Menton, M. Palmero, with Cocteau mural in the background

Left: Karl photographs Marti Friedlander at the door

Below: Marti photographs Karl at his desk, Mansfield memorial room, 1972, courtesy of the Gerrard and Marti Friedlander Charitable Trust

We were invited as a family to a rugby match between an English and a Côte d'Azur fifteen to commemorate the hundredth anniversary of the death of William Webb Ellis, the man who had picked up the ball and run with it at Rugby School, thus initiating the game (not untypically) with a foul. His grave in Menton had been rediscovered in 1958 and rededicated and adorned by the international Rugby Union. It was at that match we learned how the French sing their support for their sports teams. The words were only repetitions of, and variations on, *'Allez Menton, Allez Menton, Allez!'* [Go Menton, go!] – but the tune has a rather lovely dying fall, almost a lament, so adaptable to winning or losing.

With the room provided for the fellow to work in there were the difficulties already mentioned. It was the town's Mansfield memorial, with a brass plaque saying she had lived and written stories there in 1920, and had said that when she died Menton would be found *'gravé sur mon coeur'*.* Since Margaret Scott's departure the room had been painted, cleaned and swept, and the plaster restored; but still no power or water. Its stone walls must have been a metre thick, and the glass on the windows was green-opaque. I was already writing there early in February, and had done a bit of free-hand unofficial gardening to clear the worst of the foliage from around the windows. But while the winter lasted I needed the window open for light, and a heater. I explained this to Bernard Tardy. When I said I intended to buy myself a heater he enacted a French flurry of protestation and assurance. Of course I must not buy a heater – no no, no *no!* That would be an insult to the town of Menton. I was the *Prix Mansfield*, and the town which honoured her would see to my needs. A butane heater had been ordered and would be delivered very soon. Of course nothing came. Part of the skill of living in France, I was learning, is being able to detect when

* 'Engraved on my heart'. She had said that – but the exact words were 'engraved in poker-work on my heart' which is much more ambiguous than the French translation – and possibly even mocking.

assurances mean something and when they mean nothing at all. I worked for a week or ten days in an overcoat, and then bought a kerosene heater and carried it there. When we left eight months later it remained for whoever was to follow me, if he or she should want it.

But I was cheerful – elated even. I was free to write and far from home, and yet I had brought my home with me and they were just around the corner. That cheerfulness may have saved the Menton fellowship. The Wellington committee were growing impatient, even desperate, at the lack of any response from the town authorities to their enquiries and requests, and Celia was thinking about a transfer to Bandol further along the coast where there were also Mansfield connections. But then they had a letter from me, with some careful speculation on the Anglo-French misunderstandings I thought might be at the root of the troubles, but emphasising all that was good about the experience and minimising the negatives. The committee circulated parts of this to the press; and Celia and Cecil Manson took heart. Now they were coming on a visit. They engaged Kay and me to help them find accommodation, and soon would be taking us out to dinner at local restaurants, and to the casino, teaching us the innocent wickedness of small-money gambling which they loved. They were marvellous company, much older than us – in fact Cecil, who was British, had been in the air force in World War I, and had sat behind the pilot with a pile of bombs on his knees, dropping them by hand over the side on to enemy targets below.

I wrote a number of notes to myself and letters home about my writing intentions. I'd had to propose a plan, and was now to pursue it. But looking over these accounts I see that they were inconsistent, hopeful but uncertain; and probably the frankest and nearest to the truth was in a letter to Margaret Scott early in March:

> As for the work itself, I knew from my last sabbatical that it takes time for the cobwebs of teaching to brush off, and that

> at first one must do chores and five-finger exercises. So I am doing the promised study of KM, enjoying it; and writing some little bits of fiction, and lines of verse too, which I don't yet quite believe in, but which I have time to refine and squeeze until something genuine – a drop of the real juice – comes out. Basically Celia Manson's idea is right. This is just the situation to shake a Kiwi writer out of himself and give him a new start. It's unlucky the scheme should have fallen down in matters of detail.

To Sargeson I wrote less confidently, 'I like being here but I'm aware all the time that what's going on out there is of no intrinsic importance unless something is going on in here. Anyway I think I'm learning new things about writing fiction.'

From time to time visitors would come to look at the Mansfield memorial. Mostly they looked in, saw someone working and left. But one day when the sun was shining I left the door wide open and a middle-aged French couple came in. I tried to make it clear without being rude that the room was not open to the public, but Madame, discovering that I was a writer – *le prix Mansfield* indeed – felt it important I should know that Monsieur, who was meanwhile patrolling the edges of the room as if he could not hear her, was also a writer, and in his youth had made many notes for a book. But now, in retirement and ready to begin, surprisingly and sadly when he tried to write it he was always overcome with tiredness.

'*Madame*,' I said, '*je comprend votre mari. Je suis fatigué toujours*'* – and succeeded in ushering them out.

We wanted to be on the move in this region and beyond, and bought a car, a Simca, from an elderly architect, a Monsieur Gioanni, who had designed and built for himself a beautiful house on three levels enclosing a little courtyard-garden, the whole reached by stairways, and with no lift; so he was now, in old age

* 'I understand your husband, Madame. I'm always tired.'

and somewhat disabled, unable to get in and out of his dwelling, trapped like a spider in his own beautiful web. His wife did not drive and did their shopping on foot at the market, so the car, parked with a local *garagiste*, must be sold.

Soon we would be making weekend and school holiday visits to the hill villages round about – Sainte-Agnès, Castellar, Gorbio, Èze, and across the border into Ventimiglia; or west along the coast to Nice; and to Monte Carlo where the children, Oliver especially who was a fan, were more interested in Jacques Cousteau's Oceanographic Institute with its submarines and its wonderful aquarium, than in the palace with it dress-up soldiers and changing of the guard.

Quite early we had secured a baby-sitter, Madame Illiano, a nice middle-aged French-Algerian woman, concierge at the Menton Music School and widow of a French officer killed in the Algerian War, who would give us a night out for 15 francs. We went to the opera in the *Salle Garnier* at Monte Carlo, sometimes separately, more often together, and saw remarkable performances, most notably Tito Gobbi in one of in his greatest roles, the wicked Scarpia in *Tosca*.

News came from New Zealand and seemed interesting but comfortably remote. In the English Department there was a rebellion against Professor Musgrove for insufficient consultation with his staff, and disagreement (Kay Davenport told me) about whether I would or would not have joined it. I had no idea – or interest. Robin Dudding was sacked from *Landfall*, which it seemed was not owned, as we had all imagined, by Charles Brasch, but by Dinny Donovan of the Caxton Press. Robin was starting a new magazine and wanted me to write for it. (I agreed.) The letter from Frank Sargeson that told me of Dudding's dismissal – and other things such as that Auckland's best bookshop, Paul's, had 'collapsed' costing Janet Paul, and possibly Brasch too, a lot of money – ended typically,

Really *must* tuck up my skirts and run like a faun about
my chores –
There was an old woman who lived in a shoe
She had so many children
It was clear no-one had told her what she should do.

Around this time came a visit to Menton by an American naval ship, the USS *Caloosahatchee*. In New Zealand an election was coming in November and Labour would be campaigning against our international doormat government which contributed troops to Vietnam and remained passive in the face of French nuclear tests in the Pacific. Should Kay and I mount an ineffective protest of two (or five); or take official champagnes at the Villa Maria Serena? We chose the champagne – and then another dinner at *La Belle Escale*, this time with the captain and two or three of his officers. While we were eating, a huge storm blew up and the sailors, who had come ashore by landing craft, decided they must return to the ship and move it further offshore to the safety of deeper water. I had left our car lights on, and when we came out the battery was flat. So in the now howling gale sending spray showering over the *boulevard du Soleil*, I was push-started by these beribboned men. I allowed myself to consider this a form of protest.

Good news came of the progress of *Smith's Dream* – it was selling well and a reprint was coming; my Macmillan Casebook on *Measure for Measure* had appeared in London; and my new book of poems, *Crossing the Bar*, would be published later in the year. Bad news was that John Reid had suffered a heart attack and was out of action, leaving a serious hole in the English Department; and then there was a second attack and he was dead. It was a shock, and I counted back the twenty-one years since, as an eighteen-year-old student, I had first encountered him with his bush of thick hair which he had, only once, as if a daring experiment never to be repeated, combed upright – *en brosse* – to give his extraordinary exposition of the 'seven levels of meaning' in Dickens' *Bleak House*. Two years ago

John and I had been been promoted together to full professorships. He seemed shocked at first, but then accepted philosophically that his student had 'caught him up', and we worked amiably as colleagues. Sargeson had never forgiven him for an early negative review, believing John had penetrated the gay subterfuge of the stories and deplored – was even disgusted by – what it implied; and Frank was probably right. So he characterised Reid unkindly in *Memoirs of a Peon*. He had been quick with the recent news that John had been nabbed on the Southern Motorway for drink driving; and quicker, even triumphant, to tell me he'd had (as Frank put it) 'a daisy of a heart attack coming up through Albert Park'.

I knew Frank was not going to be saddened by the death when it came, but I was: John was fifty-six, at the height of his powers – and one can now only reflect that more recent developments in cardiac surgery would have saved him. The immediate question was how the English Department was going to manage without his quite extraordinary energy and range, or find a replacement. Allen Curnow's reaction was similar to mine: 'I will miss him. WBY says, "Men improve with the years" – all may not, but Reid certainly did.'

On the road

On 20 March I wrote 'Spring is making another of its spectacular false starts'; but they couldn't go on being false, and soon there were camping expeditions. When I look at the map of northern Italy they seem daring, even heroic. We bought a roof-rack for the car, two tents, sleeping bags and inflatable mattresses, a gas camping cooker and light, and a small folding table. We planned expeditions each with an intended 'summit'. The first, in April, took us away north to Lake Como, where we pitched our tents in sight of the Alps snow-capped across the lake; and then eastward to Venice where we camped on the Lido and were in the Square of St Mark's (the intended 'summit') for the May Day celebrations. On the way back we stopped at Sirmione on Lake Garda, in honour of Catullus and of Tennyson's beautiful tribute to the place and the poet, with its incomparable rolling-on rhyming vowel sounds:

> Row us out from Desenzano, to your Sirmione row,
> Sweet Catullus's all-but island, olive-silvery Sirmio.

The second expedition, a month or so later, took us to Tuscany, Pisa and Florence, where the summit for Kay and me was Botticelli's *Birth of Venus* in the Uffizi Gallery; and for the kids, the Leaning Tower of Pisa. In those days there were tourists, but nothing like the numbers that now invade Europe, so we could walk into the great galleries off the street, no charge, no reservation or ticket needed. At the Leaning Tower, still at that time open to the public, I climbed with Oliver and Charlotte while Kay remained down on the grassy surrounds with Margaret. Looking down from away up there, hanging on to the scary rail-less and sloping floors, we watched while a gypsy stole the pushchair Kay and Margaret had wandered away from; and saw Kay pursue and recapture that essential piece of equipment. On the same trip the chair flew off the luggage rack at high speed, and I parked on the *autostrada* shoulder and trudged back what might have been half a kilometre to recover it, and found it at the side of the road, guarded by two *carabinieri*, who reprimanded and warned me, but (because Italians are nice when small children and their parents are in question) patted my shoulder and let me return with it to the car and tie it more securely.

On the way home we stopped at Rapallo because I knew Ezra Pound had lived there, and we wandered about hoping we might see and recognise him. It was a town I would get to know very well later on through my Pound studies; but I did not then know that Ezra, though still alive, had by this time moved in with his long-time American mistress Olga Rudge, in Venice. Perhaps I passed him there and didn't know. Next year he was dead.

What struck me often, observing our children on these trips, was how much that was in each character sprang from the particular mix of elements from the gene pool. So long as each received basic nurturing and security, the character formed itself on its own terms and each was unique. Oliver, Charlotte, Margaret: this was the lovely flock Kay and I were shepherding around Europe. There was a minimum of piety among us, tears but not too many, shouting but not too much, some songs, some recitations from memory, and endless jokes. What a pleasure they were, how rewarding and enriching, and how we loved them!

AND THEN THERE WERE THE TORRENTS from Jenny North, who never let that *poste restante* address rest for long. I was conscious I couldn't write back accounts of my doings without making her more than ever conscious that we were a troupe of five and she was not one of us. I remember writing colourfully – I suppose romantically – about climbing a stone stair called the *raccourci des Colombières* (literally the short cut of the dovecots) that ran up from the *avenue Katherine Mansfield* to the *boulevard de Garavan* where there was a seat under a pepper tree, and I could sit in silence (because pepper trees required it – but mainly because there was no one else) and look down on the Villa Isola Bella, sending her Mansfield thoughts and emanations.

In one letter I must have written that she should give me up – something (though I probably didn't say so) which I did not want but knew should happen; and this produced a reply of some pages the central and severely serious point of which was, 'You're the best thing that's ever happened to me and to reject you would go against Nature.' But then her tone changed, and she was back to being the Jenny who could always charm and enchant:

> Look – it was this morning when I wrote all that radish and now it's tonight; and when I've posted this I'm going for a walk. I will wear my NEW shiny black coat with shiny white lollies for buttons, with the detective collar UP. I will stride – aloof

> and enigmatic – so that everyone scurrying home to cook spuds will sense I am somebody's mistress, and if somebody doesn't feel like writing until he's got himself all unscrambled in London that's alright with me because I trust him to love me in the middle of the night, road, occasional sandwich. '*Ne regarde donc pas à tes pieds! . . . Devant toi! Avance toujours! Fixe le but.*'*

Summer came early, and the Mansfield room was a haven of cool comfort, quiet until a train pulled in to the little Garavan station, then a brief flurry of people and action, and silence again. Our apartment too caught the breeze from the sea and stayed comfortable in the hottest weather. Television and radio were all in French or Italian. We had all been missing the English language, and were glad of the tourists, eager to answer their questions about the town and batten on them for conversations. A couple of Australian backpackers stayed overnight with us, bunking down in the sitting room. For the school holidays we planned a trip to Spain.

My mother wrote to tell me she had sold the family home at 63 Kensington Avenue, built by the Swedish grandfather. She asked me what I thought about this. I told her it was her decision, and she had made it. But I added that the night her letter came I'd dreamed that Japanese were invading the lower garden and I was throwing rocks down, trying to drive them away. That was a return to the fears of the war of my childhood; but it was also an answer to her question.

My work continued. The Mansfield project had gradually clarified. I admired the best of her stories very much, but she had died too young to reach anything like her full potential in fiction, and on the other hand I was constantly impressed and entertained, sometimes astonished by, the quality of her mind as revealed in the letters and journals. I began by thinking of making a selection of them together with her reviews; then later that it would be

---

* 'Don't look down – keep going!' This was a quotation from Chapter 5 of André Gide's novel *La Porte Étroite*, which Jenny used as a kind of mantra.

letters and journals only. No edition had ever been done that mixed the two so that, chronologically, they could be revealed in part as commentary on, in part as supplement to, one another. I decided to work towards that and see if I could find a publisher willing to take it on. Most of my reading now would be in that direction; and it would be taken further in London during the latter part of the year.

I had also responded to Robin Dudding's request for contributions to his new periodical, now called *Islands;* in fact had, or would have, work in the first four issues – a review of David Mitchell's poems in the first, a short fiction in the next, then a poem, and fourth, a review article about James K. Baxter. The unnamed fiction, which Robin printed with the title 'Horses', indicates I was already working on a narrative that would only emerge as a novel twenty years later, *The End of the Century at the End of the World.* The extract was written in the first person of a young woman, clearly a sort of Jenny North character, but with elements of the Mansfield personality (they were not dissimilar).

There were already indications that New Zealand secondary schools were interested in ordering the reissue of *Smith's Dream* – an unexpected development that would continue and grow. Appearances, one could say, were good – the Menton fellow could be seen to be making good use of it.

And yet, though always full of buoyancy and hope, I was unsure within my writing self, hesitating, uncertain of direction. I envied Maurice Shadbolt's now dependable production of novels; or, I should say rather, I *half*-envied it, because I found them hard to admire. He was like an actor; he *behaved* the great writer, and with such confidence!

For £120 we bought a British Bedford van, formerly of the Gloucestershire constabulary, from a young Australian woman who assured us it was safe and reliable. The plan was to have our ramble through Spain, then return to Menton, sell the Simca, and late in August take ourselves in the van up to Paris, then across to London where we would remain until the end of the year.

CHARLES BRASCH VISITED US IN MENTON in July with a Dutch friend and mentioned that Curnow was writing new poems, and about to publish them as a book. I wrote at once to Allen that the news 'gave me such a tremendous kick of adrenalin it seems what you do, or more exactly what you write, is of some consequence to me. So I'm writing to say Bravo, and even May I see them?' This request was 'jokey' in tone; but the excitement was real. I had spent more than ten years wondering, with fading hope, whether we would see our major poet re-emerge, or whether the efflux of 1955 had been his last of significance. Allen's letter in response seemed full of a matching anxiety about what I might think of them.

> Yes there are new poems as Brasch mentioned. If I had a fresh clean typescript handy, I would indeed be tempted to mail them to my Critic, – you can assume that role with grace, as a hard-earned right & wear it as lightly as you like: I could hardly assign it to you! I'm moved by your writing. [. . .] At 60 everything has still to be discovered – easy to say so, but this is art, & not at all easy, ever! [. . .] I would like to send one or two for samples – then I get cold feet about which – and what you think of them is of 'some consequence' to me too. Really I'd like for you to see the whole sequence, properly dressed. May I think about this? It is something to me that you would care to see them.

This was a strange uncertain tone; and Sturm's biography quotes him writing to Glover at this time, 'Of the contents, I have the usual manic-depressive syndromes . . . The weaknesses – I know where they are [. . .] here and there in the verse dynamics, the plasticity, one daren't say the form since that's a dirty word.'*

* Sturm, *Simply by Sailing in a New Direction*, p. 460.

In fact the new book, *Trees, Effigies, Moving Objects*, would be waiting as a welcome-home present when we returned to Tohunga Crescent. There were weaknesses of course, but no need for me, as the appointed 'Critic', to go looking for them. If the poems were not Curnow at his best, they were certainly Curnow at his second best, which was so much better than most they were items of great literary significance. He was writing again, and likely now to go on. And if there were weaknesses it seemed to me they had nothing to do with 'verse dynamics' or 'plasticity', but to do with that insecurity and snobbery that made too much of having been important in Washington among important people. It was the curse of the colonial which none of us ever seemed quite able to escape, and which he must have known, even though I would not mention it, I would not fail to recognise.

IN MORE THAN ONE LETTER I describe the last moments of the crash seeming to happen in slow motion, the car refusing to respond as I tried to turn the wheel into an undemanding bend in the road, a terrific rush of bright green foliage, then grey earth pouring through the windscreen and the children screaming. For a moment Kay thought she was blind in her right eye, but it was only that it was filled with blood from a cut above it. I was trapped by my elbow between the car door and the bank we had driven in to, but I dragged myself free and pulled the children out one by one, bruised and indignant but unhurt. We'd spent the night camped under the Pont du Gard, the famous Roman triple aqueduct constructed in the first century CE to take water from Uzès to the military camp at Nîmes. In the morning Oliver had paddled his orange inflatable canoe on the river, and now we were on the road to Tarascon, heading by the back roads for Spain. In a letter I told Kay Davenport we'd seen an omen, a viper crossing the road in front of us (this was true) and shortly afterwards our van had 'leapt into a ditch'.

People stopped to help, including a doctor who dabbed Kay's wounds, murmuring soothingly to her. Someone local must have called an ambulance (there were no cell phones then). They were all kind, but it was clear they thought it was the fault of the 'Englishman', with his right-hand drive, probably veering on to the wrong side of the road. In fact it was something wrong with the steering, which had refused to respond when there were corrugations in the surface, and simply glided on straight ahead by its own momentum as if in a skid. I'd begun to notice it and should not have gone on. The fault was mine, but not because I was an 'Englishman'.

The ambulance took us, siren wailing needlessly, all together to the hospital at Nîmes, and a tow truck carted the van away, still with all our gear. Kay had three small wounds that would need stitches, and was to be checked for concussion. She was admitted and I took the children to a little hotel and secured a room on the top floor, with one enormous bed. I had lost my glasses. Margaret (aged two) was distressed because her baby bottle (her *biberon*, as she now called it) was also lost, and she needed it for comfort and to get to sleep. We had a meal in the square and checked on Kay, sitting up in hospital with two black eyes, her wounds around the right eye now neatly stitched (the surgeon, trying out his English, had said, 'Closs yo high' which she made out to mean 'Close your eye'), and not displeased to have been served a nice hospital pasta and *crème brûlée* with a small bottle of the local red!

It took a long time to get the three settled and asleep in the giant bed; and then I sat wide awake in a chair looking down to the square until 2 a.m., watching the waiters sweeping the cobbles and cleaning up after the café had closed. I had the horrors, and *guilt*: it could have been so much worse.

So *l'équipe Stead* never got to Spain, which had been in our literary sights so long with thoughts of the Hemingway novels that had once seemed important. A piece of the literary patchwork of our youth had been removed and would not be put back until it was too late to seem significant. Kay was discharged next day. We stayed another night at the hotel, and took the train back to Menton. Our summer holiday would happen right there, swimming and walking and driving about the hills and over the border into Italy, awaiting visits from Kay's mother and from Marti Friedlander who was to stay with us and photograph me at work in the memorial room. A week or so later I drove the Simca back and at the site of the crash hunted for my glasses but couldn't find them. Out of the bank I dug a door handle and the right-side rear-vision mirror, both snapped off. My elbow had been between them, perhaps part-protected by them from the impact. As I wrote to Musgrove, 'how I have a right elbow that opens and closes, and how Kay has a left eye that sees, is a puzzle'. At Tarascon, where the van had been towed, I recovered our camping gear and clothes. The *garagiste* took our address. He would assess the value of the wreck and send me a cheque. Of course I never heard from him and he did not respond to letters.

7.
Critic, Editor, Poet . . .

London One and London Two

The accident opened the poetry vault and gave me a poem I called 'Under the Sun', suggesting this event, so significant to us, so insignificant to the world, was like most things under it, 'nothing new', and showing that it had happened in a region where evidence of two thousand and more years of human history was everywhere. It was 106 lines, probably not uniformly 'good', but authentic.

> Do you remember how the leaves chattered in Provence?
> They were telling us something.
> Every stone had a blood stain,
> Every rock had thrown back a human cry.

When lines like that are delivered, their internal half-rhymes and echoings all in place without forethought or deliberation – when they have come indeed 'as the leaves to the tree' – you know you're in business. Under everything, academic, public, fictional-literary, it seemed the poet still breathed. That was how it felt.*

* The poem is on p. 64 of my 542-page *Collected Poems, 1951–2006* (Auckland University Press, 2008), and there have been after that *Collected* two further collections, and new poems still get written, so clearly I still had almost everything to learn about how to access the 'poetry' mode and make it dependable.

Late in August we said our farewells, personal and formal, to Menton, sold the Simca, and travelled to Paris by train where we stayed in the Hôtel Récamier overlooking the square and the church of St Sulpice – the Latin Quarter, the Paris of Hemingway's *A Moveable Feast* and so much else that was literary – and then we were on our way again to London. A flat had been booked for us in the same Nuffield compound in Prince Albert Road on the edge of Regent's Park where we'd been quartered in 1965. Camden Town was our shopping centre and tube station, the children were enrolled at Primrose Hill Primary, and there was a nursery in the Nuffield for Margaret. We looked out on the park and ranged about in it; but there was the old familiar claustrophobia of London, always worst on Sundays when people crowding into parks, and even uncovering their white bodies to the sun, seemed to demonstrate that they were caged and unfree.

At bedtime Charlotte sometimes cried because she said she missed France and the little pink school where she'd been a star. I suppose London seemed dark and cluttered and ugly to her, after the olive grove and the yellow-and-orange houses and the land- and sea- and skyscapes of the Côte d'Azur. As the days grew shorter I used to take her and Oliver for a walk around the streets before dinner, while Kay read to Margaret and put her to bed, and we kept up a running fantasy that there were London One and London Two: One was the part we occupied and were walking through; Two was a second, mysterious, magical and sometimes sinister below-ground world we kept glimpsing as we looked down into areas (as they were called), basement apartments and sunken gardens, through grilles and into drains. Often we could hear it rumbling – the *Underground!* There was also the canal below the road, and beyond it the zoo with its murmurings, its occasional roars and howling in the half-light of evening, and the whirr of late bird flight from the enormous eerie aviary. As we passed through London One we made up stories about what was going on in London Two; and these fantasies were fostered by the fact that I was reading them *The Hobbit*.

Because *The New Poetic* had been done as a Pelican I wrote, as soon as we had an address in London, to Judith Burnley at Penguin proposing a selection of Mansfield non-fiction and she responded with interest. There were matters to be settled about contents and length; but in the meantime she offered me the use of a photocopier at their office in John Street close to Mecklenburgh Square. So Katherine Mansfield was now my day-job, and I returned with pleasure to working at the British Museum, not only in the Reading Room, but the Manuscripts Room where a number of her papers, including many letters to her British friends, were housed. Much of this material was thus far unpublished, or had been edited to avoid embarrassment to subjects still living – including her vivid accounts of watching D.H. Lawrence and Frieda rail and rage at one another, Lawrence beating his wife violently and almost dying of the effort he put into it. These had been written when the Lawrences and the Murry-Mansfields had lived in adjoining cottages in Devon. Treasures like these could now go into my selection.

In the Manuscripts Room I found Eric McCormick at work on what would finally be published as *Omai*, his study of the first Polynesian to visit London. Taken there by one of Cook's captains, Omai was presented at court, entertained by the aristocracy, examined by scientists, painted by important artists, and won praise for his social poise from Dr Johnson: it was an important subject. Eric had been at Cambridge with L. C. Knights and had come under the influence of F. R. Leavis, so we had much common ground. He liked the nearby YWCA for lunch and we went there often. From time to time there would be something he had discovered in the West End he thought I should see, and he would take me there by obscure routes through tunnels and undergrounds, always on foot and at great speed.

In Auckland Eric, who was almost certainly gay though secretive about it, lived with his sister Myra, and they went about as a couple, she looking like a more masculine version of him, he like a more feminine version of her. He and I talked about Louise

Henderson of course, our mutual friend, but he never reverted to the subject of my short story, 'A Quality of Life', which had upset him because it revealed too much.

The 17th of October was my fortieth birthday. Five days later James K. Baxter died in Auckland of a heart attack. The news when it came was of something like national mourning: it was said no poet's death had so affected New Zealand. Baxter was forty-six – another of those deaths present-day cardiac surgery would have rendered unnecessary. I remembered sadly the grim non-farewell at our gate and regretted the circumstance that had brought it about. I also felt a sort of anger with him for the stupid regime of piety and self-laceration he had endured – semi-starvation, the long barefoot walks in cold wet weather over stony roads, the flagellation with a buckled belt – its theatricality and hypocrisy. But what a talent, and what a loss! Some years before I had reviewed a book of his less than generously, chastising its religiosity and extravagance, and then had grown to love the more recent poems, the *Jerusalem Sonnets* and the ones that followed. Irrationally I was bothered by the thought that he would not read what I had to say about him now – the sense that a conversation had been cut short – but I agreed to write a review article for *Islands*.

In this same month I had been in touch with Ida Baker, Mansfield's old friend whom she had called the Mountain (sometimes the Rhodesian Mountain), sometimes her F. O. (Faithful One), and her Slave. Ida had been devoted to K. M. since their school days together in London, and had been used and abused, sometimes despised, sometimes hated – and yet had made herself indispensable. Preparing this selection I knew there were appalling things Katherine had written about her which John Middleton Murry had excised from his editions of the letters; and yet Ida, who was at the time the chief transcriber of Mansfield's work, must have known they were there, so she could hardly be taken by surprise. I was curious to meet her – and she invited me to come to her cottage in the New Forest for lunch. She sent train and bus times and a sketch map. For a woman of eighty-five, her eyesight failing, and whom Mansfield had characterised often as incompetent, all this seemed to me remarkable.

I went by train and then bus to the village of Wood Green, and then to the cottage where she had prepared a lunch and we shared it, talking endlessly about 'Katherine'. Her reminiscences were vivid, and brought me closer to a sense of the real Mansfield, the real Murry, the real Lawrence. Ida had a distinguished face, very much an old-fashioned gentlewoman, who didn't seem to have lost her intellectual edge. She kept the door of her cottage open night and day during the summer so that birds could come and go to their nests in her rafters. She acknowledged that she was not smart, quick, lively enough for Katherine who needed, she said, someone like Anne Estelle Rice (the American-born painter) for company. She was very clear that her relations with Katherine had no lesbian element. At the time she had not known what the word meant. It was only after Katherine's death that she discovered the woman who was her partner for the rest of her life. I made notes about this meeting and published them long afterwards.*

I worried that Margaret Scott, now the acknowledged transcriber of Mansfield manuscripts, might disapprove that although I would be able to check and correct transcription mistakes in letters selected for the book I was putting together, I would not be able to do the same for every passage from the Notebooks/Journals, and I wrote saying so, and outlining my plan.† Margaret replied 8 November:

> Your non-fiction anthology is of course a superb idea. For me it is her non-fiction which is her *real* writing [. . .] Of course in a perfect world you would work from perfect texts, but the

* 'Katherine Mansfield's Friend', *Answering to the Language*, pp. 172–75.

† She was at work on a complete edition of the Notebooks/Journals. She hoped to have it ready soon, but she was painfully slow and it would not appear until 1997.

> K.M. industry has flourished for half a century without them – I don't know why you would think I would suddenly at this point say Tut tut. I hope very much it will have a quick smooth passage: I shall be avid to see it.

It seemed for the moment I had her blessing, and that was important.

We had Christmas as a family with our friends Yvonne and Michael Riley and their three children. They lived in South Kensington, but for holidays had the use of a beautiful old stone schoolhouse and garden at Courteenhall, the Northamptonshire seat of Sir Hereward Wake, 14th Baronet.* The estate of some hundreds of acres included the hall, a stables, a venerable stone church with military memorial flags, and a small village for workers, gamekeepers, servants. The children had ample space to ride bikes along the gravelled walkways. We walked over the fields and in the woods, played croquet on the schoolhouse lawn, and paid a courtesy visit to Sir Hereward and Lady Julia – though this may have been no more than a chance encounter in the grounds. Secretly, I tripped the snares gamekeepers had left for foxes. The Rileys were fun to be with, ribald, civilised, but right wing so politics were mainly avoided. The Wakes had a kind of vintage Englishness – nothing remaining of the rebel forebear, stiff, formal, shy to the point of inarticulacy, posh and public-school-proper, snobbish but trying not to be – we felt we knew them well only because we had read so many British novels.

Over this Christmas period I was working on my Baxter article. I worked intermittently but often at poetry too; and it now seemed there were, for me, to be three modes: one was the constant jottings I thought of as inconsequential but necessary five-finger exercises, like practising the piano –

---

* As a schoolchild at a time when we learned quite a lot of British, and some but less New Zealand, history, I had heard one or two of the hero legends of Hereward the Wake (something about a swamp?) and his rebellion against the Norman invasion. I assume this 14th Baronet was his descendant.

In Camden Town
What do they hope for
Behind the streaming glass
Of cloth-cap cafes?
Every clock tells a different story.
Every story calls for a different end.

Next there were the hard work poems, sometimes dense, intense, 'metaphysical', which so often came to nothing, or to something wooden, where the deliberation showed too painfully. And then third, the rare poems that emerged 'as the leaves to the tree' from some subterranean shift or psychic shock – the 'Under the Sun' kind of poem.

But what I taught myself now was that the second kind did not have to emerge finally as wooden and dead-eyed. Simply, the more one wrote of any and every kind the better one got at it – and I was writing constantly. It was what I *did*, my existence. Because of that constancy I could, by an act of will, work nothing into something, and something (almost anything) into eloquence. I wanted there to be a poem about, a farewell to, the South of France, and I worked at it. It was not a long poem, but when I look at the drafts (interspersed with the drafts of the Baxter article) I see how, line after line, page after page of rewrites they go on, until something that satisfied the self of that time in my life came clear.

Cold moon in velvet, Europe's moon
Riding the slates and chimney pots of London
You walk over Paris too, in squares and gardens
The fountain waters give you back your face.

Cold Europe's moon, along the Côte d'Azur
You are finding out the little rocky bays,
The flickering bat-flight between palm and palm.
In Tuscan woods the stranger apprehends you.

St Mark, St Michael in their piazzas praise you
Who with a light that silvers Como's peaks
Can gild the Adriatic. Everywhere you discover
The stones of Christ, the glass stained with His blood.

Nothing is changed by change. You are as you were
Madonna of the skies, reminding Europe
What moon-crazed folly set a city blazing,
What story sprang from that illustrious wrong.

Cold moon, you showed me once an olive grove
And cypresses bathed in such beauty it seemed
The voices of their dead cried out demanding
The twang of an ancient wire, the words of an ancient song.

Back at the coal-face

I have been tracing the process by which the poet and fiction writer survived and emerged from under the academic, literary historian and critic. But I enjoyed being an academic, making discoveries, recognising connections, especially when criticism overlapped with biography which (*pace* my mentor Knights) I encouraged it to do. I enjoyed teaching and liked my students. Mansfield had not supplanted the field in which I had become expert. The Mansfield project would go on, but so would Yeats, Pound, Eliot and another whole book I planned to write on them.

Neighbours, including Allen and Jeny Curnow across the street, welcomed us back to Tohunga Crescent. Oliver returned to Parnell School, Charlotte began there, and Kay enrolled Margaret at the Parnell Kindergarten. When the orange inflatable canoe and the blue tent returned from France Ollie planned to paddle about Hobson Bay at full tide, mapping it.

I paid Sargeson a visit and he seemed pretty well recovered from the blow of the previous year, the death of his old love, the jockey and horse trainer Harry Doyle. He was, he told me, making new non-literary friends (one a firewood delivery man, and one a council roadworker) among the 'working class', and was writing a second volume of memoirs. He seemed sprightly, though full of complaints about rheumatism, and about Janet who had, he felt, made him a target in her latest novel, *Daughter Buffalo*. It was the usual Frame mix of brilliance with the kind of satiric grotesquery that compromises and sometimes destroys its own fictional reality, and Frank found himself in the character of Turnlung, the old writer who is making a study of death.*

The amount of his section being gardened had shrunk, but there were still tomatoes and peppers to spare; and the talk of his daily reading, the ever-flowing river of it, went on as usual. Almost too late I realised that his seventieth birthday was approaching and no one, except the gravely ill and soon to die Charles Brasch, had thought of it. Charles had sent him a cake, but there were no plans for a celebration – so we gave him a Stead family dinner, and he arrived with his haversack full of presents for the kids as if the birthday was theirs.

After the new collection, *Trees, Effigies, Moving Objects,* Allen was already writing new work which he wanted me to see, including the sequence 'An Abominable Temper' about his forebear Peter Monro. I half-liked what he showed me; but I thought the excitement of finding himself writing new poems might have been better curbed and culled for another year. In particular I thought one short poem included in the collection, 'A Refusal to Read Poems of James K. Baxter at a Performance to Honour his Memory in Cranmer Square, Christchurch', addressing Baxter as 'Jim', and with its final lines 'Winged words need no crutch / and I've none for you', was gratuitously cold and competitive.

---

* Twenty years later I didn't so much get Janet's reluctant permission as persuade her not to withhold it, to use the ninth chapter of this novel (a piece of virtual Frame autobiography) in my *Faber Book of Contemporary South Pacific Stories*, Faber & Faber, 1994.

My Baxter article appeared in *Islands* 3 in February and brought a handwritten note from Colin McCahon ending with a very McCahon-looking (that unmistakable lettering!) GOD IT WAS GOOD. Allen read the article and made no comment. It did not confirm his view in that 'Refusal to Read . . .' poem that the young Baxter was 'never better' (code for 'the older Baxter was worse'); but I knew he would have to take on board my favourable view of the late sonnets, as he did my praise of David Mitchell in *Islands* 1; and these slight shifts in his view of things were reflected in a long interview with Mac Jackson in *Islands* 4 (Winter 1973). That issue included both the interview and the whole 'An Abominable Temper' sequence, together with my 'Under the Sun'. There was a lot to talk about! Cross-crescent relations were lively, amiable and with occasionally electric sparks. He trusted my good will and knew I did not much warm to 'An Abominable Temper'. Our airmail *New Statesman* began to disappear again from the letterbox and return a few days later back in its crumpled postal sleeve, which meant that Allen, now preparing for retirement from the university by working as much as possible from home, was secretly 'borrowing' it. There were no reproaches, even when Kay caught him with (so to speak) his fingers in the till. The paper had come to his box by postman's mistake, he explained, and was being returned.

I was now forty, and the two mentors of my youth were once again in action. Allen's Jackson interview mentioned more than once that he was now sixty-one, soon to retire from the university, and writing poems which were new and fresh; and Frank at seventy was counting his recent books and pointing out how many more he'd published in the past decade than in all his preceding years. They both seemed to have head down, looking neither left nor right. It was the condition to aim for; and though forty seemed to mean advancing, almost advanced, years, clearly it need not mean anything more than 'what's past is prologue'.

Robin Dudding's success with the new journal was impressive. He had six children and I worried, as many did, that his circumstances, now that Caxton had sacked him, were probably dire. He'd had some financial assistance from Brasch; but Charles died in May of this year and no one seemed to know whether his will might have made any provision for Robin. As a member of the University Press Committee I floated the idea that a place might be found for him as an assistant to Dennis McEldowney, while allowing him to continue editing *Islands* – possibly as an AUP publication. It was an idea that came to nothing; and it was only in retrospect I recognised that McEldowney himself, while not openly opposing, made sure it didn't happen – and that he was right. Robin was disastrously dilatory, which was probably what had cost him the Caxton job. Adam Dudding quotes me as saying Robin was heroic 'but you can't go on being a hero in slow motion'.

Dennis, on the other hand, the 'blue baby' to whom the scalpel of Douglas Robb had given a viable life, was himself a brilliant editor, a man who combined his own authentic literary talent with efficiency and organisational skill. He wished Robin well; but he would not have wanted to be saddled with him in any formal and permanent role. Later Robin was to sink into the despondency, depression and domestic chaos vividly described in his son's account.*

The English Department had adjusted to the lack of John Reid, and my own timetable had not been much affected – lectures on Shakespeare, Yeats and New Zealand literature (now including Mansfield) to the big first-year classes; tutorials on Augustans and Romantics to second-years; Shakespeare's late plays to stage three; and to the MA class, literary criticism and Modernism: not all at once of course, but present or impending in the year ahead.

It all seemed to loom over and weigh on me; and yet I decided I would spend an hour each morning, after breakfast and before heading to the university, working in our small downstairs room that looked out on nothing but a green lawn and shrubs and trees, writing a new novel. Other half-completed pieces of fiction would

---

* Adam Dudding, *My Father's Island: A Memoir*, Victoria University Press, 2016.

be put aside; the idea now was to set one in the Côte d'Azur. This showed total absence of good sense or wise management; but I suppose I was like Charlotte in London, missing the place that had seemed so lovely, and simply wanting to return myself to it in imagination. Soon the effort was painful; the difficulty of combining university duties with an ongoing novel was excessive. Nonetheless a draft was completed, called *A Light off the Sea*. A year or so later I was writing to Frank about it, full of uncertainty. 'I suppose I will make something of it in the end, though it may not be of novel length.' To Robin Dudding I wrote, 'Novels are very hard work and I hereby resolve not to embark on another for a very long time. But this one must be finished.'

Eight years later, when I put together my first collection of stories, a shortened and revised version, now called 'The Town', appeared there as a novella, the centrepiece of the book.* Thirty-five years later again I rewrote it one more time, now as a sort of fictional-retrospect, looking back to the Côte d'Azur 'before the world was invaded by cell-phones and caught in the web of the Web; when intercontinental flights were not uncommon but not quite commonplace; when the Wall was still up, and Vietnam still raging, and South Africa was still an apartheid state' – and in it went, into another collection† with a new title, 'And still the sun shines'. In that novella, first eked out daily in 1973, there was a shadow of Jenny North – not a portrait so much as a wishful echo – in the character of Clifton Scarf's French girlfriend, Javine.

JAMES MCNEISH WAS THE MENTON FELLOW for 1973, and Janet Frame followed in 1974. The memorial room was unchanged but no problem for Jim because he appeared to ignore the 'rules', and

* *Five for the Symbol*, Longman Paul, 1981, pp. 65–110.

† *The Name on the Door is Not Mine: Stories New and Selected*, Allen & Unwin, 2016, pp. 52–113.

the town of Menton too. He simply took the money and lived not far away in Èze. With Janet, however, the room loomed again. She had an ally on the spot, the Danish-born New Zealand poet Anton Vogt who in recent years had left New Zealand in high dudgeon, denouncing us all in an article in the *Listener* and making it clear he would never be back. He was now living in Menton and took up cudgels on her behalf, again in the *Listener*, deploring the fact that she was so poorly provided for.

Nervous of appearing Pollyanna-ish, but afraid for the future of the fellowship, I responded with an article called 'A room much maligned'. I suppose this must have seemed to suggest Janet was making an unnecessary fuss, and she responded with a letter of her own to the *Listener*, entirely without a hint of gratitude for the award, and full of complaint. It shocked Celia Manson who wrote to me in October, 'We were quite heart-sickened by Janet's letter. It smote Cecil especially. It's been some consolation to hear from several people that it's typical of her. But most readers won't know that. I suspect Vogt is behind it.'

Well, if there was damage it had been done and couldn't be undone. I was not pleased with Janet, thought she'd been foolish, and yes, probably allowed herself to be used by Vogt with his big ongoing grudge; but I shared New Zealand's unwillingness to reproach her for anything – at all, ever. She was our Victim wasn't she? – so my response was to make light of it.*

The following year electricity, a lavatory and shower were installed, and at least two of the subsequent fellows, Marilyn Duckworth and Lauris Edmond, lived in the room. They were not supposed to; but it meant the grant was not all used up on

* But we now know that Janet meanwhile had written a novel, *In the Memorial Room*, full of grumbles, in which the people who had set up the fellowship are mocked and maligned. She chose, wisely, not to publish it, but it was posthumously published by her executors in 2013. For my review of it see *Shelf Life: Reviews, Replies and Reminiscences*, pp. 89–100. I thought it was a shocker, bad fiction and bad form.

accommodation, and they were freer to enjoy what the location offered. Gradually the size of the grant was increased, and a reliable arrangement for an apartment in the town was reached. The Mansfield Menton Fellowship had survived. It continues, but a dependable ongoing funder is still looked for.

NINETEEN SEVENTY-THREE TO SEVENTY-FOUR . . . were years full of action. There was no doubt I was home again. Keith Sinclair and I together with David Ballantyne, Bernard Brown and the three Maurices (all at that time living in Auckland) were moving to establish an Auckland branch of PEN. It was the government-recognised body that spoke for writers and had been run entirely by those on the spot in Wellington, who sometime exploited what I called their *droit de géographie* to their own advantage. They resisted our idea as needless – everything was in hand down there, and we were considered 'difficult'. Keith was short on charm perhaps, but always incisive and effective. I think it was at this time I earned the label 'controversial', which has probably stuck. Ballantyne practised the wily and ancient skills of the journalist. Of the three Maurices, Gee was our very quiet secretary; Shadbolt, because of the rapid turnover of female partners at home, was ineffective; and Duggan was seriously ill. He had finally defeated his alcoholism only to succumb to cancer of the bladder. But we succeeded – an Auckland branch was established, followed later by branches in Christchurch and Dunedin; and PEN became for the first time what it was supposed to be, a national body.

Nineteen seventy-four was the year when the new Labour government appointed me chairman of the Literary Fund Advisory Committee; also the year (so much more significant) in which Prime Minister Normal Kirk died suddenly and threw us all into confusion. I was at Ahipara with Kay and the children, and friends (the Sturmers) and their children, on 1 September when the news came, and driving back to Auckland I was composing in my head a poem in response, the first of what would be a sonnet sequence.

It began with a dream I'd had the night before about the dying Duggan. When the poem first appeared in the *Listener* I named the subject of the dream, who is addressed, as Max – but later, after Maurice's death, was able to correct it:

> Maurice, I dreamed of you last night. You wore
> A black track-suit, red-striped. Saying goodbye
>
> We fought back tears. I woke thinking you dead.
> Here in the north manuka is flecked with flowers,
>
> Willows bent in stream-beds are edged with green,
> But the tall-striding poplars seem no more
>
> Than ghostly sketches of their summer glory.
> Beyond the dunes blue of the sky out-reaches
>
> The blue of ocean where the spirits of our dead
> Stream northward to their home. Under flame-trees
>
> By Ahipara golf-course someone's transistor tells me
> The news again, and down on the hard sand
>
> In letters large enough to match the man
> Children have scrawled it: BIG NORM IS DEAD.

Robin Dudding had been asking whether I could write a critical piece about Maurice's work, one that he could see before he died. I felt I couldn't, or shouldn't. I thought 'Along Rideout Road that Summer' and 'Riley's Handbook', and to a lesser extent 'O'Leary's Orchard', were remarkable, extreme, and of their kind quite unmatched in New Zealand fiction; and that so much of his other work, by comparison, was conventional and static. I felt I could not make one point without the other. It was the way Duggan had struggled *through* to those last works, had shaken off the suit of conventional fiction in order to walk naked, that seemed to me so remarkable; and I couldn't see how I could say what I wanted to say in a way that would make the dying man feel anything but distress or irritation. These were things I would be able to say later when I edited his *Collected Stories*.

Robin's next idea was that I should interview Maurice, receding into the background as I drew him out. I agreed to this and so did Maurice. He thought he might forego the morphine that was keeping pain at bay, long enough to remain clear-headed while we talked, but the right moment never came. He declined too fast and died at the end of the year.

Quesada

Quite distinct from the fictional Javine of *A Light off the Sea*, real Jenny North, neither shadow nor echo, was still about after our return, still a student. She had a new boyfriend now, but we couldn't avoid one another and didn't want to. We were friends, and would be friends always. That, we agreed, was what mattered, and there was no need for sex. She had painted her new flat at the back of a big house in Princes Street 'Tonka toy yellow' and I had to see it and admire the way she'd decorated it. She showed me where the key was hidden when she was out at lectures, so if I called by and she wasn't there I could go in and make myself coffee. I tried to stay away but was drawn back. I liked to be there when I knew she would be out, taking in her ambience without seeming to involve myself further with her, or her with me. But sometimes I did what Clifton Scarf does at Javine's flat in the Menton fiction (which was being written at this time), and made some kind of sculpture of the fruit in the bowl on her table, with a message to amuse her. It was my call sign, as it was fictional Clifton's.

The agreed prohibition on sex lasted out the first term. One day I called when she was scheduled to be at a lecture and she was there, in bed. She told me she was sick to death of the new boyfriend and had dismissed him finally and for ever. She asked me did I want to fuck. I did. The several months that followed were like a long goodbye.

I was invited to Melbourne in October 1973 to talk to a conference of the Fellowship of Australian Writers. Somehow Jenny was gripped by the idea that I would take her, that we would go together and after that everything would change. I did not take her, and after that everything changed. What I did take was a little book called *Zen Flesh, Zen Bones*, and while there I wrote a sequence of short poems called 'Fifteen Letters from the Zebra Motel'. It was full of longing, but with a distinct whiff of farewell. It ended:

> Not to need
> Not to believe I'm needed
> Not to look into mirrors
> Not to look into eyes
> But into trees
> Into the sky beyond them
> Where the unfolding leaves
> Are patching shadows for summer.
>
> This last and solemn letter
> I write to myself.

Jenny consulted her guru on the North Shore who told her that all contact with me must be 'discontinued'. He took charge of her; she reported to him daily by phone – she was in good hands. I knew this was necessary – had known it all along – but she was absolute and it was painful. I did not want to lose her.

The poem sequence 'Quesada' was probably begun at the end of that year and the writing went on into the early months of 1974. It was written in pain and exhilaration – the pain of our necessary parting, the exhilaration of its own self-genesis. Its core was the little poem about how I would like to take her to the bush stream 'up north', the one I write about in *South-West of Eden*, sacred to my childhood, and how I'd dreamed of her, after she ran off to Jerusalem, 'beside a wide unruly river'.

Around October 1973 my younger colleague Roger Horrocks, whose PhD I was supervising, had sent me a final draft of his thesis. It was on various kinds of experimentalism in twentieth-century American poetry, but with a good deal of reference back to Walt Whitman as precursor and (almost) patron saint. Roger's intelligence was exceptional. I learned from his work and this was a moment when I was open to influence. 'Quesada' shows evidence of it; and at the same time during these months I was reading *Don Quixote*.

Allen and Jeny were overseas from the end of 1974 and left us the key to their bach at Karekare. Kay and I had not agreed about whether to build on our section at Coromandel, which I favoured; but the use of the Curnow bach changed my mind and I now accepted Kay's view that a bach within an hour's drive of Auckland was preferable. So towards the end of that year I was out there for a few days, clambering over the hills and hollows looking at sections for sale, walking down to the beach each evening to report to Kay from the pay-phone. We had only one car, and she had left me with a box of food, and would drive out at the weekend with the children to approve my choice. I wrote to Allen, heading the sheet of paper with a sketch of the scene from the front deck of their bach looking down the valley to the sea. I told him I had spent the three days 'finishing off some last pieces in my novel' – which must have been the Menton fiction, *A Light off the Sea*. A PS said:

> I read the 940th and last page of Don Quixote in bed this morning, having read the preceding 939 slowly over the summer vacation. What a tremendous book! I'm glad I didn't

> try to read it ten years ago – I don't think I would have stayed with it, or recognised how interesting it is technically.

Quixote is a knight whose grip on reality is insecure, and whose exalted love for Dulcinea belongs to an earlier time, an age of chivalry and romance. That was not a bad model for a forty-year-old professor lamenting the end of an affair with a student half his age. So Quesada (a variant on the name Quixote) became the poem's central character, and Jenny his Dulcinea. His mood is a sort of controlled hysteria, and the scene has strong elements of Karekare and the west coast:

> Quesada on the dunes hurls himself at the elements
> Howls at the sea, tries to shout down the surf
> Pushes against the wind that fathers a mountain of sand
> Catches at the sun with his glances
> Throws his name away like a rose the surf casts back at him
> again and again.
>
> The waves drive forward against an offshore wind
> That turns their crests to banners.
> They shiver in the heat haze silver and white
> Shaken against sunlight above the crack of broken rollers
> Driving up the hill of sand again and again defeated.

The poem is full of lyric intensities but also the ironies of recognition – and there are even puns and jokes. Father Frank McKay who would soon be writing an official biography of the man who told Jenny 'Tell him to fuck you or fuck off' loved the poem but was worried by its ironies, and more by the jokes. 'The real Stead is the romantic Stead' he told me. I thought the real Stead was the romantic realist, and that, along with the intensities, the ironies had to remain. So did the jokes –

Donkey Shot and Liberty Prance*
Off with your pants and on with the dance

So
  Kubla if you can
  Juan Quesada
And if you can't –
  Try teaching!

It was more than 200 lines long, and I have to say it still astonishes me, as if I had come upon it in a secret archive written by someone else. The long Whitmanesque lines couldn't be sustained just by acts of the will. They had to arrive complete and there must be no 'fillers'. Grammatically and syntactically each word must have a job to do.

No one dies of that pain, some swear by it, a few will live
  with it always,
No one mistakes it for the lamentations of hell
Because there is a kind of exaltation in it
More eloquent than the tongues of wind and water
More truthful than the sibylline language of the leaves
The cry of the injured whose wounds are dear to them
The howl of the vanquished who cherish their defeat.

'Quesada' became the title poem of a small olive-green book I published myself, under the imprint of The Shed. It was not that Dennis McEldowney would not have taken it gladly for AUP. *Crossing the Bar* had been a success, won the Jessie Mackay award and sold well enough to earn a reprint – unusual with books of

* These are anglicised versions of French pronunciation of Don Quichotte and le Petit Prince. Salman Rushdie's new novel (2019) is called *Quichotte* with the same effect on the ear when he talks about it.

poems. The Shed was just another experiment, repeated with my next book, *Walking Westward*, after which I decided to leave publishing to publishers and get on with my own business, the writing.

In 1968 when Joan Stevens put together a little book on *New Zealand Short Stories*, she used four portraits to fill the front cover: Mansfield, Sargeson, Frame and Stead. It was strange (exciting for me) that three of our Takapuna foursome of 1955 should be there with K. M. It would not have surprised Frank to find himself with Mansfield – he liked to joke that together they constituted the 'double disaster of New Zealand writing'; and by now Frame might have been expected. But neither he nor Janet would have thought to see Stead joining them – not anyway as a fiction writer.

It was the flying story, 'A Fitting Tribute', which had given me this elevation. It had appeared in the *Kenyon Review* and been praised by the famous New York literary wit Dorothy Parker. It had appeared in translation in fascist Spain and communist Hungary, as if in each case it symbolised escape from repression, a subtle subversion which could not be pinned down and prosecuted. There were translations into German and Dutch too. So it could be called a minor international success. But that was not why it figured in Professor Stevens' book. It was there because it had become a small *New Zealand* classic, anthologised, read in schools, talked about, studied, adapted for radio, a movie was made of it – and it still figures.*

No one has ever made such a case for 'Quesada'. That sequence had begun with the little poem to Jenny North – and there it had remained, as if waiting for something to happen. And then, after two years, it had taken off, losing its specifics of place, becoming

---

* 'I can't drive past the cricket pavilion in the Auckland Domain without thinking of C.K. Stead's "A Fitting Tribute", the story of Julian Harp, first man to fly (but lying on his back!).' Tessa Duder, 28 October 2015. 'But the story I thought about most is the one that broke with convention, "A Fitting Tribute". It's fair to say it's a classic New Zealand short story [. . .] about home-made heroes and non-conformity and eccentricity, but the imaginative leap Stead took seems to have been so much greater.' Philip Matthews, 23 November 2016.

general in reference, belonging nowhere, or everywhere, rather than somewhere; becoming '*literature*', which only makes a broader impact if it finds for itself 'a local habitation and a name', a public space, a role *beyond* literature.

That the balls of the lover are not larger than the balls of the priest
That the heart of the miser is not smaller than the heart of Quesada
That the same sun warms the knight and the squire
That the long lance and the short sword open equally the passages
    to death
That the barber may wear a beard and the hangman have long life
These are the opaque equities of our world.

That the breast of Dulcinea is whiter than the driven snow
That the strength of her knight is as the strength of ten because
    his heart is pure
That the empire of true love is boundless and its battalions
    unconquerable
These are the translucent hyperboles of art.

Where was Quesada whose grapes fattened uneaten at his door
Whose fields were ripe, whose mill-wheels were always turning?
He was beyond the horizon riding against the sunspears
Remembering the foot of his lady tentative as a white pennant in the
    swift mountain stream.

Owls in the poplar candles, a pheasant dead on the road
Thunder over the treeless mountain burned brown by summer
Thunder over the flooded fields thunder over the dunes
Thunder over the darkened ocean shafted with light
Thunder in the long line of the surf breaking against an offshore
    wind
Thunder in the long line
Exaltation in the defeated heart of Quesada.

Who but a Christian would sing the broken body of love?
Who but a lover would sigh to be a plaything of the gods?

But there was something else happened in the evolution of the poem, which might in the future make me less dependent on accident. It was a section which had felt different in the writing – with a great deal of put and take, trial and error, rearrangement and revision, a great deal of deliberation and feeling one's way, but no sense at all of strain or undue effort.

Our cameramen are hoisted on a boom
Over the garden
We swoop in through trees
Hearing birds, dry leaves
Seeing grass crushed in a ring.

The girls are gone
Also the lean man from the lane
He is riding somewhere
Against the sunspears

She had broad strong hands
And beautiful feet.
He wanted to go down in the dust . . .
Living inside his mind
Sailing between two lives.

Limits are not fixed
Nor are the possibilities limitless
Rainshine, sunfall, madness
Human spirit
Spirit of Quesada.

Alexander Aitken, the New Zealand mathematician who wrote an extraordinary account of his experiences in World War I,* records that he did maths best when he did not try too hard. Answers came to him, it seems, not quite as 'the leaves to the tree', but in response to patient attention to detail and easy access to memory. It was neither 'hard' nor 'easy': it was just maths. I have heard a professional golfer say the same about his game at its best. And I remember as a schoolboy runner how there was a way of seeming to relax into what was in fact top gear, top speed. I was finding the same about poetry. The mind could move so fast, so effortlessly well, but only if it wasn't pushed – if it had trained well and then was left to do the job without teeth-gritting interference of the will. Once again it was a Zen perception – something I had known from my days as a high jumper.

> Brumel, crossing the bar
> Represents nothing.
> A singular wit
> Shrugs gravity a moment off
> And falls on foam.

The account I'm giving here is an inward one – how it seemed to what Leavis would have called (two of his clunky, determinedly unromantic terms) 'a practitioner of verse'. Just ahead now for this 'practitioner' was the remembered sound of a child's piano practice echoing off the stone walls south-west of Eden; and the roar of helicopters ferrying the last Americans out of Saigon. Ahead, in other words, was the long poem 'Scoria' and my semi-public sonnets. 'Quesada' had its moment. The little green book won the New Zealand Book Award for Poetry in 1976; and first reviews were

---

* *Gallipoli to the Somme: Recollections of a New Zealand Infantryman*, ed. Alex Calder, Auckland University Press, 2018.

good – even, in one or two cases, ringingly. So let me be indulgent on its behalf and give space to a small part of one of them – Peter Crisp's in *New Argot*:

> To one fascinated by the range of language's most subtle and effective uses, 'Quesada' offers a classic craftsmanship of music, cunning and economy. And with the longer line comes a sense of amplitude and scale [. . .] The long lines, yielding to mellow impulse, skirt bombast, fashion, expediency, with a simple and single-minded directness of utterance. For every line said there are two unsaid [. . .] The clarity is exceptional. Very few poets can strip their art down to this essential music.

But 'Quesada' could never be 'a small New Zealand classic'. Where were 'the New Zealand thing, the regional thing, the real thing'? Where were the Māori, the Polynesian, the Local-Political-and-Worthy-of-World-Attention thing? It was an aesthetic act. It would not disturb the Groves of Academe (in which it had been secretly conceived). 'Quesada' had its moment, the moment passed, and it remains now in the midst of all my writing, undisturbed and undisturbing.

Postscript:
If Jenny North had lived I would not have written so frankly about her, but I doubt that she would have minded. She married Bill Peacock I think in 1975 and they had three or four children. In October 1996, after decades of silence between us, she wrote to me c/o St John's College Oxford, where I was Senior Visiting Fellow, to tell me she had cancer and only a year to live, and to say goodbye. She told me that her copy of the *Norton Anthology of Poetry* was marked 'Jenny North, Spring 1971' reminding her that I had given it to her 25 years ago. 'I want you to know that all is resolved in my

heart – and judging by your novel *The Singing Whakapapa*, all is resolved in yours. Thank you for Lydia – I took her, and the use of my letters, as A Fitting Tribute. [. . .] I wish all love to surround you in your remaining years in this "camping ground", as it does me.

Farewell friend
from Jenny
with freesias.'

8.
Wellington, Sydney, and the End of a War

Margaret rolls on the floor

Publication of my selection of Mansfield's letters and journals was delayed by a general stalling in the publishing industry caused by the oil shock of 1973; so I had more time, and on trips to Wellington to chair the New Zealand Literary Fund Advisory Committee (henceforth the Lit. Fund) I was able to further check manuscripts held in the Turnbull Library and to talk about the project with Margaret Scott, who had already given it, or had seemed to give, her blessing. But I found her attitude equivocal and unpredictable, at times enthusiastic, even skittish, at others schoolmarmish and censorious. I always respected her for her intellect and her prose; and she was reputed to be the best transcriber of Mansfield's difficult and headlong handwriting – though not, as I discovered, infallible. But she lacked confidence to proceed on her own with the collected letters commissioned by Oxford University Press, and had to accept the help of Vincent O'Sullivan if ever that vast project was to be completed. At first she was pleased about this, and grateful; but their working relationship was soon fraught with dissension and animosity, each blaming the other. I was not a friend of O'Sullivan's as I was of Margaret's; but I had to suspect from my own experience that more than half the fault was probably hers.

On one of my Wellington visits when I suggested we have lunch and talk about progress Margaret agreed, insisting it must be at her house where we could talk without interruption. There was wine with the lunch, and having drunk quite a lot she produced her corrected version of the Notebooks. With these, of course, I could have corrected any mistakes that had crept into the published versions I was using, and thus into mine. I did not ask for that favour, but I felt it was held out to me as a hint, a temptation. And then she did something I had never seen anyone except her brother Jonathan Bennett do – she rolled on the floor. There is a story somewhere about how Ford Madox Ford rolled on the floor when Ezra Pound showed him some poems Ford considered unfashionably eighteen-ninetyish. Pound recorded it as a lesson – and it is certainly something one is not likely to forget. I don't remember what was the cause of brother Jonathan's roll: only that it happened at Bob Chapman's house, when he and Chapman were together editing the Oxford *Anthology of New Zealand Verse*. Margaret's roll seemed inebriated and perhaps meant to be enticing, though if so, it was a miscalculation. After a necessary pause while she (like Monkey of Chinese legend) 'tidied herself', lunch and the talk continued as if the roll hadn't happened and as if those temptations, the corrected texts, had never been shown to me. It had always been my intention to make the best I could of what was available; and that was the project as Margaret had endorsed it when I first proposed it from Menton. I could proceed without her corrections; and that's what I did.

But I was reminded of the lunch and the roll when another Mansfield scholar, the (in my view very odd) American Jeffrey Meyers published an account of his work as a Mansfield biographer.* He began with an acknowledgement that Margaret Scott had 'very generously let me stay in her house and read all the

* 'The Quest for Katherine Mansfield' in *Writing Lives: Principia Biographica*, ed. Leon Edel, W. W. Norton, 1984, p. 144.

[Mansfield] letters while I was working in Wellington, which saved my travelling to libraries in Australia, England and America (as she had done) and reading the letters which she had learned to decipher. She also showed me her copy of Mansfield's *Journal* which indicated the unpublished entries.' So far so good – a generous and proper acknowledgement. However,

> . . . as the weeks passed and I worked furiously all day and late into the night – for it was winter in wet and windy Wellington, and I found it the most boring city on earth – Margaret Scott seemed to become jealous of my energetic achievement which contrasted so strongly with her own listlessness. She began to nag and pick quarrels with me, and we once had a tug-of-war with a pair of my trousers while debating whether or not she should iron them. Her overt hostility alternated with menacing sulks, but I was determined to put up with anything until I had finished reading the letters and cleared out just before the inevitable explosion.

In the course of Mansfield scholarship one encounters strange behaviours, but few stranger than this. But I was blamed and scolded by Lauris Edmond for sending this American academic she described as heartless and for recommending he stay with Margaret. Of course I would never have recommended such a thing; and I suspect the mistake of the invitation was Margaret's own. Lauris finished her letter of reproach saying she supposed I would think this had nothing to do with me, which she acknowledged was true but she'd enjoyed writing it!

Copyright negotiations as the project approached its end were complicated by the fact that, at his death, John Middleton Murry had left all such matters in the hands of the Society of Authors; and by the fact that the date of first publication, being often after Mansfield's death, meant that the term of the copyright in each case had to be calculated from that later date. The ultimate financial beneficiary for whatever payments were due was Murry's widow, his fourth wife Mary, who (Margaret Scott told me) took no serious interest in Mansfield's writing and regarded any little windfall from the estate only as an occasion to have her hair restyled.

The book finally appeared in London in 1977 in a very fine Allen Lane hardcover with the Anne Estelle Rice portrait of Mansfield on the cover, and simultaneously as a paperback Penguin Modern Classic. By this time Margaret was able to refer in a letter to our 'old weather-seasoned relationship'. She had said she did not want to be thanked in the book for her help, but I thanked her anyway, and dedicated it 'affectionately to Celia and Cecil Manson'. They telegraphed their delight and followed with a letter saying it 'gave them more pleasure than anything that has happened for a very long time'. I sent Margaret copies and her response was mixed: 'Your introduction is as interesting as it is impeccable. You tauten and correct the common view of her talent and ways of using it. You help me to crystallise some of my own views, so that I am indebted to you.' But she still grumbled about matters of transcription too minuscule to be significant to the general reader or to affect the book as whole.

Katherine Mansfield Letters and Journals was to continue as a Penguin Modern Classic for more than a quarter of a century; and then to reappear in New Zealand as a Vintage paperback. It was the basis of Cathy Downes' one-person show, *The Case of Katherine Mansfield*, performed many times over a number of years; and it was the book which set numbers of scholars off in pursuit of the mind that lay behind, and reached beyond, Mansfield's published stories. It was the obvious 'product' of my Menton fellowship; but so equally was the novella, first published as 'The Town' and latterly as 'And still the sun shines'. Some years later Curnow asked, 'Can the Menton fellowship ever have been so usefully productive?'

Wellington: Lauris, Fiona, Denis . . .

Labour was, as always, more sympathetic than National to

the arts, and in particular to literature, and more money was on offer. The Lit. Fund's official history describes me as 'professor of English at the University of Auckland, novelist, poet and critic, articulate, outspoken and charming but often controversial. [...] As a practising writer living away from the capital, and a well-known opponent of New Zealand's involvement in the Vietnam War, he clearly expected, and was expected, to do things differently.'* So more or less at once we used some of the available money to establish new New Zealand Book Awards in three categories, poetry, fiction and non-fiction. Although nothing in the matter of book prizes is ever quite pure, free or dependable – there is always an element of luck, of literary-lottery in who wins and who is overlooked – these were at first (I think one can say) 'purer' than later, when they became entwined with the publishing industry and sponsorship, and took on a commercial aspect. But in the meantime we had to decide what was to be done with the Hubert Church and Jessie Mackay awards, which had been up to this time the premier literary prizes. This was a matter which greatly exercised the mind of Lauris Edmond, herself just emerging as a poet and 'free woman', and Fiona Kidman, both of whom made submissions on behalf of PEN.

My dealings with Lauris were complicated by the fact that I'd had two of her daughters, first Frances, then Rachel, as very lively and intelligent members of my stage two (i.e. second-year) tutorial in Auckland. In fact when Lauris first introduced herself to me in Wellington it was not as a writer but as the mother of two of my students. There were no problems with Frances; but Rachel had breakdowns and a period in Ward 10 (the psychiatric unit) at Auckland Hospital. She wrote asking me to give her some kind of a reference that would help her get past this episode, which I did willingly. Lauris wrote thanking me and it seemed all might be

* Elizabeth Caffin and Andrew Mason, *The Deepening Stream: A History of the New Zealand Literary Fund*, Victoria University Press, 2015, p. 157.

well; but then came another from Lauris saying Rachel had killed herself. It is an example of how the personal and the public are so often intertwined in New Zealand; how few the 'degrees of separation'.

This was even more the case with Lauris because of her close friendship with Fiona. They were part of the PEN team in Wellington, and though Lauris (in a frequently badly behaved alliance with Alistair Campbell) had been a determined resister to the idea of an Auckland branch, Fiona had come to accept its inevitability and was helping to make PEN work as a national body. Lauris also lunched from time to time with Margaret Scott and could hear reports from her about our progress with my Mansfield project. And Fiona at this time was engaged in doing a version of *Smith's Dream* for radio, so with her too my relations were both semi-public (Lit. Fund and PEN) and literary/personal. The novel was doing especially well now in schools, and I had numbers of letters, sometimes from one pupil, sometimes from a group of six or eight, or a whole class, asking questions about the book and my intentions, and quite often from English teachers inviting me to come and talk to their class. I tried to answer all of these.

Then there was Lauris's working relationship with Denis Glover, putting together a selection of Fairburn's letters, she as editor, Denis as publisher. This put her in an awkward situation as the feminist poet she aspired to be, since neither Glover nor Fairburn was able to take the idea of women writers entirely seriously. 'I am prejudiced', Denis told me in a letter, 'against what Johnson defined as a poetess – "a she-poet".'

Late in 1975 Denis and I were invited by the English Association to form a panel with Allen Curnow in which we were to discuss something like 'the state of New Zealand literature'. Denis accepted saying he would prepare nothing in advance, but told me in a letter about a lunch with Lauris in which he had asked was I 'of Jewish descent', he himself 'being very pro-Israel', and offering me the following limerick:

There was an old 'Ebrew of Auck
Who was madly affected to pork.
He knew what he did
Was forbid to a Yid
But he brandished his knife and a fork.

I think our panel was lively enough, but I remember one particular exchange which revealed (something I knew anyway) that Allen could seem almost as benighted as Glover and Fairburn when it came to the matter of acknowledging merit in women writers. On the subject of Mansfield Allen remembered 'some fool' in Christchurch who had referred to her as 'the peacock in New Zealand's literary garden' – to which I interjected the correction 'Pea*hen*', and Glover topped that with 'Pi*ha*'. But Mansfield was to get no seriously affirmative word from either of them. She was some kind of obstruction to the advance of our literature, having received more than her fair share of attention 'overseas'.

Kay and I put on a party that night, partly for Denis, but inviting 'everyone', 'the usual suspects'; there was no problem getting Denis there because the path from the Curnows was all downhill; but there was the greatest difficulty getting him back again. Denis was very heavy, and (as always) very drunk, and it was the work of several strong persons returning him uphill and into the bed Jeny Curnow had prepared for him.

Denis was by now New Zealand writing's court jester, the funny man and fool who nominated Princess Anne's horse for vice president of PEN NZ, and who I remember after a literary occasion in Christchurch hollering to the skies, 'A hearse, a hearse, my kingdom for a hearse.' He was acknowledged for some wonderful early lyrics, especially the 'sings Harry' series, but was by general agreement past his use-by date; which is probably what caused me to ask Lauris a question about him. This produced an interesting answer in a subsequent letter. She began by saying she didn't know why she should be writing to me tonight except that our last conversation had left some new thoughts – and especially that she'd given a wrong answer to my question about Denis's conversation, which she should have acknowledged was remarkably inventive, full of nonsense of course, but often *wise* nonsense. She went on to tell me about a time when she was going on a beach holiday with her family and Denis had insisted on going with them, staying in a pub nearby, so that at the end of every day she had to have a session with him. She had found these exhausting but rewarding, and the family accepted the strange arrangement because they liked Denis and found him entertaining. In the end Lauris had had to put a stop to it because it was wearing her out; but she wanted me to know that Denis was not just (as so many supposed) a drunk and a fool, but a man with a great human insight and subtlety.

This was an unusual view of Denis in his later years, one that reflected well both on him, and on Lauris.*

Maurice Duggan, another serious literary alcoholic of the period, died 11 December 1974 at the age of fifty-two. It seemed another waste, like Baxter's – a writer possibly on the brink of new and remarkable things, none of which we would now see. We gave him a send-off (secular but for a few denomination-neutral prayers) from the university's Maclaurin Chapel. Frank did not attend. He had refused to go to Harry Doyle's funeral too because he knew he could not control his tears; and for the same reason had avoided Ron Mason's. Keith Sinclair gave the eulogy, and I read from Maurice's 'Beginnings' article (*Landfall* 80), with its refrain, 'And the Nurse said, "Drink this."' Eight writers were his pall-bearers – Keith, Maurice Gee, Eric McCormick, David Ballantyne, Kendrick Smithyman, Maurice Shadbolt, Bill Pearson and me. Looking back over almost half a century it seems a strange pale-skinned broederbond – and yet a genuine writers' tribute because

---

* I would like to have quoted the letter literally and in full but was forbidden to by Lauris's daughter Frances Edmond who controls the copyright.

every one of us had written significant books. Less than ten years later Fleur Adcock would edit *The Oxford Book of Contemporary New Zealand Poetry* which would represent twenty poets, sixteen men and still only four women, and yet would insist she had chosen entirely and solely on the basis of literary merit. The times 'they were a-changin' – but not fast, and not yet!

Sydney

In 1975 I was invited to take part in a 'Poetry Write-in' in Sydney organised by Grace Perry, editor of *Poetry Australia*. I arrived half an hour before I was scheduled to appear – to be, I thought, a member of a panel, but found I was expected to speak solo to quite a large audience, chaired by Louis Johnson the Wellington poet who was now teaching creative writing in one of the New South Wales polytech/universities. I was unprepared for this and asked for a few minutes to walk in the garden and think what on earth I was going to say, but Grace Perry insisted on coming with me, and talking at me without a break. Talking came to her so effortlessly, indeed compulsively, the idea that one might have 'nothing to say' was to her quite meaningless.

The presence of Louis Johnson, amiable and easy-going, reminded me of his old argument with Curnow about literary nationalism; and I had somehow picked up out of a few words said that this was an ongoing argument in Australia too, and had already been touched upon. That gave me somewhere to start, and a direction – and after fifteen or twenty minutes on the theme I was able to engage Louis, and then the audience, in a lively discussion. Somehow the hour and a half I was allotted passed. But Grace Perry must have registered my initial horror because after I'd returned home she wrote (one of her almost illegible letters) apologising 'that you were thrust so precipitately into the breach on arrival', but explaining 'that is the technique to which I attribute the potency of the product. You were magnificent.'

It was at this event that I first met Peter Porter, Queensland-born poet but long established in London and on a brief visit home. I was to get to know him well later.

> 'Peter the Rock' I called him,
> 'Porter the Carrier' – and sometimes
> (acknowledging a facility, a felicity)
> 'Prêt à Porter'
> the runaway Australian who made
> London his home
> Italy his university.*

Without any academic training, Porter was the ultimate intellectual and 'high brow' – very different from Les Murray who had grown up an only child whose mother died when he was twelve, in the wilds of the Coolongolook dairying country, teased at school as a fat boy, often afflicted with depression, and with a kind of autistic relationship to language which in his poetry took on a life of its own, almost separate from the people and things it referred to. It was the presence of these two already well-known poets that had made my off-the-cuff opening possible, and even a success, because they represented what are really the twin poles of all post-colonial writing, and had even engaged in a quiet war about it, Murray standing for the regional, the local reality, and Porter for the international – for the inherited European culture as against the locally evolved one.

The weekend of the 'Write-in' included a dinner where I found myself seated between two women writers, Penny Nelson and Fay Zwicky, both there to learn more about writing poetry. Fay, Jewish, originally from Melbourne but now living in Perth where, she said, 'we are the only Z in the phone book', I thought was the more talented poet. Penny, the daughter of two well-known and successful

---

* 'In the June rain', *That Derrida Whom I Derided Died*, p. 47.

journalists (I had seen her father's column in the *Bulletin*), was a capable prose writer, a dashing Sydney-sider with many stories. In her late teens at Sydney University she'd had an affair with a fellow-student, Bob Ellis (later well known as a political speech-writer and gossip columnist) who became convinced, and convinced her, that the Cuban missile crisis was going to lead to a nuclear war in which Sydney would be obliterated. So they had cleared out together in her mother's car, and waited in the mountains for the End of Everything. After several days with no sign of the expected disaster, they returned to find no crisis except the one their absence had created. Penny became a friend and I later used some of her life as background for the character of Samantha Conlan – Sammy – in my novel *The Secret History of Modernism*.

Back in Auckland I found Frank was suffering congestive heart failure. He could not sleep lying down and got through terrible breathless nights by sitting in a chair resting his head forward on a stool. There were three or four nights, he said, when he was hallucinating, sleeping for a time, waking and thinking 'I must eat', and then sleeping again having eaten nothing. Kay cooked some meals which we took over for him, some to eat, the rest to store in next-door's deep freeze. Barbara Duggan engaged a district nurse and they tried to find a diuretic that would clear his lungs of fluid. I rang him every day until he asked me to stop because he believed he was dying, and each time our conversation ended he wept thinking we were saying goodbye for the last time. So I kept a check on him through Barbara; and soon the report was that the new diuretic was working, he was sleeping, he was eating, he would live.

America here and America there

A visit to New Zealand by the American poet Robert Creeley, initiated by Alistair Paterson and sponsored by the Arts Council, was the occasion of interesting, even revealing, literary tensions. Creeley was one of those cult poets who attract disciples to whom a taste for his work represents enlightenment. We had our own enlightened ones, of course, though (also of course) there were subtleties and refinements, and arguments over these that might be described as theological. Creeley had been blessed by William Carlos Williams, and thus had in effect apostolic powers to pass the blessing on – and there were those here eager to receive it. I had reservations about his studied minimalism but I was more often drawn to it than to John Ashbery's or Robert Duncan's, poets with whom his name was often associated.

The Arts Council had assigned to different poets in different regions the choice of who should read with Creeley. It was my job to choose for Auckland and I decided to make it simple: three Auckland poets, Curnow, myself and David Mitchell would have ten minutes each for the first half, and, after an interval, Creeley would have thirty minutes (or so) in the second. I declined to have anything to do with housing him, since I thought he was an experienced professional accustomed to being provided with travel expenses and hotel accommodation. All this displeased Russell Haley who wanted to organise the Auckland reading and manage Creeley's entertainment. Letters flew back and forth; and some kind of compromise was reached. The Auckland reading was as I'd planned it; but Creeley seemed more than willing to be kidnapped by his disciples. He also acquired, in Dunedin where his tour began, a new partner, Penelope Highton, who would in due time be his third wife; and he wrote a kind of verse journal, running through his New Zealand stops, and onward to Sydney and South East Asia, the whole published as *Hello*.

My own position in all this, as seen by the poets who were Creeley's admirers, had been described (I think it was by Alan Loney, but Ian Wedde was also sniping from a publication on the sideline calling itself *Spleen*) as 'cluttering up the fast lane' – by which was meant I had some slight credibility as a Modernist, but was not 'Post-Modern', and so could give a kind of respectably avant-garde appearance to my dealings with contemporary poets and poetry, while really putting the brakes on 'progress'. And it's true I was bored by the fuss and the provincial passions his presence among us engendered.

But 'Bob', as I learned to call him, had enjoyed himself in Auckland and wanted to come back. I suppose the new Kiwi wife had a part in this. Clearly the New Zealand visit had marked a division in his life; and in fact the first volume of his *Collected Poems* goes up to 1975 while the second begins in 1976 in New Zealand. The only real biography at present (2018) is a hostile one by Ekbert Faas, focused largely on his early years, and with a large contribution from the much-wronged first wife. Creeley is represented as choleric, violent, depressive, often drunk and/or drugged, a 'womaniser', but progressively a less interesting poet as he gets older and sorts out these personal problems; and the story is not taken forward into the New Zealand visit or beyond.

So this was the poet now asking for a temporary post in the English Department, and willing even to accept a demotion from his current rank of tenured professor at Buffalo, New York, to a lectureship. He wrote to me asking what I could do to make this happen. He had written to Musgrove, and also to Roger Horrocks and Wystan Curnow both of whom he could count on wanting him, but (he told me in a letter dated September '77) had received no response from anyone. By the time one of his letters caught up with me in London he was angry – not with me, because I had made efforts on his behalf, but with Musgrove, who was dragging his feet and setting contrary forces in motion cancelling one another out.

In a very small book he calls *Autobiography* Creeley tells of driving somewhere with his daughters Leslie and Kirsten aged eight and ten, and Leslie suggests she and her sister compete counting telephone poles. After many miles Kirsten announces that she has a score of 3486 and asks how many Leslie has. 'Oh,' Leslie says, 'I wasn't counting.' I sometimes felt that Creeley's relations with his acolytes were like that: they were counting madly but he was not. A few pages on in the same book he writes, 'There is an awful self-consciously recognised limit to what may be called my sincerity.'

Recently I've found, in one of my letters to Kay when she was in Wellington at the Library School, an admiring response to Creeley's interview in *Islands* 15 (Autumn 1976):

> I think all the distracting mannerisms are very much of the surface. Something much better comes through it – a firm personality, a nice sense of humour (which means intelligence too) and seriousness. When he says he likes or remembers a poem because of a line in it, the line is always a good one. And there's this for example when he's asked what he thinks of Ted Hughes: 'Hughes has extraordinary emotional power, but that Crow sequence, it bored me, frankly, because I didn't want to deal with a damn symbolic crow [. . .] I would rather pay attention to a real one.'

My own mixed feelings, my inclination to laugh at Cult Creeley and yet enjoy, and sometimes admire, what he wrote, was not given expression until he died, when I published 'A/go, an elegy-pastiche for Robert Creeley'.*

> Remember Bob? –
> wore a pirate's
> patch, and wrote
>
> and talked
> somethin' like
> *this*, like the real

* *The Yellow Buoy*, Auckland University Press, 2013, p. 32.

thing, talkin' –
and (remember) the
book he wrote

after his visit,
the one he called
Hello – intricate

quirky, and himself
strangely
formal – 'Dear

fellow-poet'
seeming mostly
to mean

no more nor
less than was
said, but with

something dark
as well? – yes
maybe –

and jokes, like
the one about
Dunedin –

'Don't take the
steak, I ain't
Dunedin.'

30 years is
a long ago

Hello! (now

a goodbye)
one of those
visitations

when 'out
there' came 'in
here' and was

and was
not
everything

it was
cracked up to
be.

Bob Creeley's last letter to me concluded that 'selfishly' he hoped he and I could keep in touch. He thought it likely he would get to New Zealand or I to the US – or that we would meet in England. He was 'so damn mad' that what could have been pleasant and useful had been spoiled – but he sent his best, as ever.

IN WELLINGTON THERE WERE READINGS at Downstage with Lauris and Fiona, Alistairs Paterson and Campbell, my former PhD student Rob Jackaman now the editor of *Landfall*, and others. Lauris wrote a poem thanking me for being a kind and encouraging fellow-reader, and when I didn't respond, followed it with a letter admitting it was not very good and sending a revision, which as far as I know she didn't publish so had nothing later to regret or take back. Fiona on the other hand published a poem, 'A Man's Name – for CKS who else' about my seeming eminence in Wellington, and about reading my book *Walking Westward* in the bath. This was so positive, such an acclamation, it gave her difficulties later when she came to write her autobiography, where she took most of a page to explain that this 'embarrassing mistake' was the result of being flattered by my having praised her poems. There could hardly be a better example of Fiona's lack of judgement. If she had not drawn attention to it, the poem would hardly have been noticed; or if noticed, it would only have told her readers that she had once admired CKS, surely an excusable error and subsequently corrected.*

Lauris and Fiona saw and promoted themselves as front-runners, as they were – women writers making their presence felt. The New Zealand literary scene needed such presences and was better for theirs; but they did seem at times to ask for special treatment, as if the old male–female courtesies, by which a man stood up when a woman entered the room, gave up his seat to her on a tram, or took off his hat for her in the street, should prevail. I had grown up with those proprieties myself, and even observed them in day-to-day life; but now, as a critic, I dispensed with them as belonging to a past time, and was blamed for it.

My feeling about Fiona's poetry was much like my feeling about Keith Sinclair's: it was somewhat rough-hewn, but with each poem something interesting had happened and someone intelligent had thought about it. Lauris's was finer-tuned, subtler, but tending to be precious. Lauris was in love with Literature, solemn, even reverent about it, and suspicious of what she called 'cleverness'. After one of our readings she wrote that I had been witty and intelligent, Alistair (I assume Campbell) had revealed his soul, and she had been All Woman! She said she didn't know what it was that made her quarrel with me for being clever – but it was an effect I had on her.

---

* The poem is on pp. 42–43 of *Going to the Chathams: Poems 1977–1984* (Penguin, 1985), and the regrets about it are on p. 81 of *Beside the Dark Pool* (Penguin, 2009). She sent me the poem at the time, hoping I would read it 'in the spirit in which it was written'. I replied that I did, and that I was 'delighted, flattered, and full of grin. I even think it's a good poem.'

Neither she nor Fiona was notable for wit, or quite comfortable with it; and it was around the time of these exchanges that Lauris wrote a review in the *Listener* in which she dismissed Ken Smithyman's poetry out of hand; his was 'not a poetic mind', to which I replied deploring her 'condescending tone, which I don't think she has a right to either as a poet or as a critic'.

A long slow evolving (ultimately well-publicised) unpleasantness with Vincent O'Sullivan seems to have had its beginnings here, when he took exception to my letter in defence of Kendrick, which he considered to have been 'more than a touch pietistic'. Vince had recently moved from teaching at the University of Waikato to be the *Listener*'s books editor, and this became a new incarnation of the Auckland–Wellington literary quarrels that had gone on at the time of Curnow's Penguin.

For me one element in this was a report O'Sullivan wrote for AUP on Curnow's collection *An Incorrigible Music*. His first paragraph recommended publication, but only because the book was by Curnow and Curnow was important. Almost everything else he said about the book was negative, damning. 'Weariness', 'imprecision', 'nothing freshly creative', 'faded routines', 'verbal effects now declined into mannerisms', 'narcissism' – all this culminating in a description of Curnow's poem about Mike Joseph's novel *The Soldier's Tale* as 'a mean-spirited, grubby swipe'.

This report gave Dennis McEldowney great anxiety. Could his Press Committee be persuaded to accept the collection for publication with such a report in front of it? Those who knew little about poetry would need persuading. So he called for evaluations of the collection and of O'Sullivan's report, from me, Roger Horrocks and Mac Jackson. We each wrote separately and in some detail, disputing the report and recommending the book, which was then accepted. An obstacle was overcome; but it left me with an uneasy feeling about Vincent, especially in his role as the *Listener* books editor. In my mind he became *Measure for Measure*'s Vincentio, 'the old fantastical duke of dark corners'.

I RESIGNED MY CHAIRMANSHIP of the Literary Fund Advisory Committee after two and a half years, in May 1976 when *Quesada* was short-listed in the poetry section of the New Zealand Book Awards we had established. I wanted the new collection to have its chance, and felt I could not be part of the committee that would be responsible for the decision, even if that meant no more than confirming the judges' recommendation. *Quesada* won the award and I received $1,000. I went with Kay to Colin McCahon's show, *Rocks in the Sky*, at the Barry Lett Galleries. They were quite large works on paper, priced each at $450. We meant to buy just one but bought two and had them mounted down on board, which was recommended at the time but later proved to be unsatisfactory. They were not our only McCahons, but the only ones we ever sold. The family lived with them contentedly, dominating the sitting room for fifteen or more years, and then we sold them I think for $25,000 each, to someone who would have them lifted from the boards and reframed, at once doubling their value.

This was a period when my poetry was expanding, moving in new directions. 'Walking Westward' was a process poem, and I thought of it as just the first of four or five long poems which would be linked. It moved about in space, but was contemporary in time – a twentieth-century poem. 'Scoria', the next in the series, would move in time (including back into geological pre-history) but would be arrested in one place, the volcanic field of Tāmaki-makau-rau. Then there was to be one set in Paris, catching as much as I was able of my obsession with French language and culture. But it was also around this time that Catullus began to figure in my work. In *Walking Westward* the opening poem ('Caesar is still Caesar / even if he breakfasts on turds / before a speech in the house'), meant to suggest our rebarbative Prime Minister Muldoon, was the start of what would be my ongoing quarrying of the great Roman poet, whose ironic and economic cadences spoke to me more naturally than the sounds of Pound, and gave me a licence to be at times less than lyrical, more like the voice of reality, frank, direct, sometimes obscene, sour as well as sweet, and to curb the charm. I admired Pound's literary intelligence, and his capacity to produce effects of mysterious beauty in the midst of clutter and nonsense; but his compulsion to rattle on when there was nothing to say, or too much to be managed, meant one had to hunt in his *Cantos* for the 'good bits' still breathing under the rubble, like the survivors of an earthquake. Pound taught me a lot, but I think Catullus taught me more.

Vietnam – the end of a war

In April 1975 the American military intervention in Vietnam came to an ignominious end with the fall of Saigon to North Vietnamese and Viet Cong forces, and the scramble of the last of the American military and their supporters to escape. The country which constantly declared itself to be the most powerful, both militarily and morally, had been defeated by a small nation defending its right to determine its own future within its own borders; but it had been defeated in part also by the people at home in America, and around the world, who had not accepted the right America claimed to make these determinations. This subject had been a thread, or fine steel wire, running through most of my writing during the past ten years. It had determined my view of our world, and would colour my view of America and of what New Zealand's place in relation to America should be, for the rest of my life. I think everything I wrote, fiction no less than poetry, was against a background of twentieth-century history, from the Depression of the 1930s and World War II, on through the Cold War, Korea and Vietnam, Iraq: all of that long story of conflict, both ideological and military, constituted the big picture, against which my small stories would be acted out. Even where they are not directly referred to, they are there, part of the backdrop and the ambience. And this dramatic blow to American pride made its way inevitably into the sonnets I was writing at the time:

16

Xuan Loc fallen, Danang fallen, we wait for the fall of Saigon.
Nobody weeps or cheers, nobody puts on sack-cloth

For the thousand thousand lives we took or broke
To get our own sweet way. We didn't get it.

Does Lyndon Johnnie underground sleep sound
Dreaming light at the end of a tunnel? Holyoake hasn't been
told.

Holt swam with the sharks; and all those airy ministers
Of canister bombs and body counts took jobs

With the World Bank, UNESCO, the Ford Foundation.
Washington, Wellington, leather chairs, inflatable arses,

'Peace with Honour' . . .*

As the North Vietnamese and Viet Cong closed on Saigon the British poet and journalist James Fenton was recording it all. People were leaving at the rate of ten thousand a day. American journalists were instructed by their papers to get out while there was still time. Enormous helicopters were ferrying people from the US Embassy out to ships waiting offshore. Viet Cong wearing captured South Vietnamese uniforms were quietly entering the city, waiting for orders to take control. From time to time, with an idea of showing that someone was in charge, American marines dropped tear-gas

* Lyndon Johnson, who kept promising light at the end of the Vietnam tunnel, and peace with honour, died in January 1973. The Australian Prime Minister Harold Holt, who committed troops to the war and promoted the slogan 'All the way with LBJ', disappeared while swimming in 1967. Robert McNamara, LBJ's Secretary of Defense, became head of the World Bank in 1968 when Richard Nixon was elected President.

grenades down from the roof of the embassy, while looters entered the lower floors and helped themselves to anything useful or valuable. Local defence forces made it clear they were not going to fight to defend the city. There was extreme disorder, occasional flurries of gunfire, but very little bloodshed.

And then Fenton saw a tank heading for the gates of the presidential palace and hitched a ride.* According to one report it was not only bearing many heavily armed soldiers and one poet, but was decorated with flowers. It tried unsuccessfully to ram the palace gate, but then someone inside unlocked it and the tank rumbled through. Saigon had fallen.

My sonnet recording the date and the event looked back to our own Auckland protests, and one in particular I'd taken part in with Jenny North:

18
(April 1975, the fall of Saigon)

Our biggest march came late. It was '71.
A girl walked with me, starry-eyed, bewildered

Shocked at the war, frightened locked in that crowd –
Fifteen, twenty thousand pushing into Queen Street.

Outside the Town Hall leaves of the tubbed trees
Decked out with raindrops shivered under the lights.

Our chanting rose to the clock and the cold stars
That watch over us, that bless us rarely.

So many years we've fought that war in our sleep!
Now Xerxes at a phone in the Oval Office

---

* I was to meet Fenton from time to time at Craig Raine's home in Oxford.

Is pulling his troops out, and I remember that girl,
That march, telling ourselves 'Keep calm, keep walking –

History won't take our names but she'll maybe award us
An honourable footnote on a page of blood.'

Postscript:
Rumours of a war between me and the old fantastical duke of dark corners continued, not entirely without substance, but hugely exaggerated, until the year 2009 when we were both in Menton for the celebration of forty years of the Mansfield fellowship and someone insisted we must be photographed together, two senior New Zealand writers, both expert in Mansfield studies. As the pics were taken I said to Vince, 'If this gets to New Zealand, both our reputations will be damaged.' He said, 'I think we should say we've eloped.'

9.
UCL, ASD & Menton Again

Karl & Karl

I was to be away on leave for the first two terms of 1977, and my mind was full of that prospect when a handsome young Australian with a moustache and a head of curly hair knocked at my office door and introduced himself as Roger Donaldson. He had been living in New Zealand since 1965, an escapee from conscription into the Australian Army deployed in Vietnam, and now wanting to make a movie of *Smith's Dream*. He had engaged the actor Sam Neill who was on the brink of giving up acting; and of the cinematographer Michael Seresin. These three would go on to make such distinguished careers for themselves it's not too much to say each in his own way became famous – rich and famous; not because of *Sleeping Dogs*, as *Smith's Dream* became in the movie version, but it gave them each their start. Ian Mune was to act in it and to be one of two script-writers.

I was pleased by Roger's enthusiasm but I did not really take it seriously – in fact my attention was so focused on other things that I have only vague memory of formal dealings on the subject; but there was a contract which committed the film-makers to paying $5,000 for the option, which I would split 75/25 with the publisher, Longman Paul. I was also promised 2.5 per cent of all receipts for overseas releases and any video or electronic returns. My $3,750 share of the initial option was all I ever received, but that seemed a lot at the time, and I was astonished, then and thereafter, at the energy, practicality, confidence and general good sense Roger brought to the business of movie-making. *Sleeping Dogs*, looked back at now, seems a creaky old product, not well scripted, unsubtle and overblown; but it was a first – the first New Zealand commercial movie filmed in 35mm, and the first to have international release.

I signed up agreeing that Roger go ahead, not really expecting to hear more, and flew off at the end of 1976 with the family to London, where from time to time letters from friends, and newspaper clippings, kept me aware that the project was in fact happening at great speed. We would be back towards the end of 1977, just in time to see its pre-release showing in a small theatrette in the Civic cinema.

I had written to the English Department at University College London knowing that UCL's academic reputation was high and that physically it was conveniently placed, close to Russell Square, the British Museum, and William Goodenough House where we hoped to be lodged. This enquiry had brought an instant response from Karl Miller. I'd had exchanges with him when he was literary editor of the *New Statesman*, but had not known he was now the Lord Northcliffe Professor of Modern English Literature at UCL. What he sent was a cable, followed up by a letter, offering me a visiting research fellowship in the English Department, access to the Senate House Library and a carrel there; and possibly the use of a staff member's office if one should be available. I could also take part in Miller's course on Modern literature if that would interest me. I accepted at once. It seemed to come almost by chance, but looked back on appears to have opened many doors and even to some extent to have determined my future as a writer.

Other invitations arrived around this time. One was from Wallace Robson, whom I had last met in Armidale, now Masson Professor of English Literature at Edinburgh, asking whether I would lecture later in the year at the Scottish Universities Summer School. Another was from Bernard Bergonzi inviting me to lecture at Warwick where he was Professor of English.

Oxford and Cambridge were ancient, devout (in one way or the other) and beautiful. University College London was nineteenth-century, radical and secular, open to all races and faiths, and dingy in the way so much of London is – noisy, soot-stained, dirty-Dickensian. Its front porticos were on the cluttered thoroughfare of Gower Street, but I always approached it from the rear where it looked like a neglected warehouse. Not far away was the Senate House Library (where I would have my carrel) looming over Russell Square like something designed by party apparatchiks of the Soviet Union. UCL had been Jeremy Bentham's idea, and it was his idea also that his auto-icon, meaning his human remains, fully dressed in his own clothes, including a hat broad-brimmed enough to have been designed with modern ideas of protection from UV rays in mind, should sit in a box in one of the corridors, to be brought out at intervals for display. It was said he attended council meetings as a non-voting member, and that if the vote was evenly split, he was considered to have voted with the motion. The head, which he had wanted preserved, had not looked good after being smoked in the Māori manner, and so had been replaced by a waxwork. From time to time the actual head had been stolen by students, and was now kept somewhere safe and secure.

But UCL, though unbeautiful, was a high-powered institution, with top-ranked scholars and scientists, and I felt it a great honour to have been offered a role there. Karl Miller's invitations had been warm; so my first meeting with him was a surprise. I was to come to his office at midday and we would go to lunch. I arrived on time, knocked, and was called to come in. Karl's office was spacious, and almost the whole area was occupied by a large table around which his students sat when he conducted a seminar. He was at the head of it now, marking papers – proofs possibly, or perhaps student essays. He did not stand up but signalled a chair where I should sit while he finished what he was doing. It was not unfriendly, but not warm either, as his letters had been. It was crotchety Karl as I would get to know him. But it was a bit more than that. As I sat there and ten minutes, fifteen, twenty passed, I tried to work out what was going on. If I had been prepared for this, and of a mood, I might have taken some work from my bag and kept him mocking company. I felt the embarrassment of having nothing to do. But I was mostly just puzzled, trying to interpret this behaviour which was really quite extreme. It was difficult, but not impossible, to imagine he did not know he was being rude. That was the question: was he making a point, putting me firmly in my place, establishing his authority in advance of whatever our relationship was going to be? Or was he some kind of socially primitive beast, the dourest of dour Scots, who did not have even a faint notion of social proprieties? Maybe I should have been humming under my breath, 'Scots, wha hae wi' Wallace bled . . .'.

I was to return often to the memory of this introduction, and even after some years, and knowing Karl quite well, I had not resolved the question until, after his retirement, I read his book *Dark Horses*, and an essay there, 'Teaching English', where he made it clear he had worried, as a journalist taking up such a senior academic post, whether he would be considered, by the academic community, 'not one of us'. This had occurred to me as a possible explanation; but I had always dismissed it, because I thought of him as in every way more important than I was. What I did not take into account, because it took a long time for me to catch up with the fact, even after a graduate student told me *The New Poetic* had been 'a cult book' in his undergraduate years, was the impact my book had made on the study of twentieth-century poetry. I was not 'eminent', but there was a sense in which my book was; and Karl was asserting dominance. I thought of that moment also when I read his wife Jane's book about her life, a book she dedicated to Karl but in which she mentions him only three times. One of the three, where she is referring to herself in the third person, is as follows: 'She was learning to guard against displays of innocence or ignorance, though a few years later her husband would still have to remind her to put on her arrogant face as they wait for their hosts to open the door and usher them in.'* Karl at that first meeting was putting on his arrogant face, in a drama of his own imagining.

Despite the rocky start I got on well with him and liked him. Some years later I put a version of him (moved back in time) as the editor Marx McLaren in my novel *The Secret History of Modernism*; and it was probably because of this characterisation that he told Barry Humphries (who passed it on) that he suspected I did not like him. In fact I was always fond of him, thought he was clever, funny, good company, sometimes ridiculous, and often bad-tempered. We had some things in common apart from the name Karl with a K. As a Scot he thought of himself as an outsider in London. His political commitment was always to the left. We had both played soccer, and he continued with a local scratch team of amateurs. He had been powerfully influenced by Leavis, continued to respect him, but had grown weary of the Leavisite puritanism, the lists of acceptable and unacceptable works of literature, the contempt for the BBC, the publishing industry, and literary journalism. I shared all that. I was a graduate of a Leavisite department, and my doctorate had been supervised by the editor of *Scrutiny*; but Karl had been even closer. He had studied at Cambridge, at Downing College, and under Leavis himself, who had been a mentor. If I had taken up that exhibition we might have got to know one another much sooner. When much later I wrote a poem for his seventieth birthday celebration it included the lines:

> Scholarship Scot
> among the Simons at Downing
> you took

---

* Jane Miller, *Relations*, Jonathan Cape, 2003, p. 100.

bookish London
by the back door
making space for yourself

who could construe
ahead of time
Heaney's invisible

mending no less than
the magic of Gazza's
dancing steps.

Gazza was Paul Gascoigne the England midfielder whose skills Karl once praised lyrically in the *London Review of Books*.

Mecklenburgh Square

We were housed in a two-bedroom self-contained flat on the ground floor of Julian Crossley Court in the William Goodenough complex on the north side of Mecklenburgh Square, the female postgraduate quarters which matched up with the London House for male post-grads, on the south side. This was not ideal in that three children aged thirteen, ten and seven had to make do with two bunks and a bed in one room. On the other hand there were other children to mix and play with, a games room, and a key to the beautiful square with its enormous trees, tennis courts and lovely gardens; and for the parents, the sharing of child-minding with others in the building, so Kay and I were free to attend plays, concerts, operas as we had done in the years before we had children. Charlotte and Margaret went to the local St Albans School, and Oliver went on the tube to Hampstead School, a large comprehensive which now claims Zadie Smith as one of its distinguished alumni. He travelled there with Alistair, son of Bill Broughton, a former student of mine now a lecturer at Massey in Palmerston North and like me, on sabbatical leave.

On the 8th of January I queued in the snow from 8.30 to 10.30 in the morning for tickets to Wagner's *Götterdämmerung* at the Coliseum; and that night Kay and I went to it, having made child-minding arrangements with neighbours on our floor of Julian Crossley Court. The opera began at 4.30 p.m. and finished at 11, with a supper break after the second act. It was our first Wagner, and we were at once hooked. Later in the year it would be returning to London and we would see, the first of many times, the four operas of the Ring Cycle in their proper sequence; and although there is a sense in which the experience would get better as we learned the whole work and its history, there was never to be again for me an experience as intense and overwhelming as that first hearing of an opera I knew nothing about except that it was famous, and that musical people tended to be divided about its composer, who had been revered by the Nazis, especially Hitler. The fact that I knew so little was probably the basis for the depth of my involvement; because I was not absorbed by, or even much interested in, the story, the mythology, the symbolism, but was being taken over, enchanted, possessed by the gradually evolving, accumulating, interconnecting musical elements – by the *music*, all of it, so that by the time the climax was reached and Valhalla was burning and Brünnhilde was riding her horse into the flames, I knew that if I did not stop listening for just a moment I would faint. This is the kind of testimony, or confession, I had read others (Bertrand Russell for example) make about their most intense experience of works of art, and had tended to mock, or at the very least doubt – so I recount it with some diffidence, even embarrassment; but because it is true.

In February I wrote to my sisters in New Zealand a summary of how we were placed:

> I have been sitting under the streamers and balloons waiting for Margaret's birthday party to begin. Charlotte has just been sick on the floor, so it's not clear now whether she or Oliver will be the Fortune Teller. We've had very cold weather. The other

day as I walked through Regents Park the pond was frozen. It was a beautiful morning with the sun shining through the winter trees – the sun does shine in London these days, since the Clean Air Act of the late 1950s has proved that some things thought to be 'natural' were really man-made. Kay has enrolled for a French course – she's working her way through the text book in preparation. My work is going well. At least I should be well on my way with a new book before we go to France at the end of June. We've managed to book a flat in Menton for the whole of July. We've also booked a flat in Cornwall for a week during the Easter school holidays. A few days ago we took Oliver with Joan Sturmer to *Il Trovatore* at Covent Garden. It was the first opera Ollie had seen and he loved it and is keen to see more.* He and Charlotte are somewhat bored and homesick. Ollie began a diary in which he did a map of Tohunga Crescent and Hobson Bay labelled 'HOME: where things happen by themselves.' In view of the planning I do here to make things happen, I can't argue with that; but on the other hand the rewards for making the effort are enormous.

The Virgin in the Garden

Karl Miller ran the Modern course and I lectured on Eliot ('The Waste Land' and *Four Quartets*) and Auden, and managed to push a lecture on Mansfield into it as well. There were six or seven lecturers and we all attended every class. After the lecture the seventy students broke up into groups of ten or a dozen, and each lecturer took a seminar lasting two further hours on the subject of the lecture we'd just heard. Among the lecturers the one I got to know really well was A. S. Byatt – Antonia. She had published two successful novels but was at the time much less well known than her sister

* I later took him to Wagner's *Die Meistersinger* in Birmingham and his attention was total. We went by train, stayed in a hotel, and had a good supper at the interval.

Margaret Drabble, and there was great rivalry, and even hostility, between them.

Antonia was currently writing her third novel, *The Virgin in the Garden*, and she was that rare kind of novelist who likes to talk about the book while writing it. I was a willing listener. She was a brilliant scholar, a speed reader as I was not, so much better educated than I was I felt faintly intimidated by the range of her knowledge and her apparent ease with languages. I was never entirely sure what she thought of me. Was I a breath of fresh air, or a colonial simpleton? Possibly both – or neither – on reflection I can't say. But there was ease and trust between us. She would leave notes for me in my departmental pigeon-hole and I find I have still a number of these which remind me of the rapport that grew very quickly between us. 'Dear Karl, If you come in for this letter and are around at lunchtime it wd be nice to see you. Feel GLUM. Yrs ASD.' She was always ASD because she had been Miss Drabble and was now Mrs Duffy, despite her first husband's name, Byatt, being the one she had used in her earliest days as a writer and was now stuck with professionally.

Antonia had planned *The Virgin in the Garden* as the first of three novels based on her own experience as a young mid-twentieth-century woman, coming from Yorkshire and making her way into the world of books and theatre and academic scholarship still largely dominated by men. So I was hearing about the sisters Stephanie and Frederica Potter and their brother Marcus. Because Stephanie was older I imagined she was (though allowing they were both fictions) the one nearest to Antonia herself, and that Frederica was based on Margaret Drabble; but I was not entirely sure – and whatever the tensions between the actual sisters, which Antonia didn't deny or conceal, it was clear the novel was not designed as a weapon of sibling warfare. In fact she probably identified in different ways with both; and the question of identification was simplified in the second novel of the series, *Still Life*, when Stephanie dies in an accident.

I listened to it as a story, and it held my interest, though it was clearly going to be full of symbolism and of erudition, and in that sense quite different from anything I would want to write myself. When I read some of the pages she showed me I was always struck by Antonia's prose – good strong English prose, like home-baked bread, rich in texture, rewarding in content and without waste or surplus. It carried its story well; its characters were real; it did not allow dialogue to cruise like a default mode, but was efficient and plausible when dialogue was called for; and it gave the reader confidence that this was the work of a writer of exceptional intelligence and narrative competence.

But what interested me as much as the novel was Antonia herself, and her state of mind, which she was not unwilling, sometimes even eager, to talk about. The battle with sister Margaret was part of this picture. 'The only way I can deal with feelings about my sister', she wrote to me once, 'is to [. . .] "abdicate". It is a v common thing for siblings to be unable to do the same thing. I know identical twins who did athletics, & if one was winning the other didn't come second – she came <u>last</u>.'

But something even more important and dramatic had pushed sibling rivalry into the background. She'd had two children, Charles and Antonia, to her first husband, Ian Byatt, and two, Miranda and Isobel, to her second (and current), Peter Duffy. In July 1972, just three days after his eleventh birthday, Charles, being looked after by a woman who I think was the wife or partner of Frank Kermode, had been hit by a car. Antonia was constantly reliving the moment when someone, having taken the phone call, said 'Charles has been in an accident.' Antonia had responded, 'I must go to him', and the person at the phone had said, 'You can't – he's dead.'

She talked about this death and that terrible moment often, and was writing poems about it – in fact published one, 'Dead Boys', in the *TLS* – a dark poem in which she managed to some slight extent to depersonalise the subject. (In a letter to me later she wrote 'I wanted to write flatly and accurately about grief.') The opening line read 'One son is many sons': it did read like a cry of pain, but for all who have lost sons rather than just for herself.

But she was writing other poems that expressed her grief directly, and I have one she gave me, a handwritten copy of twelve short lines in four stanzas, the second and fourth line of each rhyming, addressed to the dead son and telling him that the ashes of her own cremation would be almost as insignificant in bulk as his, and that if she could, that is what she would choose for herself. The novel she was working on did not represent Charles or his loss in any way; but it was on her mind constantly during the writing, and when it appeared the following year it was dedicated to his memory, giving the dates of his birth and death.

One of Antonia's notes suggested a lunch with Claire Tomalin, and concluded, 'Have written a worse poem. In all day Tues, not sure about Wed, probably Thurs, certainly Fri. Home telephone 789 XXXX.' Claire was working on her Mansfield biography and Antonia had suggested that with my *Letters and Journals* due soon, she and I should be brought together. Another of her notes reads, 'Have only gone upstairs to deliver report to Valerie [secretary]. Sometimes seeing Valerie takes time but may not. C[laire] T[omalin] is a very beautiful & elegant & alarmingly sophisticated woman. Always makes me feel a frump. I make her feel frivolous. Though she is the more serious feminist.'

Claire was indeed all of those things, and with a remarkable and commanding voice to match. Karl Miller told me he had been deeply in love with her as an undergraduate at Cambridge. They were still good friends; but this fact about their past was delivered in his typical sardonic tone, as if it was something he remembered with some bitterness, yet was able to turn into a decidedly improper joke.* Karl had not been Claire's only lover at the time, and she had married another Cambridge contemporary, the journalist Nick Tomalin. The marriage had been turbulent, punctuated by affairs

* See 'Hospitality' in my *That Derrida Whom I Derided Died*, p. 100. In her memoir *A Life of My Own* (Penguin, 2017) Claire has written about her lifelong love for Karl.

(mainly, but not exclusively Nick's) and separations, moves towards divorce, and the births of four children; but they seemed to have settled into something approaching peace and harmony when Nick, covering the 1973 Arab–Israeli (Yom Kippur) War for the *Sunday Times*, had been killed by a Syrian heat-seeking missile.

At the time of our 1977 meeting Claire had recently resigned as literary editor of the *New Statesman* (Karl Miller had preceded her there) and would soon have the same post on the *Sunday Times*. She was on the committee of the Royal Literary Fund and of the London Library, and was to be a Booker judge that year or the next. She was now (or soon to be) married to the playwright Michael Frayn,* had published a book on Mary Wollstonecraft, and was currently working at the British Museum on her Mansfield book.

During our lunch, as the three of us talked about Mansfield, a person I described to Kay as 'a little old man' came shyly to our table and spoke in a whisper to Claire. She introduced us – and it was as if our conversation had conjured him up out of the ground. This was Richard, the brother of John Middleton Murry, Katherine's brother-in-law of whom she had sometimes seemed very fond and at others described as a teenage nuisance.

MY CONTACT AT PENGUIN CONTINUED to be Judith Burnley who had been so helpful at every stage of the Mansfield project, and there was a lunch with her too, disturbed by an IRA bomb scare somewhere not far enough away for comfort. Judith was a warm-hearted stylish woman who wore a lot of rings and jewellery and make-up and smart clothes and, once, an astonishing silver boiler suit like a Formula One driver. She lived in Bryanston Square, a W1 address which I thought her style matched. Her accent sounded to my inexpert

---

* Frayn and I were said to resemble one another in appearance, and I was sometime mistaken for him in London theatres. See 'Really', *That Derrida Whom I Derided Died*, p. 85.

ear exceedingly posh, and when she told me something about her friend Joanna I misheard it and said '*Jannah* – what an unusual name' and had to have it spelled out for me. There was a similar problem with a reference to Baarn, who turned out to be Byron.

Judith's first novel, *The Wife*, had come out from Heinemann in February of that year, and at one of these lunches she told me with great excitement that John Schlesinger had bought an option on it for a movie. Schlesinger's most recent movie, *Midnight Cowboy* with John Voight and Dustin Hoffman, had won important awards and had been a great box-office success so Judith's hopes were high. Neither she nor I knew then the hard truth about movie-making – that many more options are bought than movies made from them, and that what is called for in such situations is gratitude for the money, hope that the option will be renewed year after year, but with minimal expectation of an outcome. That way, disappointment is avoided. Schlesinger's movie of *The Wife* would never be made, but meanwhile, innocent of such knowledge, we celebrated as if it was a certainty.

The novel dedication read 'For F. B. with love', and I assumed this was her husband, Fred Burnley, a talented TV director, who had died two years previously after inhaling guano dust while filming something for a David Attenborough nature series. Judith was surprisingly frank about herself and described this marriage as virtually sexless, and explained that the important relationship in her life was with the writer Emanuel Litvinoff, an East End Jew. Litvinoff was a name that interested me because he was known for having confronted T. S. Eliot as an anti-Semite. Eliot's anti-Semitism was something the British literary world skirted around, avoided, refused to confront; but it was, I thought, such an essential part of the much-honoured Eliot (recent winner of the Nobel Prize for literature) it needed to be acknowledged and deplored. Litvinoff had read his poem 'To T. S. Eliot' at a crowded meeting of the Institute of Contemporary Arts, and by chance Eliot was present. Here are the opening lines:

> Eminence becomes you. Now when the rock is struck
> your young sardonic voice which broke on beauty
> floats amid incense and speaks oracles
> as though a god
> utters from Russell Square and condescends,
> high in the solemn cathedral of the air,
> his holy octaves to a million radios.
> I am not one accepted in your parish.
> Bleistein is my relative and I share
> the protozoic slime of Shylock . . .

It's not a good poem – too wordy, diffuse, heavy-handed, and runs on too long; but hard-hitting, echoing unmistakably lines from anti-Semitic early poems which Litvinoff thought Eliot should not have republished after the war when the appalling truths of the Holocaust had been revealed. On the occasion of the reading the poem produced deep shock and embarrassment. Eliot listened, his head forward against the chair in front, and was heard to murmur that it was a good poem, a very good poem, which clearly it is not. Dannie Abse, another Jewish poet, stood and made some kind of mollifying statement which no one quite heard. Then Stephen Spender stood up and protested that he was as much a Jew as Litvinoff and that he deplored this attack on Eliot who was a good man, a great poet, and a dear friend – which was entirely in character for Spender, who 'thought continually of those who were truly great', and who was not one of them, but aspired to be at least their dear friend.

That summer

On 25 June the five Steads left London in their VW van heading for the hovercraft from Ramsgate to Calais, and drove on to Arras where we camped a night. From there it was a leisurely trek from one camping ground to the next, spending a morning along the way in the region of Remoulins and the Pont du Gard looking for the place where we'd run off the road in 1972. It was all vividly familiar, the landscape, the event, and the lines of my poem, but the exact spot eluded us and we pushed through Aix-en-Provence (stopping at the atelier Cézanne), a camping ground at Fréjus, and reaching Menton on 1 July.

We were to spend the whole month there and had booked a spacious flat in 'Le Lutetia', the same apartment block where a permanent arrangement would later be made for the Mansfield Menton Fellowship. It was a repetition of the 1972 experience, though briefer, less effortful, with children that much older, and in constant summer weather; and it was this sojourn that cemented Menton into the family consciousness so we have been back many times. There were the same trips to the hill villages and across the border into Italy; the same swimming on the Menton seafront, and at the Garavan man-made beaches, or along the coast in a beautiful little bay just below the railway station at Roquebrune. Oliver and Charlotte climbed a steep path, l'Annonciade, marking the Stations of the Cross, up to a fourteenth-century monastery with a spooky basement crypt. On that path they caught geckos which they brought home and put in two or three large boxes enclosed at the top with fine wire netting, on the terrace that looked out to sea at the front of the apartment. Moths and butterflies were netted and released into the boxes, and were quarry for the geckos, which were released at the end of the month after a summer of ease and plenty.

In the van we had been able to bring books, including the ones I needed for my work, and from time to time I parked under the umbrella pines at the Garavan station and pushed on with a new chapter of my new Pound Yeats Eliot book. Everything seemed to fall effortlessly into place – everyone seemed happy: it was 'one of those times', always remembered with nostalgia, and on reflection with a kind of sadness that it had to come to an end – though not this time with a car crash, only with a timetable.

We left on 1 August and this time took the route through northern Italy, through Torino into Switzerland, then Germany and the Black Forest, Freiberg, back into France, Strasbourg, and once again Arras, where we camped, and tidied ourselves, and found a good restaurant in which to celebrate Oliver's fourteenth birthday, 7 August.

On the 8th we crossed Calais to Dover and back to London. On the 16th I flew to Edinburgh for drinks and a dinner with Wallace Robson and (my notebook says) 'a party at Arthur's Seat'. On the morning of the 17th I gave my lecture to the Scottish Universities Summer School and that afternoon flew back to London in time for *Das Rheingold*, the first of Wagner's Ring Cycle which we were now to see in sequence at the Coliseum. *Die Walküre* followed on the 20th, *Siegfried* on the 24th, and *Götterdämmerung* on the 27th. On the 29th we left for San Francisco, Tahiti, and home. In my pocket there was a letter from Wallace Robson thanking me for my 'splendid lecture', and in my head the long slow drumbeat of Siegfried's exhilarating and terrible funeral music.

Postscript:

Claire Tomalin's book, *Katherine Mansfield: A Secret Life*, was long delayed in the writing and did not appear until 1987. Karl got me to review it for the *LRB*. I admired its diligence and good sense, and especially its revelations about Mansfield's health problems and their probable source and consequences; but I could not read the description of her as 'sexually ambiguous, with a husband and a wife, and lovers of both sexes' as anything but a picturesque misrepresentation.* I accused her of slipping into the clichés and trigger words of the feminist movement, and letting the times do her thinking for her. Claire did not respond; and when we next met she simply joked about her mistake, which I'd pointed out, of taking the word 'kit' to mean a suit of clothing rather than a flax

* *London Review of Books*, November 1987, and *Kin of Place*, pp. 39–46.

carrier bag. But she must have wanted to reply and I suspect Karl talked her out of it.

My review was reprinted, however, in the collection of essays I called *Answering to the Language*, and when a review of that book in the *TLS* quoted what I had said about her description of Mansfield as 'sexually ambiguous' she took that as an opportunity to reply, and we had a spirited exchange, neither backing down.*

* *TLS*, March and April 1991.

10.
The Fellowship and a Taste of Freedom

Breaking the neck, a movie, and Muldoon

In the next two or three years I did what I think was my best teaching. The big lectures to first-years usually went well enough; and the stage two tutorials were probably better at least in being more informal and 'close quarters'; but best were my lecture/seminars to MA classes. These were on New Zealand literature, including always some aspect of Mansfield, and on modern literary criticism, where Allen Tate always figured. But I had one class and paper all to myself, on Pound, Eliot and Modernist poetry, running parallel with the book I had begun seriously at UCL and was pressing on with while teaching. At the end of 1978 I wrote to Keith Sinclair of this class, 'they are so brilliant it's embarrassing – 13 A passes out of 17, and I've marked and re-marked them'.

My own poetry was developing in tandem with my teaching and a new collection, *Walking Westward*, was about to be published by my own imprint, The Shed.

Driving to the orthopaedic clinic

A skein of ducks
and then another

rippling eastward out
high and fast
over the estuary.

Or it might have been
two lines of telegraphy
an impression on the eye
dashed down:

'11 a.m. / tide low
sun on mangroves.'

Long before . . .

Long before the sun goes out for ever
it seems the trees will take over
and the insects among their branches
and the animals underneath them.
This the gods have decreed because we subvert
their Cosmic Joke with ungodlike efforts at order.

O Brave New World
without pogroms and sham trials
without cities and the bombs to rubble them
without the shame of history! –
nothing but the mindless movement of leaves
and ignorant jaws ceaselessly devouring.

These were from 'Breaking the Neck – an Autumn Sketchbook'. Bodysurfing with the family at Karekare I had caught an enormous wave at low tide and been picked up and dumped straight down on my head into the shallow water ahead of the surge. I have a vivid memory of being swirled around bodily, with light shining beautifully through the green water and the shells and sand that were going around with me as the wave rolled in, and the certainty that something very bad had happened. I came out of the water with my left arm hanging useless. The surfies laid me down on the sand, and when I tried to sit up I experienced the worst shot of pain I'd ever felt – so extreme I didn't move again for many hours, just lay on my back in a state of terror while things were done to me. The rescue helicopter took me to Middlemore Hospital in South Auckland (known affectionately to some of its medical staff as BroRepairs) where I was X-rayed and a neck fracture was confirmed – fortunately 'stable' or I would almost certainly have been quadriplegic. I had to spend some days there, sedated (a large needle in the backside), drinking soup in a cup, sleeping with my head in a neck brace and between two sandbag pillows; and then there were many weeks in a brace while the fracture mended, the damaged nerves grew back, and the left arm regained muscles that had wasted. But all this time I was still functioning normally, and life and my teaching went on.

Kay was now back at the University Library, in the Law School, and later in 'NZ & P' (New Zealand and the Pacific) where she would be my ready research assistant especially later when I was writing *The Singing Whakapapa* with its revelations about the Church Missionary Society and the role my great-great-grandfather John Flatt played in the exposure of unauthorised land purchases. We had only one car, and because we believed in the healthy benefits of walking, one would drive to work and the other home, so each would have one between-Parnell-and-Princes Street walk with, either way, a double hill climb.

We had arrived back in August 1977 just in time to see the first private screening of *Sleeping Dogs*, due soon for public release. I was struck early on in the movie by how well it worked by contrasts, juxtaposing the calmness and beauty of the Coromandel scenes and the violence in the streets of Auckland. But as the movie went on what I am now able to think of as Roger Donaldson's (and also Ian Mune's, who was one of two script-writers) characteristic faults began to show: overstatement, melodrama, and a casualness about plausibility. I remain an admirer of Donaldson for his practicality, his charm and refusal to be stopped by obstacles (who else could have persuaded the New Zealand Air Force to provide fighter planes and aerial attacks at no cost?); and when asked at the time I spoke only positively and admiringly of what he had done. But I did regret especially the script, and the loss of any political subtlety or depth. Ian's idea of theatrical riches did not seem to relate to language so much as to volume. It was as if, when finding himself at a loss for where to go next, he had a character get very angry and shout 'You bast-*ard!*' Ian (who played Smith's friend Bullen) had also written a very long death for himself, which involved an exceedingly protracted downhill roll; and in the first few days of public screenings it was said Roger was still busy cutting some of that scene's embarrassing excess.

But the movie had a local success which would not be possible now. A New Zealand feature film was a rare event, and this one was showing all over New Zealand to full houses. Sam Neill's movie career was launched; so was Roger's, who would follow with *Smash Palace* starring Bruno Lawrence, then a new version of *Mutiny on the Bounty* for the Dino De Laurentiis company – and Hollywood.

The paperback of *Smith's Dream* was released yet again with, on the cover, a still from the movie of Sam and Ian up to their waists in a cold stream; and it seemed for some years almost every secondary school child in the country studied the novel, and usually the film with it. I accepted invitations to visit secondary schools and teachers' colleges when I could – visits that often involved scary flights in very small commercial planes.

News came that Roger and Ian would be taking *Sleeping Dogs* to the Cannes Film Festival, and its local success continued. I received thundering messages of congratulation from far-left groups (including one from the Marxist-Leninist Workers Party) who saw *Smith's Dream* as a forecast of where capitalism was taking us – into fascism and the American Way – a view which was in turn promoted by the behaviour of Rob Muldoon, elected Prime Minister in 1975. Muldoon's use of the language could be impressive, but the eloquence and fluency which came naturally to him was mostly overlooked because the strongest impression his speeches made was their uncompromising abrasiveness and aggression. He was politically unscrupulous and (for example) used knowledge that came to him as head of the SIS to make it known in Parliament that the police had been questioning the senior Labour MP Colin Moyle about 'homosexual activities' – this in order to deflect attention from the questions Moyle had been asking about possibly dishonest dealings by Muldoon's accountancy firm.

Many people were alarmed and there were calls to talkback radio referring to *Smith's Dream* and saying the character of Volkner, who takes control of the country and calls in the Americans to help against freedom fighters in the hills, was based on, or meant to be, Muldoon.

Towards the end of 1978 there was a visit to New Zealand by the West German president Walter Scheel, and the University of Auckland decided to confer an honorary doctorate on him. The event was in daylight and out of doors, in the grounds and gardens of Old Government House, and when the speeches were over our Chancellor, Henry Cooper, introduced Kay and me to Muldoon, who said at once, looking at me, 'Oh so you're *that one,* are you?' He was thinking of *Smith's Dream* – and more particularly of the movie. 'They were saying it was about me,' he said. He explained that he never went to the movies these days – his presence drew too much attention – but he'd felt he had to arrange for a private showing of *Sleeping Dogs* so he could check on why this was being said about it, and about him.

I explained that he was not so well known, and was in fact in the Opposition, when I was writing the book. This seemed to imply, 'No of course it was not about you.' I was being polite to the visitor, but Kay thought too polite.

'Yes,' she said. 'You've just grown in to the role.'

Muldoon hoisted his cheek scar and uttered his famous mirthless laugh. 'Uhk, uhk, uhk . . .'

Another person who did not normally go to the cinema was Frank Sargeson. Movies never figured in his conversation, and my guess is that if he had been to one since the old silent-screen days it might have been during World War II. But he came with me to see *Sleeping Dogs*. He looked stunned afterwards and had nothing to say. He might have thought it was awful – and just as moviemaking, I suppose it was; but I suspect if I'd asked what he thought he would have said, 'Buggered if I know, Karl.' It's the occasion that stays with me, like a little piece of our literary history.

But when I look at the volume of his letters I see that Frank had been very early to make the connection of the novel with Muldoon. To Phil Wilson he had written:

> But Karl, yes, his Smith's Dream is out at last. Very readable. He's kinda followed Graham Greene and kinda written a B.O.P. [Boy's Own Paper] adventure story, making the hero from the Left instead of the Right, tying it all up with the Cong etc. Intelligent stuff, it could be popular and DO GOOD. I hope so, though perhaps better if Muldoon read it by accident and found something had got under his skin. You'll get pleasure from this book.

The 'kinda . . . kinda' and the 'B.O.P.' suggestion sound like notes at least of uncertainty/reservation. I think the novel was for Frank, as for so many people, one that was difficult to 'place', and especially so coming from me. To Brasch he wrote a few weeks later, after the same B.O.P. comment, 'I thought it all most agreeable and refreshing reading. If K's not careful he'll become known as our Graham Greene.'*

---

* *Letters of Frank Sargeson*, ed. Sarah Shieff, Vintage, 2012; to Wilson, pp. 462–63, to Brasch, p. 465.

Bastion Point was another matter that had fixed Muldoon in the eyes of liberal-minded New Zealanders as a bully indifferent to our history and its injustices. This beautiful piece of land overlooking the Waitematā Harbour had been gifted by the local iwi, Ngāti Whātua, to the Crown in 1859 for defence purposes at the time of the Russian scare, with the idea that it would be returned when the need was past; but the Crown now claimed ownership. Land developers had their eyes on it. What splendid mansions could be built up there, looking out over the harbour towards Rangitoto and beyond. What profits there were to be made – and what a waste that it had not been exploited! Muldoon was for selling it.

Ngāti Whātua occupied the block in 1977, in protest against their dispossession, and to protect it from the developers. Over the following months the Crown negotiated and made apparently juicy but in fact derisory offers. There were elders keen to profit by the sale, but Joe Hawke, representing younger and more militant Māori, refused to budge. Outside moral support was at first welcome, and the Stead family joined in. It was a quieter foretaste of what would come for us in the Springbok protests of 1981.

In May 1978 Muldoon ordered in troops and police to evict the protesters and break up their camp. I wrote to Allen Curnow, who was away on leave and wanting local news, that Muldoon

> . . . did it on a big paramilitary scale. Flew in hundreds of police from all around the country – gathered them together at an airbase north of the harbour – then they came in a military convoy over the Harbour Bridge, in army trucks, with equipment to knock down the protesters' shelters – a huge operation, and quite unnecessary.*

This was another public event that found its way into my sonnets.

* The matter was not resolved until the Waitangi Tribunal ruled in favour of the protest, and a subsequent (Labour) government returned the land to Ngāti Whātua.

A fellowship and a novel – with Janet?

I read Frank's *Sunset Village* in 1978 and discovered he had used things I'd said in conversation, and experiences I'd told him about as a hospital orderly at the receiving end of the laundry chute in the Infectious Diseases Block, and also working in the morgue. Frank's prose in these years, which he called his 'Mandarin style', was taking his readers by surprise – so ornate, elaborate, such a radical change from the Kiwi vernacular by which he had established a new direction for our fiction. I was at first puzzled until I recognised it as 'camp', a style which made room for his identity as a gay man and a gay writer. This was an identity he still preferred not to acknowledge publicly (and he disliked the new use of the word 'gay' which he saw as the misappropriation of a useful adjective); but it was there in the new prose, signalled to those alert and attentive and sympathetic – prose with a flourish. This is something I still haven't seen acknowledged by critics writing about his later work.

He phoned and was depressed that his novel had not even made a short-list of ten for the Wattie Awards. I reminded him of the celebration just put on, with a whole issue of *Islands*, to celebrate his seventy-fifth birthday; and told him the Wattie thing didn't matter (though of course it did) – he was an honoured icon and there to stay, never to be forgotten. He said no one in New Zealand takes seriously a writer who stays and tries to make a go of it here. I knew that was partly true but tried to convince him it had changed or was changing.

At about this time I drove him home after we'd had a meal at the Peking restaurant. We walked up first to the university where the car was parked, went in to pick up my bag and he commented with wonder, and I thought displeasure, on the tidiness of my office. It was like his reaction to our refurbished house – too 'boo-geois'. I said I needed order to work in. He'd been grumbling during the meal about Robin Dudding and now he seemed displeased with me and my Scandinavian orderliness.

When we got to his place he took me in and gave me a tour of his disorder – not that I hadn't seen it many times. The book shelves were over-full and jammed tight. Letters had been laid out on the bed in the room that had been Harry's, and when the layer was too thick a blanket was laid over it and a new layer started – so it was like levels of silt, geological strata, the recent history of Frank. There were piles of books everywhere, some that had been tipped and spilled across the floor. The curtains were tatty. There was a large stain on the ceiling, and the fridge smelled of elderly cheese.

While he made us a cup of tea I suggested the break he was planning to give himself on finishing the current work might be the time for creating a radical new orderliness, and I offered to help, but he rejected that because each individual decision, about whether to throw something out or keep it, and where to lodge it if kept, would have to be his. It would involve new negotiations with the Turnbull Library, to which already he had sold a lot of his papers. They would come and take stuff away.

But he grasped onto the idea of a clean-up in that planned break, and seemed at last happier – even thanked me for cheering him up. My poem about him, 'A Warm Wind from the East', published in the *LRB* just before he died, captured that disorder at 14 Esmonde Road behind the green hedge.*

TOWARDS THE END OF 1977 PROFESSOR MUSGROVE retired as Head of Department, and after the staff had been canvassed I was offered the post. I declined and it went to Forrest Scott. At some time during that year the university had decided to establish a three-year senior research fellowship. It seemed an opportunity much more attractive than being HOD, and I applied for it. Nicholas Tarling, Dean of the Arts Faculty, at once ruled my application ineligible

---

* 'A Warm Wind from the East', *Collected Poems, 1951–2006*, Auckland University Press, 2008, p. 181.

on the grounds that the intent was to bring in new blood from outside. I could see the point of this; however the terms in which the idea had been proposed did not make any such stipulation, the advertisement made no mention of it, and it seemed to me it could be argued equally that the best applicant, wherever he or she came from, should get the post. I thought also that though the scheme was ambitious in one sense, it was penny-pinching in another: the salary for the post had been set at the senior lecturer level, so it meant that anyone of real distinction, particularly coming from overseas, would almost certainly have to be prepared to take a drop in salary. I was ready to do that myself.

Nick Tarling was English-born, a Cambridge graduate, an expert in South East Asian history, and also actor and specialist in classical music and opera whose Sunday-morning talks about music I listened to with admiration. He was a witty chap, unmarried, possibly gay but whose friends seemed to be all elderly ladies. It was as if he was one of them and they were going to grow old together. He was said to suffer very low blood pressure, and to be exceedingly grumpy in the mornings; nonetheless he swam daily near his home on the North Shore. Nick was the dragon enrolling undergraduates had to face for an approving signature (or refusal) when their chosen courses deviated from accepted combinations. I liked him, admired him, and enjoyed his jokes which were usually delivered in a sort of half-whispered growl, with his chin tucked down and a wicked glint in the eye. Kay once went with the opera tour-group he took away, usually to the Sydney Opera House, and found him delightful company.* But his opposition to my application made him an enemy at this time; he figured as such in family dinner-table conversations, and my loyal children had various plans for him, such as ordering an enormous pile of horse manure, or a pile of firewood, to be delivered to the drive of his house. A two-year sub

* I have a poem about Nick, 'who died swimming', in my 2018 collection, *That Derrida Whom I Derided Died*, p. 114, 'Unusual Obsequies'.

to the *Reader's Digest Home Improvements Manual* was another suggestion; or a taxi to take him to the morgue or the zoo – or just an ambulance. I don't think any of these plans was executed – the pleasure was in devising them.

I speak about these things lightly, and of Nick Tarling as if he were a kindly old codger; but when I look at my file on this application, what emerges is Nick as dealer and academic tyrant. He couldn't tolerate not having his own way with his fiefdom, and when he'd made up his mind on something he would get what he wanted even if it meant bending or ignoring or breaking the rules. He did not want my application to go before the faculty. First he invented a rule that I could not apply on my own behalf but an application should be made on my behalf by my Head of Department, Forrest Scott. He probably thought the department would oppose the idea but they didn't. When the application came from Scott, Nick said he would not put it before the faculty 'to save Stead embarrassment'. When I insisted the faculty be informed of my application he did this more or less in passing and without information about what I was proposing to do with it if successful, while two other applicants' proposals (both in his own subject of South East Asian history) were described in detail. Nick then proposed that my application be set aside, and when the faculty divided 15/15 on this, he used his casting vote to get his way. That led to an appeal by me to the Vice Chancellor who had then to go to a Senate Committee for a ruling.

So there were long needless delays, but I had help especially from Sebastian Black, and also from Jock Asher, Keith Sorrenson, Keith Sinclair and others in the faculty, and my application was at last allowed to go forward and was successful. I proposed to undertake three projects: the editing of Maurice Duggan's *Collected Short Stories* for AUP; the completion of a collection of essays on New Zealand writers and writing, which would also be published by AUP with the title *In the Glass Case*; and most important, the continuation towards completion of *Pound, Yeats, Eliot and the Modernist Movement*.

Half way into my second year of the fellowship two of my proposals had been completed; and by the end of the third the Pound Yeats Eliot book was well advanced. But it was also my intention during this time to continue writing poetry, and possibly fiction. 'Scoria' was added to *Walking Westward*, and new Catullus pieces were being drafted. In mid-1979, as I began to feel sure I was fulfilling what I'd promised to do, I wrote to Janet with an idea for a novel based on our shared 'Sargeson experience' in 1955.

> I had an idea at the weekend that you and I should write a novel together. I would write the first twenty pages and send it to you and then you would write the next twenty and send it back – and so on. It would be first person narrative. I would be Curl Skidmore; you would be Cecelia Skyways. Frank would figure as Melior Farbro, the old master. The first twenty pages would be devoted to what happened and didn't happen at Farbro's place 25 years ago. I have ideas about how it would go on.

Janet accepted this proposal without any hesitation: twenty pages each, by turns – she thought that was an excellent idea. It could be called *Farbro's Place*. She said that time should be recorded before it was forgotten.

We were both to be in Wellington for a writers' conference in September, and I suggested we should have a meal together. We went, just the two of us, to the Wellington Settlement where the back-and-forth plan for the novel was agreed again. She was to hear about it next when my twenty pages were done – which I hoped would be soon. It was still Janet; the sense of friendship and trust restored during my Dunedin visit continued; but a restaurant was a public space, not one she could be at ease in, and I was reminded of that shy retiring abashed woman of *autre temps*.

I was able to tell her that during my last visit Frank had been in fine form, and we'd sung along together to the fourth movement of Beethoven's 9th – the 'Hymn to Joy'; and how he'd told me about Clarry, and his eyes had filled with tears. First he'd thought Murdoch was going to be his new love after the death of Harry; but now it was Clarry. But then he'd caught a glimpse of 'Murdy' at Takapuna and had found he still 'felt a pang'.

So the dinner passed off, awkwardly, shyly – but at least we were friends, and the joint novel was confirmed. It was during this conference that Michael King caught a photograph of Janet and me together. In it I am saying 'Look – Michael's going to photograph us' and telling her to smile; and she is putting her hand to her mouth and pulling away with an expression of uncertainty. It's a picture that catches perfectly the Janet of that time and those public occasions.

The writing of the novel began on 15 October (1979), and there's a notebook which traces its development – the characters, the events, the decision to move the narrative back from 1955 to 1951 (the year of the protracted Waterfront dispute which would be part of the story) – all this without any mention of Janet's role in the writing. I was getting it straight on to the typewriter – something I hadn't done before – and it was simply racing away from me, or with me, those ongoing, long-running sentences inspired by Günter Grass's novel *Dog Years*. By 24 October I had written eleven pages, and by 9 November, thirty-one – over 15,000 words, at a rate of about 750 words per day. A month after beginning, two chapters were finished – thirty-six pages, 18,000 words; and though Cecelia Skyways and her Zen Master, Bodhidharma of the Web, and her letters, one to the Blessed Virgin, another to the Prime Minister, had all figured, there was no longer any thought of the real Janet who was supposed to be my co-author. The notes go on until this one: 'Novel (first draft) finished on Jan 12, exactly three months after starting.'

So the novel that would be *All Visitors Ashore* was written without benefit of Janet, and would become in time probably the outcome I liked most of all the work I did on that three-year research fellowship. But having done it, I took fright from it. It was so unfamiliar, so different, an aberration. It alarmed me. I put it away in a drawer and couldn't bring myself to read it, even to look at it for a long time. This was 1979, and it would not be published until 1984.

Wystan to Carlos

I had been invited to that 1979 Wellington conference to give a keynote address on the current state of New Zealand poetry. This was the lecture, much talked and written about subsequently, which I called 'From Wystan to Carlos: Modern and Modernism in Recent New Zealand Poetry'. It was a piece of revisionist NZ Lit. Hist., changing the terms in which we discussed our poetry from the nationalistic ones Curnow had put into all our heads ('the New Zealand thing, the regional thing, the real thing'), shifting the focus outward to the bigger picture of Anglophone poetry in the wider world, and the influences that had been brought to bear on the practice here; and I was well equipped to do this because the Pound Yeats Eliot book was giving me a set of terms and a framework. So I saw Curnow and his generation as products of what I called 'Modern' poetry in the twentieth century, where the prime debt was to British Auden and his cohort, and to the best of the Georgians before them; and the Ian Wedde generation as Modernists, whose debt was to Americans Ezra Pound, William Carlos Williams and their descendants. And all this was neatly illustrated (giving me my title) by the fact that Allen had called his son Wystan, and Wedde had called his son Carlos – Wystan Auden and Carlos Williams, the prototype progenitor in each case. I characterised these two schools as 'closed', the Moderns, in that they used closed poetic forms, and 'open', the Modernists who tended to sprawl and let the poem's internal pressures dictate shape and form.

It was neat enough, persuasive up to a point; but Lit. Hist. is a crude instrument, and ignores how most poets dislike being fitted into schools and categories. Alex Fry in the *Listener* described the lecture as 'surpassingly elegant . . . a superb performance . . . it will undoubtedly be heard of more'; but he noticed 'most of his auditors felt uneasy'. I noticed this too, not 'most' but certainly some – Lauris Edmond and Hone Tuwhare, for example, side by side in the audience, neither looking pleased with what they were hearing; and at question time Hone complained in an imperfectly audible hum, troubled I think (as others were) at not having been 'numbered in the song'. Ian Wedde, who had been 'numbered', challenged me as I went out the door, protesting at my having used the word 'open' to describe his *Sonnets to Carlos*. And Allen Curnow, who had probably been thinking I was someone he could count on for unequivocal praise, was not pleased to have his own critical terms threatened with displacement, and was troubled even more by my pointing out that there'd been a gap in his production of new poems lasting at least a decade. In the next session he took a kind of revenge by rejecting all 'theory' about poetic movements (as if he'd never had one) and offered instead, 'I just write poems'.

I did not quite understand why reference to his years of poetic blackout should have been such a sensitive point, even an embarrassment, for Curnow, because it seemed to me to illustrate the authenticity of his work. To use an Auden phrase Allen, as I saw it, was being 'lived by history'. There had been a gap in his work while in some interior way he was absorbing what history required of him. When he emerged from it the new poems were 'something different, something nobody counted on', least of all Curnow himself. Of course if the silence had gone on I would never have referred to it; but it seemed to have ended triumphantly, and I was trying to celebrate it, and the new work it had made possible.

In fact there was a sense in which from Allen's point of view what I had to say on this subject could have been much worse. There had been a novel I might have written brewing up, a very Henry Jamesian idea, of an older poet (this was thinking of Curnow and James K. Baxter) who fell silent as a brilliant younger practitioner took all the public attention; and who then came roaring back into full poetic life when the younger poet died. Baxter died aged forty-six in 1972, the year that marked Curnow's resurgence. The idea was fictional, but it contained a significant grain of truth. Fortunately for good cross-crescent relations there was another idea for a novel, and this was the one I had proposed to Janet, and which was now racing away without her.

I knew Allen was not pleased, but I only learned from Terry Sturm's biography that when the text of my lecture was published in *Islands* he made many pages of dissenting annotations. We did exchange notes on the subject; and as Sturm records it, it was an unusually civil difference of opinion, though now and then there was an edge. When Allen mocked the practitioners of 'open form' as 'the Open Brethren' I replied that if there was an Open Brethren there was a Closed Brethren too, and I suggested that on their behalf he might be suffering from 'critical agoraphobia'.

Oddly the one suggestion in my lecture he really couldn't bear was a speculative footnote suggesting that the irregular setting of one of the new poems in *Trees, Effigies* . . . might have been influenced by the young poets of the magazine that called itself *Freed*. This provoked his one public response – a letter to *Islands* insisting this was not so. *Freed* had, he said, 'passed unnoticed by me'. When I grumbled about this letter and said that he and his mates Glover and Davin had been 'sniping at me', his reply was immensely touching. 'Sniping at you was, & is, as far from my mind as from my heart, & the latter has been much troubled by feeling that so it must appear.'

'From Wystan to Carlos' was one of the larger prose pieces planned for that collection of essays to be called *In the Glass Case*. Another, done the previous year and published first in *Islands*, was my study of John Mulgan and his novel *Man Alone*. This was one of those pieces that caused me to be characterised as 'controversial', because it challenged the Mulgan myth, warmly embraced by our literary community, that John had been a good left-liberal denied the Rhodes scholarship he deserved by a conservative university which disapproved of his politics. It was not that I wouldn't have enjoyed affirming this myth; only that the evidence showed clearly it was untrue. A check on the academic records of the time revealed that Mulgan's performance had been weaker than his principal competitors; and that he had not rated above them in sport and social engagement. There had been no political interference and no injustice.* He had been simply less deserving.

Keith Sinclair, who was writing a history of the University of Auckland, was urged by Mulgan's angry sister, Lady Dorothea Turner, to prove 'Jesus K. Stead' (as she called me) wrong. Keith replied that he would have liked to have done this for her, but 'although I read a considerable amount of evidence, I could not find anything to suggest that John Mulgan did not get the Rhodes because of his political opinions'. Dan Davin was also outraged. In a letter to Keith he referred to Karl Stead's 'damn silly article in *Islands*' and asked 'Is he going off his chump?' And when the collection of essays was published he gave it a distinctly unfriendly notice in the *Review of English Studies*. Glover who referred to me in a letter as Allen's 'foster child', said as far as he was concerned I didn't exist.

Other revisionary critical articles that went into the *In the Glass Case* collection were ones on Sylvia Ashton-Warner, who had been pretty much ignored by the literary community, as if popularity in the United States and a Hollywood movie ruled her out of serious critical consideration, and another on David Ballantyne, who had been badly neglected. The piece on Ronald Hugh Morrieson was also included; and the introduction to Duggan's *Collected Stories*.

Ashton-Warner had combined fiction with theories about teaching (including teaching Māori children) in a way that was truly original and had been recognised in the United States; yet here in New Zealand she'd felt scorned by the education bureaucracy, and ignored by fellow-writers. She was a colourful

---

* The essay which recounts these findings will be found reprinted in my *Kin of Place*, pp. 156–96, with a postscript describing the reactions it produced. Keith gave me copies of these letters at the time.

personality, given to self-dramatisation, grand gestures and over-statement; but why the feminists who took up Robin Hyde (not that Hyde was undeserving) did not turn their attention also to Ashton-Warner was a puzzle. Ballantyne and Morrieson were different cases: they were Kiwi chaps, both boozers (one ruinously so) which made it (oddly) easier to argue the case on their behalf, and they were both to gain (posthumously) new readers.

Duggan was a more complex and difficult case. He aspired when sober to middle-class propriety and order, and yet in his best work rebelled against it – against the self who read his own work in a stagy, sort-of-posh voice, and liked always to have a new car and tidy book shelves of first-edition hardbacks. My difficulty as his critic and editor was to make clear the limits of the conventional fictions that had been most admired, and the merits of those raffish stories that (as Katherine Mansfield liked to say of some of her own) revealed the slug under the leaf.

The Mansfield essay, which I had given first as a lecture at UCL, corrected her husband John Middleton Murry's account of the sequence of her best stories and how they related to the ups and downs of her relations with him. This account had gone unchallenged for half a century, and I was able to show it was a characteristically egotistical (and wishful) fiction which would have enraged Mansfield had she lived to see it.

There were essays on New Zealand poets as well. The limits of Fairburn were (perhaps too robustly) exposed. The case I had been early to make for Curnow as poet was affirmed and extended; but his view of our literary history was challenged, and some younger poets he had overlooked were noticed with approval. Baxter in particular got his due.

Reviews of this book were good on the whole, but this or that of its pieces gave mild offence, or was challenged, or (the case against Fairburn in particular) deplored. The Mulgan article which debunked the myth was considered by men like Bertram and Davin (who claimed to know better because they'd known *him*) almost unforgivable. But the strangest accusation brought against the book was that there were important poets whose work I had failed to discuss. It was as if I had some semi-public function, and therefore a duty to acknowledge merit wherever it existed. To fail to do so was deliberate and malicious – as if I had been an anthologist and had 'left them out'. Kevin Ireland complained in *Landfall* 135 that I had omitted to discuss a group of 'well-published names' who happened to be my contemporaries.* 'Somehow things have got to a pretty rum state' he wrote 'when a noted critic can go to some trouble to lecture at us then publish his rulings on N.Z. poetry today, yet omit to mention O'Sullivan, one of our few poets of mature distinction.'

The collection was completed in the second year of my senior research fellowship and published in the third, 1981. That book alone would have justified the award. I should have dedicated it to Nick.

1980 – and the *Wanderjahr*

Nineteen-eighty was for me a year of hard work, and of a ten-week *Wanderjahr*. I was pushing on both with the Pound Yeats Eliot book and with new poems. I judged an extraordinary New Zealand Book Award for fiction, in which the short-list when we reached it included novels by Frame, Ballantyne, Wendy Simon, Fiona Kidman, one from each of the Middleton brothers, O. E. and Ian, and a short story collection by Owen Marshall. The Shed published *Walking Westward* and I was distributing it to bookshops around the country. I was on a committee to appoint a new Professor of English at Canterbury from eleven applicants. Dave Mitchell was running regular poetry readings at the Globe in Auckland and I read there from time to time. My supervision of Ruth Harley's PhD

* Kevin himself was one of these. He would have to wait until 2016 for his work to be discussed by me. See *Shelf Life: Reviews, Replies and Reminiscences*, Auckland University Press, 2016, pp. 125–34. There was a lot of ground to cover!

continued.[*] John Dutch sent me four of his novels for comment, and I read and annotated one in meticulous detail. I began writing for Karl Miller's new magazine the *London Review of Books* and reviewed fiction for the *Sydney Morning Herald*.

And then I went abroad and seemed to organise my travel arrangements more or less *en route*, changing them as I went to keep up with new possibilities that presented themselves along the way – and writing an ongoing open form poem-account as it happened, which I called 'Yes T. S. – A Narrative'.[†] The principle governing the writing of this long 'process poem' was a quotation from Louis Aragon's *Paris Peasant*:

> So I let myself go. The days glided by in this sort of baccarat
> game . . . An idea of myself was all that was in my head.
> An idea that was born gently. A forgotten word, an air.
> One feels it bound up with one's whole self, . . . like a form
> seeking another similar form with a lantern in the middle
> of the night . . .

There were surprises sprung on me by circumstance, one so unlikely it might be thought I invented it. It's difficult to convey the sense of shock I felt, arriving in Paris alone and without celebration on my forty-eighth birthday, continuing to read in my hotel bed Jean Rhys's novel *After Leaving Mr Mackenzie*, and coming on a passage that seemed almost a description of myself and my situation.

> He was forty-eight years old.
> Paris had attracted him as a magnet does a needle . . .
> He hid behind a rather deliberately absent-minded

* Ruth was a special friend and went on to an exceptional public career in arts administration in Wellington, where she headed the Film Commission, and in Australia where for some years she was chair of Screen Australia. She is currently (2019) chair of NZ On Air.

† *Collected Poems, 1951–2006*, pp. 143–71.

> expression. Once, in his youth, he had published a small book of poems. But when it came to actualities his mind was a tight and very tidy mind.

In Paris I saw *The Winter's Tale* in French, and was caught up in a street march with mine workers chanting 'Giscard, t'es foutu – les mineurs sont dans la rue!'*

I went briefly to Menton, and flew from Nice to Munich. Landing in a snow storm I heard the news that the Hollywood hack Ronald Reagan, star of B-grade movies, had won the US election. It seemed deeply depressing – even frightening – but for the wrong reasons. Everyone of liberal persuasion thought Reagan would reignite the Cold War. But in fact and *au contraire*, he would meet peaceably with Gorbachev. The real harm was to be economic rather than military. Reaganomics would link up with Thatcherite monetarism and before long would be invading and damaging all the Western economies including New Zealand's. Ahead for us lay, not nukes, but Roger Douglas and Ruth Richardson.

In Regensburg I talked to Elisabeth Augustin, an elderly German-Jewish writer, who had survived the war in Amsterdam, but had had to wear the yellow star, and had not been able to save her mother from the gas chambers of Auschwitz. We were having tea and cakes together when I said in a rather chatty undisciplined way that everyone in Germany was so kind and generous it was hard to see how '*all that*' had happened. Elisabeth fixed me with a stare and replied firmly, 'You know *exactly* how it happened. It's in *Smith's Dream*.'

And then there was a conference on Commonwealth literature in Aarhus in Denmark where I met Ulla Ampersand, who at our first meeting explained to me that there was a correct order to eat the various items on a smorgasbord. A great deal about Commonwealth

---

* 'Giscard [i.e. President Giscard d'Estaing] you're fucked – the miners are in the street.'

literature was transacted at that conference and I participated to the full – even to the extent that Carole Durix told me I frightened people. But I was somewhat distracted. When the conference ended I had no idea whether I would ever see Ulla again. She was my incandescent Dane, my excitable Viking and the representative charge to which I would always have to plead guilty. When she appeared as Uta Haverstrom in my third novel, *The Death of the Body*, she was the sexual puritan who keeps the unnamed narrator at a proper distance. In this the fictional Uta differed from real Ulla. I always felt she believed she ought to be keeping us apart. Propriety was important to her, like the correct order in which to deal with a smorgasbord – and there was her much-loved husband, and my much-loved wife, and our adored (three each) children. But there was also a Scandinavian literalness and practicality about her: against propriety, excitement could not always be denied its victories.

On the train towards Holland I added a few elegiac lines to the long 'process poem' I was writing:

> These are the high far grey clouds over Jutland
> and behind them paler clouds through which
> the weak light of another morning breaks.
> Here is a lake with trees on the skyline
> and on the far shore water lying under poplars.
> These fields with cows could be the fields of home.
>
> Soon the rails will run out of Danish landscapes,
> there'll be none left to display. No more the waterbirds
> of the lowlands will be Danish waterbirds,
> no more the hedges and the fence-lines Danish.

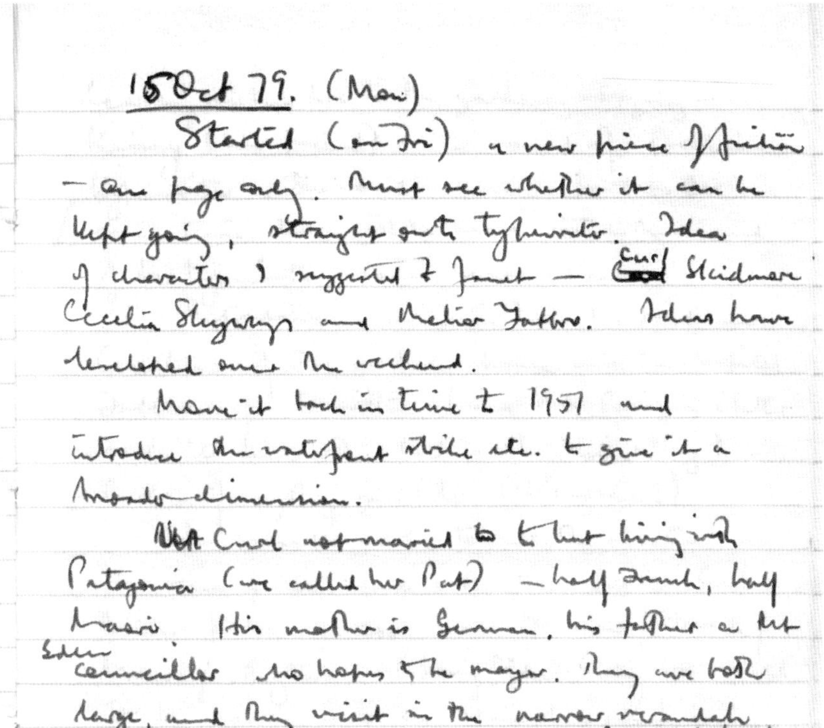
15 Oct 79. (Mon)
Started (on Fri) a new piece of fiction — one page only. Must see whether it can be kept going, straight onto typewriter. Idea of characters ? suggested by Janet — Carl Skidmore Cecelia Sluggings and Melior Fathers. Ideas have developed over the weekend.
Move it back in time to 1951 and introduce the waterfront strike etc. to give it a broader dimension.
Carl not married to but living with Patagonia (we called her Pat) — half French, half Maori. His mother is German, his father a Mt Eden councillor who hopes to be mayor. They are both large, and they visit in the narrow verandah lined with matting, bringing cake. {they want him to come home.
Carl's father is the same age as Melior's — they know one another a little — cool distance. (Comic — but not silly.)
Melior's great love is a little trade union official (better not make him a jockey) — connected with the waterfront strike. Melior is afraid of the police. Of course Carl excites him but that is not his main interest. He still cruises public loos. (Frame a scene of him

Notebook records beginning of novel *All Visitors Ashore* (with names of characters). This was the novel Karl and Janet Frame were going to write together but Karl wrote it all

Above: Kay and Karl, 1980s

Below: Karl about to be arrested on the rugby field at Hamilton after the match with South Africa had been stopped by the protest, 1981

Top: Karl receives CBE from Govenor-General Beattie, 1985

Middle: Karl with his creative writing class at Tohunga Crescent, 1985, Andrew Johnston third from left at the front, Tim Wilson (and hair) directly behind Karl – McCahon paintings in the background

Bottom: Karl and Kay with Greg O'Brien at a literary launch, 1990s

Left: Last walk with Frank, photo by Kay, 1982

Below: Karl with Malcolm Bradbury and Allen Curnow at the Curnows' bach, Karekare, 1980s

Above: Dunedin Writers' Week, 1994, from left: [bookseller], Lauris Edmond, Patricia Grace, Margaret Mahy, Maurice Shadbolt, Roger Hall, Fiona Kidman, A. K. Grant and Karl

Below: Dunedin Writers' Week, 1994, Maurice Shadbolt, Keri Hulme and Karl

Above: Karl with Janet Frame, Wellington Writers' conference, 1994, photographed by Marti Friedlander, courtesy of the Gerrard and Marti Friedlander Charitable Trust

Below: Marti and Karl at Going West Festival, 1999

Above: Karl with Max Cryer, Kay and Barry Humphries at Tohunga Crescent – Louise Henderson's cubist *Cow's Skull* behind, 1980s

Below: Allen Curnow and Karl not long before Allen's death in 2001

Karl and Barry Humphries on a rock at Karekare, 1980s

Postscript:

When writing this chapter I had not looked at Charles Brasch's *Journals 1958–1973* which offers (p. 544) a quite extreme example of a member of the writing community who could not reconcile my novel with his expectations of me:

> 15 Nov [1971] *Smith's Dream* is an affront, a stone for bread, fact without value. How can I be interested in Stead after this?

Part Three

Edging Towards the Exit

11. 1981 – and Farewell Frank

Frank, the family, Sylvia and so on

I came home to floods of mail from schools – both teachers and students, asking me questions about meaning and motive in *Smith's Dream* and about its connections to and differences from the movie. I did my best to answer them all seriously. I sparred mainly amiably by letter with Lauris Edmond who would soon be on her way to Menton on the Mansfield fellowship. Frank when I visited seemed lonely and eager to see me, so I went as often as I could. Dennis McEldowney had written a small pictorial biography of him, and Frank showed me a picture in it of himself on his one venture abroad, picnicking with friends in the grounds of Hampton Court. He told me the younger of the two women in the picture was the wife of his lover at that time – the man who had 'taught him everything' about the homosexual life, and had taken him cruising the loos of London.

On the same visit he told – or tried to tell – a story he'd heard on the radio about an elephant mother rescuing her child from a swollen river – pulling it up on to an island, and then herself being swept away downriver, but returning next day to the rescued one and protecting it. He was having difficulty getting the story told because he was interrupted by weeping. One did not often – or ever – see Frank weep; and he was illustrating the action of the mother, making his two arms the trunk and pushing or pulling the young elephant up to safety. It was comic, but it was also touching. Frank liked to be socially in charge, but for a moment his guard was down.

I was still caught up by the thought that we had an exceptional and neglected writer in Sylvia Ashton-Warner. I tried to get the university to award her an honorary degree. Keith Sinclair, who that year had awarded her autobiography *I Passed This Way* the New Zealand Book Award for non-fiction, supported me in this, but Professor Marie Clay in the Education Department was in two minds about it. Sylvia's methods of teaching reading to Māori kids, so charmingly recounted in her books, were unorthodox; and Bruce Biggs, a prominent Māori and Professor of Anthropology, saw them as a kind, or an aspect, of colonialism. But they had worked where others had failed. Would those little Māori have been better *not* learning to read English?

I sent Sylvia a copy of what I had written about her for the *LRB* and told her it was Kay who had first alerted me to her work. She invited us to visit her at Ōtūmoeti. Her house, 'Whenua', was airy, spacious, tastefully decorated, with the inevitable grand piano, and Sylvia herself was charming. She had style and a theatrical manner. She wrote to me afterwards:

> I think you are a very brave man, even reckless, to write about writers. Where is your first instinct of self-preservation? It was delightful to meet you and Kay. Good luck – Sylvia.

We spent most of two summer months at our Karekare bach, in the bush walks and the west coast surf. There was only the public phone out there, and these were the days before email and cell phones, so I was happily cut off from the world of work and daily business. But there was a small community of friends –Tony and Robin Hooper and their two sons sharing a drive with us, Allen and Jeny Curnow just a couple of hundred metres down Lone Kauri Road (which Allen was adding to the New Zealand literary map), painters Peter and Sylvia Siddell and two daughters down at the beach, and Jim and Jill Holt and a son and daughter, their pines visible from our bach, away up on the ridge between Karekare and Piha.

Mike and Libby, Miroslav and Antonia

I was invited to a festival in Toronto in May of 1981 put on by the League of Canadian Poets. It was organised by their president, Henry Beissel, but the hands-on day-to-day work was done by his secretary Elizabeth Brewitt, whose efficiency cut through all kinds of obstacles and secured for me flight tickets that would take me to Toronto and, after twelve days of the festival, onward to London for two weeks, and then home again. Hotel and daily expenses were covered for Toronto. What was even better, the seats when I arrived at the airport proved to be 'clipper [i.e. Pan Am business] class' – a new experience. Elizabeth when she met me at the airport had the red hair and freckles of Anne of Green Gables, but, as I reported to Kay, 'unlike "Anne with an e", was dashing and elegant'.

My colleague of the 1960s, Mike Doyle, now teaching at the University of Victoria in British Columbia, was waiting for me at the hotel, and we were to spend some of the next ten days walking about together and going over old times and common ground.* Mike was both poet and critic. He'd come from what one of Ronald Hugh Morrieson's characters calls 'humble early oranges', an Irish family in London, and in the 1950s arrived as a Royal Navy rating in Wellington, where he'd been discovered, or had discovered himself, at Victoria University. There he began publishing poetry

---

* Doyle first published as C. D. Doyle, then as Charles, and finally as Mike. He and I would later edit a New Zealand edition of the Canadian literary journal *Ariel*, October 1985. We kept up email exchanges over many years and I wrote an obituary article about him in *New Zealand Books*, Autumn 2017.

and became one of Louis Johnson's, in effect, anti-Curnow group. In the 1950s I had reviewed his first book of poems rather tersely in *Landfall*, but that time of strife and competition seemed well behind us. His talent as a poet was considerable, and I liked its international flavour and sophistication; but his shifting about had given him no secure base anywhere, and though he was here in Toronto for the festival he had no part in it – no acknowledged place, at least thus far, among the Canadian poets, who he said were even more inclined to 'nationalism' than our own. Mike had published critical studies of R. A. K. Mason and James K. Baxter, and a book on William Carlos Williams, and was currently working on a biography of Richard Aldington.

This festival was for poets only, Canadian, with a dozen or so invited from overseas; but the way it was run was to be the template for later Toronto literary festivals. The visiting and out-of-town poets were kept together and taken each night to a different top-class restaurant; and there was a day spent visiting the Niagara Falls. The local star was Margaret Atwood who had in those days a sort of Botticellian beauty, and read poems, even the ones about torture, in a voice that went unvaryingly over and over the same cadences with little or no animation. She looked like *Primavera* and sounded like a frog in a bog.

It began with the League's 'AGM and banquet'. Next day I and the Irish poet John Montague formed a panel to discuss the subject of poetry and politics. It was something I had made myself 'expert' in; but Montague was able to point out that he came from the same area as Bobby Sands, who had recently taken part in the IRA's 'dirty protest' (i.e. smearing the walls of their cells with their shit) in the Maze prison in Northern Ireland, and that Bobby was now in the process of starving himself to death. How could I match that, he seemed to imply? What was academic expertise compared to the real thing? Montague's reverent tone on this subject, and the fact that Sands and others were really dying, made it difficult – in fact I felt impossible – to show anything but respect for these Irish heroes; and of course I was well equipped to quote relevant lines by Yeats, who allowed even the 'drunken vainglorious lout' MacBride to be 'numbered in the song':

> He had done most bitter wrong
> To some who are near my heart,
> Yet I number him in the song.
> . . .
> I write it out in a verse –
> MacDonagh and MacBride
> And Connolly and Pearse
> Now and in time to be,
> Wherever green is worn,
> Are changed, changed utterly:
> A terrible beauty is born.

Yes I got full marks for that. But I couldn't entirely conceal that my sympathies were divided. 'The Prots', after all, had been planted long ago and felt they belonged where they were, and I wasn't sure, as a New Zealander, how much historical guilt one person could be expected to carry and acknowledge.

John Montague had something clearly powerful to say in response to this but was hindered by the onset of a prodigious stammer, something which afflicted him at intervals (I suggested to Mike Doyle it was his critical faculty trying to find a way out); but he told me afterwards what he'd been trying to say was that I was a 'scoundrel'. I liked the word – it sounded so Irish, and though he meant it as a reproach it had the feel almost of a caress.

Kay was writing me regular reports from the home front, and among these came news of protest marches against a proposed tour by the South African Springboks – thus far peaceful occasions and, as Kay reported them, the Auckland ones more like meetings of all our old friends than foretastes of disorder and violence. So there were intimations of what I would return to, but as yet nothing to suggest what '1981' would come to represent in the minds of New Zealanders. In response I wrote descriptions of some of the poets to Kay. This for example of the Scottish poet Edwin Morgan:

> He is 60 and just retired (early) from his Glasgow chair – seems younger than 60, rather shy, a bit of an unwashed inhibited Brit, with quirky originality. Buttoned-up yet highly intelligent, modest, friendly and nice. He reads a mixture of what are called 'sound poems' (Jabberwocky is a 'sound poem'), science fiction poems, and straight social and documentary pieces. He reads well, has a nice sense of humour and a highly developed sense of the poems as language – the whole effect is pretty satisfying and certainly entertaining within the overall limitation that it's a cop-out in not doing anything at all about the self except conceal it. But since the Canadian side of the festival has been full of big raw naked naïve embarrassing overweight corn-fed butter-soft egos, it's a relief to have a stalwart Brit treating himself as a mechanic of language rather than a Walt Whitman of the prairies.

Other impressions of readings included this of the Canadian Gary Geddes:

> . . . a beautiful melancholy forty-ish poet in a white Indian cotton shirt emoting in a beautiful rich deep voice. He seemed to be cajoling the audience to make us feel what he was pretending to feel. [. . .]
> Then a fierce activist Canadian woman Michèle Lalonde, and hers was just about the most powerful and impressive poetry reading I've ever heard. It made my scalp prickle. The audience was not very responsive. People I talked to afterwards acknowledged she was good but not enthusiastically – which may be because their involvement in the argument about Quebec affects their response. I told her at breakfast next morning how much I'd admired her performance and she

looked surprised as if she wasn't expecting anyone here in Toronto to feel anything but anger.

But the poet who interested me most was the Czechoslovakian Miroslav Holub who told me how much he loved to get out from behind the Iron Curtain and how difficult it was to achieve. His work had not been published in his own country in the past ten years, and when he was given permission to accept an overseas invitation he was always aware of a man from the embassy in the back of the audience in a raincoat who would be monitoring what he said and what he read. To Kay I wrote, 'He is very cool, calls himself a scientist [he was an immunologist in his daily life], and is one of the most distinct personalities here. Everyone likes him.' And in another letter, 'He's such a strange interesting individual and he enjoys himself so much.'

On our last night Miroslav and I took Elizabeth (now Libby) Brewitt out for dinner, took turns to dance with her, and took her home to the door of her apartment where she kissed us goodbye, two middle-aged poets, once each. Next day it was raining and he and I bought umbrellas. He envied mine because it had a button you pressed to make it open. We went to a bank together to cash cheques the festival had given us to cover extra daily expenses. And then we were on our way – I to London, he back to the cage that Prague was for him.*

I was very close to the end of my Pound Yeats Eliot book and the purpose of a fortnight in London was to continue work on it in the Senate House Library but also to meet with Donald Davie who was to figure in the final chapter, both as poet and as critic. Davie was that rare thing, a really readable literary critic. His writing took your interest and carried you along. He had been the most knowledgeable and best proponent of Pound's work in the UK,

* See my *Collected Poems, 1951–2006*, p. 299 'Ode to a Nightingale' and p. 335 'Miroslav Holub in Toronto, 1981'.

and yet continued to be ambiguous about it, not primarily because of its crazy economics and deplorable anti-Semitism (which was my position) but more because he considered Pound's loosening of poetic form to be a kind of indiscipline which had larger social implications and political consequences. Davie was deeply conservative, and tended to lecture the UK for not appreciating the greatness of Pound, and the US for over-respecting his ill-disciplined freeing up of the traditional bonds of poetic form. I thought this made him a perfect focus for the good and the bad in Pound who was the central figure in my book, and the final chapter was to be called 'The Case of Donald Davie'.

Davie had invited me to his club, the Savile, which I characterised in letters to Kay as the Servile. It was certainly very grand in its literary antecedents, having had among its members R. L. Stevenson, Rudyard Kipling, W. B. Yeats, Henry James, Thomas Hardy, Edmund Gosse, Max Beerbohm, A. A. Milne, H. G. Wells, Rider Haggard, J. M. Barrie, Compton Mackenzie . . . In this very British and male-only establishment (women would finally be admitted in 2017) Donald and I consumed a lot of conventional food and decent wine, and covered a lot of ground. We didn't agree but that was not the purpose of the meeting. It was really to establish clearly where Davie stood on crucial issues about the consequences of the poetic revolution Pound, together with others like William Carlos Williams, had brought about, so that I would be sure I had not misrepresented him. He enjoyed our encounter and so did I. 'I don't often get a conversation like this,' he said. We parted around midnight, though he would be staying at the club and said he would have been happy to carry our talk on into the small hours.

When the book was finished I sent him its final chapter which was largely about his critical work as exemplary in the context of Pound and Modernism, and he replied:

> I believe your diagnosis of the Davie 'case' is probably irrefutable. It is certainly more generous and more patient than what

> I'm used to getting alike from British and American readers, who all sooner or later exclaim 'Why doesn't he make his mind up'.

His letter concludes, 'It is late at night and I am a little drunk but I hope the main message comes through – I am very grateful indeed for being taken so seriously.' He also urges me to think about offering to teach at the Yeats Summer School in Sligo, a suggestion I would later act upon. But his view of my chapter changed when he'd had more time to think about it, and we were to air our differences in the Australian literary journal *Scripsi** where he reverted to his old anxiety that Pound's poetics were an invitation to social disorder, and I replied that I considered literature and politics different modes of human activity, and that disorder (if Pound's *Cantos* were disorderly) in the arts was not a licence for disorder in the larger sphere.

ANTONIA'S NEWS OF THE UCL ENGLISH DEPARTMENT was of conflict. She thought Karl Miller was finding it too stressful to be both HOD and editor of the *LRB*. He was, she said, dictatorial in meetings and the women were complaining, telling him he was unreasonable, even outrageous, while the men mostly suffered him in silence. I was to experience this the following year when, in his haste, he misread a letter of mine, accused me of 'boorishness', and then wrote 'I see from your letter I have been intemperate. I'm sorry. I can only say that the load of work I have these days makes me touchy.'

The Virgin in the Garden had just reappeared in a King Penguin and she gave me a copy and inscribed it emphatically:

> To Karl who will appear in Vol II, mutatis mutandis,
> with love, May 31st 1981
> Antonia
> Redeat et virgo, redeunt Saturnia regna.

* Vol. 4, no. 2, 'A response to C. K. Stead', and vol. 4, no. 3, 'A reply to Donald Davie'.

This aroused curiosity. Vol. II was to be the continuation of *The Virgin in the Garden*'s story of the sisters Frederica and Stephanie Potter; and a lot of our talk was about the progress she was making with it. It took the same form our conversations about the earlier novel had done, she telling the story, and sometimes enunciating problems and looking for suggestions about how they might be overcome.

I had promised Ruth Feinstein, whose reading in Toronto I'd missed, that I would come to a reading in Cambridge where she was to appear with W. S. Graham and George Barker. The programme indicated that she should come between them but both were already well lubricated before the event began, and in the quarrel about who should read first before alcohol rendered him helpless, sober Elaine was pushed into third place. I had a train to catch back to London, and she had still not begun when I had to leave. I was sorry to have missed her again; but not sorry to have heard Barker whose little pink *True Confession* Jim Baxter had lent me as a student and which I'd kept; and I still had some of his poems in my head, in particular the sonnet to his mother that begins –

> Most near, most dear, most loved and most far,
> Under the window where I often found her
> Sitting huge as Asia, seismic with laughter,
> Gin and chicken helpless in her Irish hand . . .

Barker had been never married to, but the on-and-off partner of, Canadian poet Elizabeth Smart, author of *By Grand Central Station I Sat Down and Wept*. There had been a lot of alcohol in their partnership, and four of the fifteen children he fathered were with her. On a return some years later to Toronto Harbourfront Festival (as it became) I was to be present when the same Elizabeth Smart, long since separated from Barker, remained drunk and weeping in her dressing room, refusing to come out and do her scheduled reading.

Antonia put on a dinner party for me the Sunday night before I was due to leave. The Jewish poet Dannie Abse was there, and I asked him about the occasion when Emanuel Litvinoff had read his poem reproaching T. S. Eliot for his anti-Semitism. He remembered it well, and especially his own attempt to pour what he called 'the oil of accommodation' on troubled waters. He thought Eliot deserved Litvinoff's reproach and seemed to half regret his own tendency to be conciliatory – but he agreed too that it wasn't a very good poem.

It was a summer night with views out on to a green garden, and I remember the atmosphere, and my old feeling that whichever way my life turned me, northward or southward, I was leaving something behind and with mixed feelings.

'1981'

The first match of the Springbok tour came late in July, and for the following two months the Stead family were caught up in the turmoil that gripped the whole country. Feelings ran so high we were a nation divided against itself. The UN had long been calling for a sporting boycott of South Africa, which would not permit countries like New Zealand to send mixed-race teams to visit. Muldoon had helped to frame (and modify) the Gleneagles Agreement by which Commonwealth countries were committed to discourage sporting contacts with the apartheid state, but not obliged to forbid or prevent them. This gave him the option of expressing disapproval without doing what his predecessor, Norman Kirk, had done in 1973, when he announced that the All Blacks would not be given visas and the planned tour was cancelled. Kirk had said that if he had allowed the tour to go ahead 'it would have brought about the greatest eruption of violence this country has ever seen'. That prediction was now being proved right.

In the intervening period the Soweto riots had occurred and made the South African issue more widely known and keenly felt. Black students rebelling against the introduction of Afrikaans as the medium of instruction in schools had been fired on. The number of dead was somewhere between 176 (the official number) and 700 (an unofficial estimate); many more had been injured, and the apartheid regime's brutality and ruthlessness had been exposed. The cry 'the whole world's watching' was true – it was; and it was hard to understand how a large section of our population could show indifference to an issue so much larger than the question of which country had the better rugby team. For the Steads, as for so many educated and enlightened New Zealanders, it was a question of conscience, of right and wrong – like Vietnam all over again, but even clearer, simpler, starker. It brought New Zealanders out into the streets as never before.

The family were involved together. On the morning when the second match of the tour was to be played in Hamilton, 80 miles south of Auckland, it was agreed we would be there. We had an early lunch, drove south, and joined the very large march that set off from the centre of town and headed for the park where the game was to be played. At some point marshals went along the outside of the columns telling those who wanted to be 'part of the action' to move up towards the front. I moved up, leaving Kay with the daughters. Oliver was out of sight.

At the front of the march there was a group, mostly young Māori, many of them gang members wearing heavy boots; and I have a vivid memory of the sound of those boots suddenly grinding on the asphalt as, at a signal, they broke into a run, veering left off the path we were following around the ground, and up a bank topped by a tall fence of wire mesh. All together, this advance guard got hold of the wire and pulled back. Staples flew like bullets, the fence was breached and as the young warriors clambered over, through and around what was left of it, the spectator crowd parted in fear like the Red Sea in Exodus 14. Many of those behind,

I among them, followed, and were astonished to find ourselves able to run through this gap and into the middle of the ground and gather there.

The game had not yet begun; and now two or three hundred protesters were forming a block in the middle of the pitch, while a crowd of 28,000 rugby supporters screamed at us. By now the police had closed the gap that had been opened, and the rest of the protest march continued around the ground, chanting slogans, the most stirring being the one that came from the South African protest movement: first 'Amandla' (power); and then 'Amandla Ngawethu' – 'Power to us.' There was something about the cadence of this that was to take hold of our imaginations as the weeks went by – a feeling of being part of something large and important that mixed tragedy and triumph.

It was at this point, as we gathered and linked arms, that the new squad of police, put together and equipped to deal with this kind of occasion, emerged from under the stand. Their headgear, riot shields and long Monadnock batons were of a kind that had not been seen in New Zealand before. The crowd cheered and those of us in the middle of the pitch felt fear. The police formed around us and herded us into a tight group, telling us individually at close quarters, and through loud hailers, that those who wanted to save themselves could leave now and would be protected; the rest would have to be 'dealt with' on the spot. A very few left but the rest – 90 per cent at least – stayed put. The exhilaration of the break-in was succeeded now by this terror. I suppose everyone was as scared as I was, but still no one moved. Minutes passed, and slowly it began to dawn on me that with so many TV cameras there for the game, senior police officers would not want to order their men to put the batons to use. Probably many of the force were not keen to use them either. They would need to be provoked for that, and we were simply holding our ground. So the stand-off continued. The game could not be played, the protesters would not move, and the crowd was demanding action.

News came that a small plane had taken off from an airfield in Taupō and was heading this way. I was never certain whether this was seen as a real threat or just an excuse, but it was offered later as an explanation of the fact that the game was cancelled. Already the police had begun arresting us one by one, dragging each protester from those on either side with whom arms were linked. I was dragged out and put in a paddy wagon with others. When it was announced that the game was cancelled the remainder of those still on the field were led to the exit, partly shepherded by police, while the angry crowd showered them with cans and bottles. Many were later attacked and beaten in the street. In that sense it was easier to have been arrested than allowed to go free.

I was processed with others at the Hamilton police station. Belt and wallet were taken and I was put in a cell. Tim Shadbolt (now Sir Tim, Mayor of Invercargill) was there. There were messages scrawled on the walls so I added one of my own: 'C. K. Stead, author of *Smith's Dream* was here.' I was to tell this to journalists who asked about my experience, and it became a story told over and over: how at that moment when the new squad with their new equipment emerged from under the stand it had seemed like a scene from the movie *Sleeping Dogs*; and what I had written on the wall of the cell.

During that year enquiries from schools about *Smith's Dream* had increased beyond my ability to cope with them, and just the title seemed to have entered the national consciousness. When a sporting disaster of some kind occurred for the New Zealand wicketkeeper Ian Smith, the *Herald* headline read 'SMITH'S DREAM BECOMES A NIGHTMARE'. So now with articles about my Hamilton adventure: 'SMITH'S DREAM MAN RELIVES FANTASY' was one; another, 'DREAMTIME SPILLS OVER INTO REALITY'; a third, 'DOGGED BY HIS DREAM'. I wrote an article for a Sunday paper which attracted a lot of attention. It won me new fans and new enemies, and letters came from both. I had been in the public eye before, but this was a new level of attention.

Charged with disorderly behaviour and released (I would later be convicted and fined), I was welcomed by Kay and our children, and Kay's sister Olwen and her Hamilton family, to what was in effect a party of celebration. We all felt sure the Prime Minister, currently in London for the royal wedding of Charles and Diana, would now have good reason to call the tour off and send the Springboks home in the interests of public order. We were not recognising how Muldoon would be counting on those marginal rural electorates for support in the forthcoming election, how strong the loyalty to rugby was there, and how powerful the dislike of city moralists who cared more about what happened to black Africans than about a decent test match on home turf. The division in New Zealand society revealed in 1981 is something which I recognise continues almost forty years later. No one who has read my earlier memoir, *South-West of Eden*, will be surprised that I saw it then, and see it still, as between the enlightened and humane, and the unenlightened and punitive: essentially as political, between left and right.

At a later protest in Auckland two policemen were carrying the Niuean reggae singer Tigi Ness to the paddy wagon, one holding him by the legs, the other around the throat so that he appeared to be choking. Alarmed, Kay shouted that his face was turning blue, and when she was ignored, tipped the helmet of the front cop so that it fell forward over his face causing him to loosen the hold. Another cop instantly had Kay's arm up her back and she too was arrested and hustled to the van. When the matter came to trial the police evidence was that no one was carried to the van that day. Kay's evidence and mine was discounted and the judge 'found it as a fact' that no one that day was carried to the van. Kay was found guilty but discharged as a first offender of good repute. Some weeks later someone who had been there taking photographs brought us one of Tigi being carried to the van, with the arresting cop's forearm tightly around his throat. These court cases were the first experience many middle-class New Zealanders had of how practised the police force of those days were at lying under oath, and how easy many of the judges made it for them to get away with it.

New Zealand, someone said, was now at war with itself twice a week, and after the battle of Molesworth Street in Wellington, when the police took a 'no more Mr Nice Guy' approach and laid into the crowd with considerable brutality, the demonstrators began to wear crash helmets and sometimes body armour, or carried plywood shields. Cargo containers, barbed wire, sand-filled jumbo bins and truck-and-trailer units were used as barricades around stadiums which became fortresses. The protests, led by people like John Minto and Dick Cuthbert, were cleverly organised and inventive. At strategic times motorways and the Auckland Harbour Bridge were blocked, and airport runways invaded. Balloons and kites carried messages. The court system was cluttered and cases deliberately protracted. The size of the protesting crowds increased week by week. The last test, at Eden Park, was played on a pitch that was being flour-bombed from a private plane and smoke-bombed by protesters in the stands, while out in surrounding streets fights raged between police with batons and protesters throwing stones and arming themselves with palings torn from suburban fences.

On that day the police Red Squad, which had been described by Bob Moodie, the cross-dressing union secretary of the Police Association, as invincible and not to be approached with hostile intent, decided to go on the offensive, and emerged from the protection of their cargo bins to go in pursuit of young protesters who had been throwing stones at them. The protesters turned and ran, and those not fast enough were caught and beaten. But then it became apparent that, outside their barricades, the police were much smaller in number than the protesters, and that they had made a tactical mistake. Now the protesters who had been running were regrouping, turning to confront and engage with them. The young Māori, many of whom had felt picked on and discriminated against by the police, were like a new Māori Battalion, resolute and fierce. The Red Squad formed a tight wedge and tried to hold their ground but were gradually driven back and finally were themselves running for cover. Tables had been turned; and to me (and I was far from alone) it was an exhilarating moment.

That evening we were to go to dinner at Bob and Noeline Chapman's but there was no sign of Oliver. Then a call came from the Ōtāhuhu police who had arrested him on the airport runway (with others including Allen Curnow). Because he was under twenty he would not be charged, but must be collected by his parents. So dinner at the Chapmans' was held for us. When we got there finally the tour and its politics was the sole subject of conversation. I was able to report that the English Department had been, throughout the eight weeks of the tour, solid in its opposition, and that seven of us had been arrested.

Images of all these events went around the world, and we heard then, but even more clearly later when the apartheid regime collapsed, that Nelson Mandela and his associates in prison, and the ANC at large, had taken comfort from this assault on the sacred icon of rugby.

There was a show of Springbok tour photographs put on first in Auckland, and later throughout New Zealand, by Real Pictures, and for that I wrote an accompanying text. More interesting in the light of her later emergence as the novelist Charlotte Grimshaw, fifteen-year-old Charlotte had kept a diary of the tour, and allowed me to send it to Peter Simpson who was putting together an archive in Christchurch. Peter wrote thanking me for sending it, and to thank Charlotte. 'Her narrative was read with enormous interest and enjoyment by all of us associated with the archive. We consider it to be one of the most valuable items in the whole collection.'

Frank Sargeson's last letter to Janet Frame concludes, 'All the Stead family have been prosecuted and fined over the Springboks – even down to the little girl – most improper!!!'

Antonia Agonistes

Going back a short step: I arrived back in Auckland in June and wrote to Antonia:

> It had rained before we landed but the lights of Auckland were glittering like superstars. You have to come to this end of the earth to see how the air can be empty of anything but itself, a beautiful nothing through which the otherworld can shine. I would like to have seen more of you, talked more to you, especially about Vol. II.

I also told her I had at last read *The Virgin in the Garden*, had enjoyed it and been quite won over by it, despite a powerful resistance in myself to 'Big Novels in the traditional mould'.

> You are a novelist as I am not, as you will see if you read the stories I'm sending you – they will seem to you perhaps like scenarios for unwritten novels while to me they are fictions with a strong element simply of story. ('Once upon a time there was a girl who lived in the forest . . .' as distinct from 'Mary's feelings that morning as she came through the muddy forest paths were confused . . .')

This comment revealed again my resistance to what I called 'conventional fiction'; and Antonia wrote back what she called (though it was four handwritten pages) a 'stop-gap letter since I do want to write, & promise, a proper one next week'. She had done too many things in too short a time and had invited 'ca. 120 people to my house on Sunday – only wish you could be there'. She couldn't write about her writing ('except to say it means so much to me that you like it') until she had done a day or two on Vol. II. 'I do miss you. One needs someone alive to talk to.' On the fourth page she wrote:

> I think I'll write one little poem and send you a copy – I am no poet but have a love of metaphor – just in the hope of seeing the others (yours). You are one of the few people who likes me when I'm going at full speed – most are either afraid, envious, or piously irritated at what looks like egocentricity. But you've got it yourself. [. . .] I wish you could be at this party which will be incomplete without. To give a Party in July is a landmark.* Think of me in July.

I don't have a copy of my reply to this, and the next letter from Antonia is undated but the reference to the royal wedding indicates the end of July. She is now at an upper-middle-class salmon-fishing house party in the wet Highlands of Scotland, deeply frustrated that she can't get on with her writing. She tells me she tried to run out and get killed on the road on the anniversary of her son's death.

> I daren't even write to you about my book because its bittiness hurts so. I think this claustrophobia may be some kind of analogy of yr loneliness in London – an unnatural state where the mind won't go. [. . .] I am going to use this letter as an excuse to go on a walk in the wet on my own if there is a letterbox in 10 miles. If you see in yr newspaper Novelist hit by haywain day before Royal Wedding you will know I meant it.

My reply expressed horror at the thought of her running out into the road – and sympathy. 'It's been terrible for you and it's terrible that it [i.e. the death of her son] should come back, and one can only hope it will gradually fade and that you can bear that it fades because I suppose that's the final loss. I'm not offering "advice" or "wisdom" – I have none – only sympathy and maundering. Please survive; but if you refuse, haywains are preferable to motorways.'

---

* Her son Charles was killed in July 1972.

Her next letter is dated 21 December and responds to one of mine I have not kept a copy of. She assures me I did not offend her – so perhaps I had been worried about my comments on kinds of fiction. Once again she is in a distraught state from last term's work and her inability to get on with Vol. II.

> I went on teaching – a mistake. Oh dear I am sorry. If you could see me you would understand (being you). [. . .] It was a kind of Puritanism. The teaching must be done properly & then every night I died. I wanted to write to you & therefore always did the other things.

On 13 January she wrote that things were clear now and that if she explained she thought I would forgive her. But for what? I had no idea what needed to be forgiven.

> I worked grimly harder and harder and slower and slower and spoke to no one and could not write to you about yr extraordinary poems because it was unsafe (I think you will understand) in the state of madness I was in to write about writing at all. [. . .] So I am sitting in the attic wch is now actually called my study, and trying to think how to start again – writing that is, and repairing the friendships I have damaged that matter. [. . .] Am writing a review of Ngaio Marsh's autobiography (for light relief, only it's dull) but makes me think of you simply because of photographs of unknown views and mountains you must know. A decorous lady, and reticent, but they don't make for exciting autobiography. [. . .] I shall be all right when you come back. If you write to me I shall write back calmly and sanely, I promise.

Farewell Frank

Kay and I worried about Frank Sargeson. He had seemed unwell since a minor 'vascular accident' (as a stroke is called in Janet's

Living in the Maniototo), and when I visited I found him in a state of almost cheerful confusion. He said he'd looked at himself in the mirror and it appeared he was wearing a false moustache and hadn't put it on straight. He had flooded the kitchen the day before and retired to bed convinced that Poland had taken over New Zealand. He made a couple of visits to the bathroom while I was there and explained that he had taken cascara because 'under the New Regime constipation won't be tolerated'. I thought at first that this might be some sort of Sargesonian satiric commentary on my recent public behaviour, but it was hard to see how it could be – how the 'satire' would work. Then he told me that Ted next door, who was now doing his shopping, was no longer Ted Tremain but Ted Middleton. When I questioned how this could be he agreed it was 'a bit sinister', but insisted it was so. When I pointed out that Ted Middleton was blind, he thought a while and then said 'Not *completely*.'

I rang Barbara Duggan, who was soon in touch with Jean Bartlett, and Frank was taken in to be cared for by the North Shore Hospital. We visited him just before Christmas. I reported to a friend that he hated being there, 'and I'm not surprised – the place is full of frail collapsed bodies with spirits trapped and whimpering inside'. Our last visit was late in January. We found Frank dressed and sitting in the day room with other patients, but neither taking part in conversations nor watching television. We suggested a walk in the grounds and he said he would like that if he could hang on to me tightly – which he did, while Kay took photographs of us. We wandered through the grounds, and then he stopped, released his hold on me and wrapped his arms around a veranda post as if he was determined not to be taken indoors again. His face was puzzled, and then it cleared and he said, 'The deterioration's been so rapid.' He was right, it had, but what could we say?

The moment of clarity passed and we took him indoors and settled him in a comfortable chair. I was due to go overseas again very soon and I knew this was likely to be my last encounter with this man I was so fond of and who had been so significant in my life. It was a recognition I could only glance at and could not acknowledge. It should have been the kind of 'good' goodbye I had not been able to say to either of my parents – but there had been no acknowledgement that he was dying. And there was also Frank's aversion to his own tearful tendencies – he would not have liked a fond farewell. So there was none, except in my head.

Kay visited a few weeks later and wrote to me in Canada that he had not been conscious – only waving one hand gently in front of his face, as if there were invisible moths, fluttering distractingly around his closed eyes.

I was in London when he died. Ruth Harley, now at the Arts Council, asked me to write an obituary but I found I couldn't. The subject seemed too big, too large a part of my life, of our lives, Kay's and mine. But I managed a message to be read at the funeral. It mentioned the big things that might have been quoted or performed – Caesar's lines on the death of Mark Antony, Siegfried's funeral music in *Götterdämmerung* – but they were all too grand for Frank; and I concluded with something simple, running together the brilliant sequence of titles he had invented for his autobiography:

'Frank has said it all. Once is enough, more than enough, never enough.

'Send him away with honour and with love.'

12. Cross-Eyed with the Effort of It

On the move again

In 1981 two of the three projects proposed in my application for the fellowship were published. The writing of the third project, the Pound Yeats Eliot book, was finished and the search for a publisher, preferably both in the UK and the USA, had begun. Holding the fellowship and without the constraints of a teaching timetable, I had been free to accept invitations – first the ones to Regensburg and Aarhus, then to Toronto; and now for my third year there was an invitation to come as 'Distinguished Visitor' to the University of Alberta at Edmonton. I'd accepted and would be on my way soon. But first Kay and I took the daughters for a trip to the South Island. There was little sense of the rampant tourism that prevails there now. New Zealand was all our own (though who 'we' included was still being worked on with the tangata whenua and through the Waitangi Tribunal) – vast and largely empty, reflective and resplendent, gleaming at the heavens, open to the everything, good and bad, that winds and weathers could hurl at it or bless it with.

Because there had been opposition to my having the fellowship, I submitted the published scholarly work – the collected Duggan and the essays, together with the Casebook I'd done on *Measure for Measure* and the selection of Mansfield *Letters and Journals*, for the degree of DLitt which the university duly conferred at the 1982 graduation ceremony. It was a small bonus for me and a small coal of fire for Nick Tarling that he, as Dean of Arts, had to do the 'capping'.

But there was still the Yeats Pound Eliot book, while the novel I called *All Visitors Ashore* remained in the metaphorical 'bottom drawer', and still caused me anxiety. When my mind turned to it, it turned away again as if not daring to look for long. Now and then Kay, the only person who had read it, would mention it hopefully. She had liked it and couldn't imagine it would not be a success. The anxiety sprang from the feeling that it was something new, outside the range of anything I'd done before. This was something I had observed in Curnow since his resurgence in 1972. I might have shown it to Frank for an opinion, but he would have seen himself in the character of Melior Farbro, and would have felt I had 'outed' him as homosexual without permission. It was time to look at it again and think about it. I packed the typescript with what I took to Edmonton, but still passed my weeks there without opening it.

EDMONTON IS THE NORTHERNMOST CITY in North America. Anyone who has read the first part of the title story in my collection *The Name on the Door is Not Mine* will know something of what I did as the University of Alberta's 'Distinguished Visitor' in the Northern Hemisphere winter of 1981–82. It is all there in outline, though given fictional shape and fictional supplements. The story was what I called, in letters to Kay, 'my knitting'. So much (but not all) of what that story recounts was 'what happened really'. Many of the people were the same, with only their names changed; their conversation, their seminars and writing classes, their informal 'beer and Bakhtin' sessions on literary theory and semiotics – it was all there for the taking, and I took it.

But in fact when I look at my letters to Kay I see I was much more involved in teaching and advising, less alone and lonely, than I make myself out to be in the fiction. And there are the necessary additions and subtractions, the bending and shaping of reality, in order to create a story. The character of Alban Ashtree, the famous Canadian poet who does or does not die alliteratively 'in an avalanche in the Austrian Alps', was invention, as was his friend and lover Libby Waltraut, with whom the narrator is briefly involved. I borrowed this young woman's first name, freckled nose and golden hair from Elizabeth Brewitt, recently farewelled with Miroslav Holub in Toronto.

In a way there was no 'story' in Edmonton bigger than the weather, and none so pressing as getting in and out of the clothes worn to combat it. The temperatures veered between 20 and 30 below zero; and when the bus drivers went on strike, and I took to packing on extra clothes and head-gear and walking from my apartment to the university, I had to go over the High Level Bridge where it was said the wind-chill factor took it down to 60 or 70 below.

All of that went into my story, and with it, occasions like the dinner at Chairman and Mrs Hyde's house, with some of the members of the department, renamed but not otherwise disguised: Eugene Fish with a thin moustache who looked like a band leader of the 1920s, and his wife, the nice, pretty, plump, compulsive talker wearing a dress with a design of tiny shoes that ran around it in circles; Hank Judder who arrives on skis wearing mukluks and a large Indian fur-lined coat, and Hank's 'weaving wife'; and the Hydes themselves (whose real name was Jackel), the slow-spoken professor and his quick-witted wife who has just completed her doctorate.

In London a few weeks later, having lunch with Alan Ross, I was asked whether I had anything new for the *London Magazine*. Remembering his lack of enthusiasm for 'open form' poems, I told him I'd just written a Canadian story which would need some revision to disguise the characters. He said 'Do send it to me, Karl' and I did, and forgot about it until it appeared in the issue of December '83–January '84. When I next saw Alan I told him I'd intended to amend it to better disguise the characters. He smiled and said, 'Well Karl, you wouldn't want to go back there, would you?'

I THINK I WAS THREE WEEKS IN EDMONTON and then moved on to London, Mecklenburgh Square again, a room in London House where my neighbour on the same floor was my English Department colleague Peter Dane, currently on leave and working in London libraries to complete his PhD thesis on John Donne. This was a convenient arrangement because I was his thesis supervisor and was able to read a newly completed chapter and discuss it with him at length – and any problems he was having as the work went on. It also meant I had congenial company whenever I felt the need.

Peter was a German-Jewish refugee who had been appointed to the English Department not long after me, having taught for some years in a university in Uganda. He was ten years my senior, close on sixty, a great admirer of D. H. Lawrence, and something of a proselyte for Lawrentian sexual ethics. I was not entirely sure what that might imply in practice; but it meant a kind of seriousness, even solemnity, perhaps reverence, on the subject – the sort of thing you pick up and recognise in conversation, but don't pursue if it doesn't match your own feelings on the subject. Peter was not humourless. He was at ease with himself, a lover of women, a Friend of the Earth, and neither preacher nor moraliser. He was good easy company. We often had an evening drink and a smoke together. My drink might be a half pint of lager, his, two brandies. One night I met him in his pyjamas in the corridor at midnight. He said he'd been reading Sidney's Astrophel and Stella sonnets and was drunk with their beauty. I thought the inebriation had more to do with brandy than with sonnets; but I admired his enthusiasm. Love sonnets were his ideal form of beauty, and after his retirement, when he lived up north growing avocados, he was to write many of his own.

Antonia and I met for lunches. Vol. II (to be called *Still Life*) was under way and once again she made me her sounding board. As the story unfolded she'd decided Stephanie Potter had to die. It would happen late in the novel, but it would mean Vol. III could focus exclusively on Frederica; or Vols III and IV if it should turn out to be a tetralogy. The death was to be an accident. Her cat catches a sparrow and Stephanie tries to rescue it. Cat and bird are separated but the bird goes under the fridge. Stephanie gets down on the floor and reaches under, towards the bird – and touches a live wire. Her dying thought is a word, 'altruism', and a moment of surprise at its appropriateness. I wondered could you have this thought before going unconscious but Antonia assured me it had happened to her exactly as in her novel, except that she had survived.

The Pound Yeats Eliot book had gone off to Faber before Christmas, and now at last I had a reply sent on to me from Auckland. It came from their poetry editor, Craig Raine. He apologised for having taken such a long time, but a number of people in the office had wanted to read it. The book was admired, but he'd decided, especially with *The New Poetic* still in print, he was not able to make an offer.

At the time I had not met Craig Raine, but I've since got to know him well, and have once or twice chided him for this decision. Do you turn down a book that everyone in the office is so keen to read you have to apologise for lateness in returning it? But one thing that has remained constant has been Craig's loyalty to Eliot, even to the point of insisting, and arguing publicly (and crossing swords with me about it), that Eliot was no anti-Semite. Together with that went a corresponding loyalty to Eliot's widow Valerie who was propping up the firm with royalties from the Andrew Lloyd Webber musical *Cats*, based on Eliot's *Old Possum's Book of Practical Cats*. My book treated Eliot as the author of the greatest Modernist poem, 'The Waste Land', but was not correspondingly respectful of *Four Quartets*, and deplored his anti-Semitism.

Antonia suggested I try Penguin, which reminded me of Judith Burnley. She was no longer with the company but would advise me. So there was another lunch, a very jolly and stylish *tête-à-tête* in which the Pound Yeats Eliot book was largely overlooked, Judith more than usually lit up and excited because her second novel, *Unrepentant Women*, had just been published. She gave me a copy, inscribing it 'To Karl, the unrepentant globetrotter – with love – Judith, Bryanston Square, March 18 1982'. I came away full of beans and wine and hope – back to my room in London House, its provisional, far-from-home, on-the-move impermanence, and the truth that I had forgotten to ask for advice about Penguin; that here I was with not one but two completed books, a novel I still couldn't bring myself to look at, and a literary critical study that Faber didn't want.

There was a night when I was working on something after midnight and it came to me that right at this moment Frank's funeral would be happening in Auckland, and that while the message I'd sent was being read, I was here in London, *writing* – one of the 'Sons of Sargeson' as his protégés were sometimes called, fulfilling the dream Frank had had for us . . . My first thought was that Frank would be pleased; the second, after a moment, was that this was a fantasy and of no consequence. The important question was, was I doing the right thing, for myself and *for my family* – something Frank had never had to ask, and which had always marked the difference between my circumstance and his.

It was a moment of uncertainty. What was I doing here in London, Judith Burnley's 'unrepentant globetrotter'? All at once it was my solid secure life as a Professor of English, teacher, researcher, literary historian, administrator and judge of literary prizes, supervisor of Peter Dane's and Ruth Harley's PhDs – *that* seemed the real person, the worthy professional, not this free-booting 'artist', 'poet', 'writer', enjoying himself in London, going to so many good plays and writing about them in letters home where he had left the wife he loved in charge of their three teenage children. The Pound Yeats Eliot book could ratify my academic credentials – but would it be published? And only good new poems, and (as it seemed at this moment) the novel, *All Visitors Ashore*, could give me the authority I wanted, the moral permission to do what I was doing and call myself a writer.

It was around this time I took the trip to Paris, the dip into French language and culture that was always part of my life outside

New Zealand. There were the usual excitements and pleasures. Like Mansfield I could always be head-over-heels-smitten by France even while understanding it was an infatuation that could come and go like the common cold. On this visit all went as usual, and well, until a moment when I found myself surrounded by children in the public space outside the Centre Pompidou, dancing around me, shouting 'Monsieur, Monsieur, un franc Monsieur', and holding up an open newspaper in front of my face. My first thought was to reach into my pocket for some change to give them; but then I was jostled, the noise and the action became too much for me and I had to drive them away. They vanished as quickly as they'd come, and I walked on towards the Beaubourg, ruffled because my first response had been friendly.

Inside I reached for my wallet to show my library card which would identify me as a university professor and allow me free access to certain shows. The wallet was gone of course – my pocket had been picked. At a nearby police station I told my story. 'Mais oui bien sûr, Monsieur, c'était les Yugoslavs' – which I took to mean gypsies. There was no surprise. I was taken into a room and made my statement while a weary cop bashed it out on an old manual typewriter, got me to read and sign it, and said I should show it to my travel insurer. When I emerged from the inner office I found the reception area full of people, mostly English speakers, with the same story. The gang of miniature robbers had been busy in the area, and successful. It seemed there was nothing the police could do but issue statements confirming that we had been robbed. They had at that time no powers to arrest the children, whose parents would be camped somewhere on the outskirts of Paris waiting for their troops of undersized robbers to return with their riches.

There had been 500 francs cash in the wallet, two library cards (no bank or credit cards in those days), my driver's licence, and two London theatre tickets for plays yet to be seen. But I still had traveller's cheques in my hotel room together with my passport and tickets back to London – so it was no disaster, just a considerable inconvenience. But it went together with that moment of doubt that had come at the thought of Frank's funeral. There was always depression lurking when I was away for long from Kay and the family, and though my black dog was not a barker or a biter, he could emit sinister whines and low growls at 3 and 4 a.m.

A salutary file

Marti and Gerrard Friedlander were still in London at this time and Marti invited me to dinner. One of the guests was Carol O'Brien who had just been asked to take over the Harvill branch of publishers Collins. Harvill had been famous a few decades back when it had scored with two international best-sellers, Boris Pasternak's *Doctor Zhivago* and Giuseppe di Lampedusa's *The Leopard*, after which it had been best known for offering European novels in English translation. Carol's task was to build a new fiction list. Marti had introduced me, with Marti-ish elaborations and overstatement, as an important New Zealand writer, and Carol asked did I have a novel she might look at. I said I had one but for some reason I couldn't explain, I was unable to read it.

She said, 'You don't have to read it, Karl. I will do that.' And as if to seal the deal she drove me home to Mecklenburgh Square that evening and repeated, as we sat there under the big trees at midnight, that she really was looking for new fiction and would welcome the chance to look at mine. Later I would forget all the details, all the pains and uncertainties that followed, and tell it (and believe it – it was not a conscious deception) as a simple and rather lovely story: I had told Carol I had a novel I couldn't read; she had said I didn't have to – she would read it. She had loved it, published it, *All Visitors Ashore*, it was a success, and that was why I dedicated the novel that followed, *The Death of the Body*, to her. *Simple!*

Now, getting on for forty years later, I have been back to re-read the files. In the eighteenth century there was a fashion set by Samuel Richardson for the epistolary novel, and it was mocked by some parodist in the 1890s (it might have been Max Beerbohm) with sentences like, 'Even as I write, dear reader, the villain is carrying me up the stairs'. I remember now that I was tempted to write a similar parody of Carol O'Brien's correspondence. She was always just arriving or departing, with long unexplained gaps in between.

> I have just got back from Venice to find your novel sitting on my desk. As I am off to New York on Saturday I may not have time till I'm back at the end of June.

The next was not in June but October.

> Karl, dear Karl – in four hours time I am setting off for my summer holiday (very belatedly). I moved house in August so have not had a chance sooner.

And a footnote.

> Re-reading this (it's now only three hours till I set off for France) it seems woefully inadequate.

She had liked the novel but not the political part (which was essential). Fortunately in the meantime (now at home again) I had been in touch with David Elworthy at Collins (NZ) who would publish the New Zealand edition. He was keen to publish, and I explained:

> Ultimately of course I care more about what happens here than there. But I feel vulnerable in NZ literary circles at the moment. It may be nothing more than a mild paranoia, but it seems that I annoy a lot of people here – that there isn't at the moment a warm welcome waiting for whatever I do – and consequently there could be some pretty mean reviewing. Under these conditions, and this being a somewhat

> unconventional novel, a London edition with some favourable reviews is a kind of protection.

A London edition also meant, though I didn't say so, a bigger advance, larger sales and financial returns including from foreign translations; and since I was still looking towards giving up my university teaching, money had to be part of the picture.

The London end was still silent when I wrote a letter dated 27.5.83:

> Very dear Carol
> I've just looked back through the file and by an odd coincidence the letter sending you <u>All Visitors Ashore</u> is dated 28.5.82, and I had got up early to watch the replay of the FA Cup Final live by satellite. I suppose 28.5.82 must have been a Saturday, as is 27.5.83, and I got up early this morning to watch the replay of the FA Cup Final relayed live by satellite. I also rang David Elworthy and he says he thinks you are going ahead with the novel but he's waiting a letter confirming. I think that represents a year of progress but I wonder where we will be by the time of the FA Cup Final next year . . .

Her reply came two months later, at the end of July, saying 'I feel as if for the last months I've been at the bottom of the ocean'. I had reason to wonder which particular 'ocean' this was, and didn't respond that she'd had me (and probably other writers) down there with her. She had at last however done an editing job, somewhat more severe than it need have been, but, though I didn't concede all she wanted, I went as far as seemed possible without doing real damage. Elworthy was sorry to lose some references and jokes that would have been meaningful in New Zealand; but we were both relieved to have the thing under way. Publication was scheduled for April 1984.

The Pound Yeats Eliot file is simpler, but even longer because of difficulties with Faber, who handled copyright permissions for Pound, Eliot and Auden, and whose controller of such matters, Mavis Pindard, ruthless at extracting blood from stones, behaved as if the principle of 'fair dealing' for quotations was an invention of thieves and fraudsters.

So at the end of that 1982–84 clip the two books have been accepted for publication. *Pound, Yeats, Eliot and the Modernist Movement* would appear from Macmillan in London and Rutgers in the USA, but not until 1986 when the problem of permissions had finally (at considerable expense) been resolved. Macmillan did a second printing of the hardcover after six months, and reissued it a year later in a trade paperback; and it was chosen by the academic periodical *The Year's Work in English Studies* (vol. 67 for 1986) as 'the most important and engaging book of the year'.

It is an unusual book as I remember it, tightly argued, rigorous in its referencing, notes and acknowledgement of sources, head-spinningly exact and exacting in its appendix on the dating of the drafts of 'The Waste Land', sometimes off-beat and unpredictable in its preferences, but always making sense of them. It was clear reviewers found it distinctly *readable*, but that it gave academics uneasy feelings. It was personal, not the kind of book a university professor would write, or perhaps should write. Looking back from 2019 I would say it was a measure of which 'C. K.' had won between the writer and the academic.

I engaged in battles on its behalf at either end of the earth, with Ken Ruthven in New Zealand,* and in the *London Review of Books*† with the self-confessed 'fibber' Frank Kermode, who had not forgotten the embarrassment of having been caught shop-lifting from *The New Poetic*, which he used now as a stick to beat *Pound, Yeats, Eliot* . . . Sir Frank neglected (of course) to mention that the

* *Landfall* 160 (December 1986), Ruthven's review, and 161 (March 1987) my reply.
† *LRB*, 22 May 1986 with correspondence in succeeding issues.

book he was reviewing exposed his misreading of Yeats's poem 'In Memory of Major Robert Gregory' and that he had therefore a motive for discrediting it.

The militant and ungrateful literary theorist Ruthven (I had written the reference that secured him a chair in Australia) argued that the time when 'poet-professors' had seemed 'awe-inspiring creatures' was over. Either they (i.e. C. K. S.) would have to engage with modern theory, which was 'the hi-tech of literary studies', or 'be neglected by the young'. I had watched literary fashions come and go, and had especially avoided the fashion for literary theory, preferring to write intelligible English; and I made that clear in my reply, which forbore, however, to quote the graffito I'd noted on a wall at the University of Edmonton: 'Literary theorists are Saussure they know everything, they know Foucault about anything.'

The book had many positive, even enthusiastic reviews, but they often revealed the uncertainty I've described: '. . . wide-ranging and tightly focussed, balanced and polemical, descriptive and argumentative, generous and harsh [. . .] readable and significant' (*Centennial Review*, vol. 30, no. 4, Fall 1986). 'At turns brilliant, idiosyncratic, opinionated, repetitious, discursive, punctuated by many uncommon insights and often moving in its passionate devotion to Modernist ideals' (R. W. B., *Comparative Studies*). '. . . unusually courageous and to me, moving . . .' (*Paideuma*, Spring & Fall 1989).

P. E. Bishop in *Choice*[*] put the book up against the other two notable Pound scholars of the time: 'In explaining why poets read the *Pisan Cantos* with such admiration, Stead surpasses both Hugh Kenner and Donald Davie. But it was A. Walton Litz in the *Times Literary Supplement* (10.10.86) who put my two studies in Modernist poetry together in a larger context:

> *The New Poetic* was a book ahead of its time marking a sharp break with the orthodox New Critical view of Anglo American

---

* The publication of ACRL (Association of College Research Libraries).

modernism. It was a truly revisionist work, anticipating the views of a later generation of critics. When the facsimile of *The Waste Land* manuscript was published in 1971, initiating a spate of essays on the personal and confessional nature of the poem, Stead was cast in the role of prescient pioneer. It is typical of his common sense that he now declines the gambit, believing that one orthodoxy has been replaced by another equally limiting.

This then was the interesting 'future' I was wanting to leave behind. I had enjoyed writing the book, and believed it contained some of the best literary criticism I had written – which means, since I had no reason to doubt I had a special talent for it, that I thought it was uncommonly good. But I have never re-read it since it was published, and it seems unlikely at this date (2019) that I ever will.

Back to the grindstone

The fellowship came to an end in April 1982 and a month earlier I was back to the full load of teaching. Publicity about the DLitt brought attention to my role as an academic, and then later in the year AUP brought out my new collection of poems, *Geographies*. 'Scoria' represented – asserted even – what was for me home base, that Mt Eden/Maungawhau view of the world that would become clear much later in *South-West of Eden*. But on the other hand 'Yes T. S.' was a twentieth-century circumnavigation; while the poems of 'The Clodian Songbook' reached back to Catullus as if a reminder that wherever and whenever you find yourself, and whatever the technology of the time, the Roman poet's truth endures: 'I am human and nothing human is alien to me'.* Finally

* The Roman poet-playwright was Terence, but the famous statement is in the spirit of Catullus.

in the book there were six poems in the on-running unpunctuated style being tried on both sides of Tohunga Crescent, the first two being tributes to my mentors, Allen and Frank.

On the subject of Sargeson I received a letter from his sister displeased that I had referred to him in an interview after his death as 'homosexual, with no family'. She pointed out that he had siblings, aunts, nieces, nephews and cousins. The letter went on, 'Frank was a snob – maybe only an intellectual one – and a romancer. A homosexual? He loved man and woman. I wish the word could be explained. It never is. We know little of those we know well.'

I replied apologising for leaving out his relatives and explained that I'd meant only that he had no immediate family – spouse and children. I suspected that her question about what the designation 'homosexual' meant was disingenuous, but I answered that it means 'a man whose principal emotional and sexual ties were with another man or other men'.

> Whether Frank revealed this fact about himself to his relatives, he certainly made it clear to his literary friends. It was no secret. In fact he was something of a propagandist for homosexuality. When I first knew him he lived in some anxiety because he feared the possible criminal stigma that might attach itself to him if some zealous policeman decided to look into his private life . . . He seemed to want his friends to know – but as time went on and the subject received more acknowledgement, he was still not of a temperament to go in for public declarations and 'coming out of the closet'.

I did not say that Frank had told me he'd always been in love with her husband.

In May of that first year back I responded to an invitation to give a lecture to the annual conference of the National Association of Teachers of English in Christchurch. I was known as something of a left-wing radical but with conservative views about teaching

English. I wanted students to be taught a bit of basic literary history, to read some examples of the best literature in the English language (including Shakespeare and Dickens), and to write grammatically. I was not unrealistic about this. I knew about the differences in ability students brought to the classroom – but I wanted this acknowledged by separating them according to natural talent, rather than a pretence that the difference was unreal or could be eliminated. In the lecture I said:

> You have to take notice of the fact that some will arrive in the third form having read more than others will have read by the time they leave the seventh. You can't cater adequately for all those together. If I argue for segregation according to ability I'm told I'm an elitist. But *Nature* is elitist.

I also argued fiercely against the New English Syllabus with its 'eight modes of language'. And then there was this kind of thing:

> Our social bonds are primarily linguistic – they are *verbal*. Language is power. So it has been felt the study of English should not deprive children of their confidence. If they can't read or talk, then find something they can do, and call *that* language. [. . .] I'm not in the least unfeeling about those in our society who, either through heredity or the effects of the environment they were born into, suffer linguistic deprivation and consequent loss of social status. But I don't think they are helped by a system which holds back the more fortunate ones.

I am writing now in a twenty-first-century world of electronic devices, social media and the internet, a world more dominated by images than by words, and it's no longer my business even to imagine, let alone to pass judgement on, how the teaching of English should be approached. But I suppose I can at least stand by my final statement in that lecture, that the study of literature was itself a kind of radical activity, in the sense that one learned from it 'to question *every* piety, the liberal no less than the reactionary'.

The mood of buoyancy these occasions brought didn't always last. I was impassioned because I believed in the case I was making – there was indignation, but mostly there was good humour and even jokes. But that was not my constant self, and often it was followed by a sinking into embarrassment, as if I had set myself alight for public entertainment.

In September I wrote to Alan Roddick:

> I wanted to reply to your letter straight away but went diligently to work and now it's 4.30 and I feel cross-eyed with the effort of it. I lecture on modern American poetry Wed morning, Pound Wed afternoon, and James K. Fixture Friday – a great swill of portree in the mind which doesn't put me off the stuff but rather makes me drunk with it and exhausted so I dream poems but can't remember them when I wake. It seemed terrible going back to lecturing, then it seemed interesting and even pleasant, because one goes up and down with the changing demands whereas on the fellowship I just slogged on under my own internal pressure and only noticed it was vacation when I looked out and saw there were no students cluttering up the place. [. . .]
>
> Life is fairly torrid. Oliver has a girlfriend and that keeps him placid when all is well and the reverse when all is not. Last night Charlotte found her diary of many years had vanished from under her mattress. Some time ago she buried it in the garden in despair, then dug it up and began to write in it again – now it's gone and last night there were Scenes. As Ollie said, it's like someone stealing your soul. Margaret came under suspicion but was too calm to be guilty. We suspect

a friend of C's but will never know I guess. Charlotte writes so well. What a pity to lose her first jottings – it was a book I gave her for that purpose in London in 1977. [. . .]

Kay has moved from the Law Library which was run by the eccentric Julia downstairs to Serials where she has a number of friends and which is run by the very civilised Ken Porter.

In a PS to this letter I wrote:

> I owe the double margin idea to the much (and I think unfairly) denigrated Alistair Paterson, who writes dreadfully bureaucratic prose but whose poetry is authentic and rewarding. He's the agreed bottom of the pecking order at the moment – the Kelveys (see KM.s 'The Doll's House') of the literary schoolyard. I've written to the *Listener* to complain about Mac Jackson's passing swipe at him a week or so ago.

The letter to the *Listener* concluded on a different note of comic pedantry:

> And while I'm writing to complain of the *Listener*'s standards in literary matters, in the same issue Harvey McQueen's poem 'Letter to Lani' concludes
>
> a garnet
sparkles where it lays
especially if polished.
>
> Alas, a gannet can lay in the present tense, but a garnet can only lie.

IN THE NEW ACADEMIC (1983) YEAR I began teaching a course in creative writing – the University of Auckland's first, though Bill Manhire's at Victoria had been running some years and must have been the precedent. Twelve students were admitted, from the larger group who applied, on the basis of a folder of work. They had to be third-year students of English who had already passed English II; and the course would include both poetry and prose fiction. The class for this first year included Gregory O'Brien and Chris Price, and the class a year or two later Andrew Johnston, all three of whom went on to establish themselves as significant New Zealand poets. Their subsequent success had, I'm sure, nothing to do with my 'teaching', and everything to do with natural talent which each of them possessed abundantly, and would have used without a course in creative writing.

It was during this period that I wrote the long-planned poem *Paris*, two hundred lines broken into ten 20-line stanzas, and the whole in long but essentially five-stress lines. It was something of a step back from the double margin form I'd been using, but not radically different because of the free-flowing, relaxed, somewhat surreal nature of the lines – their evocation of (as the last line has it) 'the Paris of Paris that's nobody's dream but your own'. It was as if the slight boredom and reluctance of being back in academic harness had released a nostalgia – for Paris, yes, but more for what Paris represented – the aesthetic realm, the field of art and dream, of classical beauty and the romance of a culture not my own, but not unrelated to my own.

The multi-talented Greg O'Brien who at the time had never set foot in that city but knew something, as most educated people do, of French literature and art, and especially French movies, illustrated the poem with a series of drawings that matched its mood. Dennis McEldowney was keen to publish it as a small book, and sent it out to a reader. He didn't tell me who, and I didn't ask, but it went to Allen who later wrote to me:

> I had a privileged advance read of *Paris*. How rich and finely built it is! Paris of all impregnable cities, to make the presence of C. K. S. felt . . . It's your very special genius for cities. I ought to have remembered 'Pictures in a gallery . . .'

Landfall in December of this year published a long interview in which I answered questions put to me by Michael Harlow. He asked about revisions and working over drafts of poems and this got me into a discussion of what might be called my 'whether the will is free' crux. I said I saw Yeats as a 'hard work' poet; Curnow likewise. Temperamentally I felt closer to the Keats view, that in my own case 'if poetry come not as naturally as the leaves to the tree it might as well not come at all'. That was a 'truth' which suited Keats, but probably only at the time in his life when he said it. I told Harlow that I said to my students, 'Don't work on the poem; work on your self, and your self will work on the poem.' It was a kind of Zen Buddhist injunction, which they might well have found irritating, or incomprehensible. But I gave Harlow the example of myself as a high jumper when young. You spent a great deal of time in training; and then . . . I knew it was wrong to put a huge effort into the jump.

> You measured your run-up; you stood there and stared at the bar, rocking forward on your toes, and *imagined yourself going over it*; and then there was a momentary loss of consciousness which returned as you found yourself running up to the bar. There was not a '*Now!*' – a '*GO!*' No moment of decision, no act of will; only an imagining of the action and then a finding yourself doing it. There's nothing mystical about this; it's just that the will is not enough, consciousness is not enough. 'Only the whole man / Jumps his own height.'

In this year Allen's collection, *You Will Know When You Get There*, and mine, *Geographies*, were both entered for the New Zealand Book Award for poetry. The judges' report showed they had first cut eighteen entries down to eight, and then reduced this short-list down to three, eliminating books by Lauris Edmond, Louis Johnson, Vincent O'Sullivan, Hone Tuwhare and Bill Sewell – which left Curnow and Stead, with Cilla McQueen whose book,

Homing In, would share the prize with Curnow's. I wrote congratulations to Allen and told him that since his book was dedicated to me I felt I shared the honour. Cilla's book (which I described in a letter to Mark Williams as 'frothy and blowaway') would also win the Jessie Mackay prize, now awarded for a first book: so splitting the main prize between her and Curnow seemed inexplicable. I felt it had to be the result of a difference between judges, and that it was a compromise, part reward for Allen's excellence and part punishment for his bad behaviour.

There had been a fuss about – indeed outrage at – Allen's poem 'Dichtung und Wahrheit', a grimly ironic retelling of the story of Mike Joseph's novel *The Soldier's Tale*. The poem was so brilliant, and its criticism of the novel's sanguinary piety so right, I thought it justified itself – and even that the outrage was more at the poem's cleverness than at its cruelty to poor old Mike, for whom I did feel some sympathy. So when a review by James Bertram of Curnow's Penguin *Selected Poems*, which came out in the same year, appeared to focus unduly and unjustly on this poem, I wrote a letter to the editor which referred to Bertram's comments as 'shoddy'. In the age before the internet the *Listener* was our local literary forum, and my letter elicited severe disapprovals from three writers. Mike Joseph had died very recently and that seemed to make Curnow's crime, and my defence of it, even more reprehensible. 'Professor Bertram defended a man no longer alive to defend himself', Ruth Gilbert wrote, 'and this must surely merit, not censure but praise.'

Mine was a needless, ill-timed letter. Marilyn Duckworth wrote, 'I see they're giving you a bad time in the *Listener* – predictably. Anyway you've got one loyal fan in Wellington that I can vouch for.' And of course there were more than one. This was the time of Fiona Kidman's flattering poem – the one she had later to disown – which began 'The name of Stead / is on every literary / lip'. That was my problem – more even than Allen at that time, I was conspicuous. To be prize-worthy it was better to be out of sight, quiet, modest, even glum, no threat to anyone, wearing a cardy and slippers and writing dark truths about New Zealand. From this distance I can see that I must have appeared to many like a hyperactive child, writing poetry, fiction, non-fiction, a professor and not-a-professor, opinionated and clamouring – in your face and a pain in the arse. Never mind the quality of the writing, who would want a prize to go to this remorselessly *present* person if there was any way it could be directed elsewhere?

Three years before, when *Walking Westward* was short-listed, the prize had gone to an affable but undemanding collection, *Literary Cartoons*, by Kevin Ireland, an expatriate *bon viveur*, best mates with Robin Dudding who promoted his work so tirelessly in *Islands* I used to refer to the magazine as *Ireland's*. When Kevin came home on a visit and to receive the prize he was congratulated in Wellington (he told Frank who passed it on) not for the quality of his poems but for ensuring that Stead didn't get it.

I had wanted to be 'a New Zealand writer'; Frank had warned me in effect to be careful what I wished for. I was in it now, grateful to have found, or made, a place for myself, but always half-wanting to escape.

Postscript:

AUP's reader of this book suggested my comments on Frank Kermode's review might be thought unfair. I never had any doubt from Frank's demeanour in our occasional meetings after 1963 that he had not forgotten his failure to acknowledge *The New Poetic* – and that he remembered it, not because it was at all serious in the scale of academic misdemeanours, but because he had at first denied it, and then lied about it in a way that made the lie obvious. To cover this kind of thing later by acknowledging 'fibs' was a way of 'confessing' and yet to something everyone would see at once didn't matter – nicely calculated, except that the better calculation would have been to leave it behind and unsaid. Karl Miller and I talked about this once and he was wry about it because he had been literary editor of the *New Statesman* at the time and had tried to protect his contributor.

13.
All Visitors Ashore, Allen Curnow, and Mermaids

1984

Nineteen eighty-four when it arrived had, for me, nothing to do with George Orwell. It was the year of *All Visitors Ashore*, the novel that had made me so neurotically anxious, unwilling to put it into anyone but Kay's hands. There are two occasions I remember equally vividly though separated by almost a quarter of a century. One was 1961 opening a letter which told me my thesis, *The New Poetic*, had been accepted for publication by Hutchinson University Library. The other was 1984, opening a letter containing the *Guardian* review (the first) of *All Visitors Ashore*. In both cases I remember where I was and who I spoke to – the first on the university's clock-tower stairway, and to Bill Broughton, a senior student at the time; the second going in to a department meeting, and to Sebastian Black. On both occasions I was babbling to the first person in sight about the good news just received; and was almost at once smitten with embarrassment at my own foolish excitement and lack of control.

The review by Norman Shrapnel, dated 5 July, covered four novels that could be described as 'political', one by the best-seller Jeffrey Archer, and two others, all three displaying (Shrapnel argued) the problem that 'realism' inevitably betrayed 'the trivialities, parochialism and introversion of our current state', while polemics produced only clichés. 'It seems ironical,' he goes on

> ... that for sheer immediacy, for the annihilation of distance between writer and reader, we should have to turn to a novel located on the New Zealand waterfront over 30 years ago. What's more, C. K. Stead's *All Visitors Ashore* is by no means direct in its approach. It uses puns, haikus, internal dialogue and various expressionist devices, changing gear from one narrative mode to another in a way that seems bound to prove tricky and irritating but turns out to be nothing of the kind. It contributes all the time to that intimacy and precision most novelists seek but seldom find. And here is a novel that keeps politics in their place, somewhere behind the people they are supposed to sustain. [...]
>
> I thought this an intricately clever and engaging novel and, at least as important in this context, human with it.

A notebook for 1983–85 shows that throughout that period I was earning income from my writing – book royalties, payment for reviews in the *Sydney Morning Herald*, the *LRB*, and now and then the *TLS*, as well as in local literary journals. The amounts were small but increasing and would increase further when I was full-time; and once out of the university it would be open to me to apply for Arts Council and similar grants. A good deal of this writing income came in sterling, and our intention (which had already begun to happen) was to keep a joint sterling account in London to pay for travel and accommodation in the UK and Europe. That way I would be able to remain a New Zealand writer based in Auckland, but with regular access to the other world where I felt less subject to the slings and arrows my presence and my personality (for whatever reason – and maybe the fault was all mine) seemed to provoke in my dear homeland. That is why the *Guardian* review (and the many positive reviews for *All Visitors Ashore* that were to follow) were so significant. They put me another giant step along the way to that long-time goal.

A two-term sabbatical was owing to me and I was to take it from August '84 to May '85. I would continue to do academic work, on the spot and by correspondence with the department, but I would make time also for the drafting of a new novel, which would be prelude to my leaving the university altogether.

For part of the period of my time away Kay took leave without pay from the library and we set off with the daughters, first for five weeks in London, where we rented the house of a senior civil servant, Sir Henry Hardman; then another five weeks going around France and northern Italy – after which the three ladies of *l'équipe Stead* would return home to work and school, and I would stay on another couple of months. Oliver, about to turn twenty-one and not living at home, was working at the library of the Medical School. During our absence our house would be occupied by Elizabeth Smither, Auckland University's 1984 writer in residence, and watched over by the Curnows.

The Hardman house was in Durand Gardens, an enclosed oval, a quite posh enclave in working-class Stockwell just south of the River. Kay and I had a bedroom on the middle floor, Margaret on the floor below and Charlotte above. It had a small back garden with tomatoes and spinach and beans. Indoors there was a small library, Sir Henry's books being politics and economics, his wife's literary. To some extent our daughters ranged about freely, but we had meals, either in or out, together, and went as a family to the theatre – to Wagner's *Der fliegende Holländer*, Tom Stoppard's *Jumpers*, and Michael Frayn's brilliant farce *Noises Off*. And I took the daughters to a football match – Tottenham Hotspur against Luton Town. We bought the right scarves so we could mix with the home fans and share the hysteria.

We gave a small party on a Sunday afternoon for London friends, Brit and Kiwi, including Fleur Adcock, and Sylvia Ashton-Warner's son Elliot Henderson; and there was a reception at New Zealand House for David Lange. I didn't know whether he would remember me but he did, and boomed out that I had been arrested with his brother Peter after the invasion of the Hamilton pitch during the Springbok tour.

This was the time of the miners' strike, La Thatcher (as she was called in France – pronounced Latta-chair) locked in battle with Arthur Scargill, who seemed to be leading the charge of the light brigade into the valley of death. Meanwhile under the concrete overpasses around the area of the National Theatre a whole cardboard city of the unemployed and otherwise deprived and unfortunate had grown up, sleeping rough, foraging in rubbish, lighting fires, begging and stealing.

While we were in Durand Gardens news came that *All Visitors Ashore* had sold out and was reprinting. It had been entered for the Booker Prize (along with 120 other novels) and had not made the short-list of six – and someone in the *Literary Review* was saying it should have. The winner that year was to be Anita Brookner's *Hotel du lac* – ever-so British, middle-class conventional fiction. Its opening sentence read like a warning: 'From the window all that could be seen was a receding area of grey.' It beat Julian Barnes' short-listed *Flaubert's Parrot*, a book the charm and inventiveness of which Barnes would never quite manage again. It was another lesson in the nature of the Booker, and indeed of all literary prizes.

We went by rail and ferry to Paris, spent a few days there in a hotel, not this time in our favourite precinct around St Sulpice, but in the Marais, the Jewish quarter, with its narrow winding streets with many good cheap restaurants, and food shops that specialised in poultry. Dead chooks hanging in shop windows everywhere! Then we picked up a hire car and drove first to Dijon where we stayed with Carole and Jean-Pierre Durix and their two children. Jean-Pierre had already a copy of *All Visitors Ashore* and was planning to do a chapter on it in a book he was writing about 'New

Literatures in English' – the other subjects to be novels by Wilson Harris, Patrick White and Salman Rushdie.*

To Allen Curnow I wrote at the end of October:

> We enjoyed our travels in France and Italy. Apart from anything else, just the pleasure of eating out in a French or Italian restaurant – a different one – every night for 3 weeks was a great treat. We had exhausting days in Paris, a pleasant visit to academic friends in Dijon, a marvellous couple of days in Sallanches (near Mon Blanc – we passed through Geneva then back into France) – then down to Rapallo where we spent a lot of time on Ezra Pound locations, and after two days identified Olga Rudge's house above the town; a week swimming and sun-bathing and eating in Menton – then a slow journey back through parts of France we hadn't visited before – across to Périgueux (Pound's Troubadour country), the Dordogne, Tours, Orléans, the Loire Valley, and back to Paris. The only bad event (there had to be one) was the theft of a suitcase – our car broken into at night – loss of some favourite clothes, and films with 120 photographs undeveloped.

The stop in Rapallo had been in recognition of Ezra Pound who figured so prominently in my forthcoming book. Pound had lived for several decades there in a seafront roof-top apartment with his wife Dorothy, the daughter of Olivia Shakespear. Olivia had been the mistress (as she would then have been designated) of W. B. Yeats, which would have made the older poet the younger's father-in-law if there had been a marriage; and Yeats, Pound's guest in Rapallo in the late 1930s, had written about his stay there in the introduction to the strange book he called *A Vision*. In Rapallo, he wrote:

---

* *The Writer Written*, Greenwood Press, 1987.

> I shall not lack conversation. Ezra Pound, whose art is the opposite of mine, whose criticism commends what I most condemn, a man with whom I should quarrel more than with anyone else if we were not united by affection, has for years lived here in rooms opening on to a flat roof by the sea.

On that roof, where the two poets sat talking in deckchairs in the sun, lived also the huge stone 'hieratic head of Ezra Pound'* sculpted by the brilliant young artist Henri Gaudier-Brzeska, whose death in World War I had represented for Pound the gross waste of youth and talent which were the motivation, or the excuse, for his political loyalties and economic theories during this period.

Pound, an only child, had been followed to Rapallo by his devoted parents who came to live there in retirement. But at the same time, up in the hills above the town, lived his lover, the American violinist Olga Rudge; so Pound's life for many years had been lived, as he said, 'between a door and a door', taking the once-a-week trudge up the *salita* through orchards, olive groves and vineyards, to spend a day or two with Olga who bore him his only child – Mary.† Mary had lived to write a book about her strange childhood, handed over as a baby to be brought up by German-speaking peasants in the Tyrol, the mountainous region of northern Italy, but visited once a year by an English-speaking couple, Ezra and Olga, who would take her on a summer holiday to Venice, and who, she was not told until almost an adult, were her real father and mother.

All this extraordinary lore about Pound – his taking the side of Mussolini (and therefore Hitler) in World War II and his ghastly anti-Semite and pro-Fascist broadcasts over Italian radio; his capture by the American military and incarceration, first in a wire

---

* Now in the National Gallery of Art, Washington, DC.

† Some years later I was to meet Mary in Rapallo and have lunch with her in Professor Massimo Bacigalupo's garden above the town. Dorothy's only child, Omar, though given the Pound name, was not Ezra's, possibly Dorothy's act of revenge, a quid pro quo for Olga's Mary. I met Omar later in Yale University,

cage where he began writing *The Pisan Cantos*; his subsequent arraignment in Washington for treason and confinement in an insane asylum for thirteen years; and then his release and unrepentant return to Italy – it was all rehearsed over meals and while we walked and climbed, hunting for the sites where so much of it had happened: a tragic and comic story of genius and madness, love and poetry, and all in sight of this sea, these hills, vines and olives. I like to think it was part of my daughters' education.

We found the *salita* and climbed up to Sant'Ambrogio, stopping at intervals to look back over the town I was to call Tigullio in my novel *Villa Vittoria*, and the Ligurian Sea. As reported to Allen, it took us two days to find Olga Rudge's house up there. Finally a charming Milanese insurance agent at the gate of his holiday villa pointed it out for us. He called it the Casa Ezra Pound, and referred to Olga Rudge as Pound's secretary. He seemed to know nothing of another Pound household down in the town. But he knew the Casa Ezra Pound was only the upper storey of the villa. The lower part had been occupied by a workshop for pressing olives (a fact that figures in *The Cantos*).

So Pound and Yeats: this was in part a literary pilgrimage. What about Eliot? Our days in Menton were 'for old times' sake'; but I was able to tell them that Eliot had got to know his secretary and then second wife Valerie better when they spent a holiday there with friends, and that it had been the site of their honeymoon, where a unique pic of Tom had been taken – shirtless!

A Curnow–Stead exchange

Allen wrote to me in October to report that all was well at 37 Tohunga Crescent. Elizabeth Smither had given a dinner party there for Allen and Jeny, Bill Pearson and others. He enclosed a new poem, 'Blind Man's Holiday', about which he said little, and nothing of the anxiety it was giving him. I was impressed by it and wrote back at once:

> This hotel may be in Bloomsbury but it doesn't provide a writing table (I'm writing this on a suitcase) nor an adequate light – however I did want to shoot back an aero to tell you how very much I admire the new poem. It was waiting for me together with other mail when we got back from France.

I discussed the title and picked up on the quotations, mostly from Wordsworth's 'Tintern Abbey'. I said 'the poem's physical/metaphysical conundrum impresses powerfully'. And I concluded:

> The final section is vivid and particular and seems to me (though I can't be sure I read it as the poet intends) to draw the whole beautifully together – as if pain, like death, and sex, closes the gap between the physical and metaphysical. A great poem. Nobody alive is writing such poems anywhere in the English language – I'm sure of it.

This letter crossed with one from Allen written at Karekare (4.11.84), having just read *All Visitors Ashore*.

> Melior is tremendous – something of him seems to irradiate the whole book, a presence one remembers – one will always be visiting him. Not that it isn't Curl's book. [. . .] Curl is special, he's there in present time as he was 30 years earlier. For me a mystery of your trade, how it's all done. [. . .]
> Weather and seasons – another pleasure – and the ferries, so much real and active detail – nothing skimped – novels twice as long are poorer & sometimes sloppy about such things – your noticing eye always awake – and ear too (that late autumn cicada!) Rosh is my favourite fictional dog, all dog in dog situations, being a dog e.g. p49. [. . .]
> It's a moving story, we're not let off the hook. I found Jeny shedding a real tear – she was finishing the book while I got breakfast ready this morning.

> Only afterwards one realises how beautifully it all fits together – plotting, machinery or whatever it is, expressing just the way things happen and had to happen.

I sent a postcard (8.11.84) thanking him for this:

> . . . it must pretty well have crossed with mine about your poem. I couldn't have a better reader. Thanks so much for all your comments. One does so want one's friends to enjoy one's work – never mind what the rest have to say. The response to AVA is great – but I feel everyone will be looking at me to do it again and I'm not sure I can.

Then came one from Allen (7.11.84) having received mine about his poem:

> I'm enormously grateful for your remarks on 'Blind man's holiday'. When it was finished what I needed was another new one. To get my mind off it – instead, I went on worrying about it, fearing something might be seriously wrong, examining it for <u>that</u>, and then worried because I couldn't find it. Your reading lifts the cloud. [. . .]

Some of the idea behind the poem had come from a conversation we'd had about the difficulty of representing pain in a poem. Allen had had an episode of extreme back pain at Karekare which had resulted in an ambulance trip from there to Middlemore Hospital which had got into the poem; and mine had been the broken neck. Allen continued:

> Do you remember something I said after my Middlemore experience and thinking of yours, about intense pain & the way one can't remember what it was <u>like</u>, being a possible subject for a poem? You said you had tried it ('Breaking the

> Neck'?) – I've just looked at those animating poems again, but they have their own story to tell. I'd decided you must be right, pain of itself – one's own – was an impossible subject. The kind of arrangement you see in Blind Man's Holiday is pretty close to what I did have in mind – the darkness that closes over sexuality, over war, over pain, despite all the 'pictures or pensées', that one knows what one is doing or where one is going, and it's a ride in the dark. But there was no schema – except that once I and II were done there had to be a III. [. . .] But I think it was the hospital experience we agreed was intractable? Because one's own can't be singled out without risk of fatuity, and this was the problem I hoped I'd solved in III, and now I feel pretty sure I did, since it worked for you.

Even at a distance the cross-crescent exchanges went profitably on.

The Death of the Body

After a few days back in London I saw Kay and the daughters off at Heathrow and settled into a room in London House, intending to deal with proofs of the Pound Yeats Eliot book, but mainly to embark at once on a new novel. If I was to be a writer full-time there could not be any delay. A gap of thirteen years, as there had been between *Smith's Dream* and *All Visitors Ashore*, would be the end of the dream. I had to prove to myself that I could produce novels (and their income) at regular intervals, whatever my state of mind, and whatever the ambient public view of me and my work. So I spent a day or so setting myself up in the room, and began at once, writing as always detailed daily reports to Kay.

I bought a new typewriter from W. H. Smith, blue, for £39.50, and found that by tying two empty drawers together with tape I could put them on the desk as a platform and type standing up – which was necessary because the effect on my lower back of typing sitting in a chair was too painful to sustain for more than a few days. There were books, a Matisse poster, and later a pinboard with photographs. What the room looked out on is described in the first paragraph of *The Death of the Body*:

> It looks over the square. It's already late autumn and the leaves are showering down and heaping over lawns and paths. Those remaining are still a curious mixture of green and brown. The afternoon light slants through them revealing the pattern of boughs that has been concealed.

Arrangements were being made by New Zealand House and our embassy in Bonn for me to make academic visits to Italy, Germany, Denmark, and my plan was that these should become part of the novel, in which the story, set in Auckland, will be told by an unidentified narrator who, for reasons which might or might not become clear (that was yet to be decided) is telling it while on the move in Europe. So the telling of the story would be as much a part of the novel as the story itself.

Professor Gorlier was 'determined to have me at his conference in Milan on multi-cultural influences on Australian and New Zealand literatures'; and the welcome in Kiel where I was to give a lecture/reading was going to be warm. Anna Rutherford in Aarhus was not so sure – the time I would be available (immediately after Kiel) was out of term and therefore not ideal: but they were working on it. Meanwhile I got on with the job, the new novel, and wrote to Kay on 12 November:

> 4½ pages written. I'm away – a start. Probably now I won't run into trouble for 40 or 50 or with a bit of luck 60 pages. We'll see. What a strange and dangerous business it is, writing fiction. So much investment of self in a leaking ship. No wonder Shadbolt goes around the bend with the effort. I ought to have been kinder to him. I have been a merciless sibling rival (even if it's true he's not much of a writer).

There was also news just received that Picador would be doing a paperback of *All Visitors Ashore* with an advance of £1,000.

The writing continued at a rate of between two and four pages a day through most of November, and during that month came a copy of Ian Cross's *Listener* review of *All Visitors Ashore*. Dripping with sarcasm ('a portrait of the New Zealand artist as an awful young dick') it seemed to me a complete misreading of the tone of the novel, ascribing to it the malice which was Cross's own. This review, and a long piece the following month in the same journal by David Young, also sarcastic in tone and deploring my having (as he saw it) invaded the privacy of Frank and Janet in the characters of Melior Farbro and Cecelia Skyways, confirmed my feeling of insecurity about New Zealand. Yet on the Denis Glover principle that 'you don't read reviews you measure them', I could hardly complain: I and my novel were getting a lot of attention, a lot of space. And meanwhile other, affirmative reviews kept coming, both there and here.

London House was providing ample company this time. There was an American lecturer in English from a Canadian university, civilised, gay, very tall (what we used to call 'an XYY guy'), with whom from time to time I had meals at restaurants round about. He was a Catholic, and when I asked him how he believed what that required him to believe he gave the perfect answer, 'By Divine grace.' From time to time I had lunch with Antonia at a Chinese restaurant she favoured in Lisle Street. She was no longer teaching at UCL and felt that something like calm and an ability to focus had returned. Vol. II was finished, now called *Still Life*, and soon to be published; and an idea for another novel was brewing which might have to come first, before she moved on to Vol. III of Frederica Potter's story.*

In the room next door to mine was a young woman, Dominique, French-Canadian – and also (I began to suspect) sometimes another,

* This was to be *Possession* which won the Booker.

using her floor to sleep on – a way of getting free accommodation and access to subsidised London House meals. One day this other occupant knocked on my door. A New Zealander, she had recognised my name, wanted to meet me, and had decided she would take the risk and trust me not to dob her in as an interloper. Her name was Shan, and the surname was familiar. Any relation, I asked, to the Speaker of the New Zealand Parliament? Well yes actually, she was his daughter!

'Squatting' in those years was frowned upon but not illegal if you were accomplished in practical matters and could achieve it. A group, usually young people, would break into an unoccupied house or building, reconnect gas, water and electric power, put new locks on the doors, pay neither rent nor rates, and could not be forcibly evicted without a court order. It was partly economic in intent, but was also a sort of Trotskyite political warfare against Thatcherism, and there were estimated to be as many as 30,000 people squatting in London. Shan was coming and going from a nearby squat, much preferring the comfort of Dominique's floor, and the food in the London House dining hall, to what was offering at 'home' in Euston.

I wrote to Kay that I had been offered a CBE and had hesitated to accept; but I'd been told I would have to make up my mind by the end of the day – so had said yes. A day or so later, I reported, there was a crisis. Confidence in the way the novel was going had suddenly collapsed. I set off walking – to Tottenham Court Road, along the length of Oxford Street, across Hyde Park to High Street Kensington, and on some way towards Hammersmith before I had accepted what the inner Monitor was telling me. I arrived back at Mecklenburgh Square knowing that I had to abandon the seventy-plus pages thus far written and begin again. 'Thought for the Day' I wrote to Kay, was

> . . . so blindingly simple I don't know why it hasn't come to me before: if, in any large or significant degree, you are

> inventing what happens while you write, then when you have discovered what happens it must all be written again. No matter how modern or meta-fictionist or whatever it may be, it is really just the telling of a story around the dinner table, and the art of that depends on knowing, before you start, the story you're going to tell, and then arranging its parts to advantage. How can you do that if you don't yet know the parts? You can't. It becomes shapeless. So Chapter One, now I know how that much of the story goes, must be re-done. Possibly it will be the same for Chapter Two, and so on how far? I feel stunned by the enormity of the task. I remember years ago thinking [D. H.] Lawrence was ridiculously puritanical because (I'd read) he would write a whole novel, and then, instead of revising, would write it all again. And sometimes again. It now makes perfect sense. But a terrible lethargy grips me at the thought. I feel like little Bill Pearson – some playful infant-school teacher has popped me back over the fence and I have to trudge around it again just to get back where I was.* Well, it's just a matter of patience and steadiness. I keep thinking of the Auden poem Frank liked to quote about how poets can 'dash forward like hussars', but the novelist has to slug it out slowly. I feel I can't do anything until I've rewritten Chapter One. And it's important to have chapters, each a manageable 'story'. It must have complexity, yet be clear. It must be a series of parcels or baskets – something with bulk that gets unwrapped, not a long thin meandering narrative line. I will need to buy a new typewriter ribbon.

The writing went on fluently after that. The certainty that it had been the right thing to do made the prose more confident. It was interrupted while I made the visit to Milan where Professor

* See my *Shelf Life: Reviews, Replies and Reminiscences*, p. 163.

Gorlier's conference was given rooms in the Palazzo delle Stelline (the Palace of the Little Stars) in the Corso Magenta, not far from the church of Santa Maria delle Grazie that housed da Vinci's *The Last Supper*. Since much of this visit would go into the novel, it was less an interruption than a part of the process. My mind was less firmly on the conference than on the locations, which were to be essential parts of the fiction – and especially a little café-bar just down the street from the Palazzo, and the café owner there I would appropriate, turning him into a sort of bossy arbiter of the way the story is told.

Back in London and writing again I reported 'real progress' in that I had rewritten chapters that had been causing me anxiety. 'I had intended to make these simple and straightforward but the Story won't permit that. Simple and straightforward tends to be conventional and to lack immediacy.'

Christmas came and went, with a flurry of seasonal celebrations, while the writing went fluently on. I had Christmas Day with our old friends the Sturmer family. Antonia invited me to a family gathering on Boxing Day. I wondered whether 'family' would include the mythical 'ugly sister' (who was not, of course, ugly at all – indeed rather fine-looking) but when the time came there were Antonia's husband Peter Duffy and their two daughters Isabel and Miranda, and Antonia's Byatt daughter (also Antonia), together with a brother and a sister and their spouses and children, and Peter's mother – the full complement, almost, but no Margaret Drabble.

There was a dinner with Beth Wilson and her brother Brian Horton, and Alan Hollinghurst, not yet known as a novelist but as deputy editor of the *TLS*. Both now living in Britain, Beth and Brian had been students with me at Auckland University in the 1950s. Brian had been one of our student poetry group, and Beth had married another, Bernard Clark. She was now divorced from him and one of their three children, Nicholas, a brilliant young art historian, had died earlier this year, a victim of AIDS, which was just beginning to be recognised and to cause a kind of moral/medical panic. When Alan Hollinghurst's first novel, *The Swimming-Pool Library*, appeared four years later, it was dedicated to Nicholas who had been his friend.

After graduating (well) from Auckland Brian had gone to Oxford with another of our poetry group, Rob Dyer, the one who threw a meringue at his tutor there at High Table and was sent down without completing his degree. Brian had gained a first in Modern Languages, and risen to a senior position with Reuters (European editor), and was now second-in-command to the Australian newspaper tycoon Rupert Murdoch. Murdoch's News International had recently bought *The Times* and was about to precipitate a conflict with the print unions by insisting the whole complex should be moved from its headquarters in Gray's Inn Road to new premises at Wapping. Brian spoke of his own significance in all this, and I had no reason to think anything he said was untrue. Murdoch had sacked Harold Evans as a *Times* editor, appointed Brian as foreign editor, and had given him responsibility for 'sorting out the mess' the paper was in. All of this seemed to accord perfectly with the mood of Thatcherite Britain. I therefore 'disapproved' of Tory Brian politically, but found him, like his sister (a supporter of the Lib-Dems), charming company.

None of this Christmas-time quickening of the social life was doing any damage to the novel. On 6 January 1985, two days before our thirtieth wedding anniversary, I wrote to Kay:

> When I gave up the first version at p. 74 that was 28th Nov. I passed p. 74 of the rewrite on Jan 3rd and I've now reached p. 84 with a clear view ahead. Giving up and starting again was an act of courage – I don't know how I did it. But more desperation than courage. As soon as I'd made the decision I knew it was right. The fiction is beginning to draw off itself, which means it's developing a richer texture as it goes.

Wedding anniversaries were days we mostly chose to ignore, but on the day of our thirtieth I sent Kay a loving telegram, and she wrote that she did not regret a single one of the 30 x 365 days – untrue of course but an entirely acceptable exaggeration. My CBE had been announced in the New Year Honours, and messages of congratulation were arriving, local and from New Zealand. The release of *All Visitors Ashore* for the Christmas market in New Zealand meant that these two events lent publicity to one another, and my absence perhaps made them more interesting, even mysterious. Kay's letters were constantly reporting people known to us who had heard the news and read the book; and reviews both local and from abroad came in numbers and spaces far in excess of anything that could happen now. We were still in the age of literacy, and did not know it was about to pass into the age of the image.

When I told Kay that Barry Humphries had invited me to lunch at the Garrick Club she asked was I sorry to be coming home so soon. I said I felt as though I would be leaving the party before it was over – but that was my habit, wasn't it? What I was enjoying most was not the 'party' but the freedom to write with complete concentration on a work of fiction. But I reported feeling quite unwell. There was no high temperature, no pain or other obvious symptoms. It was mostly that I felt depressed, was struggling doing my daily runs around the square, and sleeping a great deal – including in the daytime when I wanted to be working, even falling asleep at the typewriter, and puzzled about what might be wrong with me. Looking at these letters now I diagnose overwork. It didn't at that time occur to me that you could drive yourself too hard, but that is probably what I was doing. Those extra hours of sleep were taken by the body because it needed them.

On 15 January I went to lunch with Barry Humphries at the Garrick Club. At first I couldn't find it until I twigged that it would be the building that *didn't* have a name. There a lackey took me to Barry, who was wearing a brown suit that looked as though it might have been of horsehair. I was wearing a jacket and £1.99 shirt of burgundy velvet and a navy tie bought in Milan. Since I didn't have a suit I thought it best to assert what I did have. I was blue with cold from walking in the snow – the papers were reporting the previous day had been the coldest day since 1947 – and my jaw wasn't working. In the loo I heard:

'So the Chancellor won't be lunching today?'

'No – he's occupied with the pound.'

'How's it doing?'

'It's rallying a bit this morning.'

'Enough to save him from embarrassment?'

''Fraid not.'

'Poor chap. I wouldn't like to be in his shoes. Let's go in.'

At the top of some stairs there was a crowd. Sir John Gielgud was going to present the annual theatre awards, and Barry was surrounded by newsmen with flashing bulbs. He gave them a moment to get their shots and then said 'I'm not here to get an award. I'm here to take Karl Stead to lunch' – in a tone suggesting they would all know who Karl Stead was. They hid their puzzlement and put on comprehending and respectful faces. A smart little paparazzo said, 'That's OK, Guv. We might need your picture for an obit.'

We went into the smaller of two dining rooms where there was a coal fire burning and pictures around the walls of theatre and literary people – Kean, Pope as Hamlet (I said he should have been Richard III) etc. Barry ate an enormous meal and I ate a smaller but ample one. We enjoyed ourselves. I told him I found Poms impenetrable. The fact that we spoke the same language was simply confusing. As we walked out an hour or so later he said, looking around thoughtfully, 'All these impenetrables walking about.' As we parted he told me he wanted me to ring as soon as I was back from Germany and Denmark so I could come and see their new house in Hampstead. When I recounted part of this later in a review in the *LRB* of a book about Barry by John Lahr I wrote:

> Barry Humphries represents the dilemma of Australasian and Anglo-African expatriation – the loss and the gain of it. He can only be fully understood at home; but there he's likely to encounter a good deal of sullenness and resentment, which is overcome, paradoxically, by the irresistible force of fame earned where the comprehension of what he is doing must be less than complete.

Carol O'Brien invited me to dinner to meet Christopher MacLehose who was taking over at Harvill and would be my London fiction publisher, taking me with him through his own vicissitudes for most of the next twenty-five years. Christopher's appearance was striking – very tall, patrician, handsome, confident or arrogant in manner depending on who was passing judgement, with a rich deep voice and public-school accent. He had once broken his right wrist and consequently for a time had had to shake with his left hand, held in a sort of twist to match the right hand of the other person. This was piquant to me, though I didn't tell him, because my father, with his paralysed right hand, shook hands in exactly the same way. Christopher had evidently found this so satisfying and stylish he continued to do it, even though the need and the accompanying right arm in a sling were gone – eccentric, even dotty, but typical and harmless. He liked to talk to me about rugby, the All Blacks and their fortunes, and 'school', which I soon perceived he imagined (or pretended) meant the same to me as it did to him. In fact to him it meant a British public school (Shrewsbury) and boarding; to me, a New Zealand grammar school 'day boy' – though there were shreds of the British conventions retained in ours: 'house boys' (boarders), caning, prefects, the tuck shop, the fives courts, addressing one another by surname only, nicknames for the teachers ('Butch' Brown, 'Hedgy' Boulton, 'Sticky' Harris, 'Parvus' Brock) who were 'Masters' and addressed as 'Sir', and shreds of Latin, like a pass to get out early that was called an 'exeat'. Since I had read British school stories in my early teens I could usually understand that part of Christopher's conversation. Like Karl Miller he was Edinburgh born, but of grander social antecedents, and had lost the accent which Karl retained. I found him charming, but I understood when people who worked for him told me he was 'difficult', even 'impossible'. He was inner-directed, and tended to neglect small things like cost. He was very particular about visual matters, and when (this was some years later) his eye lighted on a painting by the Italian movie director Federico Fellini that would be *'perfect'* for a paperback reissue of *All Visitors Ashore* he had to have it, even though the price should have been too high for Harvill, and getting it took so long the publishing schedule was disrupted. I mention this only as an example, because to me it was disarming, even though I recognised the frustration of his staff who were almost without exception beautiful young women.*

Christopher drove me home from Carol's dinner that evening, in an open-topped car that seemed to match him in style, though getting in and out of it with legs as long as his could not be elegantly achieved. He asked me about the novel I was currently writing and said he looked forward to being its publisher. Later I would get to know his wife Koukla, who was French and redoubtable.

Mermaids

Ulla Ampersand acted as secretary for the Commonwealth Studies group in Scandinavia and Germany, and in that role came down to Kiel to hear me speak and read. There was also a representative, Lyn Dovey, from the New Zealand Embassy in Bonn; and I was welcomed by Professor Konrad Gross, head of the English Department at the university. The attempt to include a visit to Aarhus had been unsuccessful – students were still away – but Ulla suggested I should come at least as far as Copenhagen. Ferries

* Our daughter Margaret was to be one of them for a few years

from that city went across the Øresund (the now famous bridge not yet built) and should make it possible for me to visit Malmö and Helsingborg, where Christian Karlson, the grandfather whose name I bore, had been born and grew up.

I flew to Hamburg and took the train to Kiel where I was welcomed by Professor Gross, given coffee and cake with cream and red currants, and taken then to the place of execution where I talked and read for two hours to the university's Anglo-German Society. There was then the discreet handing over of cash which seemed standard in Europe: Lyn Dovey gave me 300 marks towards expenses and Professor Gross 200 for my lecture. My meal was at their expense and my hotel room booked and paid for.

We went in a group for dinner at a restaurant. The weather was ferociously winter, but calm. My memories are at once general, even conventional, and particular – ice and snow, a white landscape with villages and church spires, docks with ships locked in frozen seas. For the novel I was writing I needed that landscape, that weather, those scenes and this Ulla, who was already being built into its structure, its focus of desire and yet simultaneously its monitor and curb on desires. The mechanics of the novel and her role in it, the mystery of its halt at page 74 and return to restart at the beginning, and why and how its events set entirely in Auckland had to be told by an uncertainly identified itinerant in Europe, so that the telling becomes quite as much the story as the story itself – all that came out of inner compulsions mysterious even to me; and yet, having at this date (December 2018) re-read it, *The Death of the Body* still strikes me as exceptionally clever and entertaining.*

Ulla came for me next day and we drove north in her big station wagon, from Kiel to Flensberg, where we crossed into Denmark; then boarded the roll-on ferry from Nyborg to Korsør. The ship

---

* Mark Williams has a good shot at reading it in his *Leaving the Highway: Six Contemporary New Zealand Novelists*, 1990, but spends too much time on the supposed connection with the Mervyn Thompson affair. Reginald Berry reviewed it intelligently in *Landfall* 163, September 1987.

had to plough through shrieking chunks of ice, graunching and heaving and shuddering as it went. Sometimes the sea was an ice surface, but the ferry cracked on through it. Then we were driving again. It was a longer journey than I'd expected, about eight hours, so we were not in Copenhagen until evening, where I was delivered to my hotel and Ulla would stay with a convenient aunt. Next day and the day after I went with her to the ferry terminal and was told the ice was too thick and the ferries were not running. This from *The Death of the Body*, Chapter 29 tells it as it was:

> I was working now in a brown city locked in a white circle. I ate my breakfast in a little red and black restaurant with frilly light shades that hung over the tables. I sat at a desk in my room, and when I looked up I could see ice sliding almost imperceptibly down the red-tiled roof opposite. Now and then a piece would break off and fall over people walking in the street below. Beyond the roof the brown tower and the gold-faced clock pushed up into the cold haze of the sky.
>
> Not far away the Tivoli Gardens were closed. When I walked that way I could see through the iron gate the elegant black curves of willows hanging over frozen ponds.
>
> In the afternoons I walked along frozen canals and down to frozen docks.

That second day there was an official lunch at the expense of the Canadian Embassy – part of their 'investment in Commonwealth Literature'. In the evening we were taken to a performance by the Royal Danish Ballet of works by Martinů and Hindemith followed by Stravinsky's *Petrushka*. Next day it was an exhibition at the Carlsberg Museum of Gaugin's early work, done while he lived in Copenhagen with a Danish wife and their four children, all abandoned when he ran off (or was possibly sent packing by the Dane) to Paris. I spent a lot of time walking about the frozen city, and it might have been this same day that I saw (sublime to ridiculous, Impressionism to

Chocolate Box) Copenhagen's famous 'Little Mermaid' sitting bare-breasted on a rock at the waterfront, her fish tail tucked under her.

JUST BEFORE LEAVING LONDON FOR HOME I went to dinner at Barry's ample and richly furnished Hampstead house, with its art collection which included a Burne-Jones (Barry had sold an apartment to buy it), Max Beerbohm, William Rothenstein – the '90s painters he had made himself expert in. I had been asked to come early so there was time for me to see the house, and Barry's office (very large, with an IBM machine), and on the top floor the studio of his wife (his third) the painter Diane Milstead. She had been working for a long time on a single large canvas which was mounted on an easel under lights in the middle of the room. It was a seascape except that in the foreground was the principal subject, a mermaid on a rock. Diane talked about it, I looked at it, and Barry watched. It wasn't just the subject that astonished me but the fact that she was 'standing' on her bent fishtail, somehow holding herself upright. I was trying to think of something to say. It occurred to me that the 'Little Mermaid' I'd seen only a couple of days ago had been sitting on her tail, with very human knees bent under her, and the tail like a kind of drapery – which was more realistic, or at least more plausible. I decided it was better not to refer to the Copenhagen sculpt, and managed to say something which was nothing. What I took away from that moment was the sense of Barry as the detached observer – as if he had contrived the moment and was now watching it play out, enjoying the spectacle.

That's how it seemed at the time; but I wasn't sure. Sometimes it's a mistake to attribute everything to the cleverness of a very clever person. Innocence and simplicity are also possible, and Barry has probably more of both than most of his public would imagine. In a significant exchange with one of his biographers, John Lahr, at a later time when Diane was making a very public fuss about their imminent divorce, Barry said, 'I was so much into pleasing. I thought I was entertaining her. Isn't that my role? There's a great deal of unlearning to do.' Maybe he had simply brought his wife someone he knew would find something nice to say about her mermaid.

That divorce was to cost him a great deal, including the Burne-Jones.

Postscript:

The chairman of the Booker judges for 1984, Richard Cobb, in a letter (published many years later) to his friend Hugh Trevor-Roper, congratulated himself for having 'managed to keep Martin Amis and Angela Carter off the short-list [. . .] and manoeuvring so that Ballard did not get the prize, to the FURY of the media and the critics'. The Amis novel was *Money*, surely the most remarkable British novel of the decade. The Ballard was *Empire of the Sun*.

Sic transit gloria Bookeri.

14.
Sligo, Gateway to the World

Outrage was in the air

The two judges for the fiction section of the New Zealand Book Awards for 1985 were Lawrence Jones and Patricia Grace. *All Visitors Ashore* topped Jones's list and Marilyn Duckworth's *Disorderly Conduct*, which topped Grace's, did not figure even in his first half dozen. My novel did not figure at all in Grace's preferences – so she and Jones agreed the prize should be shared, half for each of the novels one judge considered not worthy of even a short-listing. These things seem to matter at the time and leave afterwards only a sense of cynicism about book prizes and the people who administer them. They are distorters of the market, great if you win, a piss-off if you don't, and in the years you don't have an eligible book or an interest in one, a bore. They are commercial rather than literary-critical events; and being partnered with Marilyn was no penance.

Nineteen eighty-five saw Professor Stead back at his desk, and lecturing to stage three students about Shakespeare's last plays. Current academic orthodoxy discouraged one from thinking of the last of these, *The Tempest*, as Shakespeare's 'farewell to the theatre'; and though I didn't dwell on that idea, it was there somewhere in the back of my mind. My academic revels were indeed ending and it would very soon be time to move on. This was my third and last year of the creative writing class and it included the young Andrew Johnston, who has become since one of our significant poets. Also in the class, with enormous hair and very fancy tasselled jeans, was Tim Wilson who vanished from sight (or from my sight) for many years and has in recent years reappeared as TV person and novelist. The class of the previous year, which I had abandoned in August leaving Kendrick in charge, published a selection of their work and I wrote a preface setting out some of the principles on which I had run the course.

> I try to teach my students first to consider every literary text, of whatever style, stature or vintage, as something still in process, with the status only of a manuscript. It is the principle of Valéry's 'A poem is never finished, merely abandoned.' And in their own writing I encourage each of them to discover what kind of writer he/she is, and to be it. I don't care about the kind – only that each should try to do it well. To that end I encourage everyone to be free, flexible, open-minded, willing to experiment. Finally I keep before them the proposition that the individual sensibility and intelligence are never enough. You must immerse yourself in the tradition of your art and become part of it. Imitation at an early stage is important. Reading is essential. This last is sometimes the most difficult lesson to impart.
>
> I put a high value on economy. I believe that if something said in eighteen words can be said in nine, those nine will be working harder, will be more charged with energy, than the eighteen each bearing a lighter load. There will be fewer neutral syllables, a stronger texture.
>
> It used to be said when I was young that a simile was only a weak metaphor. No one thought of putting the proposition the other way about: that most metaphors are similes pretending to a strength they don't in fact possess. There is an artificiality, an artifice, about poetic imagery, which is naturally reduced as

you approach closer to spoken language – to what Wordsworth called 'the real language of men'.

A course of this kind calls for patience, precision, tact and firmness in varying combinations. One can never be sure how far one has succeeded or failed in exercising these qualities in the right measure; but gradually, as the year goes on, they resolve themselves into something that could be called simply friendship. The effort becomes collaborative. I am able to fade into the group, and even, finally, as I did last year, absent myself altogether.

Kay and I went to Wellington in May for my investiture as CBE (Commander of the Order of the British Empire!) and around the same time Bridget Ikin's movie of 'A Fitting Tribute' was previewed at the Berkeley in Mission Bay. Ken Smithyman and I kept up reading poetry for Dennis McEldowney at Auckland University Press, and I continued as a member of the Press Committee. Mostly Ken and I agreed, but not invariably, and the disagreements involved interesting explanatory notes back and forth, sometimes including an appeal to Murray Edmond for a third opinion.

Mike Doyle and I had been accumulating material for a New Zealand issue of the Canadian literary journal *Ariel*, which would be published this year. My contribution, apart from one poem and the job of soliciting and editing new work, was a review article about Keri Hulme's *The Bone People* which had won the Pegasus Prize, an international award to go that year to a novel by a Māori. In my article I asked a question which is now considered improper: did only one of eight great-grandparents a Māori qualify Hulme for this award? It seemed the right question to ask then; in retrospect it doesn't: one has moved with the times.

But setting that aside my piece still strikes me as one of the few (and certainly the first) really acute critical discussions of *The Bone People*, which I considered to be a work of great distinction despite the fact that I was made deeply uneasy by its depiction of the violence against the child, Simon. It reminded me of Benjamin Britten's opera *Peter Grimes*, a work which also presents extreme violence against a child (in fact he is beaten to death) yet asks for sympathy and understanding for the man who commits it. 'In principle' I concluded, 'such charity is admirable. But the line between charity and imaginative complicity is very fine indeed.'

This was published in our New Zealand edition of *Ariel* in October 1985; but in that month the novel won the Booker Prize, which put any discussion of it into a quite different category of critical interest. In November Karl Miller told me he thought it the best piece of criticism he'd seen of mine. He was impressed by its clarity and eager to secure it for the *LRB*; but he seemed to be troubled by the idea that he might seem to have initiated this as a response to the Booker outcome. His solution was to ask if I would let him print it as a letter to the editor – which (I now recognise) made it an act of will by me rather than by him. I was not at all happy with this but weakly agreed – so that's how it appeared, looking as if I had been moved to write to the editor by *The Bone People* having won the Booker, whereas in fact I'd written it before the prize was even in consideration.

Nor did I think the Booker decision a bad one. Hulme's novel was said to have come through the middle, between those on the committee who thought the prize that year should go to Iris Murdoch's *The Good Apprentice*, and those who favoured Doris Lessing's *The Good Terrorist*. If that's true then an untypically good decision was reached by accident. Hulme's novel was a much more deserving winner than Brookner's *Hotel du Lac* which had won the previous year, and than Kingsley Amis's *The Old Devils* which won in 1986.

This was one of those things that was to come up again and again – that I had attacked Keri's novel when it won the Booker Prize. I had not attacked it. I had expressed admiration for its immediacy, its vividness, its sharp sense of a strange reality, where three characters bond, but

> ... their bonds exist outside biology. [...] Although a bond like sexual love grows between the man and the woman, there is no physical contact. That is the imaginative strength of the work – that it creates a sexual union where no sex occurs, parental love where there are no physical parents, creates the stress and fusion of a family where there is no actual family. [...] Both the novelist and her character describe themselves as sexless, sexually drawn to neither male nor female, 'neuter'.

This was also the year that I reviewed the Wedde–McQueen *Penguin Book of New Zealand Verse* which prided itself on being the first anthology of our poetry to include poems in Māori. Translations for these were given in footnotes and I quoted some typically ham-fisted examples and said either they were bad translations or bad poems. I acknowledged that since I didn't know Māori I couldn't say which was true; but neither, I pointed out, did the editors. Once again I was saying what was true, but unacceptable.* It prompted Michael King to say in *Metro* that I was advocating 'the ethnic cleansing of New Zealand literature'. I threatened legal action and got an apology and retraction of sorts; but now I was branded as 'anti-Māori'; and soon, when *The Death of the Body* appeared with its two activist feminists wearing (as the two I had in mind did) overalls and badges that said 'Dyke', I would be 'anti-women', and possibly even 'anti-gay' as well.

These are accusations of a kind it is no use attempting to rebut. If you chose your words carefully and knew you meant what they said, the review or critical piece and what it says must stand, to be seen and inspected closely, in the hope that the inspector will have an

* I shouldn't give the impression that everyone deplored the review. In fact letters of approval came from a number of writers, including Maurice Shadbolt, Brian Turner, Harry Ricketts, Bill Sewell, Marilyn Duckworth, Dell Boldt. Mark Williams, accepting it for *Landfall*, had said 'I love the polemical thrust of the piece.'

appetite for language, for its *life on the page*, and a sense of humour, as well as his or her commitment to whatever Good Cause may seem to have been challenged or affronted. I was a combative person, and the air of the 1980s was full of outrage. I had to take whatever came my way. I knew that King had more or less consigned me to the bin of history and its 'old-boy network'; as I, equally half-heartedly, had consigned him, along with Wedde, to the collective insincerities of what I called 'the good boy network'. Janet Frame and I, when King was writing her biography, had agreed in our secret email exchanges about it, that he was not entirely to be trusted, and there were times when he could be 'sneaky'. And yet he must have got over his ire, as I got over mine, because our exchanges just before his death were affectionate; and he dedicated his last book of essays* to me with the ambiguous, 'For C. K. Stead, who like a hanging concentrates the mind.'

Mervyn Thompson was another caught up in that prevailing air of outrage, and he was quite unable to cope with it. He was the English Department's lecturer in drama, and aligned himself firmly with the radical feminists, an allegiance he demonstrated by putting on a production of Renée's *Setting the Table* – a play I didn't admire, which had struck me as the equivalent of what used to be called in the 1930s 'agitprop'. But it had already had some success and Mervyn thought it said something important and deserved reviving. In it a group of women plan and carry out a violent revenge on a man they believe has committed a rape. In 1984, the year of this revival, a woman (never so far as I know publicly identified) made the same accusation against Thompson, and a group of women set out to re-enact the revenge of Renée's play. Mervyn was attacked at night, kidnapped, chained to a tree and threatened with castration. The appearance of a couple of walkers in the park interrupted the attack and the women vanished, leaving his car daubed with RAPIST!

* *Tread Softly, New & Collected Writings*, Cape Catley, 2001.

Thompson's trauma was profound. He claimed he had never raped anyone. The court suppressed his name from any reporting of the incident with the idea of protecting it from the unsubstantiated rape allegation, and his person from further attack. He treated this suppression almost as if it had been a denial of his right to speak, and 'went public', telling his own story and proclaiming innocence and outrage. I was deeply sympathetic to Mervyn. There seemed to be no substance to the allegation – no victim identity, no evidence of evidence – but somehow his clumsy handling of television and magazine interviews made everything worse. The theatre world, which likes to think of itself as 'liberal', turned against him in ways that were merciless. He was told that one of his plays scheduled for production would not go ahead. When he financed and put the production on himself, it was subject to an actors' boycott, and picketed. As Bruce Jesson pointed out in *Metro*, 'Thompson was being attacked as a representative of the very social forces he had spent his life opposing.'

In the midst of all this Mervyn wrote an account of it which he later described as 'unwieldy, repetitive, caught up in its own pain'. He must have asked me for an opinion because he quotes me, 'in a friendly note', telling him 'It feels like a book about horsemanship written on horseback'.*

Mervyn struggled on, incorporating his personal agonies into the drama of his life, becoming yet another example of the ongoing pains and failures of bringing life in New Zealand to the New Zealand stage. He died of cancer only a few years after the big meltdown of 1984, but more or less on his feet, acting it out to the last. He was, yes – heroic and tragic – he deserved both those big theatre terms. Kay and I both remember him fondly, and recall with disgust the mindlessness of those picketers shouting '*RAPIST*' and banging on the walls as he tried to bring his words to life on the stage of the Maidment Theatre.

---

* Mervyn Thompson, *Singing the Blues*, Blacktown Press, 1991, p. 64.

Bombs and fondness

Just before midnight on 10 July Kay and I, in bed but not yet quite asleep, heard an almighty explosion from the direction of the harbour. 'We're under attack,' I joked. Five or ten minutes later we were asleep, but woken by another, even louder. Next morning the radio news reported that the Greenpeace ship *Rainbow Warrior* had been sunk at its anchor at Marsden Wharf. The first explosion had frightened all those on board who had quickly left the ship for the wharf – which had been the intention of those who planned the operation. But the photographer Fernando Pereira had gone back for his camera, and had gone down with the ship at the second, more potent, explosion.

Greenpeace had been using this ship to monitor and inform the world about French nuclear testing at Mururoa in the Pacific, and the French spy agency, DGSE, which specialised in underwater work, had decided to deal secretly with this troublesome interference in French national affairs. Whether the bombing had been authorised by President Mitterrand, or he had merely been 'informed', was never clear, but he did not accept responsibility, and was not inclined to apologise, which would have been unpopular at home, since the French public, still smarting from the dishonour of World War II, loved its nuclear '*force de frappe*'. In the end Mitterrand sacked the head of the DGSE, and sadly accepted the resignation of his Defence Minister, Charles Hernu, both of whom he suggested had 'exceeded their authority'. None of this would have been necessary, and the official lies would have been enough, if all the perpetrators had got away – but two were caught.

The bombs had been brought down from French Pacific territory on a yacht, the *Ouvéa*, which had escaped New Zealand waters immediately after the bombs went off. Others involved, including the DGSE frogmen, had done their work and flown out before anyone had been identified and captured. But there was one hitch. The bombers worked from Ōkahu Bay where gear had recently been stolen from yachts and launches, and locals were on watch. When they saw activity – a Zodiac dinghy, at least one person in diving gear, a campervan – they called the police. The police took eighteen minutes to arrive and the suspects had vanished; but the number plate of the campervan had been taken. Next day the dinghy was found tied up in Hobson Bay not far from the boatsheds there; nearby, an outboard motor had been dropped into the sea, and a single oxygen bottle of French manufacture, of a kind used for highly sophisticated underwater operations. When the campervan was returned the two agents, Alain Mafart and Dominique Prieur, travelling with false Swiss passports as the couple Sophie and Alain Turenge, were arrested, interrogated, and ultimately charged.

The rest had got away; but France could not now renounce its own agents. David Lange's memoir reveals that 'the French Government asked how much we would want for the release of the agents'.* He replied that 'our legal process must run its course'; but he writes, 'At a time when most convictions for manslaughter led to a sentence of three years the Chief Justice grandly gave them ten' – which suggests he thought the sentence excessive given the minor role played by these two. Nonetheless he had said the sentences were to be served in New Zealand, and changed his mind only when the French threatened economic sanctions affecting our meat sales in Europe. Lange had not imagined he writes, 'that the government of France would resort to extortion, but I should have known that a government which sent agents to carry out an act of terrorism would resort to anything'.

So the agents served possibly two of those years in New Zealand jails and then, by an agreement which both countries pretended had been brokered by the UN, were to serve the rest in French Polynesia. From there they were soon brought home to France 'on medical grounds', where they were released and honoured.

Kay still has a clear memory that a couple she would later recognise as having looked remarkably like Mafart and Prieur had

---

* David Lange, *My Life*, Viking, 2005, p. 222.

come to the reference desk of the library asking for up-to-date local maps. The library couldn't help but Kay had suggested they try the Geography Department.

It had all seemed very close to home, happening in our own bailiwick of Hobson Bay, Ōkahu Bay, the waterfront. I wrote a poem about it which appeared both in the *Listener* and in the *London Review of Books*. Its subject was not just the bombing, and French political cynicism, but was also (as everything tended to be for me) literary: a rejection of French literary theory and 'deconstruction' in favour of Anglophone pragmatism – and with a shameless pun that depended on the reader knowing how the French pronounce 'Turenge'.

Deconstructing the Rainbow Warrior

In my game (and yours, reader) it was always the Frogmen
had clever theories. We did the dirty work

using the English language like a roguish trowel.
Tonight, two rubberised heads have set their Zodiac on course

from Okahu Bay. Past the Container port,
around Marsden Wharf, they're ferrying a transitive verb

called Bomb. In a hired campervan a man and a woman
smoke, check their watches, and bicker.

Turenges don't make it right, and anyway
the name is false, like their Swiss passports.

Half of Auckland, Dominique argues, has taken their number.
She's exaggerating of course. He refuses to panic.

A beautiful night. You can see the lighthouse light
on off Rangitoto, and an undercover moon

casual among clouds over North Head. Here come
the rubber boys back in their puttering Zodiac.

Remember, reader, poems don't deal in fact –
this is all a bad dream in the Elysée Palace.

Now scatter – it goes, like the Paris Metro, to plan.
Soon you will hear explosions. Someone will die.

More than a ship will founder. And the theory? Ah, the theory!
Dig a hole for it with your English trowels.

MY CORRESPONDENCE WITH A. S. BYATT continued, mainly but not solely literary. The *Rainbow Warrior*, the family – it was all there in mine. And one of hers began 'thank you for the telegram (which made me happy for days) & the letter, & the very generous review'. But there was a problem that hovered around the review she thanked me for, and something it said about *Still Life*, her sequel to *The Virgin in the Garden*:

> Byatt's novels have a great deal of intellectual and literary superstructure, which I suspect she thinks is essential to serious writing but is really just superstructure.

I did go on to say that it had been 'successfully absorbed into the fiction', and gave the book fulsome praise:

> I finished *Still Life* with pleasure, with admiration, and with something like awe at its intelligence, its sustained seriousness, its density, its accuracy of observation, above all its lack of all sham and cant and its consequent moral authority.

All sincerely meant, but would that do? In her response Antonia accepted one or two of my mild strictures but came quickly to my word 'superstructure':

> This of course makes me mad. [. . .] Super to what, Karl? By what criterion do you judge parts redundant? Is the metaphor – for it is only a metaphor – architectural? You don't help by resorting to tautology – 'superstructure is only superstructure'. Sometimes I think poets mistrust novels that are preoccupied with the nature of language. [. . .] Both my editors at Chatto – [Cecil] Day Lewis and [D. J.] Enright were poets, and both were sure that plot and characters and what dear dead E. M. Forster called 'personal relations' were the essence of the matter and everything else the accidents. I don't believe that. I admire James and Proust and Mann. I get bored by Hemingway, apart from odd rhythms.

And she went on from that to a quite long exposition of what was essentially the Hist. of Lit. (including 'the dissociation of sensibility') which she and I, more or less contemporaries, had acquired from our reading of T. S. Eliot in our youth.

The letter went on then about her new novel which had diverted her from the story of the Potter sisters; and she concluded by telling me she'd liked my 'deconstructionist terrorist poem' (which I'd sent with my letter), 'especially the lines about the Elysée', but was 'not sure about the trowels'.

My reply was handwritten and included

> . . . I knew that phrase about 'superstructure' would make you angry. It was a despairing short-cut after trying and failing in the space allowed me (which I exceeded by 200 words) to say what I did mean. [There follow some sentences about the 'strategy' of writing reviews; and then . . .] The author is never going to like the short-cuts. Also there is something to be said

against what you do in your novels – and it has to do with unity, artistic wholeness, how much of a bagful of goodies the novel can be and remain a work of art. But if you didn't do what you do there would be loss. The writer's most important duty is to be him/herself, and I accept all your counter-statements. That's all. Any more will have to come later. [. . .] Karl Miller has taken the *Rainbow Warrior* poem. Like you, Allen Curnow didn't like the trowels. I was thinking of the word 'vowels' lying hidden in the sound of it.

But I wrote again a day later, and concluded:

> I thought in bed this morning (waking at 4.15 to look at the comet [Halley's] again) of something to be said that would explain what I mean about 'superstructure', but it doesn't matter. Your prose is charged with <u>intelligence</u> – in both senses – and with your presence. That's why you will always have readers who are also admirers – and I am one. That's not to say that there isn't also a sense that this wonderful object is heterogeneous. It's the art of <u>prose</u> and of <u>fiction</u> rather than the art of the novel – but it's also a novel, and certainly not artless. And you will always be taken seriously in your fiction because it's so apparent you mean business. You have <u>power</u>, which as a fiction writer I lack (odd that, isn't it?)

It's evident that I had not found it possible entirely to conceal from her my sense that her novels were (like her letters) too full of too many disparate things, too many kinds of knowledge and a compulsion to share them never quite distinguishable from 'showing them off'. Her fictions were remarkable documents but not, I would have said if it had not been their author I was writing to, unified works of art.

She came back to the subject after a lapse of time:

> I don't want to think about *Still life* because I'm trying to do something quite different at the moment – the short stories are more concerned with artistic unity (I would argue that the novel has a sort of almost over-stressed metaphoric unity, but that doesn't counter your arguments). And it occurs to me from time to time that you may be thinking that I'm not answering out of pique or disinclination, and not because (which is the case) I can only write essay-letters or nothing – cf length of novels. But I have learned to do short things. I want to send you an autobiographical piece I wrote – called Sugar – about the deaths of my father and grandfather – also a long essay about the metaphors of Still Life.
>
> [. . .] I want to see The Death of the Body. I don't think your persona* is bug-like, or even dragon-fly – more substantial, though clean cut – Kingfisher?
>
> [. . .] I look forward to seeing you in the summer. All love

THE WELLINGTON EVENT WAS WRITERS' WEEK and it was there Fleur Adcock introduced me to Craig Raine, saying we should get to know one another, because I was the Craig Raine of New Zealand and he was the Karl Stead of the UK. I think she meant that we were both poet-critics, equally in the spotlight, often in trouble for being outspoken, too frank, tactless. Craig was best known at that time as the initiator (with Christopher Reid) of the Martian poetry movement, by which everything on earth was observed as if by a stranger from space who did not understand it – which gave the account a surreal quality. Craig had been books editor of the *New Statesman* and was now the poetry editor of Faber and Faber, the post made famous by T. S. Eliot's occupancy.

---

* She is referring to the narrator in my Edmonton story that had just appeared in the *London Magazine*, and survives in the title story of *The Name on the Door is Not Mine*. I must have said something negative about him.

He had just the year before published what was probably his most successful collection, *Rich*, which included a brilliant twenty-page autobiographical essay, and had sold 15,000 copies in its first edition. Also in that year he had been elected a Fellow of the Royal Society of Literature. The Faber stable was still the one that attracted and published the best-known British poets, and significant Americans like Robert Lowell and John Berryman. I wrote a mocking poem about it some years after meeting Craig, which included these lines about 'Tom' Eliot:

> It was Tom established
> the Faber poetry principle:
> 'Poets are not published by us
> because their work is superior.
> Rather, the work is superior
> because it is published by us.'

That poem included references to Eliot's anti-Semitism, a subject which (as I've said) Craig and I were always to disagree on (he believed Eliot was innocent on all charges), sometimes vehemently. He was also the Faber editor who had turned down my Pound Yeats Eliot book, apologising for returning the typescript so late, but 'everyone in the office wanted to read it'. Nor was I ever entirely favourably disposed to his Martian mode, which seemed to me, though often remarkable, sometimes excessive in its use of analogy/simile/metaphor. When I knew him better I was to write a poem, 'Likenesses', which I dedicated to him as both an expression of admiration and of mild reproach:

> King of Comparison, clever as the Reverend Moon
> you marry a dozen thises to a dozen thats
>
> in a flash of light, while I admire and demur.
> Nothing for example is so like a swallow

as these swallows are, describing their twittering arcs
without analogy, in and out of an archway

that opens on a village square.

We were also to disagree about Ted Hughes whom Craig revered and whose work I expressed doubts about.*

Craig left Faber soon after I met him, to take up a fellowship at New College, Oxford, and to set up and edit the literary magazine *Areté*, which I would write for from time to time; but his loyalty to Faber, and particularly to Eliot's widow Valerie (and thus to 'Tom'), was unwavering. And yet despite these and other differences Craig and I got on well, right from the first. Fleur's instinct had been right: we were natural allies, similar temperaments, destined to be friends. And there were the oddest coincidences: I was born in Auckland, he in Bishop Auckland. His mother's name was Olive, and so was mine; his sister's name was Norma, and so was mine. His only play, *'1953'*, a counterfactual drama set in Italy after Hitler has won World War II, was based on Racine's *Andromaque*, the source of the only play I had written, the verse drama that had so excited Sargeson in 1955.

These (apart from perhaps the last) were mere chances, of no real significance – I knew that – but I liked to entertain them as if they 'meant' something. It wasn't long before Craig was telling me he loved me – 'somehow'. And 'somehow' I loved him. I wasn't sure whether this meant I figured significantly in his imagination as he did in mine; or whether all the many literary people who were his friends were equally loved, and that this love (though it seemed real) was just a feature of his temperamental extravagance. I have an image of him cycling down an Oxford lane with champagne and cigarettes in the basket at the front, grinning with the pleasure in

* My doubts were of the kind expressed by Robert Creeley in Chapter 8 about 'that damn symbolic crow' when he would have preferred a real one.

store as we settled to talk and drink and smoke the fags we normally denied ourselves, in the summer garden at the back of their house.

Craig's wife was also an Oxford don (Fellow of St Anne's College), editor of the seventeenth-century poet George Herbert, author of a book on Evelyn Waugh, and the niece of Boris Pasternak. She was known as Li, and published as Ann Pasternak Slater; and they had four children, three of whom over the years would make names for themselves writing for, or directing in, the theatre. A scholarship boy at Oxford, the son of a working-class boxer/epileptic who was also a faith healer, Craig seemed to be at the time of our first meeting, and in most of the years that followed, at or near the centre, if one could think of there being one, of the British literary scene. He was close to Karl Miller, a neighbour of Ian McEwan, a friend of Julian Barnes, Martin Amis, Ted Hughes, Carmen Callil, Seamus Heaney, Christopher Reid (who succeeded him at Faber), Claire Tomalin, Patrick Marber, Christopher Logue, Galen Strawson, James Fenton . . .

When I first knew the Raines they lived in a smallish modern townhouse in Alma Place in central Oxford. Later, on the death of her mother in 1989, Li inherited a big house in Park Town (an oval 'square' in North Oxford), and with the house came some of the remarkable Impressionist paintings of Leonid Pasternak (1862–1945, father of the novelist Boris), who had spent the last six years of his life in this house with his daughter, Li's mother. Among these paintings there were some notable portraits, including an early one of Einstein and a late one of Tolstoy.

The Wellington festival was busy, crowded with talent both local and from overseas. There was a single 'hour with' Craig, and one with David Lodge (which I chaired), Timothy Findley, Allen Curnow, Mona Williams, Tom Shapcott, Alain Robbe-Grillet, Margaret Mahy – and one with me. There were in addition the usual panel discussions, readings and book launches. I remember only a little in detail: enjoying Craig's company, and David Lodge's gloomy fun, a party in the company of the Duckworth-Adcock sisters, and feeling slightly apprehensive about the American novelist Robert Stone who seemed to be on fire and looking for adventure. Craig's reading was with Janet Frame, Albert Wendt and Murray Edmond, Janet rising to it bravely, but in her 'little girl' voice, as if trusting it to keep all this masculinity at bay. I was on a panel about 'The Novel Now' with Stone and Lodge and Keri Hulme.

Craig invited me to be in touch when I was in the UK later in the year after the Yeats Summer School, and I was to be there for dinner on 2 November. By that time *The Death of the Body* had been launched and had just been reviewed in the *TLS* by Galen Strawson who was also there for the Raines' dinner. Strawson told me how much he'd liked the novel. I expressed surprise because the review had not seemed altogether happy with its complexities. His wife who was French said all Galen's reviews were like that. 'He has been reviewing me since we first met, and they are always negative.' I knew *The Death of the Body* was a novel which would delight some people and irritate others, and I could accept that Strawson was one of the latter; but what pleased me was that philosophy was his subject (and he was son of the famous Oxford philosopher P. F. Strawson) and that when I asked him about that aspect of the novel he replied – almost irritably as if it hardly needed saying – that yes, Harry Butler's thinking as a philosopher was fine. 'That's exactly how a philosopher's mind works.' I couldn't ask him didn't he enjoy the jokes? That was something he would have to have volunteered, and he didn't.

There were plenty of reviews of the novel at that time – book pages had not begun to shrink – and quite enough praise to satisfy any but the greediest of egos; but the one I liked best was by Robert Irwin in *Time Out*, which was in effect a comic rewrite of Strawson's:

> 'What are you doing,' asks my sister Bunty.
>
> 'I'm reviewing this novel by CK Stead. I'm having difficulty with it.'
>
> 'What's it about?'

> I read her what I'd written so far. [There follows a summary of most of the plot.]
>
> 'That's as far as I've got. I suppose it's not a good idea to give away so much of the plot.'
>
> 'There you are then,' says Bunty, shooing the horse out of the kitchen. 'Now all you have to do is say whether you like it.'
>
> 'It's not so simple, Bunty. This CK Stead is a New Zealand poet and literary critic, well-known for being dead-clever. What he has done is set this story in another story, which is about how the first story was written. Harry's story is being written partly in a café in Milan, and the narrator keeps changing his mind about the way the story is going and he reads bits out to the café proprietor and a highly critical Danish lady. This frame story has what we in the trade call a "deconstructive effect" in that it keeps drawing attention to the literariness of the text. I felt like saying "Get on with the story." '
>
> 'I'm not surprised,' says Bunty.
>
> 'Ah but then you see I got gripped by the story outside the story, because the highly critical Danish lady has very big breasts and the novel writer fancies her something rotten. [. . .] It's a very tricky parable about the fictionality of all texts.'
>
> 'Will I like it? asks my sister.
>
> 'I did, and I expect a lot of people will. But I'm afraid it's a bit too clever for you Bunty. You should stick to those true pony romances.'

It was after this dinner that Craig wrote a card telling me he loved me, and (though 'one hardly ever transmits messages of affection') why he did. There was nothing strange about this; but the fact that it could seem to me somewhat 'out of bounds' was a sign, perhaps, of how much more 'British' we NZers were than the British – or some of them. I had written thanking them for having me, and sending a copy of the Picador of *All Visitors Ashore* which I'd brought and meant to leave with them and had forgotten. This message crossed with his card so I had to write again: 'Your card is a bit like a pre-emptive strike. I felt like that too, about you and Li and your house and your lovely kids – but too inhibited on paper to say so. You are a lovely lot of Poms and I feel privileged to have met you' – which still fell short of what I felt, and what he was seeming to offer; but it was the best a shy Kiwi could do, at least for the time being. Thereafter our fondness for one another would grow and become more manifest, and I would learn to embrace him Russian-style, and kiss his whiskery cheek.

It was just before or after this dinner with the Raines and Strawsons that I sat with Anthony Thwaite and Peter Porter around Peter's kitchen table (five floors up with no lift) in Paddington. Anthony had been that year's chairman of the Booker judges, and had made the mistake of writing to his friend Julian Barnes saying he was sorry he hadn't been able to prevail against 'those silly women' on the awarding committee and see that Julian's novel *Staring at the Sun* made it through to the short-list. Barnes had shown this note to his publisher who, knowing what such a gem of gossip would do for sales, had told the *Daily Telegraph*. The *Telegraph* had gone straight to the other judges, who were of course outraged – so there had been headlines and embarrassment. 'Oh Daddy' Anthony's daughters had wailed (and the literary world with them) 'how could you be so *silly*?'

We'd had an Indian meal together and now sat drinking wine and gossiping. Anthony by hints and oblique signals seemed to invite me to ask how *The Death of the Body* had fared, but I forbade myself to ask the question and so, bursting to be important, he told me anyway. When they had got their 127 (or was it 144?) titles down to the long-list of twelve (which in those days was not published) my novel was still there. Someone (not Anthony – possibly one of those 'silly women') had argued passionately for it but it had not survived to make the short-list.

I said I was glad someone liked my novel as much as I did.

Peter said gloomily he always knew that no one would like what he wrote. It was a fact of life for him – like having to get out of bed in the morning.

Sligo and beyond . . .

But that was yet to come. TVNZ decided they would do a story for their *Kaleidoscope* programme about my leaving the university. There was a lot about walking – shots of me striding along Princes Street with Albert Park on one side and the university clock-tower on the other; and coming and going through Parnell – bald man with long legs, in a hurry – accompanied by my own voice-over. The family figured too as walkers; and there was a scene at home, the five of us at dinner, looking (when I see it now) young and beautiful. The film crew came to Karekare too, and there were pictures of the bach, and of the hut in the bush at the top of the section, that looked all the way down the valley to the headlands and the beach and the ocean beyond. Up there I had built a small shelf across one corner of the single room where the typewriter sat so I could work standing. It was there I had written the last chapters of *All Visitors Ashore*.

And they all came to the airport to see me off – Kay and our three children and the film crew. This was the real departure, not a mock-up. The hugs and kisses were real. Once the filming had caught me going through the departures door I couldn't turn around – I was on my way.

Towards the end of her autobiography, *A Life of My Own*, Claire Tomalin writes, 'I was fifty-three when I left the *Sunday Times*. It was my last job, and I was going to spend the next thirty years as a writer.' That exactly parallels my age and situation in 1986. Immediately ahead lay Sligo and the Yeats Summer School, and then London and the launch of *The Death of the Body* – and beyond that my life as a writer would be whatever I could make of the new freedom.

On the way to Ireland I flew through Tahiti and LA and stopped a day or two in London where I called on Karl Miller to talk about books (including Witi Ihimaera's *The Matriarch*) he had for me to review. We had one of those conversations that always surprised me, because it was the kind you have only with people you know very well – better than Karl and I knew one another – so there was something unreal about it; and yet it did have the effect of creating closeness.

I was struck, not for the first time, by how *still* Karl was – and I wondered was he ill, even dying. He told me he did not approve of Kermode's response to my letter about his review of the Pound Yeats Eliot book, and did not approve of my responding to the response. I said there was a question of *truth*. He said there was nothing to be gained from arguing with reviewers.

He said Craig Raine had told him I had said that he, Miller, was so inscrutable it was impossible to have a normal relationship with him. I said this was Craig's invention, and that I would not tell him what Craig had said about him because I couldn't remember. All this was in a tone of banter, with Susannah Clapp looking on anxiously from her desk, her green shoes peeping out from under it. I thought I probably *had* said that Karl was inscrutable; but I would also have said that I liked him, and Craig would have reported that too.

But now Karl was telling me that yesterday he had sat in the sun trying to review a book that really interested him and he hadn't been able to think of a single thing to say about it. That was strange too – strangely intimate, confessional. He walked me to the lift and said he looked forward to seeing more of me when I was back from Sligo. He had a lot of work for me to do – the Ihimaera review, then Christina Stead, Penelope Fitzgerald, Michael Schmidt . . .

I flew to Dublin and asked at the airport how I would find my way to the railway station. As one fond of chanting the final lines of Yeats's 'Easter 1916', I was charmed by the response, 'Would it be Connolly or Pearse you'll be wantin'?' I felt I was in Ireland indeed where, as I wrote to Kay, 'Nothing is what it seems – and *everything* is political.'

I was to take daily seminars on Yeats, and give the plenary session on his 1928 volume *The Tower*.* It was as if I had known the poem 'The Lake Isle of Innisfree' from birth, but now I was lodged in the White Swan Hotel, where the stream that runs out of the lake rushes by under a stone bridge and over a stony bed down to the Sligo docks where Yeats played as a boy. I was to walk on a very hot day all the way from Sligo to Drumcliff Churchyard where 'Yeats is laid', and where 'By his command these words are cut':

> *Cast a cold eye*
> *On life on death –*
> *Horseman, pass by!*†

The new friends I made during the Summer School included Helen Vendler, Ann Saddlemyer, Declan Kiberd, Cal Bedient. I shared seminars with the poet Tom Paulin and was on a panel with him and Conor Cruise O'Brien. I got to know Yeats's son Michael, an Irish Senator and Member of the European Parliament, and his wife Gráinne. A message came for me from Seamus Heaney who had, he said (and he had written it more than once in his essays), been taught by *The New Poetic* how to read and understand T. S. Eliot, and had wanted to meet me, but was held up by the imminent death of his father. That meeting would come a few years later, after Craig Raine and I had attended Seamus's inaugural lecture as Professor of Poetry at Oxford.

With Helen Vendler, America's most respected academic critic of poetry and a renegade Catholic, I formed a sort of joke 'Atheists' Alliance', which we were to continue at a Yeats conference in

---

* Reprinted in *Answering to the Language*, pp. 29–47.

† In my Introduction to *Answering to the Language* I discuss my visits to the two W. B. Yeats burial sites, the first in Roquebrune, the second, this one, in Drumcliff Churchyard. The question of whether or not the corpse in the second grave is the right one also figures in my novel *The Secret History of Modernism*.

Monte Carlo the following May, and the year after when she invited me to Harvard. With Ann Saddlemyer, who was writing a biography of Yeats's wife Georgie Hyde-Lees, I rediscovered in Sligo the pleasures of ballroom dancing. The three of us were all the same age, fifty-three. With Declan Kiberd, the Summer School's charming young host and Irish literature's most distinguished academic critic, I played informal indoor cricket and 'took a remarkable catch' in a corridor. Cal Bedient, who lectured in English at UCLA was there, not as an expert but to learn. He invited me to visit him in Santa Monica, and I would do that, and stay with him, when writing my next novel, *Sister Hollywood*; and much later I would use him partly as model for my eccentric character Alban Ashtree, the runaway Canadian poet in the later-written part of my story 'The Name on the Door is Not Mine'.

In Sligo I read in the Hawk's Well Theatre and included the recent poem 'After the Wedding', a step back in time to Kaiwaka and my childhood, which ended:

> 'Marriages are made in heaven'
>   – not so.
>
> We marry to be nearer the earth
> cousins of the fur and the stalk
>   talking together
>
> that brown water reflecting
> these green hills.

My Sligo had been a success – there is no other way of describing it – and so were the weeks in London that followed. And yet the beginning of my new life was not entirely the end of the old. My identity as an academic would not vanish overnight, and for many years I would be called upon to be 'Professor Stead' as often as to be 'C. K. Stead the novelist and poet' – including to Oxford as Senior Visiting Fellow at St Johns, to Bristol to receive another doctorate, honorary this time, and to London to be made a Fellow of the Royal Society of Literature (and sign on with T. S. Eliot's pen!).

I would live in New Zealand, still 'controversial', productive, only slowly calming down and as slowly becoming, I felt, if not always liked, at least accepted. But the travel, the 'escapes', would continue, and for more than thirty years I would never spend a complete winter in the Southern Hemisphere. There were many European summers large parts of which Kay and I would spend in Uzès, in the region of Avignon and Nîmes, in the house of our friend Tony Axelrad, translator of *The Death of the Body* into French, who retained his house there and was glad to have us occupy it while his work for the International Criminal Tribunal for the the former Yugoslavia kept him and his wife Pat mostly in Den Haag. Publishing and translation opportunities took me to Zagreb and the Dalmatian coast which would figure in my fiction. Pound connections cemented my friendship with Professor Massimo Bacigalupo of the University of Genoa, and the town of Rapallo. The Bogliasco Foundation twice awarded me a literature fellowship, and the Seresin Trust a residency at Gaiole in Chianti. These extended my fondness for that part of the world and its literature. And of course there was Menton where so much had begun, and thereafter a place of many happy returns.

But London was never out of the picture. It was my second city after Auckland, and Kay and I lodged in the Nuffield Foundation flats on the edge of Regent's Park, or in the London House complex in Mecklenburgh Square, or in Ann and Anthony Thwaite's *pied à terre* in Paddington, or in our friends the Rileys' townhouse in Ladbroke Road, or (once) in Stephen Spender's house in Loudon Road,* or, in later years, with daughter Margaret and her family in Queen's Park. If that makes me some sort of 'old colonial', or perhaps an unregenerate 'settler', I won't argue; but I would prefer

* I had spent the night of my sixtieth birthday in Stephen Spender's bed, but with Kay, not with Stephen.

to say that all my life I have been a loyal Pākehā New Zealander, with deep and abiding attachments to Tāmaki-makau-rau, which was, and is, as on that Mercator's projection world map of my childhood schoolroom, 'South-East of Everywhere'.

IT WAS ONLY AFTER MY SLIGO ADVENTURE and the London weeks that followed, in fact at the end of the 1986 academic year, that the English Department put on its farewell for two retirees, Peter Dane and Bill Pearson, and for a third, ten years younger, the professor who had left to be self-employed. It was modest – evening strawberries and cream with white wine in the courtyard. Kendrick as court jester had eked out a poem for each of us, presented in a finely printed folder. Peter in these poems was the Friend of the Earth, apologist for 'Jack Donne and Berty Lawrence'; Bill was Coal Flat's historian and the conscience of the 'Fretful Sleepers'; I was the 'Mangawhai/Maungwhau Viking' who knew that 'only the whole man jumps his own height'. I was given a painting by Greg O'Brien, *Gravity Escapes Conviction* (oil on board).

Dennis McEldowney wrote me a note saying:

> I don't think any of us realized how imminent your departure was, otherwise we would have been more prepared. It has been fun working with you all these years, both when we agreed (which was usually, and with a strong sense of rapport) and when we disagreed (less frequently but just as profoundly).

Allen's message, written while I was still away in London, was brief but (typically) both quietly eloquent and to the point: 'Most of all, my heart's with you in this well-conducted release from not-unserviceable bondage to U of A. We both look forward to your safe return.'

And it was perhaps not altogether strange that Professor Musgrove's message should have touched me as it did. He had been

HOD during my five student years and probably twenty of my years of employment. Even when I was a student he was seen as an example of what the brightest students used to call brutally 'the professorial rot' – meaning those eminences who attained chairs for life and thereafter did little or nothing new or remarkable. His MA lectures were close encounters where students could see the yellowing old notes he was working from with their shameless markers showing where the lecture had ended the year before, and the years before that. And yet there were times when Mus could take fire. He was an actor, it was Shakespeare set him alight, and he would read or quote the lines with such passion, crucifying himself against the blackboard, dying as Othello or weeping as Lear over the dead Cordelia.

Mus had not been able to attend the strawberries and cream with wine in the courtyard, but he wrote me a farewell note saying, 'I wish you good fortune. You have merited it, and earned it, and shall I say, "Nihil quod tetigit, non ornavit."' That was what Dr Johnson had written of Oliver Goldsmith: 'He touched nothing that he did not adorn.' It was very Oxford (Latin and all), very elegant, and I chose to believe he meant it.

Before I set off for Sligo the university Registrar had sent a message to say Senate had agreed that I should be Professor Emeritus.

And a telegram had arrived:

BEAUX VOYAGES
RONA LIGHTYEAR

Rona Lightyear was Cecelia Skyways; she was, of course, Janet Frame.

Postscript:
Mus and his wife Marjorie never moved from that small rented flat in Devonport. Their one child, Judith, attended (as a first-year student) the very first lecture I ever gave in Auckland and was in my

stage two tutorial before defecting to history. As Judith Binney she became the classic NZ historian, one of Keith Sinclair's dragon's teeth, recorder of, and academic spokesperson for, the Tūhoe.

Mus had written one academic book – about Herrick – but had had no luck in finding a publisher, and thereafter gave up, but guarded his chair nervously. I felt he was always slightly suspicious of me, wondering whether I hoped one day to nudge him aside. But I sometimes surprised and pleased him. We acted together in a departmental reading of *The Winter's Tale* in which I (since it was my course) played Leontes and he Polixenes. And then there was a time in a common-room conversation about Platonism, when I remembered and quoted a poem he had published years before in the *Poetry Yearbook*. I had liked it enough to read it several times, and then, because I have that kind of memory, and because it was elegant and rhymed, it had stuck. I can still quote it, I think more or less accurately:

> Within your bed were dark and light,
> Surrender, conquest, sleep,
> But do not ask how much of you
> In memory I keep.
>
> Think if you will that, purged of time,
> Discorporate, refined,
> The ideal you still moves within
> My universal mind.
>
> Nothing is lost that ever breathed,
> Or faded into, air.
> Content you, once my own with this
> Platonic love affair.

Acknowledgements

Loving thanks go first to Kay who is always the first reader of everything I write, and to our three children for being there.

My thanks to Auckland University Press who have published this book and a number before it, poetry, criticism and memoir; and in particular I record my gratitude to three managing editors, the late Dennis McEldowney, then Elizabeth Caffin, and more recently Sam Elworthy, and to all their staff over the years.

I'm conscious of a debt to the University of Auckland which first educated me, then employed me for most of the years recorded here, and to its Faculty of Arts which awarded me its Senior Research Fellowship in 1979. I am honoured still to be Professor Emeritus and to have received the university's Distinguished Alumnus Award in 2008; and I continue grateful to its Department of English and my colleagues during my years there, only some of whom are mentioned in these pages, but all of whom deserve to be.

My grateful thanks go to A. S. Byatt, Alan Roddick, Kay Stead, Kay Davenport, Patsy Dutch, and Marilyn Duckworth for permission to quote from their letters; to Hugo Manson for permission to quote from letters by his late parents Celia and Cecil Manson; to Bridie Lonie for permission to quote from letters by her late father Iain Lonie; to Dr Ben Knights for permission to quote notes and letters from his late father Professor L. C. Knights; to Professor Nathalie Mauriac for permission to quote her late husband Robert Dyer's letters and poems; to Dr Elizabeth Aitken-Rose and the Sargeson Trust for permission to quote from the letters of Frank Sargeson;

to Tim Curnow for permission to quote from his late father Allen Curnow's letters, and to Auckland University Press for permission to quote from Allen Curnow's poems; to Alan Roddick for permission to quote from letters of the late Charles Brasch; to Rachel Scott for permission to quote from letters by her late mother Margaret Scott; to the Denis Glover Estate and to Pia Glover, the copyright holder, for permission to quote Denis Glover's letters; to Sean Shadbolt for permission to quote from his late father Maurice Shadbolt's letters, and to David Ling Publishing for permission to quote from Volume One of Philip Temple's biography of Maurice Shadbolt; to the Public Trust for permission to quote Eric McCormick's letter; to Nick Duggan for permission to quote from his late father Maurice Duggan's letters; to Professor Raewyn Dalziel for permission to quote from her late husband Professor Sir Keith Sinclair's letters; to Elizabeth Caffin for permission to quote from a letter by Dennis McEldowney; to David Higham Associates for permission to quote from a poem by Emmanuel Litvinov; to Adam Dudding for permission to quote from a letter by his late father Robin Dudding; to Elliot Henderson for permission to quote from a letter by his late mother Sylvia Ashton-Warner; and to Exact Change press for permission to quote from Paris Peasant by Louis Aragon.

C.K.S.